D1000487

THEOLOGICAL TRANSLATION LIBRARY

VOL. XXX
EUCKEN'S THE TRUTH OF RELIGION

Theological Translation Library

NEW SERIES

Descriptive Prospectus on Application.

THE TRUTH OF RELIGION

BY

RUDOLF EUCKEN

AWARDED NOBEL PRIZE 1908
SENIOR PROFESSOR OF PHILOSOPHY IN THE UNIVERSITY OF JENA

TRANSLATED BY

W. TUDOR JONES, Ph.D. (Jena)

Second English Edition
Translated from the Third and Revised German Edition,
with a special Preface by the Author

WILLIAMS & NORGATE
14 HENRIETTA STREET, COVENT GARDEN, LONDON
NEW YORK: G. P. PUTNAM'S SONS
1913

34497

TRANSLATOR'S PREFACE

IT is with mixed feelings that I allow this translation to pass out of my hands. It would not have been undertaken had it not been for the affection which I possess for my old teacher and friend, and for the influence which he exerted over my life when I had the privilege of spending nearly three years with him in the ancient University of Jena. And such an experience as mine is only a specimen of what is true of thousands of other students who have passed through his classes in Jena since 1874. These students are found the world over, and are all imbued with something of the spirit of their great teacher in connection with the problems and contents of religion.

The book presents peculiar difficulties which will be immediately acknowledged by all students of the author's writings. Much is lost at the best in a translation, and especially is this so when the work is that of a prophet of religion who cannot be tied down either in thought or mode of expression to the level of the writer on exact subjects. I have been painfully conscious of the inadequacy of language to express many of the ideas presented in the book—ideas which seem inseparable from the religious experience of the living personality. The terminology in many portions of the book moves midway between Philosophy and

Theology, and I have endeavoured constantly to take this important fact into consideration. But it is a fact of great difficulty in the midst of the present-day flux of philosophical terminology. Whatever the faults may be, I hope no one will detect a lack of fairness in dealing with various theological conceptions.

I have to thank my wife for valuable help in connection with the whole of the translation.

In the course of a few years, two large editions of the book have appeared in Germany and the work has been the subject of a large number of books, dissertations, and essays, by many eminent German philosophers and religious teachers. I hope it will meet with a similar reception in the English-speaking countries of the world, and help all who have at heart the furtherance of the things of the spirit to differentiate between the transient and the Eternal in Christianity, and to labour for the growth of the Spiritual Life in the deepest consciousness of men.

W. TUDOR JONES.

HIGHBURY, LONDON,
1st November 1911.

PREFACE TO THE SECOND EDITION

A FIRST large edition of this volume having become exhausted in less than twelve months, advantage was taken of the publication of a third German edition (August 1912) to incorporate the numerous changes made by the author. Most of these changes occur in the latter part of the chapter entitled

"Characteristic Religion" (pp. 457–511). Besides this, the whole work has undergone revision and simplification, which, I hope, will render the volume far less difficult than the first edition. The changes in the book have been made in consultation with the author, and I wish to thank Professor Eucken for his unfailing courtesy and kindness.   I have also to thank the Rev. E. E. Coleman, M.A., for his kindness in reading the whole of the proofs and in making many valuable suggestions which have proved of great service to me.

W. TUDOR JONES.

19th April 1913.

AUTHOR'S PREFACE FOR THE ENGLISH EDITION

THE author of this book has found so much good-will in England in connection with his efforts that it is a great pleasure for him to see his main work on religion appearing in English. The work does not pretend to present a system of religious philosophy; but, in the midst of the present-day controversy over religion, the most important task seems to be to present with the utmost possible clearness the solid nucleus of religion, and, along with this, to show its main rights. In the conviction of the author, religion is able to attain a secure position and an effective influence only when it is founded upon the whole of life and not upon a particular so-called faculty of the soul, be it intellect, feeling, or will. It behoves us, therefore, to possess a plan of human life as a whole, and to inquire whether life as a whole turns out to indicate the operation of a Higher Power, and, hence, to lead to religion. The primary condition of this is the consideration that human life is not a mere piece of nature, but that a new stage of reality reveals itself in it. Such a revelation is actually present in the Spiritual Life; and we are not able to grasp sufficiently this fact or to understand its effects without recognising that the Spiritual Life is a Whole, and that it is present with elevating energy as a Whole in man.

In pursuing this path it becomes evident that a universal life—a cosmic depth—is imbedded in the Spiritual Life. It is only as a revelation of such a nature of life that spiritual creativeness, art and science, morality and right, can develop themselves and transform man. If, therefore, all genuine Spiritual Life is the effect of a Higher Power, religion is imbedded in it. The great spiritual leaders of the race were clearly conscious of such a fact. But a religion of such spiritual activity is still of a very indefinite nature, and receives a distinctive character, first of all, from the fact that, throughout a grave upheaval, in a conquest over suffering and wrong, a further stage of life—itself a kingdom of Divine Love—is unlocked. Herewith religion becomes for the first time an autonomous province of life; herewith it brings forth a new and unique life.

But Characteristic and Universal Religion—in the sense the terms are used in this work—must remain in living relationship and mutually further one another, for thus alone can the whole of religion shape itself into greatness, and thus fortify and raise not only individuals but the whole of humanity. This fundamental conception tests and measures the historical religions especially according to the manner in which they shape the life of humanity, and according to what they are able to achieve for the moral elevation of human nature. Here the conception decides resolutely for Christianity as the summit of all religions; but simultaneously it demands, in view of the situation of the present day, that Christianity be more forcibly referred back to its essential vital content and be given a simpler and more intelligible form, and be freed from whatever is no more alive in it but is a mere heritage of past times.

The Eternal and Divine in Christianity is the depth of life which is unlocked in it. It has become necessary to differentiate more clearly the Eternal and Divine from the transient and the human which have so intimately mixed up with it in divers forms. It is only a conception of religion which binds freedom and depth with one another, and which heightens freedom through depth and depth through freedom, that will be able to overcome the storms of the present.

RUDOLF EUCKEN.

JENA, 1st November 1911.

CONTENTS

xiii

THE TRUTH OF RELIGION

———•———

Part I.—The Universal Crisis
in Religion

CHAPTER I

a. THE PROBLEM OF RELIGION

HE who wishes to ascertain the intrinsic truth of
religion need neither trace its blurred beginnings in
time nor pursue its slow ascent, but may take his
stand upon the summit of its development. For it
is here first of all that the problem of truth obtains a
clearness and, at the same time, an urgency. We
need not trouble ourselves about magic, which accompanies and governs the initial stages of religion; and
we need not occupy ourselves with religion as a mere
aspect of early civilisation or as a mythology of
nature. Our problem begins only where religion
engenders a world of its own, and holds forth such
a world over against the remainder of existence, thus
transforming the remaining world through and
through. Thus, religion holds before man, in the
midst of his province, an invisible order of things,
an eternal existence, a supernatural life, and claims

1   1

his soul for all this.   Such a stated revelation appears
not merely in one but in several points in history ;
and, further, the contents of the " historical " and
the positive religions vary.   But the same problem
presents itself in all the manifold phenomena of
religion, and a sharp Nay as well as a joyous Yea
is common to all religions.

Nowhere is religion able to gain man for its new
world unless it frees him from the old world, and
enables him to dislike and even to hate what hitherto
has swayed and enchanted him.   There is no possibility of a genuine and effective turn of his life
without a breach with the nearest-at-hand world—
without the clear discovery of the misery and vanity
of such a world.   This world must displease man
not only at certain points but in its entirety.   All
within it not only contains much pain and sorrow,
but all within it is inadequate for man's highest
happiness.   Man is not only menaced and oppressed
from without ; he is troubled from within by anguish
and alarm.   It is only an entire revolution of the
nearest-at-hand life that can engender a genuine and
overwhelming aspiration after religion, and it is only
through such an aspiration that religion can come to
birth in the soul of man.

Indeed, the harder and sharper is the Nay, the
more energetic and joyous becomes the Yea which
religion holds out to man.   Religion as a communication of God—of the highest power and perfection—
not only alleviates in some way the pain of man, and
not only heightens somehow his happiness, but
promises an entire freedom from evil and a translation
into entire blessedness.   The new world announced

by religion signifies the highest conceivable world—
the summit of all perfection. The evanescent and
diminutive nature of man shall gain a portion in the
eternity and infinity of this new world; and, indeed,
man shall ascend to the Divine, and religion will
finally bind the Divine and the human in one.

Religion sets our life in a stormy conflict and
movement through the revelation of such immense
prospects, through the transportation of a superhuman aim within the needs and exigencies of
human existence. Our existence raises itself to
incomparable greatness and intrinsic value; and into
our being the essence of the cosmos enters and longs
for our decision. Our circle of life dissects itself into
a For and an Against; the customary valuation of
the excellences of life is not only altered but
inverted, so that now that alone holds valid which
leads us to the Divine, whilst all that holds us fast to
the ordinary world, in spite of all its captivating
brilliancy, sinks to the level of an evil. "If any man
cometh unto me and hateth not his own father, and
mother, and wife, and children, and brethren, and
sisters, yea, and his own life also, he cannot be my
disciple."

But, besides being such a denial of the world,
religion is at the same time the strongest power
within the world. Nothing has so much united men
inwardly, but also nothing has so much divided them
as religion; nothing has so much deepened the nature
of individuals, nothing has so necessarily impelled
forward the characteristic tendencies of nations as
convictions of Divine things. Whatever appears in
life as heroism roots itself ultimately in religion;

nothing can inspire man in the depth of his soul, nothing can win his entire self-surrender unless it has linked itself to his religion, or has become a kind of religion in itself. Indeed, all the belief of humanity and of the individual seems inseparable from a belief in the indwelling of a Divine in human nature—of the living presence of an eternal and spiritual energy in the deeds of man. He who has experienced the religious problem in the depth of his soul is never again able to free himself entirely from such an experience; he may cast it off and banish it to a distance, but when he does this he cannot but choose to lay his strongest affection in the realm of negation; he cannot but choose to handle the question of religion as the main question of his life, so that unbelief itself becomes only another kind of versatile belief in his inmost conviction. Thus the strongest power *within* the world constitutes in reality the conviction of an *over-world*.

But, at the same time, religion is an object which has been constantly spoken against in a harsh and callous manner. This happens not only from the outside, but also from the deep earnestness of wrestling souls. Ever anew the question raises itself whether an opening to the Divine—whether a raising of man in some way to a Divine life—is possible, or whether all assertion concerning this turns out finally to be no more than a delusion. Must not all that affects man assume a merely human form? And must not all which recommends itself to his aims enter into mere human notions? And is not all drawn into the narrowness and the gloom of the earthly circle—is not all confined within the barriers

of our nature ? Often enough what served interests
of a pettily human kind was considered Divine ; the
forces of the world tore such a Divine meaning and
reduced it to a means for their own ends. Religion
promises man a new life and new heart. But has
it not often knit itself faster to the mechanism of the
world and heightened in a most repulsive manner
hate and jealousy, vanity and hypocrisy ? And,
further, the external world does not correspond to
the conceptions of religion. How could the external
world hinder so callously the upward tendency of the
life of man, how could it concede to unreason and
injustice so much scope, if it stood under the secure
guardianship of an all-powerful Reason and of an
Infinite Love ?

Thus, doubt burns like a devouring fire and leaps
up into the external province of religion, and also
finds its way into the most holy place and engenders
a tormenting uncertainty. Deep by the side of their
yearning, ardent souls have discovered with pain the
contradiction of the appearances of things, and have
found no consolation in the customary modes of
appeasement. Indeed, with the leading religious
spirits, much that had originated from a joyous
creativeness is hurled back into the abyss of doubt.
The stubbornness of doubt changes with one stroke
the general appearance of things : the joyous high flight
is retarded ; the upward energy is paralysed ; what
hitherto appeared evident, now appears impossible ;
the over-world which is to the faithful the secure and
self-evident standard of life, recedes into an inaccessible distance and, indeed, threatens to resolve itself
into an empty illusion. Religion then appears as a

grand error of the human spirit—as an image of
man's own existence projected into the All, and as a
dream of a more beautiful life to which a reality does
not correspond, but on which he hangs his life.   He
who sees through the dream as a mere dream ought
to undertake an inexorable struggle against such a
falsification of life; he ought not to tolerate religion
patiently, but struggle against it with the whole of his
energy as a deadly error.   Here all possibility of a
third course falls to the ground.   If religion is not
the highest and most fruitful truth, it is the worst
and deadliest of errors; if it is not the work of God,
it is a diabolical testimony of falsehood and darkness.
How can we decide concerning this critical point on
which the course of the whole of our life depends?
How can we flee from the intolerable barriers which
lie between affirmation and negation?

The historical religions have answered these questions in their own way; they have not answered
them through philosophical doctrines but through
the real facts of the work accomplished; they have
not reflected and disputed merely *how* the Divine
glory can enter into the world of man, but have
undertaken to affirm the possibility of the impossible through the *fruits* of its reality.   In the personalities of the founders as well as in the religious
communities the wonder seemed to reach an intuitive
presence, the idea seemed to incarnate itself in flesh
and blood.   Religions felt themselves in the possession of an obvious reality—a reality which liberated
them from all insecurity and armed them against all
doubt.   But, unfortunately, the truth of all this was
not so simple as the believers supposed, for even that

which was to overcome doubt raised a new and greater doubt.

It is fact of an *historical* kind which is expected to consolidate belief. Such a fact must stand out from the remainder of life and develop a distinctive characteristic feature; indeed, the more individual does such a fact become, the more energetically will it work. But, as an expression of Divine truth, the same fact must hold valid for all times; it must govern and permeate the whole compass of life. Is not an intolerable contradiction imbedded in such a belief? Does not the binding of life to one special form of life confine it in too narrow a groove? Will it not cut away all further development, and must it not become a coercive burden which incites human nature to cast it off?

The most casual view of the history of religions places this entanglement clearly before us. Every historical religion borrows peculiar convictions of the world and peculiar valuations of life from its environment. The environment states the question, and religion undertakes the answer. Thus every Indian religion has as its presupposition a strong feeling of the transitoriness and unreality of existence. Can the imposed solution satisfy any one who rejects such a presupposition? And does the matter stand otherwise with Christianity? Can it speak to all men, races, and times if it maintains any definite character, and does it not dissolve itself into vague generalities?

The personalities of the founders constitute the centre of the historical religions. Nothing gives the presence of an over-world within the human circle more convincing energy than the unswerving

constancy with which such personalities are rooted in
the Divine ; than the manner in which they are completely filled by the thought of this one relation ; and
than the simplicity and nearness which the great
mystery has acquired for them.   Hearts have never
been won and minds have never been swayed without
the presence of a regal imagination which understands
how to win visible forms from an unseen world, and
to penetrate through all the multiplicity of things
into a kingdom of a fuller life.   Nothing so elevated
above the ordinary every-day existence is to be found
as this, and nothing has governed the hearts of men
in so compelling a manner as such a secure growth
and such a presence of a new world.

But all this is individual and distinct precisely
where it is great ; so that the religious life which
issues from such a source bears a thoroughly individual character.   Jesus, the Buddha, Mahomet, have
affected humanity in fundamentally different ways.
If one fundamental form is offered to all peoples and
times, does it not exclude much which humanity can
not and dare not relinquish ?

Further, the attempt to mould one religion into a
world-power on the ground of history is dependent
upon the particularity of the transitory historical situation.   Such a formation of religion requires a definite
and highly developed realm of thought, and the means
to obtain this can be no other than the environing
culture and civilisation ; yet though these latter seem
to be no more than handmaids to religion, they work
powerfully upon religion itself.   That culture and
civilisation were the products of particular peoples
and epochs ; sooner or later the whole of humanity

will outgrow them, and if religion is indissolubly bound
up with them, the breach with a past culture and
civilisation yields at the same time a divorce from the
tradition of religion.

Thus doubt upon doubt rises. The Eternal seems
to fall under the ban of time as soon as it touches the
ground of time. But again, if it stands entirely on
something that is conceived as immutable, it becomes
a hindrance to all movement and a denial of all history.
But history is ever present, and its current incessantly
carries forth something new, and an indestructible
need of the life of humanity rejects any imposed
stagnation. In connection with this difficulty it may
seem as if in the alleged Eternal it is not so much the
Divine and Eternal which reveal themselves, as that
a particular kind of human and temporal notions is
founded and sanctioned. Why should we at this
time of day bow before such particularity, and why
should we renounce the independence of our own life?

The historical element which should have supported
religion becomes thus a new burden; doubts concerning an over-world and its province seem now
strengthened all along. Then the uncertainty concerning the whole matter bars an entrance into
religion; indeed, the more we puzzle our brains and
worry ourselves, the further religion seems to recede
from us. " God is the easiest and hardest object to
know; the first and easiest to know on the path of
light; the most difficult and last to know on the path
of darkness " (Leibniz).

CHAPTER II

b. THE CHARACTERISTIC FEATURES
OF CHRISTIANITY

THE general problem of religion increases with the
turn to Christianity. The investigator as well as the
believer willingly acknowledges among the religions
of the world a surpassing greatness in Christianity.
In the first place, Christianity belongs to the higher
of the two groups into which the historical religions
may be divided. *These are either the Religions of
Law or the Religions of Redemption.* To the first,
the kernel of religion is the announcement and
advocacy of a moral order which governs the world
from on high. A fixed decree issuing out of a holy
will is announced to man for his acts, words, and
thoughts; a glorious reward awaits the fulfilment
of this law, and a painful punishment awaits its
transgression, if not in this world yet in the world to
come. Life thus in the whole of its extent is linked
to a super-sensuous world, is drawn to the daily task
and to the decision for or against God. Such a call
to man would be impossible without the conviction
that he is able to select the alternative by means of
his own energy, and that his will suffices for the

adoption of the good. On the other hand, the religions of redemption declare such a conviction as false and superficial. The capacity of man which seems so self-evident to such a conviction becomes to the religions of redemption the most difficult of problems —becomes the most weighty question and concern. Through this growth of the problem, man appears to the religions of redemption as entirely unable in his natural state to reach God, and as a being who falls continually into evil and illusion; and consequently such religions long for an entire transformation and renewal—for a sinking of the old and a raising of the new, and for a great miracle of redemption. How such a miracle is to happen may appear in the beginning entirely puzzling, because man views himself here in the midst of the most difficult entanglements. But the possibility of a deepening of life corresponds to the entanglements; life is conceived more and more as a Whole, and is stirred, convulsed, transformed incomparably more than hitherto. The very opening of such a question relegates the religions of law, despite all the merits of their greater simplicity, transparency, and rationality, to a lower level—to a level which has been reached and passed by the most important inward movement of the world.

Two types—the Indian and the Christian—are to be differentiated in the religions of redemption. As both types understand evil differently, they seek therefore the " cure of souls " in different ways. To the Indian religions, the existence of the world is primarily an evil; the world, with the whole of its natural constitution in space and time, appears as a kingdom of empty semblance. All in it is transient and unreal;

nothing in it has duration; happiness and love are merely momentary; and men are as two pieces of wood floating on the face of an infinite ocean which pass by one another never to meet again. Fruitless agitation and painful deception have fallen upon him who mistakes such a transient semblance for a reality and who hangs his heart upon it. Therefore it behoves man to free himself from such an unholy arena. This emancipation will take place when the semblance is seen through as semblance, and when the soul has gained an insight right into the foundation of things. Then the world loses its power over man; the whole kingdom of deception with its evanescent values goes to the bottom, all the excited affections caused by the world are extinguished, and life becomes a still and holy calm; it reaches the depth of a dreamless sleep, and enters, through its immersion into an eternal essence, beyond the shadows; it passes through its dissolution, into a state of entire unconsciousness according to Buddhism in its most definite interpretation. In all this, no new life with new values opens out in front of us; the emancipation is supposed to consist in a right insight, and each individual has to decide for himself; the leader can only point out the road; the energy to travel over such a road is a matter for the individual himself. A wisdom of world-denial, a calm composure of the nature, an entire serenity in the midst of the changing scenes of life, constitute the summit of life. " When I know that my own body is not mine, and that, further, the whole earth is mine, and, again, that both are mine and thine, then no pain can happen."

What a different kind of spirit breathes in Christianity! Christianity, too, finds the world full of misery and suffering. Its beginnings and its summit are not to be glided over so easily as is done by the ordinary Christianity of our day. But even all the experience of suffering will not allow the world to be simply rejected, but far more, the fundamental construction of the world appears as a perfect work of Divine wisdom and goodness. The root of evil is not in the nature of the world but in moral wrong—in a desertion from God; and it is this moral wrong which first of all brings pain and death into the world. Such a trespass enters so deeply and paralyses so completely the energy of man's nature that the world out of its own potency can never again harbour the Good. Therefore, God Himself must come to man's rescue; He does this through setting forth a redemption over against the fall of man; He does it through the inauguration of a kingdom of love and grace which bestows a new nature on man, and puts its law within his soul. Through such a conversion man is securely raised beyond all suffering and trespass to Divine holiness and perfection; indeed, the deeper has been the discovery of the previous misery, the greater the joyousness which emanates from such a redemption. Thus, there grows a pure impetus of life from the convulsion and the misery themselves; the union with God gives man a secure foothold; the domain of his life does not sink into the abyss of nothingness as in the Indian conception, but he gains a great task— a task to build a kingdom of God upon the earth, and to gain every individual soul for the kingdom. There thus originates here out of effects and counter-effects a world-encompassing drama, full of difficult entanglements and mysterious puzzles, but still of an unfathomable depth and of an immeasurable hope.

Whilst thus the Christian life binds together a world-denial and a world-renewal, whilst it ascends through deepest pain to highest perfection, and whilst, at the same time, the consciousness of trespass and suffering endures in the soul alongside of the consciousness of redemption, it develops a breadth and depth of discernment unknown to other religions, and it gains a perennial inner movement. Nothing lies further from Christianity than an attempt at palliating and excusing suffering. For what purpose then does it need a deliverance if suffering does not oppress man with intolerable gravity? But all suffering cannot stifle man and drive him to despair, because Eternal Love raises him to a new world—a Love which all the power of the enemy cannot harm. But this new world has to be wrested ever anew from the kingdom of darkness, and even within the realm of blessedness an echo of pain is heard. Thus life remains throughout guarded from inactive repose and luxurious enjoyment, and after the conquest itself the struggle does not cease to exist. Man obtains here within the kingdom of belief and hope a secure treasure which appeared at the outset as a distant goal. Thus his existence becomes at the same time a possession and task, rest and effort, joy and pain, certainty and doubt; and along with all this there yields itself that flow of inner life by means of which Christianity far surpasses all other religions.

Further, the Christian life is especially rich in that

it includes in itself two stages—the belief of Jesus himself and the belief of the Christian community in Jesus Christ. In the former we find the proclamation of the kingdom of God upon the earth—the kingdom of love and peace, the inauguration of a new world in the pure inwardness of the spirit of man, a joyous trust in the nature of man as grounded in God, an invitation to all to a share in the great enterprise and feast. Fresh youthful feeling, readiness to serve, world-pervading love, become here the vehicles of a characteristic Christian morality. By the side of the belief in Christ as fixed by the Church a darker picture of human life and a lesser estimation of human capacity prevailed. The idea of evil has now grown to mean a delight in destruction and a diabolical rebellion ; so that the counter-effect to evil must now grow. The kernel of this counter-effect is brought about through atoning and redeeming sufferings—through the appearance of the God-man for the redemption of a humanity that could not redeem itself. Suffering is thus taken up into the Godhead ; man is wholly dependent upon a miracle of undeserved grace ; the Divine Life descends deeper into the soil of humanity, and religion is raised far above all ordinary life and existence. This new stage brings forth difficult entanglements ; the danger of a darkening of life and of falling into a blind devotion and into a mythological mode of thinking takes place. But in all the entanglements and dangers mysterious depths appear throughout, and a new life not only develops through a relationship with God, but also through its collision with an envious world is led through deep reflections to

a more triumphant grasp of truth.   Christianity
through the union of these two stages carried once
more the opposites of life into wider connections and
elaborated more energetically than any other religion
its experiences ; for in the contradictions themselves a
greater richness of life and a more powerful exertion
of man make their appearance.

The fact, however, that the opposites did not lead
to an entire discord but that the effort far more led
back to some kind of union of these discords in a
higher unity is due by Christianity to the supreme
personality of Jesus.   It is true that tradition has
woven around the personality of the Founder many
lineaments which belong to the veneration and interpretation of the earliest Christian community, but
through all the disguising mist there is perceptible to
every unbiassed mind a unique mode of life and
character of incomparable unity of an individual and
intrinsic kind.   Religion has here transformed itself
into a human purity with wonderful energy and inwardness ; a sublime elevation has joined itself
to a simple innocence ; manly energy of action has
united with gentle feelings, and a youthful joy of
disposition with a deep discovery of suffering.   The
distinctive world of spirit has here acquired for
Christianity a personal embodiment and, at the same
time, an overwhelming clearness ; for life and death
a proof founded upon facts has been gathered for the
truth that it affirms—a proof to which Christianity
could ever return from all the entanglements of the
course of the world and from all the strife of parties
in order to call back to memory its own true task, in
order to create fresh energy of life, and to gain clean

beginnings for life. The personality of the Founder
has thus become incomparably more to Christianity
than the founders of all the other religions have
become to their adherents. Christianity in this has
a possession which cannot be lost—a possession that
binds souls to the Founder, but a possession that
protests against the caricature presented by the
Church. And finally the excellences of Christianity
itself must not be forgotten—excellences which its
history and its development into a world-power
testify. Originating on Jewish soil, Christianity
found its education primarily with the Greeks and
soon afterwards with the Romans. Without such a
contact it might have easily remained a mere Jewish
sect, but through these two connections it quickly
forged its way through a narrow nationalism and
opened out its effects upon wider areas. The connection of Christianity with Greece and Rome was
advantageous in two ways. On the one hand, the
new aspirant met a universal and thoroughly-matured
culture, and its effects for the ethical and spiritual
renewal of humanity found their most precious supplement in the desire for knowledge and the sense of
beauty of the Greeks, and in the energy of will and
organising power of the Romans. At the same time,
notwithstanding all the wealthy possessions of culture,
Christianity found in the humanity of the time an
opposite frame of mind. For the glory of antique
life had now exhausted itself, and dark shadows
announced the coming of the night. At the beginning of the third century especially a deep feeling of
fatigue lay over the whole of life and effort, and even
in less-resigned natures this turned into a strong

2

longing for supernatural aid and redemption. As
Christianity went out to meet this longing, its denial
of the world in its direct and most obvious aspects
and its erection of a new world could gain the entire
surrender of souls. Christianity thus shaped itself
into a world-encompassing organisation — into a
Church—which collated the belief in a present Kingdom of God with a visible object. There originated
an encompassing and governing system of life and
culture as religion, which confidently took over the
spiritual guidance of humanity. In reality, the
Christian Church became the mainstay of waning
antiquity and the educator of new aspiring peoples.

In the midst of all the transformations of the times
and in the midst of trials from without and worse
ravages from within, the Church proved itself the
most powerful ally of the life universal which we have
witnessed in all the centuries of the Christian era.

Thus, Christianity appears in the whole of its
effects and existence as the religion of religions. But,
at the same time, it contains far more problems,
meets with far more entanglements, and possesses a
more intricate content than any of the other religions.
All the fundamental points of Christianity clearly
show this.

Christianity develops from the connection of
personality to personality a new world, and explains
this as the kernel of all reality. But does not such
a world, notwithstanding all its depth and spirituality,
become too narrow for the extent and wealth of
existence, and is it alone able to encompass all sides
of the ethical life ? Indeed, does not a danger lie
here close at hand, that the inaugurated kingdom

of love, gentleness, and peaceableness, through their severance from the remaining world, should become merely subjective facts and weak inactive tendencies; that the hard opposition of the world-powers should be evaded rather than gripped; that the exacting humility towards God becomes a slavery towards man, and that a willing endurance should acquiesce to all the unreason of politico-social relations? Christianity uplifts man particularly high through the union of his nature with God—higher than any other religion. But does not the deification of man produce a humanisation of the Divine, and has not anthropomorphism taken root in Christianity far more than in the other great religions? No religion has more definitely flowed parallel with history than Christianity; but no religion has occupied itself so much with the problem how historical events, notwithstanding their particularity, can possess and discover eternal truths. No other religion spans so many different sides and stages, and consequently none has to fight so hard for its own unity; none has been exposed so much to the danger of a severance from one another of these sides and stages, and of their falling out of the domain of truth. First of all, this appeared in that the breach with the ordinary world was not made decisive enough, and did not establish itself firmly enough; and later, in that the transformation of man's nature did not penetrate thoroughly enough; and thus religion degenerates into a mere revolving around the natural life and its tendencies; soon after, a stubborn denial of the possibility of bettering the world turns towards the mere cultivation of one's own environment and

threatens the soul with gaping hollowness. Also,
the two sides of a more general and a more positive
Christianity came easily into dire conflict, and the
unity of the whole remained an ideal from which the
actual situation lagged far behind.

But it is the religious conception of the personality
of Jesus which has caused most trouble and strife.
It did not suffice the Christianity of the Church to
believe *with* Jesus, but it desired also a belief *in* Jesus
Christ as mediator and redeemer. In its doctrines
and principles the Church fought with its whole
energy for the belief that God was present in the
redeemer not only in isolated aspects and energies,
but in the fulness of His nature, and that in the
person of Jesus the Divine and the human were
bound together in an indissoluble unity. Herein is
imbedded something which Christianity can never
abandon. Christianity must in some way be certain
of an inauguration of the Divine Nature within
human life if it is to possess absolute truth and to
exert an abiding influence. But how is this union to
be made conceivable ? And has not the doctrine of
the Church concerning the Deity of Christ as the
second person in the Trinity been a mistake, because
it has mixed up a fundamental truth of religion with
philosophical speculations which hardly any Christian
can understand, and because at the same time it has
tacked on to Christianity the way of thinking of a
particular generation—ideas which threatened to
become mythological to later generations or, indeed,
which have already become so.

Also, in the history of Christianity great dangers
and entanglements met the stated gains. The antique

mode of life, whose ideas Christianity willed to incorporate, became more alien and hostile to the
Christians when they saw through its real nature.
Christianity had previously viewed antique culture
and civilisation through the medium of a religious
disposition, but now it saw that such a mode of life
had no meaning for historical epochs in any characteristic sense. Antique culture and civilisation were
borne along by a joyous belief in a reason immanent
in the world, and it was for the working out of such
a reason that all the energy of man was called forth.
Does not Hellenism with its equating of spirit and
thought tend to entangle Christianity in an intellectualism which its inmost nature combats? And do
not the Greek love of form and its longing after
artistic delineation and plastic embodiments tend to
entangle that pure disposition whose sovereignty
Christianity proclaims? Also, the Roman mode of
thought, with its dependence upon a solid organisation and with its forensic treatment of all relationships, harmonises but little with the Divine Kingdom
of love and peace. The soul of Christianity through
all this was driven back and enfeebled; the same
danger has taken place through ecclesiastical forms,
and the Church has largely succumbed to this danger.
It would have succumbed more had it not been that
ever anew particular personalities have opened out
once more the original fountains of life. Christianity
on account of so much defacement remains yet but a
high ideal.

Further, the lassitude of the civilised world at the
time of its initial contact with Christianity was a
great disadvantage. Christianity had, as its main

purpose, to work against such a fatigue with its "glad tidings," and it has in reality planted a new life-motive of a higher kind in the heart of humanity. But through the enormous influx of merely external elements, Christianity itself fell under the strong influence of that tendency of the age towards stagnation, and relapsed into a disposition and form far too passive. Saturated through and through by the feeling of corruption and weakness of human nature, man yearned for redemption and peace beyond all else ; he desired to unburden himself as much as possible of his own responsibility and to be protected by some fixed authority ; he established himself against tormenting doubt through belief in certain data, and brought forth the miraculous, the magical, and the unintelligible as proofs. To such a mode of thought, the spiritual seemed, without a sensuous embodiment, to lack a completeness of reality, and thus both the spiritual and the sensuous flowed inseparably together. The Divine seemed thus to be more highly honoured the less man and his capacity were valued. A secure rest, beyond all the life of the world, was found here in God ; but no path returned from this rest to the reality around man in the world and to an energetic possession and joyous uplifting of the world. All that is of a spiritual and religious nature in such a position was experienced by the mighty spirit of Augustine. But, at the same time, he stamped for future generations a type of thought of his own age, and brought about the severance of the Divine and the human ; he bound up the spiritual with the sensuous, the invisible with the visible Church, and the effects of all this have continued ever since. It is out of the work of Augustine especially that the religious system of the life of the Church grew, and it was through his energetic concentration that an ark of shelter was offered in the deluge of that epoch of humanity, which, however, with all its spiritual narrowness and constraint, its rigid determinism became intolerable to ages of more courage and independence.

The first shaping of Christianity consequently could not remain incontestable. The first great counter-movement originated upon the ground of religion itself. This was the Reformation. Portions of the Roman and Greek influences were eliminated, and the inmost kernel and unique character of Christianity were once more energetically grasped; through the turn from the Church to personality a more original life, greater energy of character, and a clearer discovery of difficult opposites were gained. But in spite of all the greatness of the Reformation, the whole matter stands in an unfinished state through the fluctuation between old and new modes of thought, and through the failure to come to terms with modern culture. There is thus nothing to prevent the appearance in our modern times of a movement which will call into question not only the ecclesiastical form of Christianity but Christianity itself, and, indeed, call into question all religion, and so involve us in a struggle for life or death.

CHAPTER III

c. The Movement of Modern Times
as against Christianity

Modern thought has entered into conflict with Christianity not only in certain directions but in the whole of its tendencies and efforts; and it is not the beliefs and whims of individuals but the very nature of the work itself which has led to a stern collision. Although individual responsibility is not entirely absent in such a collision, yet this responsibility is not of the kind that can be accredited and attributed to individuals. It is thus necessary to distinguish the movement against Christianity from the work of individuals and parties, and to analyse it according to its own inner structure. It is then necessary to consider in the first place the changes in the world of ideas, and afterwards turn to the changes in the domain of life.

1. *The Changes in the World of Thought*

(a) *Natural Science and Religion.*—The collision between modern thought and religion is most visible in the realm of natural science. Traditional religion has associated itself with a naïve view of nature which

24

considered the earth as the static centre of an encircling universe. Such a religion understands the
creation of the world as the work of a reason superior
to the world—a reason which holds and links nature
together, and makes it a means for its own ends.
And, further, such a religion gives man a matchless
position in which all the conditions are connected
with his weal and woe, and in which the destiny of the
All is linked with his deeds—with his fall and misery,
his elevation and bliss.

Modern science has attacked and destroyed such
a view of nature at three main points. Since the
time of Copernicus it has extended enormously its
field of operation; it has discovered world beyond
world, and has reduced the earth to a mere speck in
the universe; it has removed that distinction between
heaven and earth—a distinction which signified so
much to religious conceptions and feelings. Can
then that which is only a satellite amongst an
innumerable host of fixed stars decide concerning
the destiny of the All? And what becomes of an
"ascension to heaven" when there is no heaven in
the old-fashioned sense—no above or below in this
boundless space?

Next comes the inward change of nature depicted by
Galileo and Descartes. All psychic energies, all aims
and ends, are removed from nature, for they resolve
themselves into a co-existence of the most minute
elements which work upon one another only through
gravity and impact, and whose whole mechanism is
entirely evident. Thus every phenomenon is reduced
to the same level and nature, and follows simple
and inviolable laws; nothing individual or unique

can break this circle, and no psychic energy can turn any phenomenon out of its course.

Such a mode of thought which invests nature with entire independence and inner completion collides severely with the religious view of nature, especially in the problem of miracle; for miracle is as intolerable in the realm of this mode of thought as it is indispensable in the realm of religion. Miracle is "the dearest child of belief"; to refer each and every phenomenon back to natural causality seems to destroy religion to its very foundation. No religion has so strenuously defended miracle—even sensuous miracle—as the Christianity of the Church; "and if Christ hath not been raised, your faith is vain." Modern natural science, on the contrary, has unmercifully driven miracle out of its domain; miracle signifies to it what it signified to Spinoza — not something above nature but something contrary to nature; every particular break in the order of nature appears to modern science as a destruction of its fundamental structure, and as a denial of its validity.

Miracle is but one point of the acute collision of opposites, for in reality the line of battle extends much farther. The transformation of all into a soulless mechanism renders nature through and through equally indifferent to all spiritual values as well as to all religious and moral aims. Nature follows its course with iron laws and has no regard whatever for what is termed good or evil by man.

> " Devoid of all feeling
> Blind Nature proceeds,
> The sun shines as brightly
> Whatever the deeds;

> The moonlight and starlight
> Wrap equally too
> The saint and the sinner,
> The false and the true."

Thus, the human circle becomes isolated in the All of things, whereas formerly it felt itself the ruling centre.

Finally, in the nineteenth century the doctrine of evolution appears and sets the coping-stone on the whole of the previous work. Hitherto, the scientific conception of nature found an insuperable barrier in the organic kingdom, and consequently the religious interpretation could always return to this one impregnable citadel. Lamarck appeared, and later Darwin. However much remains disputable in the theories of each, the general meaning of the evolutionary theory has passed from the realm of discussion to the realm of fact. Scientists are agreed that the forms of life did not stand side by side as completed things in the beginning, but are causally linked with one another, and that the higher have proceeded out of the lower through natural changes. And it is also agreed that man is related to nature, and that characteristics of nature extend, too, into his life. There was thus developed a biological interpretation of human and mental greatness which contradicts directly the ethico-religious interpretation. The ethico-religious interpretation measured the values of all activities and experiences according to their relationship with God and with the Kingdom of God which was above the world; the biological explanation estimates qualities according to their use and their preservation in the struggle for existence. In the former mode of

thought, eternal values are aspired after in spite of
all the changes of time; in the latter mode, the
valuation of things must perpetually alter according
to the changes in the external situations, for what is
of use to-day may become injurious to-morrow, and
inversely. In the religious mode of thought, a pure
inwardness should construct itself, and the gaining
of the whole world could not compensate for the loss
of the soul; in the scientific mode all tendencies and
efforts are directed towards the external, and the
" soul " has become an empty word. In all this, the
irreconcilable opposition to religion is evident, and
both modes cannot possibly exist together. But
natural science is here in our midst, and has, step by
step, further developed with an inevitable kind of
necessity. It has not only brought forth an immense
fulness of results, but has even opened out a new
course of thought—a more precise insight, a clearer
line of demarcation, and a stronger affinity with
causal connections and real facts; it has, through
this work, turned against the course of thinking
that underlies religion, and has declared religion as
scientifically untenable. Is religion able to withstand
such a mighty current ?

(β) *History and Religion.*—History, to the opponents of religion, associates itself with nature.
Traditional religion in its combat with the meaning
of history has experienced a blow which has affected
its inmost nature. According to the religious view,
human history and even our earth have had but a
short span of existence, and all that appeared on these
domains received its aim and its driving energy from
the Godhead who reigned above the world. The

Godhead had preordained the plan of the whole; destiny had linked itself to each individual; prophets and heroes were sent "when the time was fulfilled." The main task of history was the education of human nature—of each individual—for an eternal life beyond the process of history, whose kernel constituted the struggle between good and evil, and which connects itself as a great drama from creation morn to the day of judgment. Everything outside this remained a mere environment, and had a significance only through its relation to the soul of the whole. It is from such a conviction that all results and experiences were interpreted, and one grew so accustomed to such an interpretation that one believed himself able to verify everywhere and at a glance such a guidance of affairs, and to discover everywhere "the finger of God."

How much all this has been altered! And the change has happened less through any sharp catastrophe than through a gradual crumbling away and a rebuilding. The extension of time, just as the extension of space, has grown into infinity; science reckons the age of the earth by millions of years; and short as human history appears in comparison with such a vast period of time, it, too, has continually extended its duration; the epochs of civilisation shrivel into insignificance when compared with the immeasurable extent of "prehistoric" times. And, further, as the presence of organic and also of mental life seems dependent upon certain indispensable conditions of existence, modern thought conceives the existence of man as a mere episode of the world-process—an episode which, compared with infinite

duration, is no more than that of a meteor in an
infinite sky which illumines and suddenly vanishes.

But the inward transformations have been still
deeper. History as well as nature has developed an
independence. As the supernatural was expelled
from nature, so the over-historical now falls under
the ban of history. Certain motive-powers were
acknowledged within the human domain ; certain
aims were exhibited ; these phenomena linked themselves directly with one another, and thus united
themselves into a great web. Each individual
example is now understood through these connections ; the highest instance is now no more
valued as an isolated miracle, but as the climax of
a movement, and such an instance grows out of the
conditions and environment. When history is thus
understood as something that has grown out of a
prior history "immanent" in it, all conceptions of
supernatural powers become an intolerable disturbance ; and it is this which renders history such an
irreconcilable opponent of traditional religion.

The same aspect appears in the knowledge that
any movement proceeds and progresses from point to
point—a fact which leads us to conceive history as a
continuous process of evolution. Thus history as a
whole gains a task and a meaning by itself; the per-
spective of a better and even an endless ascent of a
capacious future invests present existence with an expansion and a task within its own province, and raises
it above all the evils of the present. The religious
hope of a culminated bliss in the next world fades
away before such a belief in the future of *this* world.

Where there is so much to do and to alter within the

sphere of time—and, indeed, here alone such a work is able to transform reality into a kingdom of reason —such a work cannot be viewed as something futile and transitory; and consequently aspiration and hope do not depend entirely upon eternity. Simultaneously the feeling of the impatience of man disappears. He seems now, under the new conditions, thrown in the main on his own energies; he reaches his majority; he does not receive his destiny from a superior power but rather shapes it through manly deeds. And thus it is not towards a supernatural kingdom of God but towards the welfare of man and humanity that the focus of attention is directed.

The conflict into which the historical and the religious convictions enter becomes specially bitter in connection with the problem of truth. Religion understands truth as simply eternal and unchangeable; although the Divine revelation discloses itself within time, it is in no manner a product of time, it does not follow the current of time; and it views all change as a degradation. The historical development, on the contrary, with the incessant shifting of its situation and its restless progress, transforms truth into a child of the times (*veritas temporis filia*); the tendencies as well as the convictions have to correspond to the exigencies of the situation of things. On account of this, all spiritual values become fluid, all truth becomes relative, all unfolding into absolute validity of the intrinsic content of thought and belief is energetically fought against. If, however, religion can never renounce an absolute and eternal truth, all decision in favour of history will be a decision against religion.

Further, the definite development of historical investigation becomes highly dangerous to a religion such as Christianity, which rests first and foremost upon historical events. The naïve mode of thought which accepted indiscriminately the transmitted picture of earlier ages, and simultaneously combined the manifold lore into a homogeneous whole, cannot stand before an awakened will and a keen critical consciousness. We cannot disguise the fact that what hitherto has been accepted as unalloyed truth and as a genuine expression of reality contains ever so much subjectivity of conception and adjustment, that we do not so much see real facts as the veil which human opinion and imagination have woven around them. How slowly and guardedly do we climb even to-day towards the facts as towards an unattainable ideal which, to earlier times, seemed so safe and certain. Growing historical criticism will not allow itself to be precluded from dealing with religious tradition, for hardly anywhere else has it shown so conspicuously its achievements, purged so fundamentally the transmitted pictorial ideas, and transformed the transmitted picture. What appeared in earlier times as a totality or whole now discloses deep differences and pointed contradictions not merely in subsidiary aspects, but in fundamental and essential characteristics. We find this, for instance, in the New Testament—in the widely divergent pictures of Jesus and in the fundamentally different representations of Christianity; so that much which came to be regarded as the main facts by believers in later times was not such to the original witnesses, or if it were it was only in a hardly perceptible form ;

and no unbiassed mind can fail to detect a great chasm between the dogmas of the Church and their historical foundation in the Bible. All this gives rise to problems concerning the authenticity of the sources with all their contentions and minute discussions. Whether the results of criticism are positive or negative is of far less importance than that the trustworthiness of the records depends upon scientific proof, and that the Divine is not poured directly upon us, but is to be found by man through the toilsome work of thought. The criticism and conclusions reached by this mode of thought have irreparably destroyed the halo which once surrounded the tradition; the dazzling light of science has dispelled unmercifully that dreamlike semi-darkness of the religious imagination in which heaven and earth seemed to blend into one another. Thus the gains of history become a loss to religion. As a religion founded upon history experiences a loss in so far as the more precise insight and the more essential conception of the past become clear through the necessary results of a critical mode of inquiry which fixes the boundaries more distinctly between one age and another, and along with this utilises the results of the past, such a religion does not readily permit itself to be flooded and overwhelmed by the results of such criticism. Sacred history was pictorially present to earlier generations, and they saw the particular time and surroundings in the light of this history. Whilst historical criticism has rendered this impossible, it has at the same time destroyed the predominant position of sacred history.

3

But the doubt and discord reach still deeper.   The inner content of the tradition becomes a problem to modern thought, but such a mode of thought finds it impossible to establish basal convictions upon historical events.   What influences the spiritual self-preservation of man must be experienced in the form of immediacy, and must be verified by man himself; and all this cannot be imposed from without.   Whilst the *Aufklärung* for the first time brought this truth to expression over against all bare tradition, it differentiated too sharply reason and history, the individual life and tradition, and overestimated the power of any present moment of consciousness.   But even we who view history in a more friendly manner are not able to give up the self-reliance which life has gained through such a turn ;   and yet history for us to-day can never take the first but the second place, because only so much in it can be valid for our life as allows itself to enter into self-consciousness.   In this respect the words of Lessing hold good :   " Accidental—*i.e.* actually empirical—truths of history can never become proofs of the necessary truths of reason."   And if life thus disengages itself from the bond of history, it becomes an intolerable coercion to bind the salvation of man to an easy acknowledgment of historical events. " To state that an historical belief is a duty and that it belongs to salvation is superstition " (Kant).   " Let no one assert that it does no harm to cling to such historical beliefs.   It is injurious in that subsidiary facts are given equal validity with essential ones, or, indeed, are presented as the essential facts, and consequently the main facts are suppressed and the conscience is tormented " (Fichte).

The meaning of history has thus brought forth all along the line a mode of thought other than is apprehended by religion. And no religion has received greater shocks in this respect than Christianity, on account of the fact that it is more closely bound up with historical points of view as well as with historical events than any other religion.

(γ) *The Spiritual Life and Religion.*—Religion is so injuriously affected by nature and history that the most important point has not yet been touched by us. This point lies in the inner nature of life itself—a point which is the source of all practical proof and mode of thinking. Between that, on the one hand, which religions in general teach, and that, on the other hand, which modern culture in the whole of its development maintains, a deep cleft has been created, so that what hitherto held good as the kernel of all reality now threatens to vanish into a hollow semblance.

The life of the human soul, from the standpoint of an old mode of thought, was most intimately interwoven with the environment of the world; mutual energies swayed within and without in the particular and in the general, and all things seemed to find their true rest in the mind and soul of man. No kind of doubt could be raised as to the legitimacy of depicting the all-ruling Power in terms of human analogy, or of understanding the intercourse with such a Power as a relationship of soul to soul in the manner of relationship of man with man. All the values of religion thus shaped themselves by means of the immediate life of the soul of man; from such a point of immediacy alone could such conceptions as love, grace, and trust obtain a meaning. No religion, however, places the inwardness of the soul higher than Christianity with its message of an Infinite Love and of the immediate presence of the Kingdom of God.

Now, the work of modern times, as we have already seen, has altered in an important manner the position and the valuation of the life of the soul. The soul has been banished out of nature, and, along with this, out of the world ; thus it had to shape itself into a particular kingdom of its own—into a totality of life and thought within its own circle. The barriers of such an isolated life become more and more perceptible ; viewed as merely existing for itself, or considering that external phenomena exist apart from itself, or being indifferent to the inward aspect of things, the soul becomes too narrow for a spiritual work which more and more decisively develops a cosmic character. Thus, the larger and wider outlook disengages itself from the immediate consciousness, turns against the soul, and sets it in a position of a mere epiphenomenon. Thus, the particular forms of life, such as art and science, politics and technics, separate themselves and form provinces of their own, and something of this kind happens finally with the whole results of culture. Everywhere independent provinces originate and engender their own tasks, laws, and motive-powers ; they carry their own aims and ends in themselves, reject all relationship with the self-existence of the soul, and look upon all standards which value the deeper welfare of the individual as disfigurements. United indissolubly with modern culture are its impersonal character, its continuous positing on itself and continuous movement outside itself, and its alleged superiority over all human plans and "ends." Indeed, the true greatness of man now appears in that he lays on one side all mere self-existence, and transforms himself into a willing tool of the processes of civilisation and culture. No one has presented such a penetrating and fundamental view of the whole processes of modern civilisation and culture as Hegel, and his ideas have operated with remarkable effect through the nineteenth century right up to the present day.

But such a work and creativeness, brought about through actual necessities, are not able to draw the life into themselves without an entire transformation of its ideals. The subjective disposition and, along with it, all the ethical relationships of man retire to the background when face to face with the proclamation of such an external spiritual energy brought forth through the co-operation of the process of civilisation. Consequently the old inwardness of the soul with all its greatness and goodness is ordered out of the centre of life to the periphery ; indeed, the soul is now driven not only out of nature but out of its own inward life as well.

We cannot conceive of a more deadly assault on religion than all this. For if the soul sinks so low to the level of a subsidiary thing, it cannot furnish the standard for man's view of reality ; and, consequently, the whole ideal world of religion appears as a mere anthropomorphism and as an unbearable falsification of reality. Positivism, following such a train of thought, has considered religion as a mere stage of development upon which man, through a childish illusion, sees magnified human powers in the universe, and believes himself capable of conversing with such

powers. Positivism has not the least place for
religion in the old sense. If it continues to hold
some kind of conception of God, this cannot signify
anything more than a basal world-substance or a
pervading world-energy. Here no personal relationship to such a substance is gained, and conceptions
such as love and grace, belief and trust, lose their
meaning. It is not only this or that point in religion
which now becomes a mythology, but the whole of
religion itself; it becomes now a stage of life which
has been passed by mental development. And along
with the downfall of religion, the downfall of morality
takes place, for how can qualities such as character
and conviction signify a value if all independent inner
life is suppressed? Such an ejection of religion and
morality by an impersonal process of culture must
affect Christianity in a most serious manner, because it
has maintained the independence of the inner life more
confidently and has developed itself more powerfully
than any other religion. Indeed, according to this
positivistic mode of thinking, the higher Christianity
set its aim, the deeper must its fall now be.

Thus, it is not only on account of the new conception of nature and of historico-social work but also
on account of the fundamental woof of life itself
that religion—indeed, all possibility of a religion—is
driven out. All the counter-effects mutually protect
and heighten one another. This work, indeed, in
some particular points, is far from leading to such a
negative conclusion; and it is often asserted with an
honourable conviction that the special changes in our
views of nature and history leave untouched the
entire system of religion. But, indeed, when it

happens in other points—and in all other points—that
all the particular corner-stones crumble into pieces,
what becomes of the construction of the whole building? The greatness and pre-eminence of this mode
of thought is that men proceeded at the start not to
destroy in any way, but were far more desirous to
bind and to fit into one another the old and the new ;
but the truths discovered cast off all this embellish-
ment and, indifferent to human views and plans, went
their way towards their own goal. And this road
leads towards the destruction of religion.

2. *The Variation of the Direction of Life*

It needs but few words in order to show that a
change in the drift of life corresponds to the transformation of the world of ideas. Hand in hand with
natural science proceeds the development of modern
technics, and with the rise of this, man has ceased to
be powerless against nature, and has become much
rather its lord and ruler. He can now with good
courage take up the struggle against all limits and
hindrances ; he can extend his life beyond all bounds
through the appropriation of natural energies ; he can
intensify the richness of life, and shape it into greater
enjoyment. Through the progressive inauguration of
new perspectives and tasks he gains a remarkable consciousness of human capacity and human superiority.
This disposition of joyous energy and courageous faith
develops over against the life of political and social
activity. Constraint and unreason cease to be conceived as necessities laid upon him by destiny whose
effects he may alleviate but whose root he cannot

destroy. Modern man, in the use of all the means of culture and in the severe clash of energies, feels himself strong enough to shape his existence into a kingdom of reason, and to make the real rational and the rational real. However many the oppositions which stand against him, these produce a feeling of life which is far more a stimulus than a deterrent to activity. In any case, man does not expect this result to proceed from any supernatural agencies, but achieves it through his own inmost exertions. In addition to this, the new ideal of life appears with its superiority to the ordinary human situation, and with its inauguration of an immeasurably richer Spiritual Life of an objective kind filled with independent contents and moved by inner necessities. Infinitely more clearness, breadth, and reality seem to enter into our life through all this, as well as a truth which does not proceed from a supernatural communication but from our own activity.

Indeed, our environing world furnishes an abundance of work and expansion ; it is able so to occupy man with itself, so as to hold him fast in the inwardness of his being, that not the least desire arises for another mode of life. The more such a tendency in the direction of the world takes possession of the whole soul of man, the more religion loses its foundation, the clearer becomes the opposition to the ages in which Christianity gained its most important achievements, and the greater appears the whole history of modern times as a progressive transference of life from a world of belief and fancy into the world of immediate existence.

Christianity in its beginnings could never have

undertaken its work for humanity without setting up a world of belief and hope over against the existing world, and without announcing such a new world as the true home of man. When Christianity, however, achieved its triumph it laid the world "beyond" in front of a tired world devoid of any special hope; and now the hoped-for life did not seem able to proceed from the present world, but proceeded only out of a new order of things. The character of the present world is clearly depicted in this way by Augustine through the ardour of his conviction and the energy of his writings. The new world is to him no distant realm but the most intimate world, which furnishes first and foremost in the toils and tangles of existence a spiritual self-reliance, which alone justifies the will to live. But the new world drives the sensuous world to the periphery of existence, and draws to itself the work and will of man. All the ramifications of culture and civilisation, according to Augustine, had but one aim—to raise man to a higher world, to indicate that the multiplicity of things should reach a world-swaying unity, and to direct all activity to the point where its toil and anxiety suddenly change into an intuitive vision of Eternal Truth and into the worship of Infinite Love. An inmost kernel of the life of the soul is here raised above all the entanglement of the work of the world, and fixes itself securely in the Divine Life. From such a level above the world, the soul is not driven back again to the world; man feels himself most secure in the midst of the persistence of antagonism and in the midst of all the blows of toil and anxiety. "Thou hast created us for Thyself, and our heart

is not at rest until it rests in Thee." This religion
of a thorough transcendental kind experiences in the
Church-system of the Middle Ages a certain worldly
culture and mellowing, but the world of faith remained
still the main world, and it had now become the
nearest inmost world of the soul, and was designated
at the height of Scholasticism as Fatherland (*patria*).
All this meant that religion formed the kernel of
life, and that the Church became the vehicle of all
the ideal interests of humanity. But a new path
of most important significance was soon opened by
new nations with their fresh courage of life. The
prior life with its belief and hope, with its weaving
of a feeling alien to the world, lost gradually its power
of attraction; it was discovered as being too passive,
too soft and dreamy; the desire arose more and more
strongly after dealings and connections with the
world around us—after an exercise of human energy
in the struggle with the hardness of the things of
the world, and after a more awakened and more
genuine life. Man and the world were more sharply
severed; subject and object were more clearly differentiated. A new morning seemed to dawn and an
immeasurable day's work lay before humanity. Thus
meaning and thought entered more and more into
the world instead of severing themselves from it;
the natural impulse of life was changed throughout,
and this change was not favourable to religion.

But this great change culminated very gradually,
and appeared in three main stages. The new life
appears first of all in the Renaissance; the minds of
men here moved more freely, and the narrowness of
the ideas with which man had depicted human life

and the world fell away. Man now not only discovers distant lands, but before all else he discovers himself, gains a vivid consciousness of his own energy, and takes a joyous possession of the unlimited opulence of the world. What draws and holds man is, on the one hand, mainly the fulness of life which everywhere wells up, and, on the other hand, the beauty which shines through all the forms of life. From such convictions and experiences there grows an ideal of a harmonious development of the whole man; and in the modern civilised state, the effort to adorn the "here and now" obtains a fast root, for the natural sphere of life drives ever forward new tasks, and gains ever new energies. But notwithstanding all its independence, the new mode of life does not as yet enter into a struggle with the old mode: at the height of the Renaissance both modes seem to seek one another rather than to flee from one another. The natural world is conceived as beautiful and inexhaustible because it constitutes the impress and reflection of the Divine Life; religion, however, receives its most valuable development through independent art which invests the lofty contour of belief with an intuitive nearness and enchanted loveliness. Thus, religion and artistic culture walk together hand in hand, and the contradictions imbedded in such a relationship are yet to be discovered.

Soon, however, the movement passes beyond such a combination, and insists at last upon a closer and more vital unity of life. This step took place in its most powerfully creative form in the time of Spinoza. Its aim was to bind together God and the world into a unique indissoluble reality. Since the Divine permeates the whole world and gives it a depth, the world becomes more than its immediate appearance reveals, and transforms itself into a kingdom of reason without any lacunæ. The Godhead, thus drawn into the world, must, however, lay aside all that is narrow and merely human, must be conceived as beyond all the limits of human conception, and must be raised to an all-encompassing eternity and infinity. Thus, religion can no more be a particular province which governs existence from a height " beyond," but seems to fulfil its task far better the more it lays on one side any particular and isolated formations, and permeates all its work with invisible effects. The aspects which united man with the great All constituted here the kernel of existence and raised him to a cosmic life ; these aspects being science and art in the sense of an ideal culture. These create, through their world-encompassing thought and free-play of imagination, a new kind of spiritual reality over against the ordinary daily life ; and, further, they ennoble all human relations, and bestow the infinite and eternal upon man in the midst of his daily life. Indeed, the more the reality transforms itself thus into a kingdom of reason, the more does a cosmos raise itself out of the chaos of an initial cosmogony, and the more the need for any special religion disappears. Religion becomes now a kind of finger-post to those to whom the mental creativeness of science and art is denied. " He who possesses science and art possesses also religion. He who does not possess them has religion as something distinct."

But, notwithstanding its great achievements, this pantheistic ideal of culture has not had a permanent hold on humanity. On the one hand, its spiritualisation of reality signifies a stepping beyond experience, so that experience could justify itself less and less with the fading away of an over-world. On the other hand, there grows a stronger feeling of the mystery and suffering of the world, destroying the calm of the pantheistic view—a view which, in its contemplation of the whole of things, left almost entirely on one side the unreason of particular phenomena. But if our world is not a realm of reason, it necessitates us to seek an explanation beyond the domains of pantheism. And thus the movement proceeds towards a powerful contraction of life upon immediate existence, upon a development of a natural culture, which forbids all progress, interpretation, and elevation beyond the realm of ordinary life. The kernel of such a life is formed by the empirical investigation of nature, together with technics and the practical politics of human society. There then originates a newer and more secular type of life with such energy and self-consciousness as have never been hitherto witnessed. Such a type of life has justified itself through undreamed-of achievements; it has opened out a large region of new tasks which have drawn man ever more exclusively into their vortex, and which have busied him almost breathlessly. Thus, life seems prepared to value all the definite energy of man and to fulfil all his entitled hopes. But the more the spiritual activity binds itself to such a reality, the more shadowy and untenable becomes each and every religion. True, such a secular culture can well proclaim that the circle of human life constitutes but a small segment of the unbounded reality, and that,

indeed, with all its extension, it belongs only to the
surface of things, and beneath it all there lies for ever
a dark and inaccessible depth.   But as such a culture
fails to obtain any inward connection with such a
depth, all its gains are of no avail to religion.

And so the trend of modern times has been to
move farther and farther from religion, and to tie man
ever more securely to the visible world.   The union
of religion and natural culture was succeeded by a
culture which turned itself into a kind of religion,
and this was followed finally by a culture devoid of
any kind of religion.   So that the tendency towards
the world grew ever stronger, and more and more
such a tendency divested itself of all super-sensuous
connections, while at the same time it gave man
far more to do in the realms of knowledge and action ;
and in certain departments it has become so rich in
content that it seems to be able to satisfy the whole
of life and effort.

Religion, without a doubt, roots itself too firmly in
the convictions of individuals and in the organisations
of society to allow such consequences of material
culture to come into full and immediate effect,
although nowhere is the centre of gravity of duration
more apparent than in these realms.   For the individual in particular, the inwardness of his soul and the
infinite aspiration of his mind constitute a sanctuary
to which he flees out of all the struggles, and from
which he can hold forth his inner experience as a
shield against all attacks.   But this refuge of the
individual signifies no stronghold for all men.   Notwithstanding the spiritual content of his life, man
remains bound to the ordinary situation of humanity ;

it is not given to him to set forth victoriously the ideals which fill the depth of his soul against culture and civilisation, so that religion becomes more and more a mere private concern—a mere ebb and flow of a subjective kind—falling down to the level of sectarianism and the miraculous. And, finally, all cautious restrictions are insufficient to prevent an entire expiration.

Can we then wonder that the opponents of religion consider that the matter has been investigated and decided? To such minds religion is upheld by idleness and dulness or even at the best by selfish interest. Such a total extinction of religion was anticipated with certainty and in the immediate future by the main trend of thought in the eighteenth century. Winckelmann in 1768 could write from Rome that in fifty years there would not be in Rome either a pope or a priest. Such an extinction of religion which, it was then thought, would take place as a gradually dying ember, is, in our day, being sought through a violent attempt at scattering doubts and denials amongst the masses.

CHAPTER IV

d. The Reconsolidation of Religion

The priesthood has outlasted its supposed appointed span of time, and seems far from vanishing; and religion, too, does not exhibit the situation which its opponents expected. Though its deficiencies are seen by ever wider circles, and though the ordinary disposition of man does not correspond to the atmosphere of spiritual activity, yet on its heights, religion proves itself again the possessor of much energy of life— an energy which seems on a deeper view of it to show that the condemnation of religion is more of an echo of the past than of a promise of the future. The Churches show such a renewal of religion in the most tangible manner. How much has their power grown, how much more definitely have they stamped the various contrasts and values of things, and how ardently do their struggles rouse the soul! True, such energy has not been limited to causes of an inward character. The democratic atmosphere of the nineteenth century increased the power of the Church, since it heightened the power of the masses who were least affected by culture and its doubts. Further, the severe concentration of life and the growing potency of great

48

organisations have worked in a similar direction. But although such and other changes explain much, they do not explain everything—they do not explain the inner activity, the spiritual creativeness, and the aspiring power of the Churches. And this growth of religion is by no means confined to the Churches: it appears, too, outside them and, indeed, in direct opposition to them ; it forms a trait in the life of the present which grows stronger and stronger. Philosophy—the old enemy of religion—applies itself most ardently to create a free place for religion; literary art treats with great earnestness the Yea and the Nay of religious questions; the fine arts seek to approach religious forms through new explanatory forms of modern make; and finally the religious problem, beyond all these particular provinces, proceeds again mightily in the soul itself. Many phenomena point to a close affinity of our day with that early age which for the first time raised religion into a world-power ; for in the midst of all the negation and condemnation a new wave of religion seems to rise and to carry humanity along on its breast.

How is this notable change to be understood ? If the movement against religion has continued, and, indeed, has swelled out further and further, the cause of this lies in the fact that the counter-effect has grown, and that religion has exhibited a stronger potency and a deeper root in human life than its opponents had attributed to it. First of all, it has, upon a new ground, brought forth new achievements ; it has, in the midst of modern life, developed a fine benevolence over against the pompous moral and social pretentions ; it has commanded to many individuals a

4

longed-for halt over against the growing destruction
of life. On account of such achievements, the extinguishing of religion can never be regarded as a pure
gain. But however highly we may regard what
religion has brought forth in the form of love and
service, the main cause of its vitality is not contained
in such achievements ; this main cause is of a far more
indirect kind : it consists in the most difficult inner
entanglements of the very spiritual force itself—entanglements which at first threatened the progress of
religion ; it consists in the upheaval of the belief in
the all-sufficiency of modern self-satisfied and self-
conscious culture and civilisation. All wavering of
this belief works in the direction of the lessening
of the opposition to religion ; indeed, the more doubt
in culture and civilisation advances, the more is
the total position of man changed ; new dispositions
are awakened and new avenues of life open out ;
religion has once more the ear of humanity who had
temporarily turned away from it, and once more it is
able to prove that what is imbedded in it is of price-
less value.

Modern culture has had to learn that all life within
the human domain is at the same time self-energising,
and that self-development is simultaneously self-crea-
tiveness. The advancement of life's own movement
brought it against barriers undreamed of, and drove it
into consequences unwilled by the individual. Life
crosses beyond the line which hitherto had been
its haven of refuge, and at each farther remove man
appears unable to govern the current of life and to
make it a tributary of reason. Thus what might be
a Whole of life, but which through such exclusiveness

is bound to prove a deadly enemy of religion, must,
unless reason and culture are to fall to the ground,
be a mere piece of a further life.

The scientific, historical, philosophical, and social
modes of thought have developed into systems, and
have made demands upon the whole of life. But
the greater their achievements the less complete do
they appear, and the more overpowering is the
protest against them; the more is the ground
destroyed upon which they have grown; and the
more insufficient and even unbearable does the
whole situation become. It is especially in its relation to man and in connection with the problem how
to found and how to construct all activity and work
from the depth of the soul that modern culture has
miscarried in spite of all its value. We must now
look more closely at this fact.

In these systems there has originated a mighty
movement to consider nature as the sole reality, and
man as a mere product of nature. So far as such an
attempt gains any success, man becomes a piece of
a meaningless mechanism, which moves, it is true,
according to definite laws; he becomes altogether
a creature of his environment; he is by no means
able to maintain a self-reliance over against the
process of nature, and the life of his soul must
reconcile itself entirely to the standards of nature,
and is unable to bring forth anything essentially new.
Often has man desired, as he desires to-day, to retain
some old values of the more human kind in the
process of the destruction of the old world of
thought; and with such a radical denial a kind of
practical idealism seems quite easily tenable: love

and humaneness may appear strengthened although
they have been founded upon nature alone without
the aid of any metaphysic.   Whilst this is an unbearable half-heartedness and even thoughtlessness, it
further destroys the final roots of conceptions, as
character, deed, inwardness, and it has absolutely no
place for moral valuation and noble idealism.   This
appears specially clear in the biological mode of
thought, which transforms our whole life into a
struggle for natural existence, and subordinates and
sacrifices the good to the useful.   At the same time,
all questions concerning the meaning of life vanish
more and more, until the bare actuality of physical
existence exclusively holds the field.   It may be
that the senselessness and soullessness of human
existence is hardly noticed on account of the haste
and press of modern life, and the loss is hardly discovered because science itself has not been drawn
into the same vicious circle.   And the reason is
clear: a consistent naturalism is not able to permit
science of any kind.   Science is constructed through
the activity of the human mind alone ; but how could
the mind construct it if its intellectual achievements
spent themselves in a mere raising up and accumu-
lating of isolated impressions, and if such achievements never succeeded in reaching a commanding
view of the isolated impressions, and still less succeeded in welding such impressions into a Whole ?
In reality, even modern natural science, with its conquest over the naïve world-view, has become possible
only through an energetic analysis and clearing away
of the first impressions of things, through an advance
towards simple phenomena and the discovery of their

laws, through the establishing of new connections by
the aid of prior ideas.   All this takes place through
the observation of the different behaviour of things
on the one hand, and their natural relationship and
systematic union on the other hand.   Thus, through
the work of the mind, the path leads to a scientific
conception of nature.   This scientific conception
could not verify itself from the things themselves,
but the verification had to be traced within the
mind; and, in the subjugation of the external world,
science remains above all an inner result.   Now, if
all inner result breaks away from its inward source
—from independent inwardness—and if life is laid
entirely upon its connection with external things,
the result is that science, and more particularly
natural science, must collapse, or, on the contrary,
that naturalism with its equalisation of sensuous
nature and reality must be given up.   Whenever
effective mental work finds recognition in natural
science, especially where it has led to an illumination
of things, so that the total mirroring of nature was
not something given entirely from the outside but
something brought forth from the mind, it develops
itself into a critical mode of thought.   Such a mode
of thought succeeds more and more in winning
recognition upon the summits of modern life, and
exercises a decisive resistance to the turning of reality
into a mere natural thing.   And, at the same time,
the path is left open for the formation of new ways
of envisaging life; and great problems, which forbid
any ready-made solution, awaken.

Further, the historical treatment of things has
made towards the superiority and sovereignty of

thought and life.   By bringing an existence otherwise numb into motion, the historical treatment has
given life more freedom, movement, and richness ;
the present has been freed from the tyranny of the
past and raised to an entire self-reliance.   The culminated transformation has entered so deeply into
life that a simple retreat to the old situation is now
absolutely forbidden.   But wherever the new mode
of thought holds exclusively the field, there issues
out of it a destructive energy.   If all stability in face
of the flux of semblance gives way, all that is solid
and durable melts away ; truth becomes not merely
the child of the age, as of the passing moment, but
through discarding its own true nature becomes an
unreality ; even the present itself, which before all
else should have been strengthened, fades away,
whilst the course of events resolves itself into a
succession of fleeting moments.   But a life that
resigns all solid aims and permanent norms, and
becomes the mere play of wind and wave, must
more and more fall into shallowness and relinquish all
content.   But man does not seem willing to be
merged in the fleeting lapse of the moment : he holds
himself inwardly fast ; he compares and questions
different aims for his life ; he has no choice but to
differentiate, select, and reject things.   Therefore his
life cannot entirely flow on the current of appearances.

" Within the hope of man alone
    The highest goal draws nigh,
He chooses, raises up his soul
    To that which is on high ;
He can duration to the moment give,
He can in Time the Eternal live."

The fact that man experiences all changes—that
each change is known by consciousness—proves that
he does not belong entirely to the domain of flux.
In so far as he in his deeper nature is more than a
flux of isolated occurrences, the incessant changes and
alterations cannot possibly satisfy him.   The nobility
and lightheartedness which seemed to him at first to
be a pure gain proceed from an unbearable emptiness and mar the deepest life.   For how could
any kind of joyous expansion of life be possible if
moment devours moment without ceasing, if what is
honoured at one moment is thrown on one side the
next ?   The nineteenth century discovered how unbearable is such a view of things, for ideal succeeded
ideal with amazing rapidity, disposition succeeded disposition with the turn of fortune's wheel, and the duration of alleged truths became shorter and shorter.
But in the midst of all this the aspiration after a consolidation of life and after a durable truth became
ever stronger, and the opposition against the immersion of the whole of human existence in the stream
of historical life became more decisive.   Such a turn
leaves no doubt in regard to the fact that history
itself is more than a mere record of the succession of
events.   History is far more an elevation above the
changes of occurrences—a commanding view of things,
connections of things, a judgment of the manifold
material, a raising of pre-eminent aims.   Hence it is
discovered that history, viewed from the point of view
of mind and spirit, is a portion of a further total-life,
and that, consequently, there is no such thing possible
as " mere " history, for history, in so far as it is recognised in its deeper meaning, includes a confession of

such a further total-life.   The exclusiveness of history
with its alleged relativity destroys the meaning of
history itself.   And if we are not to give up the
meaning of history, it is necessary to rise above it,
and to take up once more, in some kind of way,
eternal truths.   Such a course does not lead directly
to religion ; but, at the same time, it exhibits the
effort after eternal truth in a very different light from
the ordinary mode of looking at things.

An entire change has taken place in another main
point.   The "immanent" method of considering history,
with its expulsion of superhuman aids, has brought
forth a powerful heightening of human existence and
human potency.   Man himself has accordingly to prepare his domain of life, and to find his highest aim
in the adornment of this domain ; now he has to
stimulate all that is included within human energy
into the greatest achievements ; and now for the first
time he seems to stand fast within his own world.
We can hardly overrate the fruit of such a conviction.
The awakening of individual lives was followed by
the awakening of the masses.   While all forms of
social relationship were entered into and judged by a
consideration of their bearing upon the actual life of
man, more joy and freedom, more care for others and
more humaneness entered into life ; and, further, the
province of thought gained in clearness because it was
developed psychologically from the immediate experience of consciousness.   But here again the affirmation soon passes into a negation, and a shrinkage soon
appears in the emancipation.   To abolish all invisible
ties and connections may appear as a pure gain so long
as man continues to idealise unconsciously, and so long

as the consciousness contains something of its earlier greatness and values. But such idealisation tends to become more and more obliterated before the impressions of experience. Humanity does not find the ideal of brotherhood so easily realised as it had expected, but finds more and more divisions between individuals, parties, and nations; the impulses, emotions, and passions of human nature develop more deeply and more widely; the tyranny of the petty common life becomes more and more brutal; and more and more we are threatened with the death of the Spiritual Life. Have not men, viewed from within, become smaller and smaller, because they value nothing other than themselves? And, at the same time, when it is discovered that the whole man even in his spiritual efforts is controlled by human impulses with all their pettiness and assertions, and that all possibility of a counter-effect—of a vocation in the highest and final court of appeal—vanishes, and when judgment over the true and the false, over good and evil, is surrendered to the opinions and inclinations of individuals and masses, it becomes evident why wrath and even hatred burn against the pretence of mere modern culture; and in order to preserve a genuine spiritual culture nothing seems more necessary than an unrelenting struggle against such petty and presumptuous culture which reduces life to a miserable level, and which destroys all genuine values. In order to possess such values man has to work his way up to something—something which he has to acknowledge beyond and above himself, and yet while beyond and above him is yet not alien to him. This leads once more to the problem

which religion has taken up from of yore ; and he who
places on one side the solution which religion offers
will think otherwise when he comes to realise the true
nature of the problem.

And, further, the expulsion of all the inwardness
of the Spiritual Life—the transformation of our entire
nature into an impersonal process of culture and
civilisation—turns a pure gain into a serious loss.
The independent life of man had become too small
for the content of the work of culture ; and through
its more extended labours his existence has grown
immeasurably in width and truth.   And it is from a
kind of necessity that the attention of the subject
upon himself was abandoned, and life was laid entirely in the relationship to external things.   But this
complexity of work which has thus become the main
fact—indeed, of the Spiritual Life itself—needs an
inner connection and an animated unity, for otherwise
it cannot possibly construct a Whole and work as
a Whole.   But the more the inward and personal
element is pushed aside without some kind of compensation being furnished, the more all characteristic
and inspiring energy slips away, the more each totality
loses its inner unity and animation, and becomes a
mere piece of mechanism which may be of value in
subduing the external world and in calling forth
certain exertions.   But all this fails to unite man
with a Whole and to raise him as a Whole ; and also
it inevitably tends to decay and fails to engender a
new world of intrinsic value.   Thus, the impersonal
work of culture and civilisation threatens to become
mechanical from its very centre outwards.   No
growth of inner potency corresponds to the increase

of work, and expansion by far overpowers concentration ; man becomes more and more the slave of his
work and a bundle of isolated accomplishments.
But the work itself, through its severance from the
centre of life, loses all its soul.   Can we deny that
the last decade has placed such dangers under our
very eyes ?   At the same time, a kind of compulsion
gives rise to the questions whether ultimately the soul
of life has to be abandoned, whether the emergence
of conceptions of inwardness above the old forms and
beyond mere subjectivity is possible, whether a
coherent and superior unity may through a great
struggle be obtained within the Spiritual Life itself.
If the latter happened, it would effect an entire
transformation of life ; and that would lead back,
not, indeed, to the old situation of religion, but still
to the problems of religion.

We are thus experiencing to-day a remarkable
entanglement.   The older forms of life, which
formerly governed history and its meaning, became
too narrow, petty, and subjective for human nature.
Through emancipation from an easy-going subjectivity and through the positing of life upon external
things and, indeed, upon the whole of the great
universe, life, it was believed, would gain more
breadth and truth ; and in a noteworthy manner man
undertook a struggle against the pettiness of his own
nature and for the driving out of all that was merely
human and trivial.   A great deal has been gained
through such a change and new tendency of life.   In
fact we have discovered far more than we had hoped
for.   But, at the same time, we have lost something,
a loss which at the outset brings forth no anxiety, but

which, through painful experience, proves itself to
have been that of "the one thing needful." Through
its own development the work has destroyed its own
vehicles ; it has undermined the very ground upon
which it stood ; it has failed, notwithstanding its
infinite expansion, through its loss of a fundamental
and unifying Life-process ; and in the entire immersion of man into activity his deepest being has been
sacrificed. Indeed, the more exclusively life transforms itself into mere external work, the more it
ceases to be an inner personal existence, and the more
alien we become to ourselves. And yet the fact that
we can be conscious of such an alienation—an alienation which we cannot accept indifferently but which
is experienced as an irreparable loss—is a proof that
more is firmly implanted in us than the modern direction of life is able to develop and satisfy. We acknowledge simultaneously that we have gained much
but that the loss is a painful one. We have gained
the world but we have lost the soul, and, along with
this, the world threatens to bring us into nought, and
to take away our one secure foothold in the midst of
the stormy roaring torrent of material work.

This danger was not realised so long as modern
ideas failed in precision of expression, and so long as
life without any hesitation supplied itself from the
old sources of thought and experience. Indeed, the
more an immanent and impersonal culture and civilisation were thrown upon their own resources, the
more that universal dialectic which the experience
of humanity has often witnessed revealed itself.
Systems of thought and, indeed, ideal worlds either
destroy one another or rail in their gained domains;

evolution itself shows limits ; but the discovery of the
limits leads to new tendencies—to new tendencies in
the main thesis. In the meantime, however, there
arises, as modern man with growing consciousness has
discovered, a painful situation. Men have drifted
from the old moorings, and the new ones which promised the highest happiness do not satisfy. They
are conscious of poverty in an overflowing kingdom,
conscious of the absence of a real substance in the
midst of incessant activity, and have discovered in
the midst of incessant joy and pleasure the absence
of genuine happiness. Is it to be wondered at that
desire and anxiety should turn again home towards
the whole of life ; that the question concerning the
inner clarification of life should place on one side all
other questions and reduce them to subsidiary facts ;
that the possibility of an inner elevation of human
nature—of a self-maintenance in the midst of a
threatening destruction of life—should become the
most weighty of all concerns ? And through such
a revolution in the tendency and character of life,
the ancient puzzles of human existence, hushed up
in earlier times, raise themselves once more with
crude and lively energy—problems concerning the
deep darkness which veils our Whence and Whither,
our dependence upon strange powers, the painful antitheses within our own soul, the stubborn barriers to
our spiritual potencies, the flaws in love and righteousness in nature and in human nature ; in a word, the
apparent total loss of what we dare not renounce—
our best and most real treasures. But we are now
experiencing what mankind has so often experienced,
viz. that at the very point where the negation reaches

its climax and the danger reaches the very brink of a precipice, the conviction dawns with axiomatic certainty that there lives and stirs within us something which no obstacles or enmity can ever destroy, and which signifies against all opposition a kernel of our nature that can never get lost. And if the call to us to return home to the unassailable foundation of our being is heard in no domain more powerfully than in the domain of religion, and to make what we dare not renounce our conscious possession, then the message of religion acquires a totally different meaning. Then religion appears no more as a creation of childish fancy or as a flight into some far and alien world, but as an indispensable helper of man in the difficult and seemingly impossible struggle for a spiritual self—for a soul and meaning of life. Consequently there rises once more, after a long period of brow-beating, an aspiration after fundamental depths and inner connections, after eternal truth and infinite love ; and in the midst of all the welter of our day appears a new wave of life universal which carries man into entirely other bearings, and which is but a forerunner of a flowing tide big with the promise of a better day.

CHAPTER V

e. The Explanation of the Developing Tendency

He who understands the religious problem in the sense already referred to is, in his treatment of the problem, pressed into a definite course of decision between Nay and Yea. That decadent mode of thought which, from grounds of utility, recommends a return to the old form of religion will appeal least of all to him. Modern culture, we hear so often to-day, has become entirely bankrupt; human society needs for its subsistence and development moral consolidation and energetic cohesion, which nothing other than a religion of authority is able to furnish; then there is nothing remaining but to return to such a religion, to bend willingly before its authority— perchance to Rome—and to accept the traditional confession as the best doctrine concerning things which are under lock and key to the human intellect.

The way in which the awakening of religion is to take place, in our view of the matter, contradicts such a mode of thought in the most definite manner. To religion belongs an inspiration which urges man to a great depth and resoluteness of life, to a self-reliance

over against the imbroglio of the world and to an
elevation above the pettily human bustle of life. Man
is able to experience and live a Higher and Nobler
within his own nature, and to overcome an alien and
even an envious world. And here again a utilitarian
mode of thought draws him into his pettily human
bustle and turns religion into a mere tool for his
material welfare; and consequently what enters into
man's nature is perceived as a half-truth, whilst human
nature at its deepest thirsts for genuine truth. How
high does even the honourable atheist stand above
such a mode of thinking!

It could not happen otherwise than that the knowledge of the limits of the New should occasion the
return of many minds to the Old to hold fast to it.
But the present crisis of religion has in reality altered
our standpoint to the Old. But still the Old comes
nearer to us when we recognise in it necessary problems
whose meanings have not as yet been shown in the
New. But this latter consideration does not warrant
a justification for a simple return to the Old. The
newer culture has cut too deep a chasm between the
past and ourselves for a return to be possible. And
we have to be on our guard against underestimating
the value of the New for the whole of life, because as
yet it does not mean *all* to us, and because it does not
immediately suffice for the inmost source of life.
For the penetrating and transforming effects of the
New are found in full currency ; and in no sense has
the New brought forth merely a number of particular
results dovetailed by sagacity and dexterity into the
empty spaces of traditional ideas, but it has changed
our conceptions of the fundamental process of life

itself. The gain in clearness and breadth through natural science, in earnestness through history, in other essentials through philosophy and criticism, will never be rescinded; and on account of such changes we are obliged to view the New in a different light, and are no longer able to adopt the simple-mindedness of our forefathers. Refitting and patching are always anachronisms, and nowhere more so than in this province.

Further, it is not to be forgotten that the present-day expansion and struggles affect not only the content of religion, but also its position in the whole of life. It is on the ground of Christianity that religion constructs, for the first time, a Whole or, in other words, the one worthful kernel of the Spiritual Life; and all the other provinces of life have no other problem than to lead into this kernel. In the Middle Ages the various provinces gained more ground, but they still remained under the guardianship of religion. Protestantism, however, brings to a consummation a cleavage between culture and religion. Neither of these alternatives satisfies us to-day: a mere religious life has become too narrow for us, and a mere parallelism of religion and culture can at the best be no more than a transitory phase, and by no means a final conclusion. Thus, there originates here a difficult problem, which no return to an old extinct mode of thought can solve.

Though the newer culture appears as an enemy, or at least as an uncongenial critic, of religion, its effects in no way turn out to be a danger and a detriment; but much rather are able to further the clarification, emancipation, and extension of life, as such

5

effects place new problems in front of themselves, and create a new energy for the solution of such problems. The earlier configuration of religion—formed in a weary and decadent age—entered into danger ; for in its anxiety for the suffering of mankind the fostering of its own active conduct was weakened, and its own actions were forgotten in its perpetually submissive mood.   It is a justifiable aspiration of modern times that religion should develop more and more in the direction of the ennobling of work, of the awakening of a new courage of life, of an inner elevation of all the provinces of activity ; it is an aspiration that religion should not only teach man to think little of himself as an individual, but also reveal to him the greatness of his nature.   The old mode of viewing things, through its sole dwelling on the salvation of the individual, has largely pushed the question of the vindication of the Spiritual Life into the background ; it looked too much upon the life of man as something ready-made and not as something that is ever a " becoming " ; and all this has happened because this old mode of thought could not return from its abode of seclusion and calm to the present actual world in order to impregnate it with a new spirit.

In the midst of such great changes, religion can only come to grief if the new ascending movement is fastened entirely to the old form, and if the old form is represented as being immutable in all its essentials. The representatives of religion easily carry such a procedure into a mistrust of the least scientific exactness and even of veracity, whilst, at the same time, they gloss over obvious difficulties.   By removing contradictions out of sight, precarious probabilities are made to appear as certain realities; and this most shallow mode of thinking thus receives a kind of relief in that it is effecting the casting out of incontestable truths. Religion will never gain the indispensable simplicity for far-reaching effects, nor the inward immediacy and the victorious energy of conviction if it binds the present rigidly to the past, if it fails to speak to us in the feelings, conceptions, and even words of our own day. If so much that belongs to the older configuration of religion has become anthropomorphic and even mythological and magical, are we to ignore such a state of things, and dare we ignore it when the real interest of religion itself is at stake?

Many who have relinquished a rigid hold upon the Old seek to escape from the difficulty by conceiving of religion, separated as it is to them from culture, as a pure inwardness of the individual feeling; and consequently they strive to transform religion entirely into a personal conviction and sentiment. In this manner they believe themselves able to verify and to develop energetically the distinctive characteristic features of religion. Through such a notion, all the contradictions of the work of the world do not touch religion because it rules securely and calmly within its own domain. Without a doubt, much freshness of life, enthusiasm, and joyous labour have issued from such a mode of religion, and it pulsates with great power in the character of our age. We shall have to occupy ourselves with this movement in the whole of this book, so that for the moment we can place its discussion on one side. At present we only indicate briefly wherein the religious crisis, notwithstanding its

recognition of the turn towards the purely human
mode of formation, compels us to conceive it as
an anomaly.   The pure subjectivity to which the
tendency is to turn from the embroilment of culture
as to an indestructible and even unassailable citadel
is not so secure and certain as it is supposed to be.
Our consideration of the matter has already shown us
that modern culture values subjective inwardness not
as a main but as a secondary phenomenon—as an
accompanying phenomenon—and, further, that it considers all life developed on such lines not as the entire
truth, but only as a circle of subjective stimulation and
imagination.   Such an inwardness can corroborate its
rights, free itself from a vacillating sentimentalism,
and prove itself the kernel of reality, only through its
energetic union with the work of the modern world,
and through the gain of an immanent and impersonal
culture.   In order to obtain this, such inwardness
strikes more and more into the deep, and gains more
extensive connections.   This it is able to do only
through the turn to a *Metaphysic*—a Metaphysic not
of the Schools but of Life.   Through this the inwardness will experience a clarifying and a winnowing; all
mere sentimental pathos must be stripped off, and a
firmer substance must be won.   The immediacy of the
first impressions of things is not the genuine immediacy
of spiritual creativeness and original depth, for all
the latter has to be worked out.

And, simultaneously with this, culture becomes
for us something quite other than such a subjectivism.   And now, with all our energy, we fight against
the splitting of life into subjective religion on the one
hand, and into soulless culture on the other hand.

Culture as a work in the world is by no means a mere external side of life ; it belongs to our nature, and has even in modern times affected deeply the configuration of total-life, whilst it has given life more clearness and has penetrated beyond mere subjectivity. So that a renewal of life is of benefit to culture in the whole of its ramifications, and thus the problem reaches beyond mere religion into the whole of our being.

The advocates of subjectivism as well as those of the old mode of thought, in spite of all their differences, agree in their undervaluation of the present-day crisis in religion. This crisis deals not only with the position of religion in life, but also with the fundamental process of life itself. Hardly at any period in human history has an upheaval of this sort been so thorough ; and such a struggle which calls mankind to a revaluation of its positions and possessions has rarely been witnessed as is witnessed to-day. An old form of life has proved itself, on account of the work of the centuries, too petty, narrow, and subjective ; and yet such a form seems to contain an imperishable nucleus which we dare not renounce on peril of experiencing the severest of losses. The new mode of thought which arose over against the old one has, through its breadth, earnestness, and energy so completely mastered us as to render a retreat to the old mode simply impossible. But the new mode brings ever clearer to the surface flaws perceived in the solid nucleus and in the secure foundation ; thus it is full of inner problems, and we cannot possibly enter into agreement unceremoniously with it. Now one mode hems in the other, and yet is not able to dislodge this other, still less can we expect both to flow amicably together on the current of compromise. Consequently, we witness the one tearing the other through the collision; we observe the disaster reaching ever deeper into the most original qualities; and the possession which is common to all breaking up in pieces. At an earlier time men wrestled with the truths of morality, of religion, of a world-view, in order to draw nearer to such realities; but now the truths themselves have become matters of dispute, and consequently we find ourselves contradicting ourselves and carried to the most pointed opposites. When we reflect, however, on the whole of life, we are able to discover a painful uncertainty: our spiritual existence floats in mid-air without any means of support, and our fundamental relationship to reality has fallen into entire uncertainty. There-fore, a struggle for the whole of life and for a new man has become necessary. This struggle has to be led not only by religion, but also by the other provinces of life—by art, philosophy, etc. True, each province has, as in the case of religion, its special problem and its special way of attacking its problem, but it is a condition of success in connection with each province that the Whole should be recognised as in-wardly present in the particular, and that this Whole should withstand every kind of dissolution, contraction, and torpor. The problem of religion is only a segment —probably the most important segment—of a more general problem—of the problem concerning the struggle for a spiritual existence, for the duration, content, and meaning of life; and the problem of religion dare not sever itself from all this.

It must produce discomfort to the adherents of religion and, indeed, it may produce deep depression

of spirit, to see that which forms, for the personal
conviction, the most steadfast security and the
highest good of life treated by science as an open
problem. But this is once more our destiny, that in
connection with the fundamental questions of life
what appears as our most secure possession, and what
in reality carries along incessantly our spiritual existence, should have to be won ever anew for our
own conviction, and should have to be strengthened
through spontaneous decision. Though the individual may withdraw from this task, human nature
is not able to do so. Religion in particular may
protest against all such distressing fears: religion is
either merely a sanctioned product of human wishes
and of pictorial ideas brought about by tradition and
the historical ordinance—and, if so, no art, power,
or cunning can prevent the destruction of such a
bungling work by the advance of the mental and
the spiritual movement of the world; or religion is
founded upon a superhuman fact—and, if so, the
hardest assault cannot shatter it, but rather, it must
finally prove of service in all the troubles and toils of
man, it must reach the point of its true strength and
develop purer and purer its eternal truth.

Part II.—The Fundamental Basis of Universal Religion

INTRODUCTION

WE have already seen that the problem of religion arises out of a vast crisis in the general movement of life. The old form of life, which hitherto had given its character to all aspiration, became too narrow and subjective for a general expansion of our existence and of activity in the various provinces of knowledge. On the one hand, the new life which issued out of the transformation of activity had no fixed centre and consequently threatened to vanish into emptiness. That we are able to discover the contradiction and reflect on both sides of the antithesis may undoubtedly be held as a sign that our inmost nature in some way is able to rise above the cleavage; but evidently the upheaval is much too deep for us to conceive and vivify without a great transformation and even a revolution of our nature. We therefore find ourselves in the midst of a great conflict for the whole of life, and are necessarily pressed to the problem whether religion can and must come to our aid in order to reconsolidate our spiritual existence, and whether it is possible to become the possessors of a reality superior to the world, enclosed within the living present to consciousness, which, if found, renders possible such a striving after a content and meaning of life. If, therefore, the problem of religion arises out of the Whole of life, it will mean that such a religion alone as flows again into the Whole is able to bring satisfaction. Thus, when we turn to the particular province, we must constantly bear in mind the reality of the Whole. But such a conviction involves specific methodic requirements; and, in particular, it carries us at the outset over the antithesis, which runs through the ages, of a derivation of religion from the intellect and the world on the one hand, and from the particular experiences of man in feeling or will on the other. What here first of all appears as a bare diversity of method is in reality a struggle for the content of religion itself; for the differences in the proofs correspond to differences in the religions; and the proofs only carry out, in each case, what was at bottom already decided by the choice of this or that kind of proof. Thus, in these considerations it is not merely the path to religion but religion itself that stands in question.

In earlier times, indeed ever since the time of the Greeks, the evolution of religion proceeded by placing the emphasis on the side of thought. At the height of this development the endeavour signified no mere reflection on the world—an attempt to arrive at a supra-mundane intelligence from the seeming purpose and fitness of things—but rather the hope of man triumphantly to penetrate to the kernel of reality, from this point of vantage above the merely human circle, thus opening out to him a wider, purer, richer life. Reality, apprehended thus in its very kernel, appeared as sustained by a living unity, indeed as the unfolding of such an over-world unity. In this work of apprehension thought gained a religious character and transformed itself at last wholly into religion. At the end of this path lies mysticism, with its complete immersion of all the varied characteristics of things into the All-One, and its devotion of the whole soul to that one end.

We shall find that this course of thought contains a truth which religion cannot renounce without becoming narrow and rigid. But this does not signify that such a course of thought is able of itself to found religion, and, along with religion, to open out a new kind of life. In reality this course never attains to religion through the energy of thought alone, but always, though unobserved, through an inflow and an appropriation of feeling, into and by the thought, thus giving warmth to thought's cold form. In a word, a thinking left simply to its own resources would never be able to get beyond empty forms and highly abstract conceptions. Indeed, even when thus completed by feeling the religion that arises here is still in a high degree shapeless and lacks the power for proceeding, from the one great intuition with which it starts, to the formation of a complex of life. In addition, there springs up a painful doubt which no merely intellectual form of religion is ever able to overcome. Is thought able to reach the kernel of things through its own energy, and can its highest exertions break through the bounds of the merely human circle and raise us to the divine? Are our conceptions in reality more than merely human conceptions? Is it not a mere world of phantoms which arises in them? Must not thought itself be recognised as a member of a wider connection of life, if it is to be valid as an expression of truth, and is to assure man of the reality of a new world? Precisely the convulsions of modern life, which we have already noticed, make this doubt acute, and consequently forbid us to base religion on mere speculation.

Still less, according to the experience of the centuries, can the reflective procedure which derives an over-world intelligence from the special construction of the external world suffice. In the phenomenal world there appeared, to such a procedure of thought, far more order, design, and beauty than was possible for the nature of things to accomplish of itself; consequently, every behaviour of physical things was considered as a testimony of the power, wisdom, and goodness of an over-world spirit. This train of thought won many minds in late antiquity; it won them in early Christianity; it won them in the period of the *Aufklärung*; and, because of its perspicuity and comprehensiveness, it will not lose its influence lightly. But whatever truth may be imbedded behind its anthropomorphic form, it has not a convincing power against the doubts of the present age. For one thing, our scientific age has discovered the drawback in this mode of thinking, that it puts science and religion into irreconcilable antagonism. For whilst science passionately endeavours to bring all particular events into relationship with each other, and to understand them from the point of view of this relationship, that mode of thought must consider religion to be the more securely grounded, the more immediate is the impression of design presented by the look of the world, and the more tangibly single startling phenomena contrast with the remaining happenings. If thus each gain in the scientific and inherent interpretation of things becomes a loss to religion, then religion must withdraw more and more into an unexplored region with the naïve assumption that such a region is also unexplorable, and without any certainty that the supposed mystery will, some day, reveal its secret to the illuminating light of the activity of thought. We discover, too, to-day, much more clearly than formerly, the anthropomorphism of the method which carries carelessly human modes of thought into the All, and explains the condition of this All as though a human being had produced it. Again, for our present-day outlook on the universe, there is, alongside of the purpose that may be discovered in it, so much that seems purposeless, so much struggle and suffering, so much rigid indifference to human welfare and spiritual good, so much limitation and precariousness even in the purposive, that for us the starting-point of that teleological doctrine is riddled with insecurities. And, finally, if we overcome all such scruples and recognise the superior energy perceptible in the physical universe, can we derive from such a consideration a new life, and can the discord of our inward nature be overcome? The older mode of thought could believe such results to be possible since it was under the influence of a securely operative religion—a religion which heightened the intelligence which under its

influence had, in a rather artificial way, been inferred
as present in the world to a living personality, and
which gave to this intelligence an efficacious presence
in the human soul. That mode asserted far more
than it had proved. But that influence has now been
shaken to its very foundation, and the whole of
religion has become problematic ; and therewith falls
all that lifted that mode of thought above what is
intrinsically contained in itself. However much,
then, in the world may remain an enigma for us, and
however willing we may be to acknowledge dark
depths in existence, such a method can never furnish
a secure position for a foundation and living development of religion. " The amazement of the sage in
viewing the depth of creation and his search in the
abyss for the Creator do not furnish an education of
humanity in the corresponding belief. In the abyss
of creation the investigator can readily lose himself,
and in this whirlpool he can drift about and miss
his way far from the source of the fathomless sea "
(Pestalozzi).

It was as a reaction against such an overstrain of
the intellect, against the transformation of religion
into speculation, and against the resolution of man
into the Infinite, that there followed a turning to
the experiences special to man himself. In these,
religion seemed to be able to win a stable form, a
living energy, and a full certainty. But here again
the attempt, though above reproach in its basis, has,
in its execution, led to problematical positions ; and
this chiefly because human life has been swerved
from the All and been treated as a separate province.
For then not only are we confronted by the difficult,

and even insoluble, problem, how anything that lies within such an entirely separate province can possibly reach beyond it—and such a reaching beyond is a necessary part of religion ; but there also arises the danger that such a basis for religion will keep man too much tied to himself and will simply excite his merely natural self. Thus, there would here be a lack of the necessary opposition to the merely human. A closer consideration of the two currents into which this non-intellectual endeavour divides, will show this more clearly.

It is either in the softer mode of feeling or in the stronger mode of will that this way seeks access to the Divine. Man is able to withdraw himself into his own feeling, to rid himself of all connection with his environment, and, in a condition of pure apartness and of soaring detachment, to know himself to be both far above his merely physical environment, and a part of an unseen whole. The mere fact that he is thus able to free himself from all the entanglements of things, and to plant himself upon his own separate inwardness, seems to prove a greater depth of reality than is to be found externally, and seems, too, to reveal a kingdom of the soul in spite of the hardness and senselessness of the immediate world. And in such a self-contained feeling, a touchstone for securely deciding concerning the truth or falsehood of every religious experience seemed to be won. Here alone human life seemed to win full immediacy, here alone to become autonomous. Let, then, all that claims to be religion be brought to this point in order to prove its authenticity and, in a characteristic manner, to decide

between the kernel and the shell.   Indeed, the claims
of feeling proceed even further : they prove themselves not only an unfailing touchstone, but become
the creative source of religion itself.   In these claims
are contained demands of life ; and further developments take place, in which are included a new and
divine world which has dawned on the consciousness.
Through this winning independence of the inward
there arises a longing to break through natural existence, and a desire to prove that this characteristic
and novel truth which now dawns is a real longing
after infinity and eternity and freedom ; and the
desire seems to culminate in peace and holiness
through the feeling in a form of immediacy of a
reality of such greatness and goodness.   Thus a kingdom of ideals arises and declares its content as a
definite truth over against all mere subjective experience.   In the province of religion the consciousness fastens itself to a Whole and grips the whole
man.   The culmination of a real existence for oneself is reached in such a manner ; and the full bliss
is obtained by a free floating in the ether of
infinity.

This, doubtless, contains a good deal of truth, but
the truth is mingled with much that is problematic,
and needs a fundamental clarification of conceptions
in order to separate the certain from the problematic.
In the first place, mere feeling is in no manner an
independent inward life—a still deep, certain through
itself of its truth.   Feeling testifies only to the
rousing of the subject—to the degree of the subjective
appropriation of the processes of life.   The truth-
content of these processes remains questionable and

doubtful; and, also, the rousing has varied degrees, because feeling can be shallow and feeble in spite of considerable amount of excitement, and can dissipate and consume itself in hasty agitation without its being able to affect the remainder of life. If feeling is, therefore, in its simple and natural state less full of value and content than when it displays its connection with real existing life, it cannot construct for itself a decisive touchstone; and consequently a criticism of the feelings is as necessary as a criticism of conceptions. One can adopt fully the words of Hegel: "The true nerve is the genuine thought; and only when the thought is true can the feeling be of a genuine kind."

In the province of religion the movement towards feeling takes place usually within the circle of crystallised tradition and the common order of things; although the subjective experience crystallises itself in this established order, it wins through it a support and a content, and in all his advance the subject would in no way shake off an objective world. Thus it happened with Pascal and also Schleiermacher; especially after the æsthetic enthusiasm of early youth had adopted a strong religious element into itself. In both cases the close relationship of the soul of the individual to religion brought forth a pure gain in warmth and inwardness. Quite otherwise is it, however, when the feeling, rejecting all wider connections, attempts to generate religion purely out of its own nature. Then it contracts itself through such a one-sided striving upon its own particular ability; and consequently its product proves lean and poor. This bare feeling is so fickle and soft, so devoid of stability and content, that finally it discharges itself into an entirely vague disposition. And when such a disposition attempts to weave a content out of itself in order to lead man beyond the mere human province to a rela°°° °hip with the Divine, it degenerates of necessity to the 1ᴄ 1 of eccentricity and fancy.

The proclamation of the predominance or even of the autocracy of feeling was thus usually on historical grounds a part of the inner process of the dissolution of religion. The receptive form estranges itself inwardly from the traditional form and yet fears to break away completely, so that one sought to hold fast to a portion of the subjective meaning whilst the substance was given up. One has the tendency to welcome such a state of things because it seems to be a gain in width and freedom ; but the fact is overlooked that when the real truth falls away sooner or later its reflex in the minds of men must disappear. Such a religion of mere feeling has the tendency to become more and more shadowy, until finally it vanishes completely from the mind. The turn to bare feeling is accordingly a path on which religions do not so much originate as disappear.

The basing of religion upon will seems to place it on securer grounds and under stronger motives. But here also a dilemma will soon become manifest, because the will, strictly confined within its own limits, falls inevitably into emptiness ; while with the development of some kind of content, it enters into wider connections and becomes dependent on these connections. The will, doubtless as a characteristic decision and as a carrier from the domain of thought to that of activity, constitutes a phenomenon of the

6

greatest significance. It not only affirms freedom from all mere mechanism of nature, but also promises to become the starting-point of a new kind of world. But as soon as we begin to develop such a world, and as soon as we lay hold of a law of activity present in the will which points to morality, we step beyond the mere individual will and venture to make assertions concerning the highest ends and final grounds. When this happens there happens, too, that we are compelled to recognise a kingdom of self-activity beyond all mere psychological functions. Herewith new demands arise concerning the reconstruction of life from its very foundation, and the will must now prove its particular truth out of the larger truth of this new reconstruction.

Common to feeling and will are two different reasons which make it impossible for both to give religion a secure basis. Both appear as original and immediate events; such originality and immediacy seem to confer on both the right of sovereign value and the ability of independent creative power. But this immediacy is first of all a mere phenomenon of consciousness, and as such, through the further work of thought, is liable to the possibility of error; much can be of significance in the phenomenon which seems to the immediate impression to have quite an opposite character. So it is in no way certain that because the feeling announces itself as a pure existence-for-self that such an existence-for-self actually obtains. Is there not much concealed and indirect dependence here, and could not the assertion rest upon error? It is similar with the will and its presumptive freedom. Is not the will probably a non-knowledge

and an oversight of the truth of its previous ties ?
Does not man aim at something more than merely
to feel himself free, although he is unable to penetrate
to the causes of his activity ? If feeling and will,
however, in their present fundamental significance
admit of so much doubt, how can they ever create
a new world in the sense of religion, and through this
fortify human life ?

There corresponds to this insufficiency of the basis
an insufficiency of presented content. Religion finds
it difficult to disentangle us from the contradictions
of life unless it culminates in an inversion of existence,
and unless it exercises through such inversion a sharp
sifting of the materials which present themselves as
near at hand. There is no possibility of a workable
Yea without the presence of a powerful Nay ; for
thus alone can the transformation strike into the
deep. In feeling or will, in the manner already
described, such a radical Nay is wanting, and
consequently human life in its particular circle may
aim at and further a given religion without being able
to become the possessor of the inward elevation and
the essential renewal—two characteristics of the chief
end of religion.

When the whole matter is surveyed, there appears
no possibility for any single aspect of life to conduct to
religion. Each one of these aspects is not only too
feeble for such work, but is also unable to present
religion with a sufficient content. The experiments
made in such direction are in sharp conflict with one
another: on the one side, the attention is directed
to the outward character of religion and to the
building up of a scientific province of thought, whilst

on the other side the standpoint is that of immanence
and of the immediate energy of movement which
arises out of it.   The one is as necessary as the
other, but on this path the two aspects refuse to
coalesce : the general character of religion, mirrored in
the intellect alone, endangers the inward immediacy
and spiritual warmth, whilst through the individual
results of feeling and will alone the immediacy
endangers the spiritual width and validity which
extend beyond the individual.   So that a new path
must be sought which will unite the discordant
elements.   It is certainly clear that through such
discord between the two opposites, an immediate
united push and a joyous co-operation are impossible.
The experience of history testifies to the particular
naïveté of basing religion on thought, feeling, or will.
It remains here to seek a new path which is not, from
the very outset, under the power of the opposites.
We need not, however, allow man and the world,
subject and object, activity and presentation, to fall
outside one another.   We do not proceed on this
new path from any ready-made imaginary existence,
but from the Life-process itself ; and from this Life-
process we seek to develop conceptions of existence
and strive to carry the particular sides of our consciousness far enough to meet within an essentially
unique Whole.   That such a Whole exists—it has all
probability on its side—appears in the fact that the
contradictions of our existence could not be experienced collectively unless there existed a living
unity spanning the separate aspects of existence.
But where is such a unity to be found ?   And when
found, is it able to be of effect without causing a

reversal of our naïve view of things? These arc
other questions. And it may be held as certain that
no proof of religion is possible in the same way as that
in which a fact of the connection of external things is
proved. The path to religion leads through the contradictions of life; and allows itself to be discovered
long before a clear conception of the overcoming of
these contradictions is ripe. It is the marked characteristic of religious problems that a great contradiction shall become visible, and also that it shall be
overcome by the entrance of something within the
human circle that will lift man beyond that circle.
This demands energetic analysis and essential gradations. The first representation (of the contradictions)
must be recognised and must become more effective
in us than has hitherto been the case. Thus when we
are battling with the question of religion, we are at
the same time battling for a more complete picture of
reality and of our own real existence. And it may
be, indeed, that we shall find much that is provisional
and full of contradictions. But who has given us the
certitude that the universe in us and we in it are
complete? Is it not far more probable that the main
value of life lies in the very fact that we are allowed
to combat with alien elements?

PART II.—THE FUNDAMENTAL BASIS OF UNIVERSAL RELIGION

(Continued)

CHAPTER VI

a. The Complexity of Human Life

1. *The Dualism in Human Life*

The movement of the Life-process in the direction of the religious problem has before all else to ask if it fashions a characteristic and continuous Whole, or if it produces essential differences, and especially if it exhibits a thorough-going dualism. Such a dualism might probably offer a thread which might guide us further. Now, an unbiassed view, undisturbed by particular one-sided tendencies, holds that our life in reality contains two different aspects: that it includes the two qualities and stages of *Nature and Spirit* within itself. This hypothesis will be elucidated as we proceed. Such an antithesis is quite other than those between body and mind, object and subject, extension in space and conscious activity, as these were brought to the foreground in the period of the *Aufklärung.* Our antithesis lies wholly within consciousness itself. The particular psychic life shows a twofold characteristic: on the one hand, it merely carries forth its sensuous surrounding nature and adapts itself within the bounds of nature, while

86

on the other hand, and contemporaneously, new
energies, ends, and forms are produced whose connections lead to a new kind of reality over against all
mere nature. This difference is so fundamental for
the whole of our investigation as to render a clear
illumination and a sufficient basis for it impossible
without an investigation into its very nature.

Modern Science itself has proved visible nature,
out of which we have sprung, to be a varying web
of purely particular elements or forces lying in immensity. Speculation may, accepting some supposed
ground of the multiplicity and the inward connections, resolve the universal reciprocal actions as well
as the course of the whole universe into simple
fundamental forms. Natural Science can push back
such connections and provide all explanation from
the simple elements themselves. For all phenomena
grow out of relationships, from step to step, on the
ground of experience ; one phenomenon is influenced
by another through their reciprocal causal inter-
action. Nowhere does the guidance of the movement seem to proceed from a Whole, and nowhere
does life itself seem to rest upon an elevated and
collective end of self-maintenance. What finds itself
in amalgamation is nothing other than a construction
of things side by side in space. The external contiguity, on the whole, does no more than bring the
elements together ; an inward participation collectively is throughout impossible and, indeed, unthink-
able. Speculation may no doubt complete this picture
by stating that the elements cannot possibly pass
wholly into the mutual relations, and that they must
possess some individual existence. But such individual

existence lies inaccessible beyond the phenomena and remains unexplored for all times. Along with this, each question concerning final "grounds" unfolds another question, and there is here, therefore, no discovery of the Why and Wherefore; the scientific investigation of the processes of nature shows them as no more than mere occurrences.

As such an existence from without, with its myriad forms, surrounds us, it extends itself also deeply into the province of the soul. Also, human activities are above all driven by the needs of individual self-preservation and self-elevation, and it is the execution of this alone which gives value to man and things; here activities are not meant for alien aims—they are not meant for any existing Whole beyond the realm of the life of humanity. Our life, primarily, creates its content out of the external relations and connections; it is nothing other than an intercourse with the environment. What is called "inward" is only echo and ashes of what originated through the friction of the connections. Our ideas or conceptions, for instance, are mere sensuous presentations; that alone can be termed good which our position utilises in the sensuous existence; all happiness, in the last resort, is rooted in sensuous stimulation; what is termed non-sensuous or spiritual is in truth only a sensuous of a finer make. Also, the connection of the psychological movements corresponds entirely with the order of nature. Isolated elements unite and link themselves simultaneously or in turns, stir and displace themselves; and it is the association of their mechanism which largely governs our life and makes out of it a complicated machine which much rather moves independently of us than helps to shape our own particular product.   No superior unity spans and stirs the manifold, so that there is no room here for either ends or activities.

As, however, our position remains bound in this network, we infer that we cannot be carried beyond that position.   What in themselves these things may be, we cannot know at all, and there is no need for us to know ; in such a beyond we could neither interest ourselves nor attain our ends.   We see, too, that the psychic life in its initial stages remains within the domain of nature, and through and through exhibits the character of a mere existing thing : it comes and goes, it mounts and sinks, it is tied to sensuous appetite and to mechanism—a life without ends or aims, without meaning or reason, entirely sinking to the level of bare and barren existence.   If we survey this psychic life in its extension over the expanse of nature right up to man himself, we find it nowhere resting in itself, but it appears with all its performances as mere means to the mere natural conservation of its own existence. What purpose does the richest equipment in the animal world serve but to put on war-footing the individual and the species in the struggle for existence ?   And hardly more does the merely psychic life perform for man, for it remains in him, too, a mere piece of the natural Life-process.

But though this kind of life has governed humanity almost exclusively in its initial stages, and though it has carried the natural and commonplace to the throne, yet such a kind of life does not remain isolated, for along with it there develops a new and higher kind with other configuration and direction.   Step by step transformations appear and form an essentially higher standard. Thus human activity is not wholly held fast by self-assertion, but also reaches out in the direction of the welfare of others. Consequently, inward connections of the community arise and win the individual up to the point even of sacrifice of self for the aims of the community ; in other departments of life the spiritual activity draws the man unto himself and places his striving under an actual compulsion ; in art, science, law, technics, etc., great connections grow up and urge man into their service.

Such work could never have been linked together into a Whole had it not been that a transformation had proceeded out of a Whole in the inward web of the soul. An inward representation of these connections must be possible ; the thought of a Whole must span the manifold, and the entire mass must be transmuted into a system. Indeed, this points in reality to the erection of a connected world of thought —a general organisation of culture.

Of more importance still is the fact that the Life-process disengages itself from its mere connections with things : the process deepens the life of the soul in itself, and strives to pass beyond the mere appearance of things to their nature. This Life-process is carried further and cast into a new mould by receiving into itself from the external world ; through this new forms and energies appear, and the inwardness attains the capacity for production, as, for instance, we find on the heights of science that the conceptions are not a mere thesis of sensuous presentations but characteristic creations of thought. More and more the inward world links itself together into a unity ; it

seeks and finds original tracks, and exercises a counter-
activity to all the mere environment. An activity
arising out of characteristic energy and decision now
places itself over against all mere hap and hazard.
To such an independence of the individual soul
corresponds the greater self-activity of humanity.
The latter prepares a particular kingdom—a kingdom
of civilisation—over against the realm of nature ; and a
corporate Spiritual Life, founded in itself, bridges all
the branch provinces and calls men to a new existence
far beyond the reach of nature.

At the same time, a new relationship towards all
natural things is won.   It suffices us no longer to know
what the mere connections of things are; we must forge
our way in the direction of the connections of things
and transport ourselves into the midst of their characteristic existence, and participate in their characteristic life. This is accomplished not only through
mental discernment and its longing after truth, but
also through the whole of the life of the spirit. What
differentiates definite love from sensuous excitement
but the reception of the " other " into one's own soul ?
How could a fact with its compulsion move us, were
it not born in our characteristic striving ? This
signifies a breaking through the narrowness of natural
existence as well as the most fundamental transformation of all greatness and goodness.   It is only when the
Life-process draws this seeming " beyond " into itself
that there arises a problem of truth, and that a good
(one of the most enigmatic of all terms) grows over
against the useful and the pleasurable. What satisfied us previously as happiness—the maintenance and
enhancement of the individual—becomes through the

inward expansion of life small and lean, and, indeed, a hindrance to definite welfare.

This new direction of life develops into an objectivity and exhibits an activity of the soul of a very different nature from the activity known on earlier levels. This new object never gains an independence and an inward present moment from sensuous impressions, but only through its deliverance from these; this deliverance is, however, a work of the activity of thought, for thought transplants us into the very centre of things, and it is through the conception of the things as great thoughts that the things can produce in us a living movement. Thus every further expansion of life means, at the same time, a transition into the province of a world of thought, of the non-sensuous, and of ideals. Indeed, there follows an inversion of life in which the work of thought operates in the interpretation of the earlier stages of things and of the foundation of all; and through this process the sensuous aspect of things withdraws to a secondary place and sinks to the periphery of life. This basing of life upon thought is, at the same time, a gain in transparency and freedom. True, the object which we ourselves appropriate exercises a strong constraint against our previous condition—an inward necessity of our nature dispels all arbitrary choice. But this constraint of the outward fact does not work through physical pressure, but all along through the intervention of a characteristic activity—an activity which eliminates arbitrary choice and thus establishes freedom. All investigation comes under the necessities of the case, but the strongest external sway of things cannot force open a turn to investigation; æsthetic creativeness could not discover and obey the necessities of the object that it deals with had not the imagination previously linked that object to itself. The thought of obligation is an absurdity without an acceptation of the fact of a moral organising power in the will.

Thus a new life unfolds itself in manifold traits; a bi-lateral life and a parting of the ways towards wider and more decisive points of view now become needful in order to obtain a complete view of things. In the one, our acts are more and more flung back upon ourselves and thus strike a depth in the soil of independent inwardness; in the other, it becomes possible to plant ourselves on new objects and be filled and moved by them. The collective flow of things found on the natural level is now entirely discarded; subject and object, man and the world, activity and its object of treatment, have all separated themselves and work upon one another as independent energies. But the cleft which frees our life from numb subjection cannot signify as yet the final conclusion; indeed, the sharper and clearer that cleft becomes, the more do we discover it as an intolerable situation, and are driven with all our available energy to seek to establish again some kind of unity which had succumbed during the initial stages of the inward movement. The road to a Yea lies through a Nay; we must separate in order again to unite, and must depart from our ordinary state in order again to return to it. There enters thus a negative element into the work of life; all definite departure on the new road follows through toil and struggle, doubt and pain; but in all this aggravation of existence the man is raised to a higher level, and is ennobled through the inward compulsion which drives him forward. Intertwining movements and revolutions break the ban of the fixed actuality which lay upon natural existence. Much still remains dark and mysterious, and, indeed, becomes more and more so; but already the clear discovery of the darkness heralds the beginning of a coming enlightenment. We are not allowed now to accept the phenomena as they merely fall upon us; we cannot now leave on one side a standard and a judgment, a sanction and a disapproval; over all the particular questions there arises the question concerning the aim of all action and the meaning of all life. The whole manifold must fasten itself together and obtain a characteristic view of things.

There is, thus, no doubt that our conscious life is not a mere furtherance of the movement of the natural order, but that within it a new art of life is to be recognised; our life constitutes not merely a simple superficies, but it includes two qualities fundamentally different in kind. That such a view of life is less simple, and that scientific investigation demands a greater labour out of it, must not prevent us from recognising such a fact. Or, shall we bend, enfeeble, and trim such a life in order that we may join together those conceptions alone which will produce our mere individual comfort?

2. *The Contradiction in Human Life*

The point of contact of two different stages of a life signifies in itself no contradiction; such con-

tradiction would arise only if a conflict between the
two stages were to arise, and if the relationship of
both became something other than what corresponded
to their separate inner significance. And it is this
which actually happens. The Spiritual Life presents
itself as pre-eminent and as being called to wield the
sceptre ; it has often to content itself with a humbler
position ; it will thus, true to its own nature, rest in
itself and construct its own particular province ; but
through such a treatment of it the man remains still
tied to the natural order, and the higher life seems to
accompany that order as a mere addendum. Such a
contraction confines the effect not only on the external side, but also brings the internal formation to a
standstill : the Spiritual Life, through that dependence
upon an alien power, seems not able to accomplish
the purpose of its own nature, and consequently must
be wrecked in its search for a More, which lies on a
coast beyond the natural province. Thus it becomes
in itself a contradiction, and what promised to illumine
our existence proves itself now a difficult riddle.

(a) *The Weakness of the Spiritual Motive-Powers.*
—A loosening of the activity from the natural instinct
of self-preservation and its liberation for aims of a
conjoint and actual kind are essential to the Spiritual
Life. This shows itself especially in the province of
morality. In however devious ways morality may be
conceived and founded, that it is a contraction of the
instincts and signifies a direction upon common aims
cannot be doubted. How do things stand in reality
with the evolution of such a conviction ? Over the
whole field of civilisation there extends an appearance
of morality, self-forgetfulness, and willingness for

sacrifice; the corporate organisations hold before themselves great aims; and mutual co-operation, love, and esteem find their way by the sheer force of their own inherent assurance into organic society. But he who accepts this appearance for the whole truth is soon disillusioned, and finds pretty quickly that the gold pieces prove themselves to be copper coins; and that that which constitutes the real experience of life is in its foundation nothing other and nothing less than an insight into, and a loosening from, the mere appearance of things. So that from of old the credit of an insight into human nature belongs to the pessimists and not to the optimists. The organisation of co-operative life, however, treats the particular interests of individuals as the whole driving-power of all effort; such an organisation wins such a power not through the presentation of elevated aims beyond the circle of immediate life, but through the benefits which it is called to further, and through the drawbacks which it is called to obviate. Indeed, the closer these individual movements link themselves to the system of society, the securer becomes their actual strength; how poorly would the movement proceed in its love for the good if it left on one side its abhorrence of evil! Religions, in spite of all their differences, are united in the fact that they change in some degree the moral achievements of man. The optimistic character of even the religions of law does not confine itself to the natural good of human nature, but expects an obedience to the voice of Divine command which promises, on the one hand, great rewards, and threatens, on the other hand, heavy punishments. Philosophy, too, deals incessantly with the wide gap

between the moral potency and the actual conduct of
man; indeed, the deeper the great thinkers, as, for
example, Plato and Kant, have penetrated into the
depth of human existence, the more they have discovered that contradiction; but the thinkers who, as
Aristotle and Leibniz, presented the facts in a more
friendly manner, yet became, in the further development of their thoughts, living witnesses against their
earlier outlook, and in favour of another view of
things. For as soon as they turned towards the
expanse of life and trod on the impressions of experience, the favourable picture was inverted into
its opposite. Thinkers are far more united concerning their judgment of man than could be expected
from the strife of their different conceptions; for
example, they present the same truth in different
forms. Art also tends to the same convictions as
philosophy and religion when it does not falsify the
reality with shallow embellishments, but endeavours
to illumine it and learns to see it in a truthful way.
How many confusions has such Art brought to the
surface, and under what strong contrasts has it exhibited human existence!

In great moments, however, individuals and nations
have exhibited a character free from self and capable
of heroic sacrifice. This is true of particular moments
when human nature was under strong stimuli, and is
a phenomenon witnessed but seldom. But does not
the circumstance prove, when it is considered more
closely, that such achievements—prized as something
miraculous and conceived as something superhuman
—condemned root and branch the ordinary natural
ways of man?

7

The problem does not limit itself, however, to the moral province in any definite sense; it is not only when man is required to sacrifice his own self, but also when he is called upon to display some earnest participation in the affairs which lie beyond his self, that the ability is denied him for such an accomplishment. It may be an activity concerning the state and society, or art and science; everywhere the ordinary mode of life shows a lamentable callousness and apathy, everywhere the effort proceeds not so much upon the thing itself as upon the advantages which promise to accrue to the individual. In order to win any energy for the actual thing itself, it becomes obligatory to take solitary circuitous paths and perilous enterprises, and then the situation seems to need a stern defiance, and soon, too, a daring assertion of one's own self; but, soon, on the contrary, the particular interest has somehow found its vantage-point, and transforms the rigid apathy into the closest attention and the most strenuous interest. If it is now felt that the situation at the height of this creativeness is a better one, this in its turn is clearly discovered as an exception, and serves more for the corroboration than for the refutation of the assertion.

There remains, therefore, no doubt as to the weakness of the spiritual and moral motive-powers. But strangely enough man stands up in strong opposition to the acknowledgment of this fact. Throughout the whole of life and of corporate organisations there proceeds a striving to represent things in a better light, to show them to be nobler and greater than they actually are; an open conviction and calm acknowledgment of the real facts of the case have vanished, and men practise hypocrisy not only towards one another but even more towards themselves; and even in front of his own consciousness the man speaks and imagines himself on the heights. This incessant drama has evoked, from of old, the bitter jests of the satirists, the fiery indignation of the friends of truth, and the deep pain of all moral natures. There is imbedded here a problem: Why do we shrink from the recognition of that mysterious Something whose actuality is undeniable? Why do we not acquiesce in the ordinary state of things which surrounds us on all sides? There must be some kind of concealed counter-effect operative; whence that concealment—that darkness—came and whither it goes nobody knows. And thus our existence continues largely under the power of opposites, and we are unable to see how the spiritual can prevail, although the necessity of our nature even against our will holds us to it.

(β) *The Spiritual Impotence of Man.*—Hitherto the subject has on the whole dealt with the strength of the spiritual motive-powers in man; the will as yet has not corresponded to the demands of the new standard. But the question arises, whether the will in particular is responsible for the fault, or whether, rather, the confusion does not extend to the very foundation of our nature. Is man able, primarily, to pursue something beyond his present situation? Can Spiritual Life, in the way it expresses itself within the limits and subjectivity of his own nature, come to actual realisation? Will not all things—not only mere appearances but even truth—be drawn down to the level of ordinary nature and thus destroyed? And will not the same happen to what could have raised man to a domain beyond the natural—to a life of fulness and veracity, to a life which enters into the soul of another?

The aspiration after knowledge becomes truth—the particular truth of things beyond the bare impressions which surround the mind in sensations and which are deposited into percepts and ideas. The sensuous presentation of the idea disengages itself from the idea itself in order to present before the mind the existence of things in space. But how do we step beyond the province of the presentation? Does not the idea, the more it withdraws itself from its object and stands upon its own particular potency, become more empty and shadowy? Moreover, within the most sublime ideas sensuous presentations adhere. With what ardour and toil has religion, from of old, striven to obtain pure conceptions of the Divine; and always in this procedure how clearly has it discovered anew the limits of our powers! Must it not then acknowledge even in its highest flight that all human knowledge attains to no more than a metaphor? But even so much signifies that the distinctively human way of thinking holds man with inexorable power.

What is true of the idea is true on the whole of knowledge. Knowledge ought to subsist upon reality as it is "in itself," and yet it is held in trammels by the subjectivity of the soul. The subject remains always with himself, and can extend and extend this particular circle, but is never able to break through the situation and transpose himself into the object; what we occupy ourselves with is never things but only our presentations and images of things. The idea itself of any thing is not given from the external but originates in our own characteristic way of thinkir Thus there stands continually between us ˉ   ᴄᵤity the ghost of our own particular thought and reflection, which threatens to reduce the world to a shadow; instead of seeing the things we see only a haze with which they are surrounded, and we only substitute one haze for another when we believe we have unveiled them.

Hence to all great thinkers the conception of truth has been the most difficult of all problems as well as a riddle full of mysteries. To such thinkers the work of knowledge presented itself not as a wandering on a paved, secure path, but as an incessant wrestling to find the main goal and the main direction of a new track. Philosophy, therefore, must take up anew the question of the possibility of truth, and must consider that the question is not altogether settled by previous work upon it. In spite of all toil the goal seemed to recede into an ever farther distance. The Greeks considered the problem simply as the unbroken connection of man and the world, and the truth was conceived as a harmony between subject and object (*adæquatio rei et intellectus* of the Middle Ages), and found such harmony quite attainable through the accepted kinship of nature on both sides. The growing inwardness of human life slackens and parts asunder such a connection with the environment; it corresponds to the most important position of Descartes when he tore off the subject from its entanglement with the physical universe and undertook to construct reality out of consciousness. But even he, at the same time, held fast to the existence of an independent actual world of man in consciousness; and therefore it became necessary for him to find a connection between subject and object by a new method. That happened with his successors in the doctrine of parallelism between thought and existence. Each of the two unfolds independently of the other; a pre-eminent power—of an immanent or of a transcendent nature—causes at least here and there a harmony of results. But to conceive of the truth of the problem in this manner is not to solve it so much as to push it backward; it must soon reappear as an intolerable contradiction alternately over against the world and upon the world. Such a criticism culminated with decisive acuteness in Kant; to him a truth seemed possible only in the degree it is conceived apart from all its relationships with things, and thus the problem is laid entirely in the particular thought-province of the subject. But when it is not recognised that a world of things persists by the side of this thought-process and that the subject is nothing without such a world, our world transforms itself into a kingdom of appearances; and then it becomes questionable whether a truth in any definite sense remains, and whether we are not standing on a province between knowledge and non-knowledge. A way out of this dilemma as well as a conclusion of the most important movements were sought by the German speculative movement, in which the leaders allowed the things to remain on one side, and endeavoured to bring forth reality out of their own thought. That such an investigation signifies an overstrain of human ability, and that, at the same time, it robs the reality of all content there is no doubt, as is clear enough from the consequent disillusion which followed the speculation. What has this most important speculative movement arrived at ? It seems to teach nothing other than the inaccessibleness of truth for man, and the insight that the sum of all knowledge forces us to acknowledge something unknowable. But out of all the changes and transformations of time arises clearly the one dilemma : *Either* the striving after truth points to some kind of existence beyond the human circle, and then our inability to attain a *direct* intercourse with the things will prove itself ever anew and ever clearer ; *or* we create the whole reality out of our thoughts, and then such a titanic plunge soon breaks the reality into pieces, and the overstrain of the human powers will take vengeance through the increasing emptiness of our existence.

The position of science in its dealings with ordinary life and in its incessant work and results can very well tolerate such doubts. Science can incessantly codify and extend results only in so far as it stands upon an average height and shuns the highest summit and the deepest abyss, and in so far it pushes further off or places on one side the problem of a final and definite truth. Such is a kind of indispensable compromise and no more, which has to take place in the co-operation of the work of science and in the continuance of life ; and to see the solution of the main problem within such a province can only mean a self-satisfied superficiality. As soon as we demand to pass beyond mere awareness to a genuine knowledge, we discover our deplorable poverty, and must confess that what is termed certain seems on clearer investigation to rest upon a totally insecure foundation.

When we turn to the realm of action, the matter appears worse than in the realm of thought. The moral inadequacy of man has been, as we saw, an object of complaint from of old; but the complaint seems often to have forgotten the question, whether the "given" and benumbed nature of man is able in some fashion to handle things otherwise. We cannot act without motives, and these adjust themselves to the good striven for; but a good for us can only be that which furthers our particular will; therefore we can strive only for ourselves and never for some external existence. In particular, it is our subjective existence—our independent and self-centred particularity—which seeks the one thing and flees from the other; to arrive at a thorough understanding of causal relations within this sphere is, for our activity, as impossible as it is to understand the generation of our sense-presentations. Pleasure and pain drive and control our life; they may be refined far beyond their raw, sensuous forms; and our subjectivity, too, binds us to great refinement, so that in the last resort we seem to act for nothing other than our own particular condition. Also, this condition may interlace and link itself to the world and man around us, in the most varied manner; we may imagine that we are striving not so much for our own welfare as for the welfare of another; we may conclude, in order to strengthen such an opinion, that we do this for another because it promises pleasure and has already proved itself of value to ourselves, so that when dealing with the seeming external we are really always dealing with ourselves; we thus find the self, in the furthest remove from its starting-point, bound to its own subjective happiness, and unconsciously striving towards it. All transformation and seeming excellence never seem to yield an exit from that embarrassment—never bring forth a transplanting of the life into the realm of over-individual and over-subjective actions. This impossibility, however, is the strict demand of morality, and with it morality stands or falls. This demand renders impossible the enclosure of man within the web of his own small self; the demand not only places his acts under definite aims but also calls him to mount to a region of definite self-denying love; it holds its message before him not merely as an agreeable play of phantasy, but as an imperative problem upon whose solution the content and value of life are decided. Thus there appears as indispensable something which is not yet discovered: it does not reveal itself, and the problem is: How may we discover it?

All through the ages thinkers have laboured to solve the problem; but the liberation of man from himself would not yield to any proposed solution; all ardent labours have alternately entangled and disentangled the skein, and the goal has always receded further away. On the summit of Greek life the good attracted man on account of its inherent beauty as an object of disinterested welfare, and not on account of its utility or its enjoyment; on account of its powerful influence on the imagination man seemed to win the good and the beautiful. Happiness (εὐδαιμονία) welded compactly together sensation and act, subject and object. But this supposition involved presuppositions of a problematic character; it reckoned with nature conceived as great and noble; it interweaved minutely the psychic nature of the observer with the objective world, and placed the increased inwardness of life as something inherent in the external world. But the question was not raised, whether this refinement of nature works in the direction of the liberation of man from nature itself and from egotistic narrowness, or whether, finally, all such attempts do not end in the mere inclinations of man. However hard and unfair the opinion may be that " the virtues of the ancients were splendid sins " (*virtutes veterum splendida vitia*), it is not without some reasonable ground.

Christianity has, as one of its great accomplishments, freed morality from mere nature, and with incomparably greater clearness than before placed the moral problem in front of the soul of man. But the solution was not, on account of this, rendered easier but more difficult. Holding all human ability as useless, there remained only the resort to a miracle of Divine grace: such alone could create a new disinterested life. But is not the centre of gravity through this shifted outside us? And do we not sink to the level of lifeless instruments and mere indecisive receptacles of Divine decree? Also, it remains in darkness how such a regenerated man could escape from the toils and tangles of his own nature, and how his life and actions could free themselves from subjective conditions. Christian love is much praised, but it is often forgotten in the midst of this praise to ask if such love is possible, and if it really exists. Thus the knot is not untied but rather

Is the situation thus, or is there some kind of help, some kind of passable exit ?

(γ) *The Insufficiency of an Alleged Remedy.*— Modern life is convinced that it has a ready exit out of the entanglements that have been brought out upon the particular ground of experience without any kind of transformation of reality, and it hopes to become equipped to deal with the problem by holding and overcoming the particular energies which are misplaced in the problem.   The solution is to take place through a belief in the power of the progressive evolution of humanity aided by society and history— two factors which the modern man holds out against all doubt, and which enable him to take up life with a joyous courage.   That such a course of thought, as it presents itself in the foreground, is peculiar and problematic, will appear more clearly as we proceed.

Such a course of thought understands the band of society and history as the energy of the Spiritual Life making itself apparent.   Bred in the chaos of individual opinions, it affirms society as a connecting world of thought, and, at the same time, develops common aims and goods over against the bare self-preservation of the individual.   But, as it was with the simultaneity of events, so is it, too, with succession —it originates a combination and summing-up of energy ; a later time takes over the achievements of an earlier time ; the stones of the building fit into each other and rise into a pyramid of civilisation ; the succession of generations eliminates the transient and subsidiary, and couples and fastens the essentials, and thus augments the fundamental inheritance of our domain.   Thus humanity is able to build up a kingdom of reason far beyond the capability of the mere individual and the mere moment; although the ideal is certainly not reached at one stroke, yet, little by little, it is brought nearer home.

This unbounded capacity of the world of experience to ascend seems to render superfluous the need of splitting up reality into two different provinces. For what purpose, then, does man need religion when his wishes and hopes, little by little, come to realisation entirely on such a ground? Thus evolutionary thought becomes a fierce, and, indeed, a most dangerous enemy of religion.

It would have been difficult for such a thought to win the mind of modern man with such convincing power had it not been that there worked behind it a significant new tendency of the life of civilisation itself. The nineteenth century developed with characteristic energy an historical point of view; over against the eighteenth century it might be designated as the century of history. Not only do we occupy ourselves as investigators far more with the past, but also we interlace it more closely with our own present work; we seek to introduce the inheritance of the ages into our work, and in this manner to establish a richer, clearer, and more concrete work. Thus it is in law and religion, in science and art. At the same time, in consequence of easier and more rapid intercourse, more reciprocal relationships and co-operative work originate; we feel ourselves more closely bound and connected together; we experience in such results a powerful ascent of our abilities over against all earlier times. Such an energetic development and such a clear consciousness of historico-social modes of life make it conceivable how, from such a development, an answer to the main problem may be expected.

A deeper and more penetrating reflection is, however, necessary in order to read more correctly that opinion of our day, and in order to perceive that history and society in all their accomplishments on the periphery of life heighten rather than lessen the problem at the centre.   With compelling force the following dilemma raises its head: History and Society are *either*, as evidences of the mere greatness of experience, testimonies of a confused and conflicting situation which has appeared clearly before our eyes; and if so, history and society participate in the entanglements of the situation, and cannot raise themselves beyond the situation or inwardly free themselves from it.   *Or* there result in history and society such actual effects of elevation and freedom; and if this happens, they do not work out of their own energy, but there is imbedded in them a superior power which prepares them as ways and means.   Then it is not history and society but something that in the meantime remains completely unknown that consummates the transformation.

What gain could issue out of the recognition that man, as he lives and suffers, merely links himself to his equals ?   The energies of man gather themselves together without much toil and act upon things: activities perform their work and reciprocally supplement and unite themselves, differentiate and particularise themselves, and thus a powerful increase of behaviour and a thorough consolidation and refinement of work take place.   This work, through such

energy, has transformed the contour of our existence
and drawn our life more and more into its own vortex.
But does such an advance of the external signify
the gain of an inward harmony; and are men in
conviction and character—in the whole of their
being—brought nearer to one another, so that the
true and the good for which they strive become easier
and gain a conquest of reason over all dangers
and resistance? Experience on this point reveals
the very opposite. A growing disunion of mind is
rendered necessary in order to support the amalgamation of work; we observe, opening out amongst men,
more and more contrasts, which swell to ever greater
passion and hatred, thus causing individual to stand
against individual, vocation against vocation, race
against race, nation against nation, empire against
empire. When, indeed, was humanity so full of
dissensions as to-day, and this despite all the
coherence of united practical work? Also, the
admission and the belief themselves do not verify the
statement that a real union of individuals is possible
without a further addition of reason, or that through
such a contact with one another a fixed truth easily
and quickly springs forth. If we view, however, our
parliaments and the great gatherings of the people,
it seems clear how very little so-called public opinion
is able to differentiate between the definite and the
indefinite, and how defenceless it often falls before
robust force, and, indeed, even before audacity and a
daring to plunder. When we become aware of this,
we shall think less confidently of the alleged summation of truth. There is, indeed, no joyous activity for
humanity without a trust in some kind of conquest of

reason in its own sphere ; but this conquest must be something other than the gain of the ordinary and the commonplace ; and when such a conquest comes to its own, a different kind of energy of thought must sway humanity than that which lies in the opinions and interests of individuals and masses.   Also, the evident strengthening of the convictions and tendencies of human society gives not the slightest security for their actual truth.   Moreover, stubborn errors can strike here their fast roots, and with a kind of sacred authority grow from generation to generation.   Later times then revere calmly the undisputed truth which the tradition of the centuries has sanctioned.   But this sanction is of a purely human kind ; and if there stands not something more than human behind it, sooner or later the day must dawn when the usurpation is seen through and the alleged truth is stripped of its mask.   And then a powerfnl upheaval results, and each and every truth falls lightly into doubt.

These considerations lead us further into the province and problem of history.   Here, also, a significant achievement is unmistakable ; but the question is, whether such achievement, through what it receives from the doctrine of evolution, is able to create a definite cleavage between reason and unreason and to possess the security of a growing mastery of reason. In certain respects there results evidently an increase of material as well as a progressive adjustment of work ; this is to be witnessed in the exact and positive sciences and in technics.   What the particular movement here achieves is a gain in the duration of its material, and in the linking together of epochs into

8

a consecutive chain of activity and production. But will this bond of union be reached if the inner existence and convictions of man are laid on one side, if the question of absolute truth remains in the background, if the activity revolves around the circumference and not around the centre of life? Was the historical movement a progressive gain in spiritual substance? Has it clarified our fundamental relationship to reality, and overcome the previously explained contradictions of our nature? Have we become greater, nobler, happier men, and has daily life transmuted itself into a kingdom of reason? Our particular consideration of the struggle for the true and the good has already given us a decisive answer; the solutions that seemed ready to hand proved themselves insufficient, and when we dive ever deeper into the chaotic abyss, we discover an ever greater cleft between wish and capacity. More and more our life tears itself away from a simple standpoint and seeks new paths. But the energy of the denial does not correspond to that of the affirmation: energies and movements are found in abundance, but no definite aim which governs, secures, and raises them.

The strenuous efforts to understand the past and the development of a historical consciousness must heighten the impression of this situation; what these efforts gain in knowledge threatens to overbalance in the loss to life. When a keen outlook on history presents before us the abundant multi-coloured material of human striving, and when it shows alternately slow and rapid changes and transformations of ideals and their ever fragile nature—material which the man had achieved with toil and which had filled his soul—then the question raises itself imperatively, whether all human toil for truth and reason is a labour in vain. With what right may we hold and defend truths as being definite and settled simply because they were so in earlier times, when they are now seen through as errors ?   The Indian words, " We were what you are, you shall become what we are," should recall us to a consciousness of the shadowy character of such relative truths.

Let us consider impartially the situation of the present.   Historical inquiry stands in magnificent blossom, it extends its kingdom ever onward, and ever more accurately it explores its ramifications.   More assured, indeed, than we realise is the validity of truth to the great investigator.   But do we gain, with all our insight, a more secure support for that which is valid to us as truth ?   And are we not inwardly poor in the midst of this overflowing kingdom ?   At the best we seem to get a particular positive or pragmatic truth which is carried to us on the current of history. The insight that all is to be conceived as in a process of flux, and that all the later comes under the influence of the earlier, is not likely to make valid the belief in a particular truth in the sense referred to.

This joyous belief in history has an hypothesis which it cannot verify and which soon suffers a shock. This belief accepts as true that the movement of humanity from of yore has transmuted itself into the elements of reason, and that through this the movement obtained an unassailable foundation, and consequently is able to erect its structure step by step. But reason is not a ready-made thing given to us, but presents itself to us as a task ; doubts and strife ever anew draw us back, and the reasonable character of the whole turns again and again into doubt. And on this account our belief in such an evolution falls to the ground. Such a denial signifies in no manner a complete transmission of history into unreason. But if any kind of reason works in history, it must originate out of a source that is above simple experience and simple historical growth ; and such a source will hardly find its highest aim in a superstructure of the kingdom of history. History can never, out of its own capacity, create pure reason, but remains a turbid mixture of little reason and much unreason.

The untenableness of the evolution theory also is corroborated through its own history. History shows it as giving support to various diverse modes of thought and afflicted with an inward contradiction. Modern thought believed itself to have grasped directly, through the ascending scale of life, an absolute truth, and to be able to carry this truth fully into the human province. Such a course of thought took up, first of all, an attitude of antagonism to history, and placed the explanations of its discovery before a powerful tribunal of reason ; there resulted, however, in a calmer mood, the view that history should be conceived as a revelation of reason—indeed, it was conceived as a gradual evolution of the whole of reason. History appeared for such a mode of thinking not so much as that which is able to engender reason out of itself, but as that which is encircled and carried along its course by a timeless reason, thus placing the main standard of life *not within* but *above* Time. Then followed the change to immediate existence through the realism of the nineteenth

century ; and to that changed view the life that stands
above historical development became a mere illusion
and bare impossibility ; history was placed entirely
upon the ground of natural immediate experience.
But through this arise the characteristically modern
way of looking at life : the old view is fundamentally
rejected, but the assertion is to be fully allowed that
the new view is able to perform less than was thought
possible.   The historical movement should be understood more on its empirical side ; but, at the same
time, it appears as a witness of reason which held
unswervingly to a belief in the strong reign of law, in
an incessant ascent, and in a progressive conquest of
the good.   Such a mixture of different kinds of mental
procedure tends necessarily to a blunting of the
problem, and obscures the sharp *Either—Or* which
doubtless lies here ; and the mixture becomes a serious
danger to the energy and truth of life.   This danger
is rapidly growing on all sides, and the doctrine of
evolution on its empirical side, with its confidence in
the culture of society and in history, has now reached
the masses.   But on the height of spiritual activity
such a doctrine has been broken and overcome.   The
untenableness and even violent contradictoriness of
limiting life within the merely human area appear
constantly before us.   Where man sinks wholly into
relationship with the human environment, where his
anxiety for his position in the mere simultaneity and
succession of things allows him to forget all else, then
he loses in inward independence, in depth of soul, and
becomes inevitably a shallow and babbling nature in
which finally all characteristic life and all truthful
present consciousness disappear.   We witness with

painful clearness to-day a strong decline of inward culture; more and more, leading minds fail in creative power ; ever less does man find definite satisfaction in all the bustle of our modern mechanism ; ever more is the inward life lowered in its pitch to the commonplace ; and ever more clearly it becomes apparent that all the gain on the periphery of life is insufficient to counterbalance the loss which occurs at the centre. In the last resort, it is true that we live our existence from out the centre, and although this fact may be forgotten in our relationship to the environment, it can never be permanently lost. If, therefore, the proffered solution of the evolutionary theory fails, the main question faces us again with a harsh distinctness : *Either* the complete surrender of reason and, along with this, an inward subversion of life, *or* an ascent beyond the ordinary level and a new energy which not only grapples strongly with the contradictions, but also lifts the inward life out of them and sets that life to work against all obstacles. It is a great gain in the midst of all the chaos of the present time to realise that all attempts to run away from this dilemma are more and more seen through as a delusive hybridisation of life.

CHAPTER VII

b. The Progressive Autonomy of the Spiritual Life

HITHERTO the movement in the direction of the Spiritual Life has appeared as a particularly difficult contradiction. The Spiritual Life presented great problems, and we find in ourselves no energy for their solution; it demanded a cosmic character and yet was coerced through the narrowness of the self; it promised a clarification of existence and yet it was through itself that the darkness of existence became evident. A contradiction which comes suddenly upon the inmost kernel of life does not allow itself to be placed calmly on one side—at least not for a strong nature with its corresponding strong thought. If the aims of life are simply unreachable, every attempt to reach them must be excluded, and they must vanish out of our existence as deceitful illusions. But, at the same time, we dare not allow so much to perish; for all this exhibited what gives eminence to man above all else, and what constitutes the good and the noble in his life—in fact, what constitutes all the inner onward movement of humanity and all the meaning and content of life. Is such a complete collapse inevitable, and does no path offer itself to evade the catastrophe?

There is one and only one possibility. The ultimate cause of the contradiction consisted in affirming that the Spiritual Life appeared as an activity of the mere individual self, and that it was bound up in the situation and custom of this self. Man forms out of his surrounding conditions a special province over against the great All; reality stands over against him as something alien, and his life appears as a pendulum swinging between his own particular province and this great All of things. Things being thus, if the Spiritual Life is called to bridge inwardly the gulf, to unfold the infinite on a definite point, the impossibility of such an achievement becomes evident, and all attempts will be wrecked on the rocks of the contradiction. This intolerable situation is to be escaped only if the Spiritual Life be not railed simply within the human province; if it contributes in some way to the winning of an independence and of a power to draw reality into itself; and if it be able to expand from within and become a universe of its own. Through this the Spiritual Life would be raised above the opposites; man would win, through his participation in the new life, freedom from the narrowness of his subjective existence; and in that which at first seemed to oppress him—as an unfulfilled demand from without—he would seek and find the inmost nature of his true self. For the insufficiency and even the contradiction of life within the merely human circle reveal themselves ever more clearly. Then an activity of a spiritual order is no

longer satisfied to accept languidly a rigid and indifferent kind of existence such as accrues from the
mere motive-powers, but is able to penetrate to the
depth of one's own nature and to attain to the might
and ardour of self-affirmation.   Thus the opposition
of subject and object, of one's own individual standpoint and one's external material, can be taken up
into the Life-process itself and here overcome.   If
this happens, there results a hope of such an illumination over the whole meaning of the Spiritual Life as
was not possible so long as that Life signified only a
particular speck in a universe of chaff and dust.   In
brief, an avenue opens in a new and opposite direction,
provided that the possibility of such a Life is more
than a mere possibility, and provided that it reveals a
corresponding reality.

All continuation of life's movement and all success
depend on the existence of such a reality.   The
many problems and entanglements connected with
the existence of such a reality constitute a further
problem : in the first place, it is necessary that our
anxiety concerning that question should not blind us
to the real fact itself.   The attention must be set on
this fact alone, and set against any incidental reflection which prevents us from claiming this new path,
for this is not a pert merriment in knight-errantry
but that which Goethe characterised as the best of
counsellors—*Necessity*.

That a new actuality, however, of an independent
kind rises in us becomes more and more evident ;
through this we seek to effect an emancipation of the
life from the small self and from the merely human
level, in order that we may overcome the inward

opposition and gain a new self. Our object in this work will be to survey the whole of this new life, to estimate its significance, and to examine the transformation it effects in our view of the world and of life.

1. *The Several Stages*

(a) *The Emancipation of Life from the small self and the merely human order.* — Thus all spiritual manifestations appear but vaguely in the isolated individual, and we need only view such manifestation from its content in order to verify the fact that it forms new connections which produce transformations upon the individual. We observe the Spiritual Life always linking the elements into a Whole; the separate elements not only come together from without, but bind and complete themselves, too, from within; within this embracing Whole each special act has to seek its proper sphere and to prove its significance. It is most distinctly so in science, and it is so wherever movement of thought extends—we find everywhere a change from a mere bare aggregate to a system, everywhere general movement and dependence of the individual upon the Whole. Life, through such an extension, alters itself as well in its single states. Life thus appears, in so far as it is of a spiritual kind, not as a matter of the mere individual, or as something pivoted on its own special point; but what the individual obtains through great effort carries in itself the assertion to all others of its validity and power to bring something of value to all, and seeks to demand from all a recognition of its claims. Truth is ever a matter for the whole of humanity and

never a private possession; in the assertion of truth
the individual may feel himself as a representative,
indeed, as a tool of the Whole; and through this
inward presence of the Whole he is lifted out of the
chances and changes of his individual position.
Springing from his work an inward necessity issues
its call, that what he with labour achieved shall
become the possession of all; and it is such a possession which specially gives activity its tenacity and
success its joy.

The Life-process, however, could barely go beyond
the severance of individual from individual did there
not lie in it, on the whole, a superiority above the
merely human and above the web of external presentations and interests.   Thought with its truth could not
possess the certitude of its validity for all men if
it did not hold valid over against all men; it could
win no inward present moment with man without
the initiation if not the culmination of a transformation in himself.   The independence of truth over
all human opinions and "may-bes" has constituted
since the time of Plato the basal confession of
science; however enigmatic the matter may be,
we cannot rid ourselves of the conviction that
truths originate in a sphere which lies beyond
the mechanical work of ideas in the brain; man
does not engender such truths, but discovers them;
and they are not measured by him, but he is
measured by them.   It is from such a source alone
that the joyous belief in the power of truth,
which inspires all striving, interprets itself; and it
is out of such a belief that the energy is available
to stand, if necessary, against the whole environment,

and to feel one's self on the side of the right against all others, and also to take up courageously the struggle against deep-rooted errors in all their forms. Indeed, man becomes a problem to himself; he can examine and sift, and with longing and energy strive after a transformation of life. Thus, there results through the living power of the truth-content a rearrangement in man's whole view of things. On the one hand, truth shall be held valid not as one's own individual opinion but as a thing *in itself*; and on the other hand, truth is accessible within one's own individual life alone. Thus there exists and works in man something more than human, and consequently he does not become a mere bottled-up kind of vessel.

The movement from utility to good appears in a form very similar to that of the movement from opinion to truth. The useful corresponds to the material of the natural or social self-preservation, and is able within a given province to maintain and to improve its particular situation; evidently here the effort governs the broad ordinary level of human existence. But the effort is not able to accomplish this without opposition. Man can have no choice but to feel the useful, with its natural and social self-preservation, as indispensable; and he has no choice either but to see that all proffered happiness is too narrow and petty, and to long for wider and nobler aims. It is something of this nature that comes to expression in the idea of the good; in such an idea something is aspired after which raises man beyond his easy smugness; what appears to him now of value is to be found through struggle and pain, and stands in direct opposition to the aims of his merely natural welfare.   If such an idea of the good operates as a gravitating force on man, if it wins his particular energy and conviction, therefore it must be something grounded in his very nature, something which proves this nature to be more than a mere advance upon an intelligence which issued out of the highly developed animal world.   What is gained here through emancipation from the ordinary effortless situation and from the small human mode of life finds its richest expression in the fact of morality.   It is true that we are aware to-day of manifold opinions concerning the content of morality, yet its slow "becoming" on the field of humanity appears to us clearer than to former times; but the primal pheno- menon of morality asserts itself victoriously against the one time as against the other.   Though the realisation of the good may be a difficult problem which may rend asunder peoples and epochs, yet the fact remains that in all places and at all periods of the historical consciousness something appears as binding and as a law above mere arbitrary action, something which abandons the mere standard of utility.   What one, however, accentuates and reveres as a good is not some one thing lying by the side of other things, but something considered as a sovereign, governing thing which demands universal recognition.   If, further, the good in man has climbed slowly from faint beginnings to a condition of per- sistent clearness, what has altered its nature?   True, the good is in that movement often brought nearer to the useful, and seems, indeed, to issue entirely out of the useful.   But all this confusion of the two

currents of the good and the useful in man lessens in
no wise the distance between their different natures;
for however much the useful may receive by an
appearance of good, to become the good itself is impossible for it. It is true that in regard to the good
the movement seems to proceed from without inward; much of the good which seems to ascend
directly from within has been imported from the
social environment, education, custom, and other
sources. But even here the inward assimilation and
the acceptation into one's will remain as a special act
—as an independent achievement; all the effects
from without would glide in vain as over a hard rock,
and they could not pass beyond a clever parrot's
prattle, had not such effects awakened an inherent
consciousness in human nature. The initial custom
can become a moral activism, but so long as it remains
a mere custom and nothing more, it is not yet moral.
What, however, may be designated as moral suffers
in value the moment it is considered as no more than
an evidence of mere custom.

Morality thus remains an inexpugnable primal
phenomenon of the Spiritual Life. In the Spiritual
Life, however, there lies an entire transformation
of human nature as well as the most fundamental
emancipation from the smallness of the mere natural
order. When it turns away from the "ends" of
natural self-preservation, and turns towards the absoluteness of its demands, morality appears first of all
as a categorical imperative and brings into birth such
typical and imposing conceptions as "the ought," duty,
and law. It appears usually, in consequence, to the religious conviction as a revelation of a world "beyond"

and as a Divine injunction to man. But such a meaning includes one side only of the fact and needs necessarily a completion; if that "beyond" does not in some way transplant itself into a "here and now," the purity of morality is cast into the greatest peril.   What works upon us from the external only could not move the soul in any other way than through the holding out of consequences—through the promise of reward and the threat of punishment. Through this, however, man would be thrown back upon the position from which morality should free itself, and the narrow circle within him would not be broken through.   Man can unfold his own activities only in so far as they appertain to his own particular nature; the law, in which these activities appear, must be an inward self-willed, self-given law.   Such an assimilation of morality in our own existence is, however, impossible unless a growth in the inward parts beyond the small self takes place, and unless morality casts aside the notion of a coercion.   An "ought" which we ourselves help to establish must carry in itself a will—perhaps a will lying far behind the passing moment; and such an "ought" must also labour for the emancipation and the expression of life. As every energetic Nay hides in itself a Yea, so is morality in the denial of the old at the same time an affirmation of the new; in its onward march on this positive path morality grows to a self-affirmation, and wins a portion in all of an inward and abiding affection of a strong and joyous kind.

The testimony of experience corroborates this with a clear voice.   It refutes from its very foundation that which perceives in moral activity only an abandonment and denial, a diminution and depression of existence; and also denies the evil attributed as a mischievous result to human activity. The denial was not at all of a specifically moral kind when it proceeded out of an unwilling and coerced frame of mind; for love and joy failed it, and consequently it had in an inward manner no value. Humanity, indeed, in its energetic moral movement stands in no way dependent on the perception of limits and pressure, and does not feel itself timid and humble, but experiences and perceives a raising of its own nature in all its struggles and sorrows. Thrown back, as it were, upon the primal source of its own energy, it could feel itself secure in the midst of monstrous doubt, rich in the midst of external poverty, a free lord of things though surrounded by powerful oppression; and in its seeming setting and even collapse it is able to herald the dawn of a new spirit, a new life, and a new world.

How, in the memory of humanity, stand the men whom we most have to thank for the development of the ideal world of morals, and in what did they find the kernel of their work—men such as Plato, the Stoics, Luther, Kant, and Fichte? Were they small, nervous, depressed natures, or were they not rather free and energetic natures—heroes of the spirit? Men of brute energy they were certainly not, for their freedom carried in itself a shrinkage of the mere self; and it was clear to them beyond any doubt that there was no affirmation of a spiritual kind without a denial of their merely natural existence.

Morality could become a power and reality in the common life only through such an energy of affirmation. And this it has become in spite of all the contradictions of daily life and in spite of all the scorn of opponents. However much morality remains ordinarily in the background, it needs only greater stimulus, impulsion, and emotion, to break forth with rapturous energy as an independent force, and consequently to unlock through its own energy a new nature to man, and to offer him a fixed support and a reliable succour. All such blossoming epochs invariably breathed over humanity a renewal of the religious life ; and then the nothingness of all mere natural and social existence was perceived with painful perspicuity ; the deep abyss in which all human life and effort move became fully visible. But even in the denial of all customary help, and, indeed, in the submersion of the whole existing world, the conviction of the indestructibility of our inmost nature unfolds itself with overwhelming energy, and out of the failure of all the customary hunt after happiness there dawns the hope and even the certainty of a newer, more definite, and a purer bliss. Particular nations have shown themselves capable of a deepening and transforming power in kindred directions when their very independence was in danger, and when they had to fight for their very existence. Also, the movement and the renewal reached into the smaller circle of private life ; here, indeed, where all external lustre and the renown of historical acts fail, where all the fortified energy of society fails, the greatest heroism may yet develop, full of ardent love and joyous self-denial. Thus are the pessimists and sceptics wrong throughout when they assert that the matter is ended and done

9

with in the downfall of the sham appearances in which daily life and the common impulses had wrapped themselves. For behind the idea which testifies this lies a further idea ; behind that mechanism of life lies a depth which holds its own against all the stir and strife of the small and common on the highways of human life. Without this activity of its present moment of consciousness, human existence must fall to pieces. All energetic activity for humanity relies upon this " beyond," and comprehends a belief in the possibility of an inward renewal. The same may be said of all great practical, political, social, and educational manifestations. These alone give man an inexhaustible possession which he seizes in all his dire need. All culture which disowns this beyond through depreciation of morality robs itself of indispensable motive-powers, and becomes in the whole of its extent, in spite of its otherwise brilliant performances, shallow and hollow ; it threatens to fall into decay unless it possesses that which gives salt to life and which turns the will from mere natural impulse.

Morality is thus in its seeming weakness a mighty power, and is in its seeming strangeness the most original energy of our life. When, however, that which otherwise stands outside us is taken into the will, when a new order of things—an infinity—drives the man from within so that nevermore does he seem to stand alone, but seems as if carried by a majestic flood of life, then clearly results a deliverance from the small self, and a cosmic life, a superhuman life, reveals itself actively in the form of immediacy.

Morality is in all this not a particular province of a

man's own but carries the evidence of a new life out of the Whole, out of Infinity. As clear as daylight the fact stands before us that spiritual activity knows no bounds, that it tolerates no external hindrance, and that it regards all which it as yet has not made its own as a resistance and a reproach. In this manner an all-inclusive life dawns in man, and at the same time morality shows that nowhere is he more himself than within his moral province. Must not this kind of thing then alter fundamentally all the prior views of man?

(β) *The Inward Antithesis overcome.*—We have already observed the dawning of an infinite life in man as well as that stirring which liberates him from the small self and the mere ordinary level of humanity. But a doubt may arise, whether this change is energetic enough to reach the root of life; whether the cleft previously referred to between subject and object, between the individual standpoint and its opposite, does not confine man within the mere surface-level of things, and does not hold him fast to a merely subjective mood and agitation. Our next concern and question will be to see whether this cleavage can somehow be bridged, and whether the life can disengage itself from the destructive antithesis.

The treatment of this question may easily diverge into a false path when it mistakenly assumes that such an antithesis has not originated in nature itself but in the course of history. The sensuous beginnings of life allow the consciousness and its object to move in perfect unison, the psychical impressions swim on the current of the environment, and the human sphere has not yet opposed individual and society one to the other. But the movement of thought grows and everywhere works towards differentiation and perspicuity; in such work the subject begins to realise itself, and at the same time acquires greater rigour and independence; and, consequently, life finds itself more and more posited between an antithesis, and through this is driven further out of its previous unity. But the liberation of the object from the immediacy of sensation is in no way its complete banishment out of life; indeed, it remains present in a freer kind of way; for we saw a counter-movement originate in which the very same thing that is pressed back on the one side is again appropriated on the other. How could thought itself without such an adherence and a reapproach of the object mark out its own frontier over against the mere presentations? How could the idea raise itself above the impressions of sensation, the judgment above mere association of ideas, and the causal nexus above the mechanism of presentations, if they were not able to transplant themselves into the very midst of the facts, to develop their duration, and to maintain their necessity in a region beyond the mere impressions of sensation? The Spiritual Life thus never falls entirely on the external side; so that another side presents itself and occupies our attention because it belongs to our existence and is encompassed by our life.

Now, however, this life develops a further movement which brings both sides together into closer contact, which leads the two to some kind of union, and thus enables the one to grow by means of the other. It is the gravitation of the object from the region of work or mere external activity which

translates the outward into an inward.   Such inwardness alone—such reception of the external into the
particular life—makes it conceivable how work can
become one's own aim, how we can love it and bring
to it sacrifice, and how we are able to drown all our
sorrows and needs in the joy which lies beyond them.
The task is laid upon us mainly through an external
necessity, and often in the initial stages it is discovered as a painful burden.   But when the task
enables us to fasten it to an inward staple, when
it is able to become a thing of value for us, and
when out of the obligation freedom and joy burst
forth, then the seeming stranger proves itself clearly
enough to be a piece of our very life: we affirm
and uplift ourselves whilst we serve the necessity
of the facts.

The most varied provinces of life indicate this
with equal clearness; each province, however, shows
it in its own special way.   That there is no definite
knowledge without a relationship with the nature and
necessity of the object has been already often noticed
and needs no further explanation; but in Art it is
shown even more clearly how a Life-process of a
spiritual kind encircles both inward and outward sides,
and enables them to act in concert; and how, out of
the contact, an inner development issues.   On its
highest summits, as in the life-work of a Goethe, Art
is neither a mere reception and copy of an external
world surrounding us, nor is it a mere setting
of a ready-made inner life; but both inward and
outward are raised into a region of corporate life, and
here in one another and through one another are
carried further.   The inwardness gains a solid con-

figuration and a distinctive individuality in this recasting mould; the object, however, could not mean much to the Life-process had it not itself received an inspiration from within, and had it not been able to communicate with this. All this is distinguished as clearly as possible from a vague parallelism of both sides, for only where the initial chaos is overcome and a clear division has resulted can Art begin its work; since it finds itself first of all facing an opposite, and has to labour to penetrate beneath the surface-content of both sides. But this labour overcomes the opposite and holds it fast; and while it does this, if on the lower level the one might suppress the other, yet on the heights a reciprocal relationship is reached; the opposing forces of a subjective and an objective, of an idealistic and a realistic division, yield to a treatment which may be designated as the sovereign treatment in so far as here the Life-process is freed from all dependence on the "hither and thither" of things, and is raised to the level of a full self-reliance.

The creations of Goethe are admired on account of their objective quality; but this objectivity signifies in no way a slavish adherence to an external material, for in this very material the spirit of man proves its superiority, since Goethe posits the material within the ground of the inner life and fills it with life anew. Through such a course alone can the material reveal its own nature and provide for the whole of life. And herein is a further striking development: the object, even in its assimilation by the subject, does not lose its own independence and its characteristic features, but through this assimilation develops those features.

Thus the consciousness itself grows by means of the object, and the whole of life wins, in being raised above the opposite of mere empty sentimentalism and of dead matter, an objective and even an essential character.   We can now say:

> " Nothing is within alone,
> Nothing is without alone,
> For what's inward is, too, outward,
> And what's outward is, too, inward."

The double-sidedness and inward reciprocity of life appear in another aspect through the relationship of man with man and through the superstructure of political and social connections.   Out of the surface-content there could never issue an inward communion and interchange of life without the ability of man to transpose himself into the soul of another, to think and feel with that other ; for through this there is granted him an independence and a power to move within suitable bounds.   Without such an inward pressure of another upon the individual, there is no good-will, no sympathy, no definite compassion and no common judgment concerning right and obliga-tion.   The idea of right shows with special clearness our ability to distinguish that " other " from ourselves, to transport ourselves upon his standard, and to think and measure out of his standard ; thus the " beyond " is simultaneously a " here and now," and the separa-tion is not abolished, but life is raised above it. Only by such a detachment from one's ordinary sphere can a conjoint order of human relationships become possible—an order which strives after a king-dom of righteousness.

Encompassing all these individual provinces, activity

achieves an inner scale of values for the individual as well as for the whole of humanity. If all which we take up in our work draws incomparably nearer to us and becomes a piece of our life, then the whole of such activity itself may form a self-reliant province and become what we designate as our " calling "; a piece of reality is thus appropriated inwardly by us, granting thus a stability to life in itself and against itself as well as a superiority over whim and caprice. In fact, it is a consciousness of unassailable worth which is secure within its inward citadel in spite of the immensity of the alien and of the inconceivable without. In a similar manner, humanity itself progressively prepares a province and a world of action out of an alien world. What appertains to this world of action may include, indeed, many problems, but it signifies undoubtedly an actuality; it constructs a starting-point for all further labour; it holds men and things fast together, and binds single periods of time into a continuous chain; it resists a dissolution into the small and egotistic, and resists, too, the constant change of that current which flows on the surface of time; it stands against all arbitrary action concerning the contour of things; and it feels bound to come to an understanding with what is able to produce effects in the depth and duration of things. In all such expansion the man discovers his real self through his own soul, and finds that he is incomparably more in himself than he could possibly be through the cultivation of his purely natural self; he becomes far more his own true self than when under the dominion of natural impulses. Indeed, the man is now more, and comprehends his life as more than is revealed by the

first look of things; consequently, effective transformations of this first appearance become urgent.

Activity alone gives man a secure feeling of
reality; without activity life threatens to vanish as
a shadow and a dream. Activity invests life with
such a consolidation through the progress of work as
a superior and upholding force. Such a progress binds
together activity and work. The " becoming " of such
a work is a highly characteristic transaction; even in
the first rude outline of it there originates a kernel, an
idea, a governing centre, just as has happened in the
growth of the physical universe and in the formation
of organic life. The kernel shoots up more and more
around the centre, the rough outline grows and shapes
itself, it stands before our thought as a self-reliant
essence which strives to pass from the region of
quasi-existence to that of a complete reality; and
through such movement it becomes a driving and
judging force within the life. The initial insecurity
is then overcome, the multiplicity of energies find
their way back towards the centre, mutually form
their boundaries and determine themselves in turns;
the different possibilities which, at first, treat one
another peaceably, are now urged to a decision, and
life as a whole is driven into a definite arena. The
work develops an experience by itself; and it is only
when the two sides of work and conscious activity
are related to one another in a comprehensive
and fruitful manner that a definite experience
originates over against a bare empiricism. Also, the
work does not require that the truth should be
corroborated through external proofs; the corroboration is in the man's own triumphant effort, in his own

deduction, and in the active ascent of his life. In all this there is present a withdrawal from self and a return to self; and, at the same time, there is an inward crystallisation of a reality which is durable within one's own province. Such concentration and crystallisation of life raise the man above all the groping and lingering of mere mental reflection, and make him yield to a power which may be termed the necessity of the fact, and which without question brings forth a further development of life.

But action cannot accomplish so much as all this so long as it moves merely sundered by the side of other actions. But the more it reaches a spiritual character, the more it outgrows that isolation until it becomes the expression of a universal characteristic, and a piece of an all-embracing aggregate action. Again, is not every work of art and of thought in its individuality a confession at the same time of the Whole, and is there not in it, in spite of external limits, a conception of the Infinite? And is there not in the struggle for the right of this Infinite an essential truth and a universal *Weltanschauung* contended for? Thus in definite spiritual activity all individual actions are spanned by an aggregate living activity; and it is through reaching such, and in no other way, that life can gain an inner unity and a solidity—gain the character of a definite reality. Such a reality can never fall on us from without; it is obtained through a great struggle in the welding-heat of subject and object which results through a turn towards activism. This welding-process, however, takes place not somewhere between the inner and the outer world, but purely in an inner world which has taken up into itself the antithesis. It is out of the Spiritual Life alone that there issues a reality for man.

Through such inwardness of the activity—especially of the comprehensive life-activity—there is also present a formation of the spiritual nature of man.   When labouring along with this, he labours on the heights of his own nature and obtains in the struggle a spiritual individuality.   This, which appears from one point of view as the construction of a new world, appears at the same time as a construction of his own nature —a lawful work against his own lower self.   The mere expansion of activity is not of a proper kind unless the man struggles with his own self and thereby wins the energy and the fulcrum of self-dependence.   But, on the other hand, the inwardness of his characteristic nature does not reach this through brooding and sorrowing, but only through a stepping out of his own subjectivity, through a virile wrestling with things, and through a clarification and a further development of all things on the line of their greatest resistance.   Thus we seek ourselves, but we find ourselves only in the plasticity of things and in the construction of a new world.   So that, after all, we are within ourselves although we seemed to have stepped outside ourselves ; and in the struggle we have won a truer and larger province of life.   All this shows clearly enough that a bridging of the cleft reaches down to the deepest ground of life; and through a recognition of this we find ourselves undoubtedly engaged in the creativeness of our own spiritual individuality.

When we base our individual work upon such

a foundation of aggregate work and of a spiritual individuality, it appears evident that the work of great souls retains a worth when all the surface-appearances and the incessant leakage of time pass away. It is clear, too, that those souls held the transitory appearances of things with a loose hand. Goethe made such a confession: " I have ever viewed all my work and accomplishments as no more than mere symbols; and in my deepest experience it seemed to me pretty much the same whether I made pots or pans."

How spiritual individuality develops into a life-work, and how it steps forth and grows alongside such life-work, has been shown by the leading minds with illuminating perspicuity. Such a work as that of Kant did not possess its most characteristic features and its greatness from its originating as a mere natural product. Such a work acquired its originality only after a long and toilsome quest through which at last the striving energy burst out into blossom and fruit. In all movement he held before himself a fixed goal, and in all multiplicity a governing unity. Such a method led the energies to their highest tension, dispersed all that was alien and irresolute, and gave to the individual for the first time his distinctive stamp. Thus the characteristics of the Whole can enter into the humblest details and fashion each and all according to the pattern of this Whole.

If this work of the spiritual " becoming " of man signifies so much, the decision concerning the success or the ill-success of his enterprise lies above all else in this: whether the ascent to such a level is accomplished or not. The inner course of life as well as the nature of the final convictions are determined throughout by nothing other than the manner in which this ascent takes place—whether such ascent is easy or difficult, whether it takes place through the quiet development of natural construction or through powerful feeling and renewal. Indeed, if the decision failed here, life would soon appear as an offering of fate, later as a work of free activity, later still as filled with the harmony of existence, and finally as moved by its own contradictions.

What is true of the work of the individual is not less true of the work of the race. To a participation in work many are called; to the furtherance of definite culture few are chosen. It is only spiritual individuality bent on its life-work which gives culture an inward connection, a full self-reliance, and a living soul; and such spiritual individuality alone is able to span all life's various provinces and to work with a rousing and durable energy upon the whole of it.

What differentiates people differentiates also epochs. Great are those times only which fasten their strivings to an undivided task in which man is able to take part with his whole nature; where this does not come about, all fulness of work, all exertion and movement of the individual and of the masses, produce neither stability of character nor joyousness of disposition; moreover, the advance of petty-human interests is not kept sufficiently at bay, so that the life will fluctuate aimlessly between a soulless performance and an empty frame of mind. It is only with a life-encompassing work that the otherwise fleeting and unreal time obtains the consciousness of an immanent eternity and of unassailable worth.

Finally, there proceeds through the whole striving of humanity the desire to grasp the entire infinity of existence in one characteristic reality, to transform existence into a totality of production, and, at the same time, to gain for the self a characteristic spiritual mode of life. All genuine culture is also intrinsically a striving of humanity after an inner unity of its own life and nature; for if the striving remains less than this, culture remains something which merely hangs on us externally in spite of its feverish industry, and which finally becomes quite indifferent to the main spiritual problems of life. But if culture is found in close relation to the characteristic mode and self-maintenance of life, life is raised securely above all merely natural and civic existence, for it has won a new world within itself.

There arises, therefore, in activity and production a rich reality; it arises, too, in problems and struggles. The Life-process reaches within itself an altitude above that of its prior hindrances, and bestows upon man, so far as he participates in it, an existence on the heights, out of which, as out of a solid kernel, there issues a counter-effect to the natural disintegration of things. This power has shown itself to belong to a higher level of life, but it signifies not as yet the final issue of life.

(γ) *The Winning of a Universal Self.*— Work as a consummation of activity forms the summit of life as well as the goal of effort; it remains the axis on which all further development has to turn. But with all its accomplishments it is not yet the final

aim.   That which renders work great signifies at the
same time its limits; and the greatness itself seems
unreachable without the aid of energies which the
work far more presupposes than produces.   In a
word, the Spiritual Life demands more unity, more
freedom, more soul than work is able of itself to
produce.

(1) In work the inward energy and the external
object reach a point of contact and a reciprocal
impregnation.   But such a bond of union within the
consciousness is at the same time a switching off of
the external; nowhere more than here is verified the
maxim that all close determination is also a negation (*omnis determinatio negatio*).   Also, work, as
an embodiment of a general conviction and as a
Weltanschauung, retains a specific and abstract character; the transference of life into work and effort is
thence a differentiation which, if made final, becomes
dangerous.   The complete immersion of man in the
sea of work consigns him inevitably to a narrowness
and may easily resign him to an egoism; also the
spiritual individuality contains a lofty self-existence
which quickly and pointedly rejects and excludes the
claims of the mere external.   That the work that
binds at the same time disunites is clearly shown in
the union of men as labour-groups; here originate
the jealousy of different "callings" and a passion of
class-struggle which in a spirit of the wildest hatred
against its opponents believes itself justified in the
advocacy of common interests.   And is the situation
otherwise when nations fight for commercial ascendancy and for world-dominion ?

Such disunion and cleavage reach beyond the individual mind into the whole mode of thought. The speciality of work prevents us from seeing both aspects of its characteristics; it cannot develop certain energies without coercing others ; work thus prepares for individuals, nations, and times, in their own life-circle, a special province and a special kind of existence, and yet we can not and must not renounce the truth that we need co-operation in a sphere of life common to all, need exchange in our work, and need to think of and to live for one another. Indeed, humanity as a whole is unable to consider the need of winning a spiritual individuality for the highest aspiration necessary to it unless it yields itself to the claims of a universal truth.

(2) The strengthening and calming of life are a further product of work. But without the counter-effect of liberating energies this very quality sinks into a numb fixture and an intolerable bondage ; the fluctuation inevitable in all work threatens to overwhelm and to suppress man. Does not work hold such fluctuation ? Work needs for its success not only external conditions and favourable surroundings, but far more an inward ability which prevents our will from being placed under its heel, and which makes work devolve upon us as a good and a gift. These guests, however, decide concerning the result of our efforts and the happiness and worth of life in so far as they rise into work and activity. So much hardness, so much injury and even cruelty, are not discovered in connection with work so long as its happy results and victorious achievements are kept before our eyes. But a pure result is seldom enough to be found ; and amongst the favoured minds scarcely

one was truly great who failed to discover a wide cleft between wish and will, and who had not far more to say than his opportunities allowed him.   Now, is this surplus presented to such minds to be treated as an indifferent and worthless thing?   And are all those wide and predominant provinces of life, which are lost by peoples and times, to be denied of their rich and far-reaching effects?   We resist such an assumption and hail joyously the teaching of Jesus in the parable of the talents, that there appears, beyond all the distinctions of the men and beyond the whole field of their several activities, what is located in the decision and character of each individual.   But does not this itself awaken the desire for a new life?   And how is such a life grounded?   How does it rationally justify itself?

(3) In the main, the entanglements originate from the relationship of work with the soul.   The work was to us no external performance; it proved its presence and its greatness within the soul through the fact which culminated in freeing the man from all bare neutrality and subjectivity; it was found to be something resting in its own essence, something moved to further development by its characteristic energies.   Work could accomplish such a feat only in so far as it drew into itself the very life of the soul, and in so far as this life set forth characteristically a light reflected from itself.   But this emancipation of work has also an obverse side.   The emancipation can become numb and exclusive; the connection relaxes and parts asunder from the centre of the soul; the work tears the self-sovereignty that is within itself, and through this the life does not only move in a track

10

too narrow for itself, but also sacrifices its freedom to a mechanism of its own acts ; and finally its specific spiritual character is turned into an iron mechanism. Whilst work itself tears away so much from man and turns round as master upon the originator, life transforms itself into a soulless mechanism in spite of all the straining of energy ; the character retreats before the activity of work ; the work overpowers the man and finally makes him its slave. So it has happened where the whole Spiritual Life has been transformed through a logical process into a particular movement of thought-process ; so it happens in a more evident and painful manner still where technical work with its headstrong aggressions monopolises all thought and judgment ; and so it happens everywhere when man is held as a mere tool for the progress of culture, and when the waves of the most sweeping movements carry and drive him along without the participation of any power of his own.

Work, without a doubt, though it withdraws itself from the life of the soul, is again drawn back to the whole of the soul, is proved, valued, and energised ; it is only through a constant movement back to its own origin and through a continuous overcoming in the strength of a spirituality superior to itself that it can unify the spiritual character and serve the inward growth of life. If it is true that man is more than his work, then the whole of humanity is more than the production of work ; it must be no less than the creation of a culture and spiritual individuality.

Thus through a kind of necessity there arises a desire after a further development of life beyond the

level of work—after a life which returns from its
immersion in work to itself, which abides in itself,
which holds fast the work and also allows a self
superior to it to unfold.   Does such a desire correspond with any kind of reality within our experience?
We answer in the affirmative; for above the levels
of work, justice, culture, and mental individuality,
the movement proceeds upward to a level of creativeness and of love, of a spiritual personality and a pure
immanent existence.   Religion and Art especially
use the conception of this creativeness; the former,
in order to exclude all union of the Divine effect with
an alien material and dark fate; the latter, in order
to explain its own work as a donum of free imagination and as a proof of the originality of the artist.
Neither could appropriate the conception were it
not rooted in the whole of life, and especially were
there not a deepening possible in the fact that work
having previously ruled and tied life is now overcome
by life itself.   This happens, however, through a
transformation into the free development and reflection of the Spiritual Life.   Herewith life outgrows
the heaviness and numbness which its prior development adhered to; now all dark residuum vanishes—
the alien becomes a governor and the outward
becomes an inward.   On such elevation above the
sphere of work and through a liberation from all the
coercion of the numb "given," life becomes a completely immanent existence, a definite self-life, and an
ascent to the heights; and it is in this that all lies
which carries an uplifting energy and good cheer
in itself.   This creativeness strikes its roots into the
soil of all the particular fields which contribute to the

growth of the Spiritual Life as well as into those of science—a science which previously sought to relate itself inflexibly in an opposite direction. Science must abandon its highest aim — Knowing — if it renounces this creativeness. For without such a creativeness the ascent from mere awareness to a true discernment is impossible. Definite discernment is never found through that which is alien to us, but always through that which is native to us; definite discernment is always a discovery of our own life, a finding of ourselves in that which at first was alien. How could this be possible except through the fact of an advance of life having taken place, thus reaching the level where our limitation becomes a personal testimony, and an activity of the self is discovered? How far and under what conditions man is able to accomplish this, is a question apart, but he could never even strive towards such a height were he entirely chained to a lower level.

The higher levels of life attain a greater clearness in the region of character; for to the forward-movement from work to creativeness there corresponds here the movement from justice to love. Though this conception of love has different levels of interpretations, and though unhappily the daily life weaves it in the most heterogeneous ways, yet notwithstanding all the tangle definite love asserts itself as a turn of life which is both indisputable and a great mystery. Love in this sense brings not only the particular elements into secure relationship and directs life from point to point in its progress, but it also raises the relationship itself out of its isolation and kindles a new corporate life in which the singularity does not

vanish but is raised and transformed beyond its
initial position. That which does not create out of
man something new and better is not definite love.
With love the existence of another obtains a full
inward present moment in the soul, and becomes
immanently a piece of the very life. All elevation,
however, is effected through a willing self-denial and
sacrifice. " The first motive in love is that I shall be
no individual person for myself, and that if I were
such, I should feel myself defective and incomplete.
The second motive is that I win myself in another
person, that I value in her what she in turn finds in
me. Love is consequently a most painful contradiction which the understanding cannot untie, and in it
there is nothing harder than that this exactness of
consciousness is negated and needs still to be affirmed.
Love is both the affirmation and the solution of
the contradiction : as solution it is moral harmony "
(Hegel).

This occurs in the first place in the realm of
relationship of individual with individual ; but in such
a construction a cosmic phenomenon reveals itself, for
through the development of the inner connections
over against the numb co-existence of bare nature, a
new grade of life appears. In addition to this, love
frees itself from the shrinkage upon an individual,
and welds together whole nations—the whole of
humanity ; everywhere it becomes a product of the
whole life, a product that not only brings existing
elements to a level of reciprocity, but which also re-
news the whole existence of man with creative energy
and with a renewing flow of life. It is trust in
such creative energy of love that makes it possible

to penetrate clearly through the existing situation of humanity, and yet enables us to hold fast to cheerful work for humanity. There can be nothing held out for man in the painful entanglements of his own soul and his seeming abiding helplessness when face to face with the problem of his own being but what religion offers as a trust upon an Infinite Love, which unreservedly awakens a new life in him and lifts him beyond the range of conflict.

What, however, drives forward such rich developments in special directions must resolve itself into the Whole of a new form of life; and the longing after such appears in the ardour and tenacity wherewith the nineteenth century as well as the present revolve around the conception of personality.

Since Leibniz each of the great thinkers has given us something original, but they all sought for a new and all-comprehensive goal of life. The meaning of our view, however, needs a further development; first of all because we have not shown that man has ascended to the level of spiritual individuality. In spite of all his most brilliant performances he does not altogether reach such a level; he can cast a glimpse at it from below; he can posit it in the life of other individuals and through this view it in greater completeness. This he is compelled to do in order to become superior to the accidental and problematic in his own life, and in order to be able to eliminate the indefinite from his nature and to energise the definite. Through this the life desires a standard where it can survey the different levels and transform the contents of each into its own possession, and where it can focus Infinity and possess an immanent self.

Life here remains occupied in itself although it appears as turning to the external; here is the level of mere achievement overcome, and the characteristic elevation of life forms the governing aim of all toil. This corresponds to the Christian conviction of the infinite value of man in his pure inwardness—a conviction "that for the riches of the whole world not one individual soul can be purchased" (Luther). How could such an estimate be justified did there not arise in the depth of the soul a new manner of life, and did there not here become visible that which forms the inmost kernel of entire reality?   Since the matter is usually conceived as a desire of a mere subjective and inactive sentimentality withdrawn from the great world into a private nook, it has no sufficient basis, and indeed, threatens to end in empty words and phrases.   The above estimate of Luther is justified only if a new stage of reality manifests itself in the depth of the soul; and this can never come out of the energy of any one individual point in life, but can only come through the impact of Infinite Life with Infinite Life, and through the formation at this spot of a point of intersection and concentration of such life.   Goethe seems to refer to the matter from a similar point of view in those noteworthy words of his: "God meets always Himself; God in man meets again God in man.   Hence there is no cause to esteem ourselves lightly in comparison with the Greatest."

The matter, then, does not resolve itself into a reference of life to one special point and a subjection of it to that point's particularity, but consists in the immense task of bringing life to its own depth and giving it a support within itself. Reality can become our own life only if our activity transforms itself into a self-activity, if it brings to expression a living self; and this can happen only when the encompassing unity remains no mere point of relation, but when, through the strenuous elaboration of a thorough-going and durable life within it, it wins a substance and a nature which affects all the remaining life. Within such a course life finds its own; without it, it misses its own. Only out of such alternate separation and reunion, out of such a scale of values and reference to the Whole, arises the question concerning a content for the life; it is only when the encompassing Whole overcomes the scattered manifold and appropriates it by a gradual and thorough reconstruction that there arises a reality resting within its own essence.

Whether such a life may be called a personal life may be disputed. In any case the ruling unity lies not by the side of but within the life, and through the unfolding of such a unity life deepens and expands; such deepest life can be in single points only because it was previously and is now in the Whole. In all this the situation is what it is, not through severance but through something entirely the contrary. It has come about through the formation of the most inward connections with things—indeed, through a connection with Infinity—although not without an energetic penetration into, and far-reaching transformation of them. The language used by great thinkers points in the same direction. Ordinary parlance, on the contrary, too much connects with this conception of a deepest unity and life the notions of seclusion and of opposition, and too often degrades this conception to the designation of a merely natural force, for us to be able to advance in our investigation without continuous reservations against these several popular views.   Hence it may be better for us to speak of autonomous life and of autonomies.   Both expressions become fairly indifferent when the facts of life stare us in the face with sufficient clearness.   To us there lies before all else the fact that in the Spiritual Life itself a movement towards the growth of a nucleus and towards a transformation into a self-life is wide-awake and on its course; and through such a turn of the Life-process a world of inwardness dawns, signifying something quite other than the shadowy inwardness of the mere subject himself.

Corresponding to such gradations of autonomous life, we find in the most important work the passing out of the spiritual movement beyond the realm of culture.   Necessary as culture is, the main standard for the final convictions of life is not in it but above it.   If culture were the highest aim of man, he himself would be a mere tool of this achievement; the culture, however, which is not clasped and vivified by a life superior to its own could not contain any meaning and must, without such a completion, sink more and more into a lifeless mechanism.   Culture is a contest of the Spiritual Life with an opposed and seemingly hostile world and not an accumulation of accomplishments; it comes to its own truth only when it flows into the current of a Spiritual Life of the self.

Laborious enough it is on the ground of human history to wring such a superiority out of mere culture. It is gained first and foremost in the centuries when antiquity clashed with Christianity—in a time when an old culture sank and a new one had not yet arisen. In such a situation life would have fallen into emptiness had it not found a world of its own as well as a full security in its concern with itself, in the diving into itself. This becomes clearly evident upon the Græcian side in Plotinus, and upon the Christian side in Augustine. Both are agreed in the need of carrying the work of culture beyond itself, and of placing it at a stage where it revolves around the apprehension of eternal truth and the development of the configuration of an all-inclusive superior life within itself alone. In these connections the thought dawns that the nature of reason is not a mere piece of the universe, but encases within itself the whole of the universe— is a microcosmus. "We are each and all a spiritual universe" (Plotinus). Doubtless the men of those times were too much shut up in a superior world of retirement and solitude; they would not return to the work of the world and employ the life that had been won. So that a sudden reaction was bound to come. But the gain of a pure immanent existence of the Spiritual Life as a cosmic life, and its inward superiority to all mere culture remained intact. There occurred, too, along with such a gain, an aim and a standard to which all that shall henceforth satisfy the spiritual nature of man shall have to correspond. This appears valid enough to-day and forbids the finality of the conclusions of culture.

This adjusted standard and this comprehensive coming-to-itself of life are a resort for us in the quest after aims more than possessions, problems more than achievements; but this conclusion is at the same time the carrier and the indispensable presupposition

of the earlier standards. We saw effort released
from the natural self, and through such a liberation
developing new energies and tracing out new aims.
Whence should these energies come, how should the
new aims justify themselves if a specific self-subsistence did not arise in the Spiritual Life, if a new
self did not come into birth, developing and asserting
itself in the movements of life? The upward march
of life to a true and real level overcame the cleavage
between subject and object. Is such a conquest conceivable unless the life returns from the province of
work to itself, and unless it transforms its achievements into a raising of the self? That we in
spiritual work develop our own inmost nature and
struggle for our true self is manifest at a glance.
Why do we, for example, allow the current of experience to mount into our presentations? Why
not allow these presentations to pass over us
calmly? Why do we practise self-defence and
seek to overpower these external impressions and
transform them into our own conceptions? Why
suffices it us not to float on the perpetual flux of
things? And why are we driven by an inward
necessity to follow the infinitude of the All into its
ultimate concealment? Such transformation and expansion must belong, indeed, to the culmination of
our own particular nature; and its furtherance must
involve a movement of this very nature within itself.
Further, Art could never have become the mighty
factor of life it is, and its form could not have been
transformed into an elevated power, had it not driven
man to his work—not merely to his subjectivity but
to the foundation of his being. That scientific and

artistic labours won such a height in the struggle for the spiritual self only on certain points of the summits does not alter the facts. What is reached wholly in the long-run would not have been reached at all without the conquest of points on the summits, and had it not been that the great personalities had taken the facts in that great sense, and had found the salvation of their life in scaling the heights of truth. Such an installation of the whole life alone has made possible the conquest of such heights and has tilled the soil of daily work and the results of its accomplishments for the reception of this seed. The work sinks rapidly into a lifeless mechanism when it severs its connection with such creativeness and barters its originality for bare diligence on the surface of things.

All these movements, viewed from the ordinary surface-existence of man, may appear as mere possibilities. But they are possibilities not in the sense of vague imaginations but in the sense of urgent tasks and driving energies. They could not work so powerfully in us and make that existence which satisfied us previously now insufficient for us, were they not realities; were they not realities out of the deep we should not have struggled with them for the winning of a spiritual self, and at the same time, for the meaning and content of our life.

2. *Epitome and Survey*

(a) *The Meaning of the Spiritual Life.*—We have already viewed the Spiritual Life developing its characteristics in three grades. It grew out of its isolation and dissipation, and simultaneously dis-

entangled itself from merely human mechanism; in
the overcoming of the cleft between subject and
object it forged for itself a self-reliant and sovereign
character; in the comprehension of infinity for its
own self, it gained in itself a fixed foundation, and at
the same time a superiority to the world around it,
and it became an autonomous life.   All these aspects
work towards one another, side by side they support
and clarify one another, and bind themselves into a
connected totality.   This picture is, however, far removed from the ordinary conception of the Spiritual
Life.   According to the ordinary conception the
Spiritual Life is conceived from its very beginning
as strewn piecemeal on separable and solitary points,
and it is only much later that any kind of connection
is brought about; it appears, too, as an attribute and
an activity of an existence lying entirely beyond itself,
and consequently finds itself hemmed within a given,
ready-made world, and busies itself in various ways
with such a world.   Our consideration of the matter
has presented the subject in quite other light.   Before
all else it appeared clear that the Spiritual Life
is only possible as an inward connection, and as a
life out of the Whole; it is participation in this
Whole which invests the isolated points with a
spiritual character; never can its own world, towards
which the Spiritual Life aims, originate through mere
external combinations.   However, this total-life did
not originate from any dark existence, but it engendered by itself centre-points and concentration-
points; for all the conceptions of the existence of its
material arose within the life itself, and through it
received a full illumination.   The Life-process has

not, therefore, to execute an achievement from the outside: it finds its problem in itself, in the bringing of its own nature to its proper fulfilment. This signifies an overcoming and an assimilation of all that lay outside, and that seemed at first alien and hostile. In such a movement not merely is this or that thing within the province of a given reality altered and bettered, but it is obligatory to bring to clearness a Whole of reality. This reality does not feel itself as one thing by the side of another, but—with its direction towards the self as the vehicle of life—as the compact and comprehensive reality, as that which deserves the name of reality in the truest sense, and which cannot tolerate anything foreign to itself.

This Spiritual Life with its reality surrounds man not as a mere environment of his; it attains in him as a Whole a present moment of immediacy, and becomes with its infinity his own life and nature. Only such an inward abiding of the spiritual world makes it conceivable that the spiritual tasks work directly on man, not through the ravaging agents of his particular interests, but through the fact that individuals, in spite of all their differences, are able to find an inner co-operation of activity, and to raise themselves out of bare subjectivity to an independent inner life and to a kingdom of inwardness. Through the presence of such an immanence of the Whole the rigid cleft which hitherto separated man from the world is overcome; now in the individual points the energy of the Whole can work and can build for itself experiences of the whole. Thus man gains in himself different gradations of life. The Spiritual

Life is thus seen to be no mere contrivance of a purely human kind, but the taking up of a difficult struggle against such a human mode—an emancipation from such a mode as an intolerable narrowness.   This new world, however, should not rest satisfied with a merely human raiment wrapped around itself, but should contain its own truth, and through its transportation into the Spiritual Life reach its own characteristic nature.   The Whole would have been a great falsification had not infinity with its translation into spirituality reached its proper depth.   It appears similarly in the direction of spiritual activity. A truth which shrinks and is valid only for the individual is no definite truth at all, but a hybrid of many colours.   If all the investigation does not draw the main motives along with it, how can the narrowness of the circle of mere-human notions be broken through, and a new world of thought valid for all be opened out?   For the value and the grandeur of the Good, it is essential that all human interests should be repelled, and man enabled by himself to rise above himself.

It is important that we should come to this characteristic depth through the Spiritual Life.   In such a province the individual's own nature is not isolated, but is interwoven inseparably with the whole of the All, and turns to this source for its own life-content. Thus there is no depth in the individual portions if they do not exist in the Whole, if they are not able here to unfold themselves; in each point a struggle for the Whole takes place, and this brings the Whole into activity.

Finally, it is to be borne in mind that the Spiritual

Life in man could never arise against the power of nature if it were no more than a purely human thing. Nature surrounds us as a boundless kingdom of energies and laws; it not only surrounds us from without, but strikes deep into our own soul with a thousand incessant effects. How could the Spiritual Life, which finds itself first in our aspiration, in any manner force its way against all this did we not stand upon inward connections, and had there not worked in us, over against that which is given in the surrounding world, the energy of a new kind of world? Transformations in the Whole could only arise out of a Whole.

It is now evident that the movement to spirituality cannot be considered as a work of any separate individual faculties of the mere man; but that it is a movement of the All, which certainly in our position needs our co-operation, but which, at the same time, takes us into itself and makes of us something quite other than we were on the first view of things. The universe itself now finds its own depth through such a movement to spirituality; from being a kingdom of relations it becomes the kingdom of a definite reality. The inward life, which is otherwise a mere appearance of things, now gains a self-reliance, and develops its own particular kingdom—an inner world. The nearer qualities of this inner world do not allow themselves to be known through general conceptions such as existence-for-self, self-activity, etc.: these give only the frame within which alone the mounting experience of life is able to set forth its qualities. For example, the Good and the Beautiful are characteristic developments and revelations of life, possessing an incomparable individuality and actuality which are later discovered in them.   So in connection with the Spiritual Life, it constructs a new ground upon which boundless avenues open out and a whole kingdom of new actualities becomes accessible. Through this we become discoverers and conquerors, but it is not into a strange but into our own world that we climb more and more.

Leibniz was of opinion that no nature could arise in man without some kind of self-subsistence, and consequently he sought to base all reality upon living monads.   Whether his theory, through such a turn to the bare individual nature, is in itself correct, may be doubted; but it cannot be doubted that there is no definite reality unless the total-life in a conjoint manner forces its way through, and holds together, all the manifold.   Without a foundation-stone all the universe becomes a mere occurrence; and thus receives the character of a mere addendum, a subsidiary and shadowy thing, and one which must finally pass away in a senseless flight that cannot be stopped.   Only a total-life can hold fast and bind, can construct a self-activity over against bare mechanical activity, can along with this reach an existence which does not belong to an inaccessible " beyond " constructed through analogy from the scientific picture of the natural world; but such a total-life finds its own more and more in the furtherance of itself, and through this gains an ever-richer content.   Only this depth of existence of the Life-process itself may be termed " substance "; such a substance lies not behind us but in front of us; and it is towards it as an all-inclusive goal that the movement now reaches out.

11

This movement of such a substance produces in the particular province of man's nature a separation of activity into that which is empty and that which is substantial, as well as a separation between the development of physical energy and that of self-activity. Evidently there arises much activity which is not gripped by the whole of the self—an activity which sets mere energies in movement; such an activity governs the initial acts and impulses of man. But there is also an activity which lies within the whole of life, and through which life is able to grow. It is only such an activity as the latter that gives life a support and a meaning in itself, and only out of such an activity are conceptions such as character, conviction, etc., possible—conceptions which sprout in spite of the presence of subjectivity and passivity, and which, as proofs of the Whole, carry along with them an elevation of the level of life. Through the strict commands of such a self-preservation, all other kinds of activity must appear empty and untenable. Through such a self-preservation in the things a new conception of truth originates far above the ordinary intellectual notion; for now that alone becomes true to life which includes, expresses, and furthers the Whole as a present moment in consciousness, whilst the separate isolated activities which have released themselves from this and which believe themselves all-efficient, sink into untruth. The main movement of life—encompassing all the separate points and shaping itself characteristically in each, and especially overcoming the opposition between theoretical and practical reason—becomes a striving which longs to pass from this region of the untruth, which at the start surrounds us, to the region of truth ; the longing after truth and real existence becomes now the main motive-energy of the Spiritual Life ; as in the province of nature, so it now becomes here a longing after the self-preservation which rules all movement; but the longing is after a self-preservation quite other than that found in nature.

In all these transformations our initial problem has stepped into a new and richer position. The movement which aimed at a level above the natural and which wrecked itself when conceived as a mere-human fact, has now succeeded in showing itself more than human, and yet has fastened man to itself. It works now with characteristic greatness and energy, but all depends on man being a participator in that elevated life. In all this there are dangers enough, but such dangers can be faced, and must not frighten the man at the outset. Let us see somewhat closer how, through this transformation, the view of the world and the problems of life are altered ; and in the meantime we shall not directly view the religious problem, and yet shall not lose sight of it.

(β) *The View of the Universe.*—Our main thought of a " becoming " independence, of a coming to it-self of all reality in the Spiritual Life, clashes most strongly with the prevalent view of the universe, and must demand against such a view a powerful trans-formation. With the prevailing view, the visible universe is held as the main world ; and what rises up in the inner life is thought of as a subsidiary phenomenon, which is hardly able to bring forth any-thing that is original. According to our course of thought, however, there is imbedded in this inner world a kernel of reality, and all else becomes a mere environment or a preparation, and thus we obtain *an inverted order* of the customary consideration and valuation of things. Will such a view be able to hold its own over against the overwhelming impressions of the external world? It can do so only through a standard of thought, and if the inner life has become conscious of its autonomy, and if from this standpoint it undertakes its work. If this happens, the demand will certainly not be denied; but the fact is to be seen and explained not from without within but from within without. Hence there is achieved in this revolutionary thought a complete transition from a Ptolemaic to a Copernican standard.

An independent life is thus to be found within, but it is highly improbable that in all the wide universe it is to be found in man alone. But even if positive proof of this were lacking, yet the Spiritual Life remains a cosmic fact; for it encloses a depth of reality over against the surface-appearance of nature.

Viewed in this manner, nature cannot possibly signify by itself a complete and finished kingdom. Its whole incessant mechanism of movements and relations reveal nowhere a self-life; in the last resort these are viewed as empty and meaningless, but yet, however, the world-process itself reveals in the Spiritual Life an imperative longing after a meaning. There originate in nature in its wending towards the animal level numerous and clear evidences of psychic life, but this animal psychic life heightens rather than lessens the conflict of opinions regarding nature.

This psychic life, which also belongs in the greatest part to human existence, remains throughout bound in the mechanism of nature, and develops over against it no kind of independent thought.   So far as we are able to see, all psychic performance on this stage of life means simply the self-preservation of the individual, and with it of the species, in the struggle for existence.   So that here a physical equivalent is well able to take the place of a psychical performance : what a higher intelligence or a closer union with its kind furnishes to one creature is furnished to others by strength of bodily organisation, swiftness of movement, etc.   Nowhere here does the inner life reach an independence, and nowhere is it able to found a kingdom of its own ; nowhere is it able to pass beyond the environment in order to view and handle that environment as a Whole.   But the inner life remains scattered and enslaved, a mere piece of an alien world, empty in the midst of all the passion of the animal impulse.   If now—not in man himself, but yet within the range of humanity —a clarification and a liberation arise, if here the inner life becomes independent and a depth of existence opens—that such a fact has happened from simple beginnings and by a very slow process does not alter the main fact in the least,—then nature cannot any more signify the whole of reality, but can only signify a special stage of it—a stage beyond which the world-process proceeds to an existence-for-self.

This new fact is far too original and signifies far too much an inverted order of things to be understood as a mere furtherance of the mechanical move-

ment of nature itself; rather must it be a cosmic
life superior to nature which thus breaks forth—a
cosmic life which works also in nature but which
proceeds beyond it to a stage of self-completion.
In such a connection the Spiritual Life cannot
at all be viewed as only a result; it must also be
valid as a principle; it can be the aim and the
culmination of the world-process only if it also
forms its foundation and presupposition, and if that
which at first appears as a mere result works in and
through the whole movement. An energy of the
Whole must be active from the outset if the manifold is to be united into a Whole, and through such
a union is to rise to a higher plane. How could an
All bring forth an independent inner life if it were
soulless in itself? Nature and the unfolded spirit
become herewith stages of the world-process which,
beyond the juxtaposition of nature with its bare
relations, progress to a total-life which overcomes
the cleft between obscure substance and unsubstantial
happening, by making the Life-process independent
and developing all substance from it. At the same
time, the All-life can no more be a stream flowing
nobody knows whither and which nobody experiences. But, in a union of beginning and of end,
a superiority is won above all mere movement,
and an Eternal appears as an essential condition of
all the march of Time. This alone gives a standpoint
whence truth, and, indeed, any striving after truth,
first become possible; at the same time we attain
to the conception of a cosmic inner life, as a
presupposition of all striving after an interior
world. But he who contracts the kingdom of

thought of humanity merely to presentations of the
external world renounces at the same time knowledge
and truth.

The recognition of such a cosmic inner life signifies
in no way an introduction of interior energies and.
movements into the province of the science of nature,
for this science of nature must reject such a procedure
as a disagreeable and dangerous disturbance of its
work.   But that recognition announces that this
science, with all its means, does not create the whole
deep of reality.   The higher stages can now throw
backwards light upon the lower stages; they do that,
for example, in the Theory of Knowledge, where the
fundamental construction of nature is turned into
a problem, and the contact between this and the
mental organism is set forth; for thus we obtain
universal truths which are distinguished from the
merely human forms of life and its presentations.
Also, the higher stages accomplish this through
artistic reflection; here the inner life of things seems
to be experienced.   Fundamental facts of the life of
nature, which otherwise had been considered as self-
evident, become now a problem, and carry us to a
deepening of the total-view of things; as, for example,
in the thorough-going subjection of all to law, effects
of change, constitution of forms, the ascent of the
world-movement.   We must never contract the
exact and speculative consideration of things, but
neither must we misconstrue the conclusions which
issue from such a consideration.

In such a connection there exists between Nature and
Spirit a characteristic relation—a relation of opposites
as well as of union.   First of all, let us consider the

opposites. Where Nature and Spirit stand in opposition to one another, as has already been shown in the present work, where a hemmed-in life and an independent life rise sharply one from the other, there the greatness of the spirit cannot possibly mean the same as the simple ascent of nature; for thus the ascent of spirit can signify no more than what the classical epoch of literature in Germany stated concerning it, viz., that upon the higher stages the development and the formation had arrived at only a greater consciousness and freedom than were apparent on the lower unconscious and hemmed-in levels. To such a view the phenomena seem different only here and there through the heightening of the functions of the intellect. In our view, on the contrary, the difference reaches back beyond the intellect into the Whole; the kingdoms of relations and of the total- and self-life widen themselves further and further. Therefore the two sides which ordinary notions and also language allow to flow together, must before all else be clearly separated, and the boundaries between them fixed; a constant struggle is needed against their admixture with all the sleepiness which attends it. Herewith the passage from the one to the other will not appear as a peaceful and secure growth, as we are led to suppose through the doctrine of evolution; but the higher must first of all loosen itself in a new direction and find a fastening in itself; and then this higher can turn back to the lower and discover its kinship in it. For a fact can certainly not remain in a state of full and pointed opposition if the All is not to fall asunder. Also, nature must somehow serve the aims

which come forth in the Spiritual Life ; the powerful
stirring of energies which culminate in nature must
somehow assist in the development of a self-life, and
the ascent to this life bring forth a further development and intimacy.   Therefore points of contact and
points of exit originate where the lower suddenly
seems to pass into the higher.   But with the recognition of such a chain of life the independence of the
higher must always be guarded, for the lower stage
may bring forth something to the contrary of what
the higher brings forth.

The total-view shows us in the relationship of both
provinces more opposition and more insecurity than
the pantheistic view which runs through modern
culture presents, but it shows as well more expansion
and more progressive acts.   And also along with
the movement depth is gained.

, (γ) *The Place of Man.*—The attitude of man is
essentially changed when the greatness and the
success of life depend on a participation in a superhuman Spiritual Life.   In the first place, he appears
to be set in strong antagonism to the customary
notions of things.   We are accustomed to view man
as the meeting-point of divergence of worlds, and to
attribute to him on account of his characteristic
nature an incomparable worth : this cannot any
longer be asserted of him.   For the New and the
Higher lie in the Spiritual Life as openings of an
independent inner world, and not in man as mere
man.   For a long, long time he hardly left the
bounds of nature, and when at last the Spiritual Life
dawned within him, that life was not so much his
own work as the communication of a superior

standard. When the Spiritual Life developed further in the human province, that province was in no way won. Much rather does the lower mode of life remain, shows the most stubborn resistance, and draws the Spiritual Life down to the lower level; thus the ordinary situation becomes one of a semi-spirituality in which the greatness and originality of the Spiritual Life is lost. Such a sharp divergence of man from the Spiritual Life places the problems in a new light and increases everywhere the extension of the activity. Thus, for example, morality may never be held as a natural quality or product of man; what even the ordinary life produces does not raise itself far above the animal instincts and impulses; definite morality with its shifting of the centre of gravity of life is fundamentally different from such instincts and impulses, but such morality becomes possible first of all from the Spiritual Life, and the ascent to this life remains a continuous problem, and, further, succeeds but in the smallest measure. Thus the decisive turning-point appears first of all in the life of a man; it does not appear with his entrance into this world as mere man.

All this doubtless involves a deep humiliation of man as mere man. But there corresponds to the degradation an elevation, as to man there opens the possibility of a participation in a new grade of reality which lies beyond the entanglements of the human province. All that characterises the Spiritual Life—its universality, its sovereignty, its autonomy —can become the possession of the man who mounts; now the spiritual contents can rise above

the purely human forms of life; now the anthropomorphism which had turned the whole of reality
into a mere reflex of human thoughts, feelings, and
strivings, can be partially if not entirely cast off, and
can be gripped by a superior standard; now the
struggle of man against the merely human becomes
possible, and world-experiences enter into his narrow
province, and through such effects his whole
attitude is changed. Out of the Spiritual Life and
not out of the mere-human are all the problems to be
seized and all the provinces to be formed. Right and
morality, art and science, are spiritual in the sense
that they are not developments of the bare man, but
developments of the Spiritual Life in man. Also,
the religious problem must transform itself in an
essential manner, in which it will deal not concerning
the preservation of that which is merely human in
a narrow sense but concerning the Spiritual Life
in man.

Further, life as a whole receives throughout a
special character in the fact that its main connection,
its fundamental relationship, becomes evermore the
Spiritual Life. This characteristic becomes clear
through comparison with the historical and traditional types of life. The religious type of life
which men have most welcomed gave to the life
the main connection with God, and allowed all the
tributaries of life to flow into the current of religion;
there came a time, however, when such a conception
proved too narrow, and when the fundamental connection passed into a region of grave uncertainty.
And as the life through this effect turned from the
"beyond" to a "here and now," it split into two

main portions—the cosmic and the social. In the cosmic portion it is mainly the force of the intellect which opens the door of the universe, and through the winning of such an insight the whole of exist- ence is raised; here now issues the construction of relations to the human environment; definite con- clusions are arrived at; and strong co-operations of humanity take place. All this ought to bring greater warmth of feeling as well as stronger reason into human relationships. This tendency has produced great and influential results, but none of these results individually has satisfied the whole nature of man, and even collectively they have failed to do so. The cosmic guidance of life threatens, in spite of all its breadth, to become cold and empty; and the social guidance, with all its nearness and warmth, threatens to become narrow and confined. These guides of life, however, have the common disadvantage in that the fundamental relationship does not lie within the individual life, but appears as something without. It is only in the drift of the Spiritual Life that the Life-process becomes itself, for here it deals with nothing other than the inmost nature of man. Thus it is here alone that the life proves itself, and it is here, too, that a comprehensive foundation is gained, upon which the relationships to God, the world, and human society have to be grounded and constructed, and a counter-effect to all one-sided forms of life has to be brought forth.

If that in which we recognise the inmost nature of man is to be found here, then the man's view passes from his immediate existence to a far-off goal. In man there are different degrees of reality, different meeting-points of worlds, and thus the man's own decision must not fail.   But such a decision lies not in individual resolutions and acts, but it goes through the whole of life.   And it is not to be understood that the individual portions of his nature would offer him for selection different worlds merely from the outside, and that he could merely have an option which to accept or reject.   Man is always carried by the total-life of the All; this total-life must be effective in the particular portions if it is ever to win the new stages of life.   But however mysterious this may appear, the Whole issues not into a Whole without the vivification and characteristic decision of the individual portions; here the movement of the All culminates through our own appropriation alone; the movement issues only through a joyous affirmation of that which belongs to us, and which, without recognition, cannot become ours.   Through this we become co-workers, and, indeed, are called to become co-carriers of the All; thus our life gains an ethical character from its very foundation—a character which shows the meaning of our adoption of the Spiritual Life as our true nature, as the ascent to our proper heights and to infinity.   This work is no longer that of a special province, but it penetrates the whole circle of life, and places activity at all times before an *Either—Or*.   At the same time, rigid determinism is broken, without our having to admit that decision depends on the chance of the moment.   For it is the fundamental presupposition of determinism that it places man definitely within a particular world-order, and allows him to be bound entirely by such an order. Thus all man's acts from their very beginning are fixed, and life is divested of all expectation. But, on the other hand, the meeting of two worlds places the fact in a totally different light ; the life now is enabled to transform its main tendency into a free act, and through this to gain a genuine present-moment of consciousness.

According to our method of treatment the Spiritual Life transforms itself from being a possession that can be taken for granted to being a difficult problem ; and this places the main tendency of life not in any one particular act, but makes the Spiritual Life a fact of unutterable toil, and so gives humanity as well as the individual a real history. The Spiritual Life was not on our view a mere form of life which could be assimilated in a hurried resolution ; but through an inverted order of the first impression of things, a new and definite kind of reality is wrung from it which draws the whole periphery of life into itself. The life has now to discover an all-encompassing unity from which each particular province is shaped in a characteristic manner. This, however, is an enormous problem, and forms the soul of all historical work. We do not find ourselves from the beginning in spiritual connections, and do not track our way securely ; but the main direction can be found and before all else it must be sought—sought through toilsome experiences and on perilous paths. But primarily some kind of life-connection, some kind of governing aim, must rise out of the initial chaos, for such connections and aims are the salient parts—the hypotheses—of life, full of risks and dangers, but yet indispensable, because thus alone can life as a Whole become a current, thus alone can questions concerning the Whole become

possible, thus alone can experiences of the Whole
originate which in their turn become a standard in
the total-existence of life. Now opposition grows,
hinders the movement, and drives it out of its course.
But new points of concentration may grow and undertake the erection of reality. It this connection the
growth does not take place—be it through a peaceful
movement or through a spiral of opposites—through
mere associations furthered by a kind of surface-
necessity ; things do not fit into one another as in the
raising of a pyramid, but ever anew, doubt and violent
emotion strike down to the foundation of life ; ever
anew one has to struggle for the Whole. What issues,
however, as connections—so far as it is of a spiritual
kind—issues not in a ready-made manner from any
part in our nature, but has to be brought forth
through our own exertions. In this manner, history
cannot become a struggle for the content of the
Spiritual Life unless the main standard of life is laid
beyond the bare results of the times in a timeless
order. The attempt to view things *sub specie æterni-
tatis* holds not only and mainly for knowledge, but in
the first place for the whole of life. The Spiritual
Life could not seek in history itself the unfolding of
its own nature unless history possessed in its kernel a
nature that goes beyond mere history. Time is something of a phantom, and all life in it something of an
appearance and a shadow if the foundation of an
eternity fails in it ; and if, out of its changes and
transformations, nothing rises up to save man for an
eternal existence. And if all depended on the brief
flash of the fleeting present moment, which endures
but the twinkling of an eye only to vanish into the

abyss of nothingness, then all life would mean a mere exit into death. Thus without eternity there is no spirituality, and without connection there is no content of life. But what is enthroned in itself above time becomes for the man who wins such a spirituality, first of all, an immense task which allows itself to be grasped on the field of time alone; and, also, the Eternal which works within us and which hovers before us on the horizon of eternity can become our full possession only through the movement of time. To wish to check this movement and to arrest the course of time, means not to serve eternity but to ascribe to time what belongs to eternity.

We see accordingly how our conception of the Spiritual Life heightened powerfully the significance and the span of history, but ever only under the hypothesis of an Eternal Order of things out of which history is experienced. A full abandonment to history, which is often witnessed on the ordinary level of life, becomes an inward subversion; with all its significance, history can only be the arena of the struggle for the Spiritual Life; it is always only a second and never a first. But even as a second, history grows powerfully, so that it signifies not the mere extension of a given thread but an emergence of a new life, and through this life it handles not the web of a bare outline but the growth of a full reality. What, however, holds valid for humanity holds valid also for the individual: the individual's life contains a great problem and an original decision; values such as personality and spiritual individuality do not fall on him as a shower, but have to be wrung manfully in the inward ascent of life. Also, the individual

will give all these movements a spiritual character,
and will be able to verify them only if he wins a
character above the flux of time; and from this
standard, through all the multi-coloured manifold
of the external tasks, seeks before all else his own
self—his own essence.

(δ) *Conclusions for the Method and the Task of Life.*
—Spiritual Life can unfold itself in man only when
significant transformations take place in the inward
web of his being, and new paths of reflection become
necessary. We shall follow these changes here only
in so far as they bear on the religious problems to
which this work is dedicated.

What precedes the Spiritual Life in man cannot
be grasped by science until science constructs a new
method and marks out such a method from all
others. There is, however, a double aspect of the
original manner in which spirituality develops within
the human province. It develops itself, for example,
under the conditions of empirical psychic life, and,
indeed, with energies which have to wrestle with
such a life. But spirituality is never a mere product
of the empirical psychic life. This psychic life is
bound up with the bodily organism, is scattered in
the individual, is conceived as an incessant flux; therefore it never longs, through its own potency, to reach
a connected world or a durable truth; and without
such there is neither Spiritual Life nor Spiritual
content. To turn the Spiritual Life into a mere
procedure of psychic existence is to destroy it in its
very foundation. The Spiritual Life must not only
possess from the beginning an independence and
self-value, but it must also maintain these; when it

12

develops under the conditions of empirical psychic life, it must, with an unswerving nature, shine through all the strangeness and transiency of human psychic life. At the same time, spirituality, first of all, works as an indefinite and low potency. It has to find its own nature which, on the one side, builds a foundation, but which, on the other side, has to come to an understanding with the psychical existence and gain its own energies for higher ends. To leave such a psychic existence calmly on one side is to set back the energy of the Life-process and to rest satisfied with a pallid and rigid spirituality. Both sides are to be distinguished clearly, and at the same time brought into a living connection.

To this double-sidedness of life there corresponds a twofold method. These methods are *the Noological and the Psychological Methods.* To explain noologically means to arrange the whole of the Spiritual Life as a special spiritual activity, to ascertain its position and problem, and through such an adaptation to illumine the whole and raise its potencies. To explain psychologically, on the contrary, means to investigate *how* man arrives at the apprehension and appropriation of a spiritual content and especially of a Spiritual Life, with what psychic aids is the spiritual content worked out, how the interest of man for all this is to be raised, and how his energy for the enterprise is to be won. Here one has to proceed from an initial point hardly discernible, and, step by step, discover the way of ascent; thus the psychological method becomes at the same time a psychogenetic method. The main condition of the successful handling of this question is that both

methods be held sufficiently apart in order that the
conclusions of each, while they are prevented from
flowing in the same channel, may yet form a fruitful
completion each of the other.

Such separation and union of both methods and
their corresponding realities make it possible to understand how to overcome inwardly the old antithesis
between Idealism and Realism.   The fundamental
truth of Idealism is that the spiritual contents
establish an independence and a self-value over
against the individual, that they train him with
superior energy, and that they are not material for
his purely human welfare.   In the noological method
this truth obtains a full recognition.   Realism, however, has its rights in the forward sweep of the specifically human side of life with all its diversions, its
constraints, and its preponderantly natural character.
Viewed from this standpoint, the main fact is,
that life is raised out of the idle calm of the
rigid indifference of its initial stages, and is brought
into a current; in order to bring this about, much
is urgently needful by man, which cannot originate,
prior to the appearance of the spiritual estimation
of values, but which becomes his when he is set in
a strong current; then, on the one hand, anxiety
for external existence, division into parties, ambition,
etc., and on the other hand, the mechanism of
the psychic life with its association, reproduction,
etc., are all seen in a new light.   These motive-
powers would certainly never produce a spiritual
content out of man's own ability; such a content is
only reachable if the movement of life raises man
out of and above the initial performances and the

initial motives. No mechanism, either of soul or of society, is able to accomplish this; it can be accomplished alone by an inward spirituality in man. Through such a conception, Realism and Idealism are no longer irreconcilable opponents, but two sides of one encompassing life; one may grow alongside the other but not at the expense of the other. Indeed, the more the content of the Spiritual Life grows, the more becomes necessary on the side of psychic existence; the more we submerge ourselves in this psychic experience, the greater appears the superiority of the Spiritual Life.

The noological method is new in name only, and in the following connection : it actually extends everywhere where logical, ethical, and æsthetic conceptions are differentiated from the empirico-psychological conceptions. In Kant, and since his time, such a differentiation has been made with great clearness. This differentiation is, however, indispensable, because there is no possibility of an independence of the particular provinces without an independence of the Spiritual Life as a Whole. Such a conclusion comes to expression in the noological method. It is different throughout from the old method of an ontological metaphysic. This latter sought especially to make phenomena intelligible through world-conceptions which had been gained through theories of a strongly subjective type—theories, in the main, which were shadows of the living content and concreteness of reality. On the contrary, the noological method understands the particular out of an encompassing and basal Whole of life. The principle of explanation is not brought in from without, but is inwardly

present, or at least allows itself to be brought to a
present moment in consciousness : it is in the last
resort, with all its arrangements through freedom,
a fact and an experience.   Herewith not only is a
higher degree of security won, but the linking of
each element with the Whole must lead to an inward
renewal and deepening as well as to a clearer impress
of the characteristic features.   Therefore, the foundation of religion must be of a noological and not of a
speculative kind : the psychological method accordingly stands in a secondary place.

It is, however, necessary not only to raise up the
Spiritual Life from the empirical psychic life, but
even within itself it needs a further separation.   In
the Spiritual Life we recognised a total-life—a world ;
but our ordinary immediate life flows in homogeneous
individual acts as a succession of events and activities,
and this seems to exclude all definite spirituality.
This contradiction is to be overcome through an
inner gradation of life alone : in individual acts a
Whole must be able to be present ; but the life
acquires an entirely different character according as
it discovers such a Whole present or not.   Were the
life to shift back beyond the surface of the individual
events, then what appears tangible to the individual
must in some kind of way become conscious, workable, and accessible.   The possibility of this is really
discovered and appears in clear results.   It is only the
presence of a Whole that enables the individual
thoughts to become an expression of a *Weltanschauung*, and enables the individual acts to become
the expression of a moral character ; for it is only a
continuous construction of an elevated thought that

can mould the material and weld a systematic order
out of the whole particular provinces.   This presence
of the Whole in the particular can have very various
grades.   For example, great are those thinkers alone
whose total method reaches into each particular, even
into the smallest achievement; great is that moral
character alone which sets its stamp on each particular
act : thus do *Substance* and *Existence* differentiate
themselves in life.   Substance is to be conceived not
as an inaccessible entity, but as the kernel of the
Life-process itself; not as a species fixed for all
times, but as something conceivable only through
the process of its construction, and as something
gifted with power through the process of its transformation.   The development in which the Spiritual
Life unfolds itself in man strikes itself into the
substance as well; and it is in this that the main
extension of life lies, because in the movement a
struggle for the substance itself is taking place.   The
first achievements are mere attempts which yet have to
stand the test of experience, and which, through such
a test, can be driven forward to a further development
and even transformation.   Such tests and experiences
need a development towards particular activities;
this is the substance itself now assigned to the
existence-side of life.   But in order to make some
contribution to the solution of the problem, the
existence-side must found a certain independence
over against the substance, for if the substance meant
nothing more than its immediate momentary expression, the life would remain tied to a situation
reached once for all.   And thus life could never
become a problem and never desire a movement;

and without both there is not possible for man, in the midst of all his unreadiness, any further development.

Thus, once again, we find a double-sided aspect of life, which carries an incessant problem in itself, and at the same time carries a germ of entanglements of opposing kinds. What is imbedded in life from the substance has continually to be transformed into a free activity, and is to be explained through such an activity. The free activity, however, needs a return-movement to the substance in order not to fall into vague indecision. The individual as well as the community show an opposite tendency. Men and times can transform their lives simply into a movement—into a play of free-energies—without grasping the radical foundation, or without even striving after such a foundation. Then shallow men arise who, in all their agility and industry, possess no souls, but merely exist—bare creatures of the environment, and of barren times, though full of excitement and business which yet possess no spiritual base ; men and times that seek to fill the needs of life through endless variations and combinations of a free and disconnected activity.

But the contrary is also possible : a substance ready-made does not enter into the sphere of explanation, and consequently never becomes the full possession of man. It is so with individuals and so with times. Not seldom do we find a spiritual foundation ready and at hand, but it is not worked out ; although in one's own possession, it remains as something alien and inaccessible. Thus is it with the dull and helpless men and times that cannot find their own depth, but follow in the direction of the shallows of life and not in the direction of what the deep contains. Also, in spiritual provinces and especially in religion, the explanation of the substance fails often to correspond with, and, indeed, often contradicts, its validity; what is willed and estimated at the base can often lie beneath a growing crust of thought. Throughout the whole history of Christianity this cleft between substance and its explanation appears; ever arises the need to prove the latter, and to seek the former.

Where the analysis into substance and existence is recognised, the kernel of life is never sought in the so-called faculties of thought, feeling, and will— neither in any one of them nor in their sum. These different phases of the one consciousness belong to the substance just referred to, and never out of their own power can they produce a spiritual content; far more do they develop in a connection with some kind of Life-substance. Such a deepening of reality alone is able to free us from the intellectualism which we recognise to-day, but into which, notwithstanding all our troubles and toils, we tend to sink back ever anew. We remain without overcoming so long as the existing activities signify to us the whole of life. In the provinces of such existent activities the intelligence stands in the foreground; that which struggles to reach up to the level of a spiritual content has to explain itself at the bar of intelligence and work from that judgment into the remaining provinces. When the fact is recognised that thought itself, in so far as it is of a productive and not merely of a reflective kind, possesses behind itself a basal and directive activity of the Whole and brings forth its creativeness from this basal region, a secure conquest over intellectualism is gained.   Then it becomes clear that in the movement of life the handling is not concerned with an assimilation of a "given" reality, but with an ascent to a definite reality ; the struggle is not concerning interpretations but concerning contents.

Thus the problem of life is raised above the antithesis of intellectualism and voluntarism — for voluntarism is a mere reversal of intellectualism, and remains bound on the mere level of bare experience.   The powers of intellect and will thus cannot form the kernel of man's nature, far less can they be carried into the universe and be raised to the substance of the All.   It is not from the forms of phenomena but from the substance of life that any hope arises of illumining the deep night which wraps our life and our fundamental relation to reality. All pictorial conceptions of these forms of phenomena are mere human projections, intellectual plays of a fugitive imagination.

While, however, the recognition of that depth heightens powerfully the task of life, it heightens at the same time the inward movement of life, and the attention extends over the whole expanse of life. For now the truth of the Whole becomes anew in each individual position a problem ; each point has to prove, to strengthen, and to adjust its truth.   This yields also a characteristic organisation of the work of culture.   Here the general view of life is not now included in one particular province, as, for example, in religion or in metaphysics, which is supposed to be able to include and to further all the other provinces ;

the main problem lies on the other side of all the branches and runs through them all; each particular province can take the whole question into itself, prove it in its own experience, and answer it in its own way. In all great achievements within the particular provinces there is implied a grasp of the Whole and at the same time a furthering of the Whole. This signifies an equality of rights among the different branches; it forbids all hierarchic gradation and subordination of the mediæval type. The differentiation of substance and existence works in that it renders life more eventful, freer, richer.

Accordingly, we see life all along taking a characteristic shape, and we find this characteristic extend from an external outline into the innermost web. What always yielded itself to the individual drew its strength and found its connection in a particular governing and thorough-going thought—the thought of the opening of a new grade of reality, of a kingdom of independent inwardness within the province of man. And this thought will lead us further into the province of religion. Our previous discussion has been necessary in order to obtain a fixed foundation; now we are to handle the matter direct.

CHAPTER VIII

c. THE FACT OF UNIVERSAL RELIGION

1. *The Transition to Religion*

(a) *The Problem of Religion in General.*—In connection with the transition to religion, it is necessary before all else to establish what is essential and indispensable to religion—to religion in each and every sense. Before all else the main point is this : religion holds up before us, over against the surrounding world, a new kind of existence, a new order of things, and divides reality into different provinces and worlds. That religion may be obtained without a belief in God is proved by Buddhism in its oldest and most definite form ; but without a dualism of worlds, without an outlook on a new existence, religion becomes a mere empty sound. The mere acknowledgment of a higher order, however, gives us in no way a religion. That higher order must not merely exist in itself : it must also be effective for us, it must place our existence on a new foundation, and must be conceived by us as a main fact ; otherwise it remains, it spite of an external acknowledgment, inwardly strange and indifferent. The mere existence of deities was conceded

187

readily enough by the Epicureans. How barren for religion were all the diggings for the final "grounds" of things and all the so-called proofs for the existence of God! There is not, therefore, any definite religion without the living presence of a higher world within our own domain, without the clash of two worlds with all their entanglement and irrationality. But even in this irrational there appears especially clear the original character, the transforming and renewing energy of religion.

Such a projection of a new world into our life is a question of an actual kind; and thus appearing as a fundamental fact, the question is not to be placed on one side but to be solved. But with all its actuality, the question does not deal with something that is individual and obvious. ECKHART ridicules such an attempt as this: "Many people hope to see God as one sees an ox." The question deals with something that is a Whole and an invisible. Such an object cannot come to man from the outside and overwhelm him with sensuous impressions; it is only an inward movement that can bring man to the point where truths, otherwise concealed, reveal themselves; and data, otherwise loose, can bind themselves into a Whole of Reality. True, such movements desire as well the work of thought, but such a help remains in the service of the main actual question.

(β) *More Detailed View of the Problem.*—The whole course of our investigation has shown the characteristics and greatness of man to consist in the working within him of a total reality; along with this the Spiritual Life became the centre of all the investigation. This must verify itself also in connection with the transition to religion. It is not the entanglements of the mere-human but those of the Spiritual Life which urge us to religion ; it is not the deliverance of man to human happiness but the self-reliance of the Spiritual Life which stands now in question. All this announces such mighty transformations against the customary mode of life—transformations which aim to present before man the truth that something more is indispensable than a smug arrangement of things.

Such a method does not only place religion on securer foundations, but, in the formation of its content, meets with evil entanglements. So long as man as an isolated existence stands over against the All, he is never able to go forth out of his own movements and needs to the certainty of a new world. What he possesses and develops on his subjective plane can never mean anything more than that which holds good for his own circle of presentations ; if things were only so, the danger becomes evident that all things will soon be explained as a mere brain-spinning of the subject himself. If, before all else, the presence of *a world within man* is not recognised as well as the fact that he can be raised to a world-life, he can never win a secure conviction of a Whole of Reality, and never be certain of the opening of a new world.

This first question of truth requires a noo-centric and not an anthropomorphic standard ; the thought-world of religion will remain under the reproach of anthropomorphism so long as Spiritual Life and the human form of existence are not differentiated. The old thinker was correct in stating that men constructed the gods in their own image; but when such conceptions were refined, they were more and more transformed into objects of thought. But the refining of the conceptions easily makes the error even more dangerous, and entangles the objects of thought still deeper in the anthropomorphic process. This anthropomorphism, however, meets with a strong opposition the more the progress of knowledge explains to man his position in the All of things. Indeed, the more his dependence on nature and, at the same time, the speciality of his species are illumined, the more apparent becomes the failure to raise man to the All-Life and to fill up the ground of reality with products from the quarry of human analogy.

More serious still are the dangers into which such an anthropomorphic conception of religion brings its inner motive-powers. A religion of the merely human kind inevitably makes the quest of man's happiness the centre of all activity; it rivets him to the inactivity to which he seems to subordinate and even to sacrifice himself. Of what avail are all obedience and all sacrifice if man only renounces in order to gain more of the very stuff which binds him? In the customary order of religion the hope of a great reward threatens to adjust the character in a prevailing manner to the results of action, and to link that character with the particular external worth of things and thus to injure greatly the pure joy in the good and true, and to endanger the inner independence. It appears then as if the whole world-order were here in order to satisfy our " dear self" with all its pettiness and meanness, and to bring it to full indulgence; it

appears as if "God had forgotten all His creatures
with the exception of us alone" (ECKHART).   True,
the deeper atmosphere of all religions withstands all
such shrinkage upon the small self, and demands against
such a notion an ardent battle for the purification and
refinement of the soul.   But into this struggle the full
energy does not enter so long as a fundamental liberation of life from the merely human and from the anxiety
for its small happiness has not taken place.   And in
order to obtain this liberation, radical transformations
are necessary, as we have already seen in the acknowledgment of the Spiritual Life and the changes it
brought along with itself; there is no ejection of the
small human assertions out of our inner world without
a new view of ourself, and there is no unselfishness
of character without a nature superior to that of the
bare self.   Man does not remain a mere man—a kind
of well-equipped animal — a kind of special and
vanishing point in infinity; he is called to acknowledge the inner presence of a *world*, and to reach
such a world in spite of his mere singularity.   Only
the effort for a deliverance can free him from the
anxiety for his bare happiness, and only the placing of
the centre of gravity here makes it possible to place
the mere inactivity in the background and to create
actions and energy; otherwise his particular nature
brings forth no fruit and, indeed, his further existence
is endangered.

The content and aim of the world of religion everywhere fall short of realisation by the natural man, but
are known by the Spiritual Life in him.   Difficult as
all this may seem, and sure as it may appear that the
natural ways of man accompany all his work and strive

to enter into this, yet through the energetic separation of the merely human from that which transcends
humanity a struggle for the maintenance and purity
of the spiritual substance is taken up, so that we do
not fall defenceless to the lower plane. As in culture
on the whole, so, too, in religion, the progress of the
developing thought appears not anywhere as a mere
disentanglement of an initially childish kind—as a
destruction of an anthropomorphism—but as a rebuilding undertaken through the discovery of a
new life and nature in man. Were there no road
from the denial to the affirmation, the work of thought
would more and more destroy the living content of
reality; indeed, the more energetically that work of
thought proceeded, the more certainly it would reach
a complete agnosticism with all its hollowness.

When, however, a religion of the Spiritual Life
leaves behind itself the merely human, it must be
by itself of a universal nature. For here it is
not the aim of religion to further, through the
introduction of a new world, this or that side of the
Spiritual Life, but, before all else, it is the energetic
longing to maintain the Spiritual Life as a Whole,
and to carry it through in the midst of seemingly
insuperable obstacles. A religion which performs
this must not consider itself as a special province
of the remaining life, but must encompass and permeate the whole life. That the *Universal* mode of
religion does not form its culmination, for, indeed,
it never leads to an independent religion, but that
it far more leads to a *Characteristic* religion—all
this will be shown later; but it will be shown, too,
that this characteristic mode presupposes the uni-

versal mode, proceeds out of its experiences, and has
to unite itself with it.

Spiritual Life was not in our view a quality of
another existence; it proved itself as a life existing by itself, which had to develop all its existence
within the life itself. The problem of the truth of
religion therefore owes its existence to the fact
that an absolute life, superior to the world, is recognised as effective in our sphere. Through such
a recognition the conception of the Godhead receives
the meaning of an Absolute Spiritual Life; out of
this all the remainder of life is to be moulded. This
yields a decisive break with the old methods of
proof—methods that sought before all else to prove
an existence on the other side of the human circle,
and to set oneself in relationship with such an
existence. Through this the intellect gained inevitably a leading position, for by what other means
could we perceive an externally existing reality? On
the contrary, the revelation and the appropriation of
a turn towards the Life-process call upon the whole
man, and prompt to a forward act of the whole soul;
all this certainly enters into ideas and has to be set in
doctrine, but even these have to relate themselves
and be adjusted to the Life-process, for they cannot
proceed as rigid dogmas which would govern the
very powers themselves. From this point of view
there results for religion a characteristic relationship
of the eternal and the temporal, of substance and its
forms; now only such truths are valid as fundamental
as are necessary to the vindication of the representative Life-process. The nature of that which presents
itself in the existing situation as an incontestable

13

truth, and which is estimated as indispensable by a standard for the act, has to be proved ever anew over against the changes of time, and ever anew does it become a problem. This is so because the historical course of the religious life of the Church has the tendency to extend further and further the importance of doctrines, and, along with this, to relax the connection with the living foundation, or to construct a particular side of the nature at the expense of the whole. Therefore, the return to the ground-process and the elimination of all the superfluous as a burden and a hindrance become an ever necessary problem ; the great renewals of religion thus appear as a simplification of life, as a return out of the darkness and distraction of time to an old and eternal truth.

Finally, the raising of our problem involves a raising of religion above the ramifications of the psychic life—above the so-called faculties of the soul ; the problem concerns itself with a particular development of a Spiritual Reality which certainly unfolds itself in thought, feeling, and will, but which proceeds not from any one or from any combination of them. All the strict fulfilment of religion in the provinces of the so-called faculties of the soul yields a formation only at the periphery, beyond which remains unexperienced and undeveloped a centre of life—the matrix of original moulding and creativeness. Let us consider the religion of the Church system of the Middle Ages, which even to-day presents itself with such an obtrusive air as the one true religion. A system of doctrines is transmitted to the individual, a complex of duties is laid upon him ; also the entire resignation of the subjective feeling—a mysticism with its organ of feeling—can be brought about through doctrines and precepts presented in such a manner as not to appear as a burden and a constraint. Thus the whole man seems to have been won, and religion seems to have become the possession of his soul. But is it so in reality ? Or does there not remain implicitly behind all the expansion what is really the fundamental fact—man as a superior Whole, as a participator in infinity, as a warrior for a spiritual self ? This depth of his nature has now come to a full consciousness, and, along with this, it has become clear that such a fact alone grants him stable security against unutterable dangers, tribulations, and doubts ; so that he will found his religion upon this rock, thoroughly weary of the debate whether intellect, or will, or feeling, plays the main part in the business. Here as everywhere else we do not find anything new in such a fact ; for wherever religion was the moving energy of life, there stood behind it man with the whole of his soul.   But this ancient truth was woefully darkened, and prevented from coming to full effect in the common life of humanity through human conceptions and especially through the Christian Church.   So that it is still something new when it is recognised fully in principle, and when it is able to defend itself more energetically against it own disfigurement.

(γ) *The Reality above the World.*—What calls forth the problem of religion out of the Spiritual Life ? The Spiritual Life in itself does not produce religion in an immediate manner. It is certain that it signifies a higher degree of reality than nature ; this degree of reality can develop itself fully and live out its potencies in our world, and can prepare all it needs

for its aims; as things thus stand, we have in the
Spiritual Life a new stage *within* the world, but we
have not as yet a *new world*—we have won no over-
world as yet; in all this we have reached an idealism
—this worn-out expression is used here for the
purpose of brevity—but we have not as yet acknowledged religion. The question concerning an over-
world leads us first to ask whether the New which
carries such a fundamental transformation within
itself knocks itself in pieces upon the hard obstacles
of our world, and is thus unable to win any secure
position against such obstacles. If things are really
so, either the whole has to be dropped as a treacherous
illusion and all activity to reach and to maintain it
has to be suspended; or we are to seek a deeper
ground in what occurs within our circle and to protect the gain throughout. But when such a matter
of fact allows itself to be proved, and when it leads
to the recognition of an absolute life above the world
of sense, even yet religion is not won. That comes
about when the life not only comes in contact with its
own results, but when we seize life and appropriate
it as a Whole, when we pass from the effects and
set ourselves upon the causes, and participate, in a
form of immediacy, in the absoluteness of the Divine
Life. But in order to reach such a decisive point we
must first of all run through the earlier stages of life
and seek to show that the Spiritual Life has no secure
ground in the ordinary everyday world, but meets
in such a world the hardest contradictions, and yet
in spite of these contradictions maintains itself and
exercises energy in order to take up first of all the
decisive question.

(aa) *The Peril to the Spiritual Life from its Surrounding World.*—How little the Spiritual Life
governs ordinary immediate existence has been seen
from the beginning of our investigation; it was this
fact that made us raise it so essentially above that
existence.   But the inner energy yet presents in no
way a triumphant advance over against the world.
The clash has become sharper rather than milder, and
the contradiction reaches deeper into the foundations.
In the meantime the Spiritual Life brings forth from
within a new kind of existence, and desires for it new
forms; it remains throughout committed to a fundamental construction of the same reality and yet it
longs to advance and possess more of this reality,
and is thus affected with a contradiction right through
its course; its energy and its truth are endangered
by the greatest obstacles.   It signifies from within a
comprehensive life, and yet this is split up among
particular individual tendencies; it signifies a timeless
truth, and yet underlies wholly the power of time, and
it is carried along powerless by the ever-restless
current of history; it must hold itself as the main fact
—as the kernel of reality and the complete aim of the
individual self—and yet it is handled throughout as a
subsidiary fact, as a means to other aims.   At the
same time, a characteristic timidity restrains the man
from confessing openly his inner apathy towards the
Spiritual Life; rather he will and can allow this
appearance of a " better " to have some kind of place,
so that there originates a general unveracity with all
the impotence which is inherent in such unveracity,
with all the hollow pomp which makes the man
himself vexatious.   This hard conflict between the

nature and the existence-form of the Spiritual Life is the deepest ground of that hypocrisy which runs through and poisons human life, not only in its union with the life of culture, but also in the deepest recesses of the soul. Such a mere semblance of character—such unveracity—is bound to corrupt all the individual activities and situations : knowledge, love, happiness —all receive a multi-coloured hybrid form ; all these might be and could be *more* than this ; everything through such a disunion lacks the courage either of a decisive Yea or of a decisive Nay. With such half-heartedness how could a new world arise or be built up over against nature ? We have already convinced ourselves that the examination of the historico-social life offers not the least hope for such a new world or the possibility of altering essentially our position in respect to the Spiritual Life. Therefore, the whole movement towards the Spiritual Life is either a great and an inexplicable error, or there is more behind it than appears clear at a glance.

(*bb*) *The Assertion of the Spiritual Life over against the World.*—That in reality *more* is entrenched behind the appearances is shown by the fact of the conflict itself ; for this fact is of a twofold kind : it shows the hindrance, but it also shows that *something is hindered* which asserts itself in spite of all hindrance. If the surrounding world with its unspiritual nature were the Whole, how could the Spiritual Life arise universally ? How could it, if it were no more than a mere appearance, exercise so much more power now that it has recognised the fact than it exercised previously ? Whence even the striving after appearance, after mere semblance, if all resolves itself into a

phantom ? There thus must be something higher in
the very truth which works in our potentialities and
in the whole of their province. That this is so is
brought into yet clearer view by the fact that the
Spiritual Life, with all its hindrances and restraints
in the environing world, does not simply conform to
this world, but asserts itself over against it and holds
fast to its own aims. It does this in the directions
we shall now point out.

1. In the midst of this kingdom of distractions one
thing clearly emerges—a most powerful movement
towards unity.   Individuals, peoples, and epochs
believe in the possibility of mutual understanding
in the midst of all disintegrations ; all assertion of
a spiritual kind is valid not only for the individual
or for a special circle, but for all ; also the particular
branches of the work of reason may diverge for a
while but not for any length of time ; and finally all
the manifold of effort must flow into a unifying
truth, for all particularity becomes rigid and lifeless
when severed from such a unity.   The striving towards
unity in the midst of all distractions is precisely that
which rouses human life, which sets it in motion,
which entangles it in unutterable strife, but which
proves itself a mighty power through it all.   Whence
arises the conflict unless from this issue—that each
shall become the Whole, the governing, the universally
valid, and that each tends to lose its value if it suffers
another to lie untouched by its side ?   Such strenuous
and even passionate striving is an irrefragable testimony to a power superior to the dispersion of the
parts and also to the whole environing order of
things.

2. However the content and the value of the Spiritual Life may be made by man to fit in with his aims, yet they withstand a complete adjustment into the merely human situation, and exercise from their side a counter-effect to that situation. No less an authority than Kant pronounced it as "highly objectionable that the laws concerning what I ought to do can be drawn from or confined to what is merely done." How does such a superiority of the norm of all action justify itself above the position of man if there dwells not in his whole nature such a superior arrangement? This arrangement in man's nature appears in the general movement of history, first of all, as a power of a directive and unravelling kind. Men and times draw the Spiritual Life into themselves, and lower it as a means for their aims; they give it a moulding which corresponds to their fleeting wishes. Thus they may carve and bend it, and make themselves appear as seeming lords of things. But such a method has always a measuring rod brought to bear on it; sooner or later a counter-effect makes its presence felt and then the merely human fashion lives itself out, its emptiness and meanness become manifest, and the final decomposition is not far away. Thus we find an incessant return to the Spiritual Life from the human perversion of it—a return to man's own nature; and consequently an energetic return to the demands of man and his independence.

This is an effect of a more negative kind; but the Spiritual Life declares its ability also positively within the human province through a persistent effort to move outside the "given" situation, through a tracing out and a holding forth of ideals,

through a longing after a more complete happiness
and a more complete truth.   Why is not man satisfied
with the relativity which so obstinately claims his
existence?   Why has he a longing for the Absolute
in opposition to such relativity, and why does he
plunge himself into the deepest sorrows and distractions?   This has happened not only in special
situations of individuals, but in the whole process of
culture; indeed, the upward march of culture would
have been impossible without a striving of man from
a level above his "given" position and even above
himself.   Was not subjective satisfaction more
easily reached by him in the semi-animal stages of
his existence than in culture with all its toils and
tangles, and does the progress of culture with all
its apparatus make him in the mere human sense
happier?   What else could compel him to step into
this perilous track of culture but the necessity of his
own nature revealing to him at the same time the
presence of a new order of things?

3. Then Spiritual Life not only asserts itself
within the human circle, but it exhibits in the midst
of all obstacles a capacity to draw the lower to
itself, along with the energy to overcome the lower
and the power to ennoble it through a higher.   There
proceeds through our life a movement from the
outward to the inward, from the natural to the
spiritual.   Any spiritual stimulation which comes to
us may seem in the first instance to proceed and to
work on us from without, and may thus appear as a
mere constraint which can only be neutralised by
counter-effects.   But what at first seems to work
on man more than *in* him soon begins to strike its

roots within him, allows itself to be gripped as one's own possession and to be transformed into free activity. Without such a growth of one's own life, without such an inverted order in the direction of the movement, all education of humanity remains a "dead-level" training, and all moral instruction remains a mere appearance; the spark of the inner life would never be kindled were such a life not imbedded in man's very nature, and did it not enable him to carry his very life further in the direction of his goal. So that it is not through the mere working of psychical mechanism, which could never awaken man and which could never originate an inner unity and an active disposition, that the progress from custom to morality, from external relationship to inner harmony, from a collection of self-interests to a unity of character, reveals itself and explains itself as a phenomenon of the inwardness of human life and existence. Through this the effort is raised beyond its original motive, and the man is led out to a region beyond himself. What appeared to him previously as mere means for his egoistic aims, begins now, through his own character, to draw him and set him in motion; this is more and more taken into his own life and raises it. The necessities of existence are directed at carrying man to his work; and how many inward movements and how many blessings proceed from such aims! But all this is to be understood only under the presupposition of the presence of an elevated Spiritual Life exercising itself actively within the human circle.

What we have already considered in connection with these three points and directions is a develop-

ment of the one and same ground-fact which testifies
in a corporate manner that there works in us a Spiritual
Life which does not explain itself out of the relations,
but which points to a higher order of existence than
the world-order which surrounds us.   With all this
is won only an hypothesis of religion, and not religion
itself.   Though the consciousness of the effect of a
higher order of things in the midst of our circle of
experience is able to give a true assurance, and to
strengthen our faith in some kind of conquest of the
good, still the power remains a dark secret, and an
inner relationship to it is not yet given.   It is only
with this latter inward relationship that religion
originates.   Let us therefore see if the experience of
life shows an entrance hither.

(cc) *The Revelation of an Absolute Spiritual Life
in our World.*—We need not enter upon any laborious
and lengthy investigation in order to prove that a
Spiritual Life superior to the world not only touches
us with its effects, but that it is also present in us
as cause with all the fulness of its energy.   It comes
to us as a great revelation that a Spiritual Life can
rise up as our *own* life : and this actually happens.
The significance of this fact can be fully judged after
we have recognised that a general and comprehensive
life presents itself in the Spiritual Life; and that in
this total-life a new degree of reality arises, and an
inverted order of the world-process takes place.   Such
a turn could not proceed out of the potency of the
individual elements of life, but has to proceed out of
the energy of the Whole.   Therefore, this Whole
must be, in a form of immediacy, present in us ; and,
also, the great change must ensue as a gain of our

own life. Now, the life of the spirit does not develop itself in us merely in isolated achievements or from the external; we have already seen how it returned to itself from each performance and constructed for itself a nucleus which became the carrier of all activity, for thus alone could the autonomous life develop itself. Whatever the personality and the spiritual individuality may receive on the merely human and natural planes could not arise and initiate any kind of movement unless there worked on such planes some kind of autonomous and original life.

The great change of life from being a mere web of relations to the founding of a total-life in itself, and the transition of reality to its own depth—all this is a fact which does not march in front of us, and it could not arise in us at all had it not gone forth out of us and had we not become along with it active co-carriers of reality. The dawning of a new world in the midst of our province, our experiencing an inward revolution of human existence—this is the great miracle in which the presence of a new world manifests itself with great clearness. He who does not find the miracle here is not likely to find it any-where else, and will seek in vain for it in the "far, far away," for the words of PARACELSUS hold good in this respect: "You are long-sighted; you see in the distance, but you do not see close at hand."

That the fact of an autonomous life in our own circle holds valid as the decisive proof of the presence of a Divine existence is contradicted only by the external clothing of the idea. "Autonomous," one may say, and so says one with the mediæval mode of thought, "implies the denial of all dependence, of all

relation to another will; religion, however, desires
unconditional dependence, obedience, submission;
thus the two are complete opposites." But they remain opposites only so long as God and man are set
one against the other from the outside in a childish
anthropomorphic manner as two isolated natures
—one side seeming to take what is given from the
other. We could think but little of man if we
allowed everything to come in to him from the
outside, if we denied him all inner movement towards
the summits of religion. And the new world, too,
would be cut off entirely from our world, and, through
its inaccessibility, the " beyond " would vanish.

But it is quite otherwise when the autonomy, now
showing more inward and less anthropomorphic modes
of presentation, appears not as something contradictory of the Whole but as an independent " becoming" out of the energy and presence of the Whole,
and, at the same time, as an essentially new grade of
life. Must, then, this independent life separate itself
most pointedly from all narrow selfishness and
from all stubborn self-assertion? It is certainly a
mystery how the highest self-activity signifies the
immediate extinction of all mere egoism and signifies,
too, a life out of Infinity. But he who puts this
mystery on one side must either cast away all
religion or shape it in a purely external form of the
understanding.

Through the inward presentation of the total
problem the thought of a world beyond the world
of sense signifies much more than a flight to a bare
" beyond." True, there results a separation — a
division of reality—for without this religion is not

possible. But this does not imply that a " beyond "
is to be thought of as a kind of fixed and inviolable
foundation of our existence entirely over against the
present world—a " beyond " that has to be adjusted
through special helps ; but it does imply a " beyond "
in the sense that the existing Spiritual Life relegates
the present world to a secondary place. Such a
Spiritual Life becomes the fixed norm for all life, and
in its renewal it becomes not some kind of a More of
an already existing life ; but in it, first and foremost, a
really existing and truthful life is won.

Thus, religion has been found real wherever it
possessed this thorough originality ; and its own
truth was the most certain of all things—a truth
in which all else found its permanence. Thus an
Augustine took flight away from the hardest shocks
of human life to the immanent Divine presence in
his own soul—to what first of all disengaged itself
from the threatening overthrow of life, to what won
him for himself. So that the Middle Ages conceived
this Divine Order as the Fatherland (*patria*); and
ventured to believe that we know God better than
we know the creature (*Deus notior creatura*).

After all this there can be no doubt as to the
nature of religion. Religion rests on the presence of a
Divine Life in man ; it manifests itself through the appropriation of this Life as one's own nature. Religion,
too, subsists in the fact that man in the inmost
foundation of his own being is raised into the Divine
Life, and participates in the Divine Nature.
Christianity was right when it found the kernel of
religion in the union of the natures of the human
and the Divine ; and even the unfortunate dogmatic

representation of the two natures in Christ could
not destroy the transforming and elevating energy
of this truth.

But the full vivification of the Divine in man and
the gaining of a new plane of life can never occur
without a recognition and an assimilation on the
side of man.   Religion can never originate unless the
Divine enters into the conviction of man, unless the
whole of his soul turns towards the new world.   In
this sphere there is no place for any mechanical
instillation; and there is no growth possible without
a responsiveness on the human side.   Hence religions
constantly long so ardently for the consent and
repentance of man; the nobility of the soul and
its membership with God must be acknowledged
if it is to be able to experience His Divine Energy.
For " what would it avail a man if he were king and
knew it not " (ECKHART).   It will appear in a fuller
manner later in our treatment that religions could
not consider human capacity as the measurement
of the activity of the Divine; but that to all religions,
in their best conclusions, human achievement was
considered as the highest proof of grace.

It is not possible that so much should lie imbedded
in such a recognition did it not signify more than
a passive approval or a setting of act and work.
If things did not mean more for our life, not much
more would be won than a decorous and pretentious
etiquette.   In order to bring forth a genuine renewal,
the recognition of the Divine must translate itself into
an energetic selection and rejection of the elements
which present themselves in this world.   The greatness
of this conversion of man consists in that the Spiritual

Life is led through its freedom from the entanglement
and anxiety of the world-situation to a pure distinctness of its own nature and to a full self-reliance.
Thus, a conspicuous distinction between essential and
non-essential becomes possible; and through such
an analysis the life is powerfully roused and set in
motion. Religion throughout is not mere contemplation with its corresponding characteristics; but is,
after the nature of its nucleus, the highest activity,
the separation of the existing chaos, the concentration
of the Spiritual Life within itself, and the setting
forth of such a Spiritual Life against all the alien
elements which threaten to overwhelm it.

2. *The Content of Religion*

(a) *The Idea of God.*—The discussion of the idea
of God belongs to the close of our investigation.
But the discussion of the subject is to be considered
not as if the idea of God had already been discovered
in advance at a certain stage in the evolution of
religion, and had driven forward all further development out of itself; but on the contrary, our investigation considers the idea of God as that which
brings to expression above all else the characteristic
properties of religion, and which makes the main
direction of the striving of religion palpable. Therefore, one was in reality fighting for the content of
religion when one fought for the conception of God,
and it is in the recognition of this fact that every
conception of religion has to justify itself.

The pathway which leads to the conception of God
leads us at the same time to the content which the

conception can have for us.   It signifies to us nothing
other than an Absolute Spiritual Life in its majestic
superiority to all the limitations of man and the world
of experience—a Spiritual Life that has attained to
a complete subsistence in itself, and, at the same time,
to an encompassing of all reality.

Before we view what such a foundation and development of the idea of God, in and by the Spiritual Life,
yield as to content, we must discuss how this way
of taking the idea contrasts with other ways, and
especially how it is qualified to overcome an antithesis,
which, beyond mere conceptions, disunites and endangers the religious life itself.   This antithesis is
that of anthropomorphism and of ontological speculation.   The former has endeavoured to keep the idea
of God as near as possible to man ; the latter has
endeavoured to lift the idea as high and far above
man as possible.   Anthropomorphism controls the
ordinary conception of religion from remote antiquity.   Can we deny that man is here wont to
project into the universe a somewhat magnified
and ennobled replica of himself, and to deal with
the Deity as with a man-like being ?   The insufficiency of this was not only brought up as a charge
against religion, but it was also fully felt within
religion's own circle.   Hence the effort to drive out
such a human notion ; and this elimination seemed
to be most thoroughly effected by ontological speculation which excluded every closer determination of
the Godhead as illegitimate, and retained as valid
for the nature of the Godhead pure Being without
any qualities and above all concepts.   This appealed
with specially attractive force to some philosophic

14

minds, who then evolved a mode of esoteric religion which seemed to be lifted high as heaven above all the smallness and selfishness of man. But with such a loosening of its bonds with man, religion threatened to forfeit not only all clear qualities of the Godhead but also all effective energy; it passed more and more into a passive contemplation, and, by this, into a direct counterpart of the anthropomorphic religion which accomplishes too little in the inward transformation of man, and which serves too directly his desire for mere happiness.

With such a divergence the two modes of religion —the esoteric and the exoteric—cannot possibly be directly united and conjoined as has happened in the main in the historical religions and especially in Christianity. In reality the Christianity of the Church has not one but two conceptions of God— one anthropomorphic and the other ontologic-speculative; they involve different forms of religion, so that any juxtaposition of the two forms cannot possibly be a solution of the problem, but can only represent a tolerable compromise which insistently proclaims the two requirements of every concept of God and of all religion. Anthropomorphism contends rightly that religion, in order to be a power of life and not a mere view of the universe, must remain close to man and must strengthen him in himself. How little ontology is able out of its own power to do this, and how little in its speculations it leads to religion—all this would be quite evident if it were not wont, furtively, to complete itself from a more positive kind of religion, and to substitute mere empty conceptions for true forms, as mysticism evidently shows. On the other hand, ontology possesses a right in the undertaking because it lifts religion out of the circle of presentations, and especially out of the circle of the interests of the mere individual; for through this, ontology really forms something new out of man, and does not merely confirm him in his smallness and narrowness.

Now, the two claims—the psychic nearness of religion and its liberation from the merely human—become united with the promulgation of the Spiritual Life. For this deals not only with the preservation of the merely human but with its spiritual substance; and it forbids all anchorage in any merely human province and all binding of the conception of God to merely human conceptions. But when, at the same time, the truth stands firm that the Spiritual Life has to win our true self—the depth of our own nature—then religion, with all its elevation beyond the merely human, preserves a nearness of soul; and, moreover, the conception of God can gain a positive content without falling into anthropomorphism. All this will happen through the fundamental conception that man himself signifies no bare isolated existence, but is moored upon Infinity; and that only in the realisation of this fact is he able to discover his own definite nature. Also, the highest human mode of designating the Absolute Nature will not suffice, for a human colouring always clings to the conception of spiritual greatness. But these conceptions, through the annulment of the sharp opposites, can well serve as pathways and symbols; and, in spite of all their insufficiency, can present us with true contents of life.

From such a reflection on these things the effort concerning the personality of God is to be judged—a fact which reaches back to antiquity. Much is here a strife over words. In the expression " personality " differences along with the most striking resemblances lie imbedded : one side thinks, in connection with the expression, of the individual human nature with its opposition to other natures and with its natural limits ; another thinks of the " becoming " independence and self-comprehension of the Spiritual Life in man. But the whole of the difference is not a strife over words. The direct denial of a Divine Personality aims at the denial of a superiority against the world-process, aims at a pantheistic melting of the Absolute Life in the world. An unconditional affirmation, on the other hand, works in the direction of humanising and drawing down the Divine. It becomes necessary, then, for a further development of the Spiritual Life sufficiently to guard its foundation against the flow of all into merely human qualities and relations ; and it is not easy to overcome this danger on account of the rooted significance of terms. Therefore, it may be recommended for a scientific expression of the fact, not to transfer at any rate the expression " personality " to the Absolute Life ; or, at the most, not to employ it as more than a symbol. Indeed, one may ask whether, in order to avoid the dangers of the conception of personality, religion of a universal kind has not to turn from the expression " God " to that of " Godhead." Whether the passage from the *Universal* mode of religion to the *Characteristic* mode constitutes such a turning, and at the same time gives a better right to the conception of personality, can be shown only by further developments and experiences.

These investigations include also the question concerning the place of mysticism.   If the Spiritual Life is, first of all, a comprehensive life, then no true departure to the religious province can take place without a liberation from narrow definiteness, without a counter-effect to the merely human, and without the setting of human life in a more comprehensive life. That mysticism sets this forth, is its great service; indeed, all the moulding of religion fails unless it takes an element of mysticism—the living soul—into itself.   But mysticism fails because it turns this necessary portion of religion into the sole content. To it religion is nothing other than an absorption into the infinite and eternal Being—an extinguishing of all particularity, and the gaining of a complete calm through the cessation of all the wear and tear of life. Thus even here the Nay and not the Yea remains in the ascendant; and this will rather lower the natural difficulties of life than wring from them a new power superior to them; and consequently the life fails to find an exit out of the sphere of irritation and of its ordinary pitch to a region of active work and to a fundamental transformation of reality.   Mysticism, however, holds valid as a weighty and indispensable motive of religion, though it does not constitute the whole of religion.   We cannot dispense with it, but dare not rest in it.

If we now turn towards the demarcations and securities, it is clear that such can never result from vague reflection but out of the experiences of the Spiritual Life.   All speculative gnosticism fades where the Life-process constitutes at once the point of departure and the limits of all reflection. The idea of God signifies to us nothing other than an Absolute Spiritual Life—a Life freed from the limits and entanglements of our experience, a Life in possession of a complete existence for itself, and constituting the substance of reality. It is thus alone that the idea of God can possess a content, that the characteristics of the Spiritual Life can long for a purer formation, and that these characteristics, uniting among one another what appeared previously as merely external qualities, can now set these very qualities in the nature itself. Through such a turn from effects to causes, from surface to foundation, the unity of the total-life raises itself to a more complete clearness; the timelessness of all spiritual content leads to the idea of a Divine Order; the truthful and the worthful now desire a full union, and the good becomes the governing power of all life. Thus the Spiritual Life, through such an ascent to the Absolute, reaches a full development of its own nature, and, at the same time, obtains an incomparably greater power and superiority over against the merely human powers.

(β) *Godhead and the World.*—In connection with the problem of the Godhead and the world, two movements have struggled for prominence, each of which is able to show a good reason for itself. On the one side, it appears necessary before all else to distinguish clearly the Godhead from the world, and to raise such far above the world; for it is only thus that we are able to preserve the purity of the conception, and only thus does an elevating effect seem to proceed from such a conception.   On the other side, the Godhead is drawn as far as possible deep into the world, and as far as possible the particular nature of the Divine is bound with the particular nature of things ; for it is only thus we seem able to reach a living present consciousness and lasting influences from the world.

> " What sort of God were one that merely planned
> The world from outside, shaped it with His hand !
> Rather is He that inner life of all that seems and is,
> In Him is Nature born and bred, and He in Nature lives."

Thus we reach the opposition of transcendence and immanence, of dualism and monism, of super-naturalism and pantheism. The terms themselves announce but little, and the mutual charges of heresy are wearisome. That the matter is not so simple as the partisans, on the one side or the other, imagine, appears clear from the fact that whole epochs have stood under the influence, now of one, now of the other : waning antiquity could not, on account of a feeling of weariness, separate widely enough the Divine and the world ; our growing modern life, with its fresh strain, could not sufficiently unite both.   Indeed, soon the impression of limits and entanglements predominated ; later the impression of energy and of beauty won the upper hand.   Alternate aspects of inability and ability drew the character hither and thither. We have to see if the development of religion through the Spiritual Life is able to raise man above the vacillations of times and of dis-positions.

The starting-point of the Spiritual Life evidently

rules out such a crass dualism as governs the ordinary mind. For the Spiritual Life was no separate domain which forced open an entrance to alien things, but it proved itself to us as the characteristic depth of reality, and as the turn of life to its own nature. Therefore, if the conception of the Godhead develops out of the conception of the Spiritual Life, the Godhead must be most intimately connected with the nature of things; and this nature of things must be founded and grounded in the Godhead, and, finally, the Godhead must be all in all. The positive religions could not evade such a conviction; and religion dare not surrender what was the experience of the great apostle who felt that "in Him we live, and move, and have our being," and that "we are also His offspring."

When dualism misconstrues this, it isolates the Godhead to the uttermost, and thus loses all power to give the Godhead a content; inevitably a partially transfigured mirror-image of the reality nearest at hand is set up for a new world. The projection of this "here and now" to a "beyond"—this reduplication of the world—must, however, create a contradiction especially in the province of religion, for with such a method there results too little inward transformation; the natural impulses are not sufficiently broken; the bitter Nay fails in religion, and without such a Nay the Yea gains no energy and depth. The same thing happens in connection with the customary hopes of immortality, which conceive of man as being immortal even in his body with all its natural limitations, which are carried with all their worldly qualities into infinity. Indeed, is there

not a religious disposition conceivable which has as
its motive some kind of conservation of the "dear
self," and which finds the hindrances against such a
conservation unbearable ?

Thus, not only all philosophic thought, but also
definite religion itself, withstand such a dualism ; but,
again, a renunciation of it glides easily into pantheism.
An exclusive and complete pantheism, however, is
securely obviated through a development of religion
out of the Life-process. To such a pantheism our
world in the whole of its existence becomes a
phenomenon, a development, an emanation, or, as
the usual wording has it, an absolute essence. All
differentiation of things appears to such a line of
thought as a weakness and an error of the human
mode of thinking ; there is, to such a view, only
one essential reality, only one essential life. The
government of God according to this theory falls
fully into unison with the characteristic effects of the
things, and the unity spreads itself over the whole
multiplicity. Such a mode of thought has the
tendency to win man to its side ; especially when the
consciousness of his energy stirs within him, and
when his eyes are opened to the fulness of life and
the beauty of the world. It is the self-consciousness
of the work of culture—a consciousness of a truth
beyond the individual himself—which, through a
strengthening of itself, raises pantheism to a religion.
Its atmosphere of vastness, its effort to reach beyond
the antitheses of life, and its giving reality a depth,
are the chief recommendations of pantheism.

Such things are no small merits. But, in spite of
all its lustre, pantheism discovers no contradiction in

the inmost nature of man ; and such a failure makes it untenable, and transmutes its development into a subversion of the self. It remains an indisputable fact that all conversion to religion originates out of an opposition to the surrounding world; the thought of an over-world arises and gains a power only because the world as it immediately presents itself to us does not penetrate into a problem whose solution must not be abandoned. Herewith, it is characteristic of and essential to religion that it develops its power from within to without in opposition to the surrounding world; and where the opposition fades or fails, its energy immediately relaxes. The idea of God becomes unstable where no inner contradiction carries man beyond the world and furthers a life above the world. All movements within the world and all the deepening of the things existing in it can, of course, further their own particular conceptions ; but they cannot justify a breach with external things, and it is through such a breach that the idea of God results. Such an idea of God holds within itself a great transformation of life and of reality; it issues also a call of the whole of reason to the struggle against unreason and for the renewal of life. All this lies far away from pantheism.

The contradiction referred to checks the development of pantheism and drives it out to great divergences. If the ideas draw God and the world in opposite directions, the two ideas cannot possibly flow together side by side ; the one tends to overcome the other, and seeks to absorb the other into itself. Where the movement to the Godhead is most influential, the world escapes more and more to the

realm of night, as is shown in mysticism ; where
the movement proceeds mainly in the direction of
the world, the idea of God evidently fades away,
until finally it becomes an empty word which transforms itself from pantheism to atheism.   The development of modern life down to the brand-new monism
of the present day makes this apparent.   Pantheism
often dresses things with a vague glamour of the
Divine, and deceives us as to the sharpness of the
opposites of things.   Often pantheism is no more
than an echo of a real and energetic religion which
has been transformed into a sickly sentimentalism—
by a process which means the dissolution of real
religion.

But in human existence the hardest inner contradiction in no way hinders a true realisation and
development of power, so that this remains an
historical fact in spite of the poverty of pantheism.
But pantheism has rendered the service of antagonis-
ing the tendency to anthropomorphism in religious
conceptions, and has cast its glance on the particular
connections of things and on the presence of reason
within the world ; and especially has it opposed the
egoism not only of the individual but of mankind,
and has further insisted that reality is to be possessed not through words and doctrines but through
the opening of a new life out of the Whole and of
Infinity.   But its mistake consists in that it conceives
the highest aim as already attained, and declares all
divergence from such an aim as a mere appearance.
This ready-made kind of reality has doubtful results
in varied directions.   If there is to be recognised as
valid only such a ready-made reality, and if it is not

shown that the reason of things can only be attained
through labour and struggle, then life transforms
itself into a mere contemplation; and the reconciliation
with reality then lies merely in a bare contemplation
of an artistic or scientific kind. This stage is reached,
however, at the cost of freedom and ethical handling,
for neither of which is there any place in such a
position. At the same time, there arises a disposition which is made partially evident even at the
outset, to regard evil as trivial and venial; hence the
danger of a quietistic optimism arises. Here, the
whole of the Spiritual Life receives too much of a
merely natural character; it may be conceived as a
supine substance or as a continuous process, but it does
not appear so much as the freedom and the destiny of
man. Thus the tendency is to overbalance and to
fall to the level of the merely human, and to come
under the ban of purely natural conceptions—a position in which it is extremely difficult for the Spiritual
Life to express its definiteness and depth. In reality,
all this merging of the Divine into the world has the
tendency to conceal the opposites and to weaken the
energy of movement. True, religion must also seek
for the Divine in the world; but it can find it only
when it has developed and stamped its impress over
against the world; for such is the only possible way
to distinguish between reason and unreason, to drive
out the enemy and to uplift the kinsman. It is
characteristic of religion that the Divine world has by
its side another world which somehow strikes its
roots into the Divine, and which also presents the
aim of its worship as an impetus out of its own
energy; which impetus, moreover, attains to this aim

not by its own energy, but only through being lifted up to it by the Divine world.

In the primal phenomenon of religion a twofold aspect is involved: the Absolute Life must be effective *above* and *within* the world; the movement must proceed beyond the world and return to the world. It is this fact especially which gives religion its driving force, its incessant life from ever fresh sources. The two things are not separated one from the other, but are present the one with the other. Religion thus needs a continuous overcoming of the opposition of dualism and pantheism, each of which pursues only one of these opposites, and thus soon reaches a disastrous state of fatal stagnation.

(γ) *Godhead and Man.*—In connection with the problem of the relationship between the Godhead and man, there exists especially the danger of making them to move, within the realm of religion, outside of each other and to labour against each other. For if Divine and human action are brought into such an opposition to each other that the gain of the one signifies the loss of the other, all the freedom of man and all human activity become contradictory to the all-power of the Divine, as well as to an unconditioned surrender of man; and both of these are absolutely necessary for all religion. If such a one-sided course is adopted, religion will as much as possible restrict human freedom up to complete annihilation; indeed, this line of thought has made all explicitly religious characters determinists in their attitude. If consideration for the practicalities of life enforced a mitigation in these matters and required the admission of a co-operation on the part of man also such behaviour was evidence rather of a practical adroitness than of a religious depth and logical conclusiveness. If, however, the consequences are thought out without any consideration for human opinion and individual feelings, determinism induces an apathy of each and all of our activities, it brings a blight on all moral endeavour and introduces the most deadly enmity between morality and religion. Then, all redemption is supposed to lie in a fixed miracle; a materialism threatens the substance of the religious life, since good is simply infused into us without being transformed into our own act. All this easily leads to an over-strain and an untruth; when this track of thought is followed, it depicts man as impotent, depraved, and bad, in order to allow the Divine grace to shine all the clearer against such a dark background of human existence. We have thus obtained the unfortunate doctrine of original sin which drew Christianity into Manichæism; and thus we reach the view of Luther that man does not acquire righteousness but rather that righteousness is imputed to him by faith. Such an opinion, if thought out, resolves the great struggle of the world into an appearance and a play.

Such consequences—unavoidable and unbearable at the same time — reveal clearly a mistake in the initial direction of this line of thought. In the last resort, it is a mistaken, anthropomorphic, and inadequate course of thought for religion also, to attempt to heighten the conceptions of the greatness of the Godhead and of the Divine action through the debasement of man and his capacities. This is in the end nothing other than the measurement of the Divine by the standard of man at his worst.

In reality there is only one solution to the problem : the opposition of the Divine and the human has, in the main, to be abandoned, and the development of the one and the strengthening of the other at the same time has to take its place.   The freedom and the self-activity of man are not a withdrawal of the Divine power and the lessening of Divine grace, but they are the verification of these—the highest verification of all.   Morality and religion do not strive for different provinces ; but, rightly understood, morality itself is the main proof of the fundamental fact of religion—of the presence of an Absolute Life.   The fact that man is raised to a level of a definite Spiritual Life over against his own weaknesses and the contradictions of a boundless world, is the greatest of all miracles, for it carries within itself the power of a world above the world.

How all this is possible, how freedom arises out of grace, and self-activity arises out of dependence—this primal phenomenon eludes all explanation.   It has, as the fundamental condition of all Spiritual Life, a universally axiomatic character.   This shows itself as no isolated problem, but as a higher stage of a more general problem, viz., how out of the connections of the world an individual nature of a psychic kind— a feeling and willing nature—has arisen, and has led its own life in opposition to all the environment ?   If we were fortunate enough to solve this problem, we should then be equal to any other.

But what remains a great riddle to speculation has been transformed into a religion by life through its achievements.   Also, even with the great determinists who possessed great natures, this truth has been verified. They were not inactive natures merely waiting upon providence; but even in the proclamation of their highest conceptions and in the shaping of their own inmost nature they were carried as if by a superior power, and became instruments for the fulfilment of their most characteristic aims. The highest achievement of freedom carries within itself the strongest consciousness of dependence. Paul more than any other brought determinism into Christianity; but at the same time he worked more than all his contemporaries. One needs only follow Augustine in his life-work in order to acknowledge him as one of the most active of personalities; and Luther's energy needs no proclamation on the house-top. Further, in wider circles of activity, freedom and dependence can run together; as is proved by Calvinism, to which the entire conviction was present that all has been determined solely and directly by God; and yet such a conviction became the strongest motive for the assertion of independence, and for the breaking forth of fervent work. Thus a problem insoluble by the understanding has been solved by religion.

The solution, however, must not be restricted to those personalities and those epochs where the original welling-up life was strong enough to drive back and to render harmless all the errors of the psychical impulses and of conscious contentment. The solution must be recognised clearly, and must govern the universal configuration of religion. In all this the activity does not revolve around a struggle of bare opinions, but around the content of life. Wherever antagonism between the Godhead and mankind remains operative, the life enters into a dilemma—

into a vacillation to and fro between irreconcilable opposites. On the one hand, we may simply be convinced of our dependence, and then all our activity appears as useless, and, indeed, as a blasphemy ; thus religion becomes almost entirely passive and receives a gloomy, doleful, and unmanly character ; it becomes a danger to the freedom and the energy of life ; it easily engenders, in its turn towards pietism, a dejected and cowed character—a character of painful unveracity wherein the man imagines that he is great in his nothingness, and so superior to another who seems to be conscious of his own powers. All this happens the more the man magnifies and confesses the feeling of the unworthiness of all that he possesses. When, on the other hand, in the reaction against such a disposition of mind a fresh and frank courage of life arises—when the man holds fast the opposites, the previous danger is escaped, and the man feels, unfolds, and enjoys his own energy ; such a feeling heightens to a defiant self-consciousness and to the repudiation of the Divine. The consequence is that culture thus takes a turn against religion, and treats it as a mere expression of weakness and as a refuge for sick souls. But all this leads rapidly to a reaction. The more such a development of culture eliminates from the contents of life everything absolute and all the problems of the Absolute, the more it extinguishes the gleam of the over-world which surrounds our existence. Then life, in spite of all its activities, becomes inwardly shallower and emptier, until at last it turns again home—turns in search of a content, in search of a spiritual self-conservation within the domain of religion.

15

If such a change for the worse in the realm of culture is to be traced in our day, the more necessary it behoves us to raise religion above this situation by means of the nature of its *substance*, in order that it may assert its superiority above the mere mentality of the day, and in order that eternal truth may be rightly held up against all the fluctuations and errors of human existence.

(δ) *The Psychic Connections of Religion.*—It is a main feature in our method of investigation to differentiate clearly between the foundation of the spiritual contents in the characteristic connections of the spiritual world, and their stimulations in psychic existence; or, in other words, to hold separate a noological and a psychological treatment. Thus the previous investigation of the religious problem needs a completion through the presence of the psychic motives which prepare and incline man for religion.

The discovery of a pointed contradiction in our life—the strong contradiction between need and reality—constitutes the starting-point of all the transition to religion; for how could we in any other way come to strive so eagerly to reach beyond the province of that experience which threatens to break the connection of the world and the unity of our own existence? This contrast is in the first place a fact of feeling. Feeling constructs the psychic starting-point of religion; but it certainly remains fundamentally different from the spiritual root of religion. But the observation of a contrast—the painful discovery of a contradiction—has an indispensable hypothesis in spiritual things. Such a con-

tradiction could not have entered into the life had
not some kind of movement been already awakened
in us—some kind of impetus after a higher kind of
happiness been initiated; for purely external misfor-
tunes produce no shock in the deepest recesses of the
soul and engender no feeling of the real nature of the
hindrance.   We see often, however, in the political and
social spheres, the most stubborn evils and grievances
enduring for a great length of time without engendering a feeling of pain, and without calling forth a
strong resentment.   The inertia is even so great
that the external events pass over the soul without
any reaction on its part; and the immediate impressions do not link themselves together to form a
Whole.   But there is involved in the discovery of
the contradiction some kind of longing after happiness: a positive need of life is the first thing found
in the foundation, driving life upon the track of
religion.

If such a need of life met with no hindrance, no
kind of entanglement would arise; if the opposition
could be conquered through external circumstances,
though not at once yet in the course of time, life
and striving would be held fast by such external
circumstances rather than raised above them.   A
breach can only take place when the opposition appears as insurmountable—insurmountable for present
and future, for achievement and for hope.   In such
a situation either the striving is to discontinue a
hopeless struggle, or it must open out new avenues
of a completely transforming view of the world and
of life.   A closer investigation of that wherein the
hindrance and the problem are discovered shows

how deep this inward revolution goes, and in what directions it carries the man. We see in the course of history itself more and more elements moving from the outward into the inward and thus deepening the inward itself. Although in the beginning all this might have been the external entanglement which our own energy could not remove and which called for supernatural aid, yet soon the *inward* condition becomes explicit and insists on a spiritual redemption. Also, it makes an important difference whether the entanglement is discovered in what a man thinks or in what he does; whether the contradiction roots itself in an existence laid upon the man by a destiny which does not correspond with and even contradicts his inmost nature, or whether the hindrances belong to the soul itself and whether man can sanction his own striving and being in the attempts to remove them. In all this the pain becomes violent, and the awakened soul is hurried along if the impressions and feelings remain unscattered but unite into a Whole of experience and judgment and work with the energy of a Whole; and through this revelation of the nature of our life the whole level of our ordinary existence becomes insufficient and even intolerable.

This judgment in its turn will reach its greatest emphasis, and the situation of the soul will reach its greatest tension when the main cause of our malady is seen to consist not in that we can never reach worthy aims, and must always remain in a state of imperfection; but in that the very aims themselves are now in doubt, that they promise no definite happiness, and in that incessant courage and

work appear worthless.   If, then, such aims do not
suffice, what shall we hope for, and whither shall we
turn ?

The crisis now comes to a full outburst ; the
previous situation is seen through as untenable, and
it now becomes necessary to go backward or forward.
Either every striving after happiness and after the
noblest things has to be viewed as a tragic error,
and has to surrender itself to a total dissolution ; or
a great turn results, a new point of departure is won
for the life, and a new world is discovered.   All
attempts to weaken this *Either—Or* lead to sickly
compromises, to the deadening of the feelings, and to
the one-sidedness of life itself.

But through such a turn to his inmost nature,
there originates in man a critical struggle concerning
Being and non-being.   Often enough has the negation
conquered with innumerable individuals, with whole
times and epochs, and has gained the overhand in
the particular province of religion as is shown so
evidently in Buddhism.   But it has not always
conquered, for the affirmation, too, has become a
world-power, and it is this affirmation which rightly
preserves human life and effort.   The point where
such a decision falls on the individual—and it is this
fact which occupies us here—lies largely on the other
side of the province of " grounds " and aims, and
there appears in its existence something axiomatic,
original, and elevated.   The decision is concerned
with the question as to whether an impetus for life is
to awaken—an impetus that no upheaval can destroy,
and which shows that, with all the surrender of the
natural self and all the overthrow of prior happiness,

something remains in man—something he cannot destroy. It cannot be destroyed because man acknowledges it not as a special possession of his own but as the inward presence of a new world which makes itself felt and efficacious in the greatest catastrophes of life, and indeed, is able to grow on account of these very things. Through such a turn the presence and mystery of the suffering itself become the beginning of an elevation beyond it.

Thus we discover the co-operation of two factors in what leads man to religion, and in what exercises a power over his soul, viz., a deeper discovery of the hindrances of the world, and an iron energy over against the hindrances right up to the achievement of a new world. We saw how the discovery of the actual situation could not have been made without some kind of ebullition of the active energy from within. And it is this stirring existence which drives the energy beyond its natural initial stage, stimulates it to a progressive depth, and advances the physical tension of life into a metaphysical tension. The whole of this is a movement of life all along the line through difficult hindrances; it is the assertion, and, at the same time, the transformation of a Yea in the midst of the strongest negation. Indeed, it is the holding fast of a Yea in the Nay; it is an ascent of the nature whose freshness and truth can only be asserted when both sides are held forth and ever anew are experienced. Thus there is set forth a dialectic not of ideas but of life—a focusing of deep experience and of manly energy and a purification of one through the other, an ever-freer elevation above the antithesis of bare natural energy

and effeminate weakness, and finally the dawning of
a heroism of the most inward kind.   All this sets a
world against a world, and out of the catastrophe
itself a new life is born.

(ε) *The Characteristic Features of the Religion of
the Spiritual Life.*—Religion does not deal with the
conservation of man as mere man, but with the conservation of the Spiritual Life in man; for in connection with religion there stands in question the
winning of a definite Spiritual Life; and religion
must set forth in a characteristic manner the particular features of such a life as well as its total-view.
In reference to these particular features we must
present at least some of them.

1. Where religion is directed upon the winning of
a new and elevated life superior to all human impulses,
its sublime nature must contend with special energy
for a province beyond all human interests and parties.
Religion is never concerned in a Yea or a Nay
with political or social problems.   Religion has
nothing whatever to do as to whether monarchy
or republic, individualistic or socialistic presentation
of economic relation, is the better condition of things;
and he who draws religion into these spheres, even if
he is of the opinion that one of them is useful for
humanity, will find an opponent who thinks quite as
strongly in a contrary direction.   No less injurious is
it to exploit religion in the interests of a political or
social radicalism, or to defame it in the interests of
the privileged classes.   How meanly would one think
of the nature of man if religion meant no more
than this, and how little would man think of himself
if the abandonment of spirituality and, along with

this, the abandonment of the content and meaning of his own life came about so easily !

2. We have already shown how the Spiritual Life with its development of a reality discovered within itself goes behind the psychic form of life with all its ramifications ; and how it has reduced the whole province, in so far as such a province had connections with such a life, into a mere appearance. Wherever this truth suffers eclipse, there are called forth difficult entanglements and passionate discords which affect deeply the configuration of religion.

Thus, inveterate intellectualism turns the greatness of religion into a hybrid of many colours. Religion should be a fact of the whole man and of his own decision ; though it may fail to possess more than a purely intellectual character. Through this, the main fact of religion is stunted in its growth, and conscience and conviction are oppressed. This is most apparent in the conception of faith. The welfare of the soul can never link itself to faith unless that faith means more than an authoritatively transmitted doctrine, and unless the man in the inmost substance of his soul stretches forth towards the belief. The ecclesiastical form of religion has succeeded but little in working out this connection of belief ; and is unable to succeed on account of its confusion between the *substance* and the *existence-form* of the Spiritual Life. The Divine Life, whose reality stood in question, transforms itself unfortunately into a doctrine—a doctrine of the redemption of the soul and of " last things," but still *a doctrine* ; and the more such a doctrine surmounts reason and even contradicts reason, the greater seems the sacrifice of the power of affirmation and of the heroism of the character. Now, heroism certainly belongs to religion—more heroism, indeed, than belongs to any other fact in the world—but this heroism must set itself in the right position, for otherwise the valour becomes a caprice and the consolidation becomes a torpor. Such heroism is not brought about through any kind of doctrine which constructs the object of life, but through the presence of an Absolute Life in our own nature; consequently belief is no mere agreement with any doctrine, but there is involved in it an ascent of the whole of our nature, a longing for the heights, and a progressive certitude of such heights out of the energy of the Divine Life. Thus, faith in its foundation rests upon one thing alone; but that one thing is the nucleus of a new world. At the same time, faith is naturally a source of new convictions; but these convictions will not be developed without ranking themselves with the general position of the Spiritual Life and without utilising the experiences of life.

Such a quality of faith alone makes it clear how its contrary — doubt — can play so great a part in religion as in reality it does. So long as faith rests upon bare doctrine, it remains unintelligible how doubt agitates the soul so powerfully, and how it can shatter the life so deeply. We have seen, however, how in the ancient world that, when the religious problem stood in the background of the Spiritual Life, doubt and scepticism were recommended by clever men as the best expedients for the comfort of the soul. But Christianity is something quite other than all this; because, through the relationship to

God, the gain of a new nature—the salvation of the threatened soul—became the great quest. But if the matter deals with the question concerning spiritual existence or non-existence, the strength of doubt leads quickly to despair. The shrinkage becomes so painful and the coercion so intolerable when orthodoxy places doctrine between us and life, and decides as to the place of church dogmas in connection with the welfare and salvation of man.

A complete driving out of intellectualism from this and other religious conceptions (as, for instance, in the ordinary conception of revelation) is necessary in the urgent need for religion. But such a conquest will only take place through the recognition of the elements of truth in intellectualism, especially in its desire after a world of thought; it will not take place through putting ourselves in an entirely contrary position to the world of thought, or through attempting to found religion upon bare feeling or will. For if the conquest is touched with the suspicion that it is only reachable through the setting-up of a contrary valid doctrine, it is easy to see, on the other hand, that bare feeling or will yields a spiritual substance quite as little as bare knowledge. Strong subjective feelings and strong subjective acts of will may contain but very little spiritual substance. The appearance only of a success is reached in such a manner; for, often unobserved, something becomes a spurious image of what is deeper, more essential, and more substantial, and which makes its appearance as feeling or will, but which does not reach the higher stage of a feeling or willing entity. What brings the opposition of intellectualism and voluntarism to naught are the problems within the Spiritual Life; these problems deal with the different sides and tasks of life which on the surface are at variance with one another and play against one another, whilst in reality they depend on one another and belong to an encompassing Whole. If something did lie beneath and proceed out of all the "isms," we could say that *Noeticism*[1] alone is able to afford a sound basis for religion; and it is out of this noetic synthesis that the struggle against the discord begins.

3. We have seen that religion has to do with the whole of life, and that it is pledged to uplift this whole; therefore it does more than construct a special province over against the remaining portions of life; it must strike its effects in all directions, and it works less directly upon the particular provinces than upon the transformation of the total-life. All the direct effects of religion, as, for example, upon science, art, the state, have grave dangers and lead easily to coercion and contraction, and are rightly rejected. But it is a fundamental mistake, when such direct actions are rejected, to reject the indirect actions as well. Since religion transforms the whole man, it will also change, through its ramifications into the whole nature, problems into energies, and aims into points of attack. But such changes do not occur through any arbitrary command from the outside, but through a tranquil—and, certainly, a mighty—effect

---

[1] The Substantive "Noeticism" is not found in English Philosophy. The terms "noetic synthesis" and "noetic consciousness" are found, but in a somewhat different sense. *Cf.* Stout's *Analytic Psychology*, vol. ii. ch. v.; Martineau's *Types of Ethical Theory*, vol. ii. pp. 443–445, where he deals with Cudworth's "intelligible ideas" (νοήματα).—TRANSLATOR.

from within without. Conceived of in its universality (although this universality does not form the final conclusions of religion) religion needs no special organisation, but is able through an invisible sway to penetrate into the whole work of life. Indeed, the deeper it works, the less it steps into publicity, and the more securely it signifies nothing other than the tranquil and yet powerful soul of the whole. Thus in the great souls whose convictions were filled with such a universal nature of religion, the incomprehensiveness and the inscrutableness of the Highest Essence do not discourage and lower the pressure of such souls, but work both in a gravitating and in an elevating direction. Thus, we find the deeply-religious Plato stating that it is difficult to know God, and impossible completely to communicate with Him ; and also Goethe affirms that a man hardly confesses his belief in a Divine Nature without at the same time confessing the inscrutableness of that Nature.

But still in conformity with this, all the conceptions of religion must carry the character of universality ; they must extend themselves over the whole life and, through this, fasten together and strengthen what does not proceed to a full development through the isolation of the various elements of life. Human life, right down to the abyss of pain and sin, is full of evidences of a superhuman Divine life which in manifold ways appears as an elevation above all smallness, as an illumination of the darkness, and as a dawning of love and mercy in the midst of all egoistic instincts and impulses. Religion must gather together, through the energy of its universal nature, such external and scattered effects, and

understand and revere them as parts of a more general
life.   Such *universal* religion does not exclude a
turning to *characteristic* religion ; but if religion is
to extend its power over the whole of life, its
values must possess an all-comprehensiveness and an
omnipresence.

This is shown, for example, in the idea of sacrifice.
Sacrifice is a supremely important conception in
religion, since only by its acceptance does religion
attain to full seriousness.   For without a thorough
renunciation, and indeed, without a seeming collapse,
there is no secure ascent to a new summit —
no attainment of a real life.   But let not sacrifice
be limited by religion to specific religious performances, but let religion reveal it as present throughout life, and let it weld together and inwardly raise
all this sacrifice.   As the energy of love is measured
in human circles by the greatness of the sacrifice it
is capable of bringing forth, so there is no genuine
movement towards truth without denial and renunciation—without an inward sacrifice.   But in the
survey of the whole it becomes clear that sacrifice
does not restrict itself to the surrender of this or
that good, but offers nothing less than the whole
natural impulses of life.   When religion works in
such a manner that we are made to see and to experience the Whole in the parts, the great in the
small, it works therewith for the purification and
sanctification of life right down to its most insignificant details.

It is similar with the conception of faith.   Faith
which the customary mode of religion confines
far too much within an isolated province, and which

it conceives in far too intellectualistic a manner,
extends, in reality, its strengthening and elevating
energy to the whole range of life. Faith, according to the customary teaching of religion, has for
its object something invisible and seemingly impossible. But where was there ever a progressive
striving in spiritual things which did not, at the
first glance, appear impossible, and which did not
believe in its own capacity for exaltation and in the
possibility of creating a new man? How, without
this, would any kind of scientific or æsthetic creativeness of an elevated kind be conceivable? How any
confiding love? How any joyous action for man's
purification in spite of all the superficiality and all the
meanness of shallow experience? And, again, all
faith has the characteristic that we cannot become
its possessors through the might and main of our
own labours, but that it rather devolves upon us as a
favour, and must be offered to us as a free gift. This
is so, not only with faith in another, but also with
faith in ourselves, in our tasks, and in our life-work.
Nowhere do we enter into genuine work and creativeness without a conviction of an axiomatic character,
which refuses to be analysed into reasons and which,
indeed, precedes all such reasons. What, however,
is desired at the single points, and is there affirmed,
though often unconsciously and unwillingly, gains a
clear light only in its integration into a Whole,
and through the recognition of the inner presence
of an infinite energy from which an indestructible
trust and a capacity for unlimited ascent can proceed. Again, it is religion which has to raise to
the power and clearness of a principle what indeed

now penetrates the whole of life, but which there,
in the breadth of life, remains manifoldly scattered
and obscured. Thus, while religion integrates and
brings into activity as a whole whatever of noble
and elevating force lies hidden in our lives, it effects
a transfiguration of life without denying its dark
side; it shows the Divine in the things nearest at
hand without falsely idealising the ordinary situation
of life.

4. This integrating energy would prepare many
a danger for religion if there did not co-exist with
it an acuteness of discrimination; and such a dis-
criminating energy is developed by religion even
of the general kind which occupies us here. For
as certainly as religion aims at the whole of the
Spiritual Life, does it desire such a life in its full
purity; but it is able to do this only through a
decisive discrimination in the human situation between genuine spirituality and its mere semblance.
Because religion dives into a substantial Spiritual
Life and constructs its nature from the Life-process,
while it will exclude much as being adulterated, it
will find more depth in what it approves as genuine;
and it will raise the genuine out of its isolation to
a union, out of its chaos to a cosmos, and out
of its merely parasitical quality to a characteristic
act and full possession of the spirit. But a hard
struggle has to take place in order to carry through
a true Spiritual Life against that semi-spirituality
which satisfies the ordinary situation of human
life, and which treacherously makes man feel comfortable. This is nothing less than a struggle for
reality against appearance, a struggle for a true

spiritual culture over against a merely human culture. True, the amount of life, now restricted to its
genuine constituents, is thus greatly reduced ; but in
what remains incomparably more is seen. There
arises now a hard conflict with the customary mode
of thought, especially because this mode of thought
attributes spirituality, and with it greatness and
dignity, to its forms of life, as though they were the
latter's natural properties ; whereas religion already
clearly shows that only a certain kernel of spirituality,
or a movement towards spirituality, is present from
the first, and that these have to attain to more by
a hard struggle. But, at the same time, a new
order of things and the presence of a new world
appear in the Spiritual Life. Man, indeed, is not,
in the whole of his existence, straight-away a personality ; there only lies implanted in him a power to
become a personality—a power over against a nature
of a very different kind, and which has to win its
way through such a nature. But this becoming a
personality is now recognised as an emancipation from
all existential dependence upon an external point and
an elevation to a self-life of a universal kind. Morality
signifies now not a quality pertaining to man as a
natural being, since what the ordinary life manifests
in the way of social instincts and of occasional sympathy forms, at the most, no more than a step
preliminary to morality and can be ranked without
hesitation as a mere continuation of the animal level.
Genuine morality does not arise earlier than at the
stage of the Spiritual Life, and it is a matter of dispute
how much or how little of this we meet in human life
by itself ; but, much or little, morality appears in our

domain, and along with it there appears a kingdom of a higher kind. So that the man in the transformation may lose some of the experiences of the natural level, but certainly his nature has gained in depth and breadth through such a transformation.

Man has been well termed an "historical nature," but most of what is termed his history is distinguished too little from what is found in the changes and deposits of nature. History, understood as distinctively mental and human, never originates through the bare succession of time; but throughout in the sense that something is held fast, experienced, and its nature brought into an inner connection. Such an achievement, however, can be effected only through the presence of a standard superior to time, which creates the effect of an order of things above time. But with such elevation history transforms itself from being a mere fact to being a difficult task. And the matter does not stand otherwise in connection with the problem of society. Society, too, in the distinctively human and mental sense, is not any ready-made thing, but has to be evolved, and to it belongs an inner unity of life—a comprehensive life. Little enough of this finds its way to our experience; but the little that does find its way refers back to an order of things superior to nature and its scattered elements.

There is thus universally imbedded in human life something deeper, although it may appear first of all only in the faintest manner; and it is religion which raises up, binds, and energises this deeper quality. Thus, religion everywhere effects a dissection of human life; sets the life, through the working out of its deep, into a portentous ferment, and calls it to a

16

strenuous struggle. Religion, in all this, is very far from explaining life as being on its natural plane something superior or even tolerable ; far more through its very elevation religion casts a gloom over the provinces of life with all their hindrance and their shallowness; but in all this natural opposition to religion, religion cannot be destroyed, for the presence of an Absolute Life verifies a fixed nucleus and the certainty of a conquest.

Thus religion stands above the opposites of optimism and pessimism, for it is able to acknowledge the total fulness of wrong without forfeiting the joy of belief or even diminishing it. Indeed, religion has won the hearts of men especially in times of bewilderment and dejection. The clear call of an Absolute Life must bring the wide differences of our existence to consciousness and, along with this, work for the heightening of the suffering. The contradictions of our existence appear, when the situation is seen as it really is, far too pointed, and the unreason far too powerful to be disguised by an optimistic mood. But the clearest discovery of the contradictions and their agony cannot create a hopeless pessimism ; but it is precisely the appearance of a new world—the presence of an Infinite Life—which makes our ordinary existence inadequate.

This twofold aspect gives the total effect of religion a twofold character. On the one side, it means a loosening, a freeing, a redemption from the old world ; and on the other side, an elevation into a new one. A uniform development and an incessant reciprocal action of both sides do not take place if the life is coerced and is morose, or if it considers the main fact in a superficial manner.

Further, inasmuch as religion appears as a kingdom of continuous development—as that which constructs the fundamental facts on their Divine side, and as that which is present in the inmost depth of the human soul—it has to be won ever anew in human life, and ever anew it has to be sought, struggled for, and perfected. Thus the fact becomes a task ; the possession becomes a problem ; and with the differences of the points of departure, the one and same life can include certainty and doubt, calm and tempest, bliss and sorrow.

Thus, through and through, religion proves itself a kingdom of opposites. When it steps out of such opposites, it destroys effectually the turbidity and the evanescence of ordinary commonplace life, and separates clearly the lights and shadows from one another. It sets our life between the sharpest contrasts, and engenders the most powerful feelings and the most mighty movements ; it shows the dark abyss in our nature, but also shows illumined peaks ; it opens out infinite tasks, and brings ever to an awakening a new life with its movement against the ordinary self. It does not render our existence lighter, but it makes it richer, more eventful, and greater ; it enables man to experience cosmic problems within his own soul in order to struggle for a new world, and, indeed, in order to gain such a genuine world as his own proper life.

3. *The Proof and Confirmation of Religion*

(a) *Religion and Science.* — We have hitherto followed the main lines of our investigation without considering the side-paths, and without discovering the relationship of our material to the remaining world of thought as that world is represented by science. It is impossible for us to withdraw entirely from this task, and to pass silently by the facts which at all times have come to the surface in connection with religion, and which have discovered a concealed contradiction. And this they have often done in no spirit of light-hearted jest, but in deep seriousness; for the facts of science have struggled against religion because science regarded religion as a falsification of reality and a disfigurement of life. Science and religion often appear as sworn enemies; each develops a truth out of its own province, and each can present only its own truth; each traces out an image of reality, and these images seem to preclude one the other. The one seizes special experiences of humanity, and indicates from this point as its ruling centre all the spaciousness of the All. The other holds itself fast to a Whole, and interprets out of this all the content of human life. Religion is inclined to reduce science to a soulless sphere; whilst science readily interprets religion as anthropomorphism—as an illegitimate inner mirroring of the reality through human presentations and interests. The attained objectivity of science appears to religion as cold and unfeeling; whilst the particular inwardness of life appears to science as subjective exaggeration and fancy. Religion does not believe itself able to guard its independence without the creation of a knowing-organ in belief; and even so it meets with the hardest contradiction, and often falls within its own province to the boundary between knowledge and belief where all kinds of entanglements prevail.

The adherents of religion are at variance among themselves; some draw the ideal world of religion quite close to knowledge, whilst others separate most pointedly knowledge and belief. Thus the struggle surges hither and thither through the centuries and the millenniums; but each situation is ill understood without the historical connections. The defence of religion to-day is strengthened by the rebound from the intellectualism which for a long time checked the ideal world of religion. From the beginning, the doctrine of the Christian Church was strongly leavened with intellectualism; in the Middle Ages the intellect served less as a foundation than as a check; and, in the period of the *Aufklärung*, science disengaged itself from all external authority and believed itself able to develop the Spiritual Life as well as religion out of itself, and speculation heightened and ennobled such an undertaking. Now, at least in the opinion of our day, speculation has collapsed, and the insufficiency of intellectualism has appeared with convincing clearness; we not only mistrust the ability of the applied intellect, but it seems also to us to rob us of a religion of true immediacy and inspiration. Therefore we range ourselves entirely on the other side, and in the founding of religion put the intellect in a secondary place, and even partially disconnect it. Thus we obtain the turn to feeling—to the explanation of religion as merely an affair of " personal " life, and to the attempt to derive the religious content from judgments of value, etc. Such a course appears natural enough, and has some degree of truth in its favour; but it is afflicted with a marked one-sidedness, and seeks to accommodate itself to such a retrogression.

Religion in reality dare not isolate itself from the universal world of ideas. It dare not do this for its own sake. Its vocation throughout is essentially and indispensably to bring forth the final and all-encompassing truth; and it cannot possibly be one thing by the side of other things, for it must be the soul of the Whole. But how could religion verify itself as such without occupying itself in a fundamental manner with the whole world of ideas? Unless it does this, not only does its truth remain set in painful doubt, but through such an isolation the danger menaces also its content; and thus the content is unable to free itself sufficiently from the petty-human mode and from selfishness; for in the midst of all the waves and bubblings of feeling, and in the midst of all the agitation of the individual, the content wins too little of a spiritual substance, and, consequently, exercises too little transforming energy on the whole human situation. Such a substance is attainable only by wrestling from a Whole to a Whole. Religion, however, undertakes this feat, and, consequently, comes to some kind of agreement with science concerning the Yea and the Nay of things.

Whether such an agreement is possible depends before all on a more accurate statement of the meaning of science and of religion. Such a meaning alone can decide whether what appeared at the first glance an irreconcilable conflict can be brought to a happy settlement. Let us see first of all what the religion of the Spiritual Life for which we contend signifies concerning the whole of reality, in order that we may try to discover the method of proof. Here an

independent Spiritual Life superior to the world is
asserted as the ground and kernel of all reality.
The Spiritual Life can be autonomous only as a total-
life—as an inner connection; but its superiority to
the world reaches the level of self-reliance *not after*
the event of becoming superior to the world, but,
according to the whole of our investigation, this
self-reliance carries such a superiority in itself, and
proves it through its own development over against
a very different kind of world.   This Absolute
Spiritual Life signifies not an isolated province, but
wills to be the foundation and the apex of all reality.
But this cannot be asserted without relegating nature,
and, most of all, the near ordinary existence, to a
subsidiary world—to a lower level.   There is no
religion without an analysis of the reality and without
stepping beyond bare nature; for a merely immanent
religion can announce and command only a painful
weakness and a halfness of thought.   But through such
a turn as we have already seen the whole reality
gains an inner connection and a depth.   Even the
movement of our world appears, at least in its decisive
phases, not as a simple development of the higher out
of the lower, but as a further driving-power out of
the Whole of the All.   Through such a turn to the
world, religion inevitably confronts science, and the
meeting of the two becomes quite early a collision.
Religion not only holds certain assertions over against
those of science; but works for their promulgation,
furthers the treatment of the world-problem, and thus
becomes itself saturated with the efforts and objections
of science.   Religion is an irreconcilable enemy of the
naturalism which sets up nature as the whole of

reality, and which treats the spiritual world as a bare epiphenomenon; it is, too, an enemy of the history which is unable to overcome the mere flux of time, and consequently unable to climb above the relativity of the scientific view to an eternal and absolute truth; and it is finally an enemy of the psychology which resolves the life of the soul into elements of the lowest common denominator, and which thus is not able to bring forth an independent Spiritual Life. In its connection with all these, religion develops a thorough-going affirmation, and, indeed, an aggressive character; it prescribes, with a strong decision, a definite track for thought and life; and he who seeks with special zeal to weaken the fact that religion itself is able to sustain a joyous and friendly disposition towards the most varied expressions of thought, shows a dimness of his own mind and a weakness of his own character. No energetic Yea without a decisive Nay must hold valid, especially for religion with its assertion of the final kernel and meaning of reality. Religion is intolerant, and must be intolerant, not against men—for every man is an infinity, and thus far supersedes all forms and confessions—but against a shallow course of thought and the flimsiness of its egotistical nature.

Upon what, then, does religion—meeting with so many high demands—" ground " its own rights, and by what means does it verify its own truth? It deals with a unique fundamental truth, viz. with the reality of an Absolute Spiritual Life within our own circle. Evidently such a Life cannot originate merely out of individual data, whether of nature or of history; it does not allow of being evolved out

of the natural world.   It is only within the Life-
process itself, as its own foundation and further
development, that it may be brought forth.   Consequently, it is concerned not so much with the
seeking for new things as with the discovering of the
new in the things we already know; it is concerned not
so much with ready-made results, as with the plunging
into the existing movement of a current ; it aims not
at discovering a world already existing merely by the
side with our present world, but at securing for itself
the depth of the reality which will necessitate the
reduction of our present world to a secondary level.

The decisive thing in connection with all this is
the advance of life itself.   The act must precede the
proof ; the reality of the representative act transmits
the main proof of religion.   Individual propositions
or performances are not alone here in question, but
the possession of the Spiritual Life as a Whole, as
independent, as superior to the world, and as our
adopted situation in such a life.   What now is it
that drives the man hither ?   Nothing other than an
acknowledgment of the Spiritual Life as his own
nature, and the placing of the centre of gravity of his
life and existence in it.   As soon as this happens,
and as soon as we possess an inward relationship to
the world and to ourselves, the man can do no other
than bind together the Spiritual Life as a Whole and
as a self-reliant life ; and thus he is sure to reach
an inwardness which will make clear the contrasts of
life as well as his own superiority over against the
environing world.   The decisive main proof lies
in the fact that an autonomous Spiritual Life
arises in man and in humanity ; and that we are

able to discover our deepest being and construct our new world through a process of selection and rejection as participators in such a Life. This proof, however, needs no minute adjustment, for it enters into every soul in the form of immediacy whenever such a soul struggles to step out of the bondage of the world, struggles to create its own laws of ascent, and to enter into its true personal life. Through this the life gains an absolute certainty. Next to this in importance stands the fact that the corroboration results through the demonstration that the Spiritual Life is barren in its ramifications until it roots itself as a Whole in an Absolute Life; for there is possible neither art nor science, neither right nor morality, without the fundamental truth which comes to expression in religion. The Spiritual Life is not a Whole in its ordinary existence; but only as an elevated arrangement of the things which present themselves within and without. But when it is not a Whole, it inevitably breaks in pieces in the isolated situations of life. Such a state of affairs concerning the Spiritual Life is a testimony to the truth of religion. We are able to give up religion, but only if we give up at the same time our Spiritual Life, the spiritual character of our existence, and our spiritual individuality. But is it possible for anyone to abandon religion so completely as all this?

Such a condition of things makes it impossible to win anyone to religion through the mere intellect; for the problem lies deeper, and the mode of intellectual activity—right down to the heart of the problem—depends on the total Life-process. He who places himself in the position of a mere spectator of the great world and accepts his life as an assigned kind of fate, he who undertakes no struggle concerning a "becoming" independence and concerning an inward relationship to things, cannot take into himself the Whole with all its problems, cannot participate in a cosmic life, and is unable to carry forward the energetic movement of religion. But he who has discovered an inner relationship with the world and with his own self, he who is held fast by the inner movement of life and is led to an inner union with reality, obtains a new insight of reality and becomes fully certain of the truth of this reality— far more certain than of the axioms of the sciences. For with such axioms the matter dealt with is that of detached portions of life and of the work of thought; but in religion we are dealing with the vindication of life as a Whole. Nowhere more than here does the movement itself prove the validity of the presupposition from which it issues.

Through such a consolidation in the deepest "ground" of life, religion can confidently look forward to an understanding with science. This is certainly not so simple as it seems, for we often witness to-day a pointed dualistic mode of thought. This mode of thought believes itself able to solve the problem after a fashion, but much rather shuns it, and it presents us with the notion that science is concerned solely with the world of experience, and, along with this, that it has to contract itself into a mere relative knowledge. From this point of view religion is supposed to deal with final "grounds" and "ends" alone; thus both spheres of science and religion fall entirely outside one another, and only an entanglement can issue from any attempt to bring them nearer to one another. Either science transforms its empirical constructions into metaphysical constructions, as has actually happened with our speculative scientific investigations; or, on the other hand, religion touches the province of science. All this contains much that is true, but it does not exhaust the facts. Science is not a summation of rules, but develops a characteristic course of thought; and this course of thought can very well come into conflict with religion, or rather, with religion of a special historical kind. Religion, however, cannot explain the standard which it accepts and to which it brings its proofs without coming to a settlement with the whole of science.

This problem acquires a driving-power especially through history. The traditional kind of religion and also of Christianity has grown in intimate connection with a view of the world which has been annulled by modern investigation. Indeed, as was shown in the introductory part of this book, it is not only destroyed in individual places but in its whole mode of thought. The older mode of thought appears to modern investigation as a thorough anthropomorphism — as a projection of human greatness into the environing world. Modern science, through its discovery of inflexible laws and through the restriction of all phenomena to causal sequence, has rendered the old view impossible; it has driven the soul out of such a view of the world and threatens to do similarly in the province of religion. Thus positivism especially, with its three stages of religious, metaphysical, and positive thought, formulates such a plan; and attempts

to place religion on one side as a childish stage of
human development which has no right whatever in
our day.   Can we deny that such a view reaches, too,
far beyond the special circle of positivism, and that
a prevalent disposition of our day views religion as
a stage on the road to be disregarded in the general
movement of humanity and its new view of the
world ?   Now, the protest has to be made that
religion, in its inmost nature, is not a view of the
world but the evolution of a new life—an ascent to
a new stage of reality.   But such a new life carries
in itself convictions of the whole of reality ; and
these convictions, together with the whole of the
standard, must somehow be scientifically vindicated
against such a positivistic mode of thought.   Such
a vindication is really to be found, and it is a vindication which makes clear that it itself opposes from
the outset the pettiness in human nature ; it is a
vindication that the development of the physical and
mental sciences, viewed from within, signifies only
the conclusions of mental constructions ; and, finally,
it proves that if something is lost on the one side,
something of incomparably greater value is won on
the other.

Philosophy shows us that reality does not exist
for us merely at hand ; it exists only in so far as
it becomes our own experience.   Philosophy also
shows that a scientific and mental configuration is
not reached unless a new outline of reality is traced
out in the Whole ; and that a new foundation is
won only when there has resulted a new connection
of the manifold in accordance with the laws of the
mind.   Thus nature becomes a mental experience

and a subject of scientific work only in so far as it touches us with individual impressions not merely from the outside, and only when these impressions are combined into a total-view; and such can arise only from within through our mental organisation. History in the human and mental sense, as has so often been shown, originates in no way through a mere succession of events and an accumulation of effects, but only when a superior standpoint experiences, comprehends, and values the phenomena through a separation of the essential from the non-essential. Our own life of the soul could not be surveyed and brought to a unity did we not in the kernel of our nature stand above the bare succession of events, and had not this succession a background for itself. In all this there is developed an inwardness of a mental and spiritual kind, which is all along the line different from the merely subjective nature. The subjective nature remains under the power of the opposites of subject and object; but the mental and spiritual nature seeks to overcome this opposition through a supreme formation of reality. The former adapts itself to the mere-human; the latter adapts itself to the Spiritual Life, and through it alone can man possess an elevated self-life. Evidently such a turn from the naïve situation of life is no mere natural growth but involves an inverted order of things, and this naïve situation of life appears now a kind of Ptolemaic conduct of life; for, instead of viewing life from without within, it is now viewed from within without.

In all this there is vindication for a standpoint of an independent Spiritual Life, as is represented and

made a main fact by religion ; and again, religious
history appears in a new light.   True, the early
anthropomorphic forms get more and more dissolved ;
but in their place a spiritual form is gained and the
movement to the spiritualising of religion is not prescribed from without, but arises mainly from religion's
own inward longing after truth.   Thus, religion
proceeds from external observances to inner religious-
ness, from the self-conservation of the natural man
to a salvation of spiritual values and a redemption
of the soul, from a duty towards isolated aspects of
the Spiritual Life to the raising of such a Life as
a Whole.   The positivistic mode of thought sees
in this the loss and not the gain ; it fails to see
the rise of a spiritual inwardness over against a
subjective one, because such a mode of thought
directs its attention to external results and not to
inward experiences, and because, over its dealings
with the results of the Spiritual Life, it forgets
the Spiritual Life itself.   The logical conclusion of
such a mode of thought is to resolve man into a
mere machine—a complicated reckoning-machine—
and such machines can be constructed.   Only the
mystery would remain, how such a machine could
produce the great revolution from a naïve to a
scientific, and from a natural to a spiritual, condition
of life.

So far, however, as science works out the central
phenomenon of the Spiritual Life, and illumines the
world from such a standpoint, it becomes speculation.
Thus, religion cannot lack such speculation for its
own scientific development.   But speculation needs
religion still more urgently.   For the aim of specula-

tion is futile from its very foundation, and it becomes
a vain assumption, unless there exists a hope of finding, in contrast with merely human presentations,
a universally-valid thought. But how could such
a thought be possible without the immanence of an
Absolute Life in our circle? So that from of old
religion and speculation have been in close contact;
in all speculation a religious element is easily to be
discovered; and religion has lost in breadth and depth
whenever it has placed all speculation on one side.
True, with the divergence in their starting-points,
quarrels have not been wanting; but they were quarrels
between friends who, in all their differences, strove
for a final mutual understanding, and who could not
do without each other. Speculation and religion
presuppose an inner movement of life; this movement cannot be forced upon anyone, but it can be
shown that, without it, no Spiritual Life in the Whole
and no genuine spirituality are possible. The words
of Plotinus are valid in connection with all this:
"The doctrine reaches as far as the road and its
course; but the intuition is the possession of him
alone who chooses to see."

(β) *General Considerations.*—If religion primarily
deals with the inward ascent of life to a Whole—
with our apprehension of the Spiritual Life as our
real self—then the inward inertness of man constitutes the strongest resistance and the most stubborn
hindrance experienced by religion. Such inertness is
satisfied with scattered fragments of life; it remains in
a merely external relationship to reality, and undertakes no struggle for its appropriation. Accordingly,
in a time of marked expansion as is the present, it is

easy to understand how religion may often appear as
a tissue of illusions; in the absence of a movement
to a Whole, the opposite opinion would be surprising.
But this inner inertness of life would never have
assumed such self-complacency and made a virtue out
of the calamity unless there had gone along with it a
great confusion of thought, implying the possibility
of solving the essential spiritual problems without a
movement to the Whole, and hence without religion.
It is remarkable how often men here turn against
religion that which, without the independence and
superiority of the Spiritual Life, as championed by
religion, becomes simply untenable.   Thus, morality
is often supposed to serve as a substitute for religion,
although a morality without a new world would be
more inconceivable than religion itself; thus, one
flutters to and fro towards an "enthusiasm for
humanity" without giving the term "humanity"
any kind of spiritual content; thus, one appeals to
the immediacy of personality and of personal life as
if personality could have a meaning and value without
the awakening of a new world at this particular
spot.   Personality is either an empty and mislead-
ing term or a confession of a world of independent
spirituality.

The *Either-Or* truly present here—independent
spirituality or no spirituality—may for a long time
veil itself from us, because we live in a spiritual
atmosphere which has developed under the mighty
influence of religion.   For by means of this atmosphere
the hostility to religion gets unperceivedly supplemented, and thus those formations existing in our
midst are erroneously credited with what only the

17

original energy of the Whole is able to accomplish. Thus it is made to appear as though it were possible to retain in the subject and in the results what has been given up in the substance and the foundation, and as though the mere man were able to accomplish what man can achieve only within spiritual connections. Such a mode of life may even appear, in the beginning, as a gain in freedom, freshness, and immediacy. But this can proceed only for a time, for life itself will engender a reaction. For the more those survivals from the older formations of life are driven out, the more all inward connections slip away, until the man finally stands on nothing broader than his own subjectivity; thus the movement breaks up more and more, and the life becomes emptier inwardly and as a whole, and more and more individuals set themselves at variance with each other, and the scene becomes one of a Babylonian confusion of tongues. Evidences of all this are sufficiently at hand; but in the meantime the struggle against religion and substantial spirituality may appear still as a pleasant occupation and, indeed, as a struggle for freedom. After this comes the reaction, and brings new dispositions and strivings into the life of humanity—it may be through painful upheavals—and then our problem enters into a new phase of universal history. For the history of the world is mostly wont to prove things in such an indirect manner as this.

In the meantime, however, the direct proof which religion transmits through its effective stirring and elevation of life is not to be misjudged. Religion does not so much add something peculiar to life as that it effects an integration, a clear discrimination, and a liberation of what already lies in the life itself, but which, without such concentration, is unable to discover itself. It is through this concentration that the Spiritual Life first gains a durable kernel, and emancipates itself from the limitations of the existential state in order to construct a characteristic world, and to become a new starting-point of life.

This integration into a Whole, and this elevation to action of the whole man, may appear less important and urgent so long as human existence is conceived to be free from acute conflicts and in process of secure advance. As soon, however, as difficult entanglements supervene, the ascent of the Spiritual Life has to overcome enormous obstacles, and is, through these, threatened with paralysis; a return to the Whole and an actuation of the energy of the Whole become indispensable. Such obstacles appear clearly enough, so that there can be no apology for, and no doubt of, the necessity of religion.

Religion finds a main proof of its truth in the fact that it forms the indispensable culmination of the total Spiritual Life; and although man can be spiritually active here and there, he can never take up the Spiritual Life as a Whole, and transform it into his own act, without religion. We have shown sufficiently the general outlines of this fact; and it remains for us now to show how all the main separate movements which endow our life with a spiritual character fail to attain completion and, indeed, lose their anchor and foundation if the turn to religion does not lead them to a Whole, to

Principles, and to the Absolute; so that ultimately the truth and the right of our Spiritual Life hang on such a turning-point. Since, on the one hand, the specifically religious conceptions permeate the whole of life, and, on the other hand, the movements which issue from that whole ever-increasingly demand an elevation to a principle, and hence a turn to religion, a firm interweaving of religion with the whole of the spiritual effort is accomplished. Thus, the whole of this effort speaks and works for religion; the more energetically the Spiritual Life develops itself, the more it becomes conscious of the opposition of its substantiality to a world of appearance; and the mightier the impetus to religion becomes, the more certain becomes the truth of religion itself.

(γ) *Special Pathways.*—If we now pursue the problem through the ramifications of life, and seek to demonstrate that the main movements of life point toward a religion of a *universal* kind, and that without religion all movements must collapse, religion is taken by us throughout not merely as the end of a movement existing prior to itself, but also as this movement's fundamental presupposition; since that spiritual effort could not originate without the presence of the Absolute Life which manifests itself in religion. But since religion clearly reveals that presupposition and the interconnection of life, and bids us incorporate them more energetically in our activities, it will work for the illumination, consolidation, and elevation of all the remaining life. This fact will appear clearer in connection with the following special points.

(*aa*) *The Aspiration after Infinity.*—The man of experience finds himself enclosed firmly on all sides; he is, as a mere portion of a causal order, conditioned and bounded in his aims and energies; the duration of his life has but a brief span to run, and he must acknowledge himself usually as a finite existence. And yet as a tremendous resistance to all this, his Spiritual Life is filled with a longing for Infinity. The idea of Infinity signifies not merely that an immeasurable expanse ever lies beyond the limits of the circle which we traverse. For such an " outside " need trouble us but little, because it does not explain the stirring and forward-driving energy which lives within the thoughts of Infinity. Such thoughts evidently bear witness on the whole that Infinity does not emerge beyond the bounds of life, but that it belongs to man from the beginning; it is the clash within us between the finite and the Infinite which brings forth such effects; and it is only out of this point that the idea and the feeling of the sublime are to be explained, for they do not originate from without, but are an original testimony of the soul.

The movement towards the Infinite proceeds not only into the quantitative, but far more into the qualitative. It is not the surface of reality which suffices us, but far more do we appropriate its whole depth. All the effort after final ends and all-inclusive aims, all investigation concerning the Why of Whys, all the longing for perfection and the highest blessedness over against mere satisfaction in the given situation—what is all this but an evidence of the depth of reality? Everywhere in connection with the idea of the Infinite we discover our liability to lose ourselves in the pathless expanse and the danger of an over-strain of human ability; but we also find a mighty ascent of our nature, a tracing of tracks and a progress upon them, and a challenge to battle against all the narrow and petty-human modes of life which have now become an intolerable barrier. Such a longing—partly revealed and partly concealed—was somehow present in the works which resulted in the great transformations of life and in the inner progressive development of man, so that the impossible itself appeared possible if what ought to be reached is now in reality reached; for out of self-satisfaction and timidity nothing great has ever been born.

What then is the basis of such a movement? If it is a work of a merely human kind, it can mean no more than a mere bolstering up of the self in one's own fancy, a futile presumption of the self, a deceitful illusion. At the same time, all the inner fruits of culture and all that ever presents itself as the spiritual uplifting of man prove themselves as a tawdry veneer on old goods and chattels. Or, on the other hand, the movement has a deeper foundation in the inner presence of an Absolute Life. If things are so, then it is religion which embraces and expresses the whole of life. Through such exertions religion at the same time attaches and rouses itself to a striving after Infinity; and, in order to accomplish this, it calls the whole soul to its aid, and wins a strong conviction and character. Thus, in connection with this special point, it is religion which brings life to its full depth; and what is wrapped up in the aspiration after Infinity becomes the evidence of religion.

This is corroborated, too, by the experience of history. The antique method of viewing the Spiritual Life—a method which largely allowed the meaning of religion in our sense to remain in the background—gave full sovereignty to the ideas of extremes and limits; the All is here limited, and the life of man moves between fixed aims and given energies; there is now no need to cross the frontier into the Infinite, but especially is there a timidity to cross beyond the natural defined boundary. When did the idea of Infinity gain acknowledgment and power, and when did it step into the very centre of life itself? It accomplished this through the tendency to religion, a tendency which culminated especially in the philosophic sense through Plotinus. Since his time the idea has often enough been obscured, but it has never been extinguished. And what appears to us new and great in modern life is indissolubly bound with the reception of Infinity into our own character and nature. For whence otherwise the fixed superiority over the world—the fast rooting of the personality—after which we at least strive? Shall we retreat once more within the old limits in order to avoid entering the pathway of religion?

(bb) *The Aspiration after Freedom and Equality.* —The experience of life shows man bound on all sides and in constant relationships of dependence, shows him bound to other men, bound to the environment, bound to his own nature. This subservience often obscures self-consciousness and continues to persist. But, at the same time, there goes through humanity an ardent aspiration after freedom. This is evidenced, first of all, in the relation of man to man as the demand of independence of each individual over against the human environment, or of the independence of a class over against another class. Through attaining such a freedom man seemed to gain an otherwise unknown dignity and an incomparably greater energy; his life seemed to experience an essential elevation, and for the first time to possess an original worth. Thus, the struggle for freedom was able to kindle the strongest affections and to make light of the most difficult sacrifices.

How does all this find explanation, and how can something essentially higher issue forth from life if there is not more present than a mere rearrangement of energies within an enclosed system? It is explained only through the fact that a new order of things has created a new breach of life, and that life through such a turn has gained an originality of an inward kind as well as a new content. But how can life gain all this if it possesses no depth, and if a reality *subsisting in itself* does not exist? If the Spiritual Life fails in this, what is there besides contained in the representation of religion? History shows, without a doubt, the longing for freedom usually coupled with eschatological ideas; ancient Christianity with its advocacy of the freedom of the religious conviction (*libertas religionis*) took up a great universal struggle for freedom; out of the age of the Reformation has the freedom of our modern times gone forth; indeed, it seemed as if no effort for freedom could stir the whole soul unless it became a kind of religion to man and raised him above mere ordinary experience. This contention holds good, too, concerning the radical

movements of the present day; they could not have
taken such a strong turn against religion had they
not moulded themselves into some kind of religion.
Whenever the struggle for freedom is not inspired by
new ideals of the whole life, it tends quickly to relax
and to enter under the dominion of egoism, be it
egoism of individuals or of classes.

But the aspiration after freedom extends deeper than
the relationship to other men; it reaches the fundamental relationship to the world and to reality.   Man
seeks in spiritual activity another standpoint in regard
to things, and, indeed, to himself, than is verified by
the nearest-at-hand experience.   In such a surface-
experience all is given and fixed, all is opaque and
alien; and, further, the nature of all this appears to
man as something external so long as it does not allow
itself to be set in his own act and there transfigured.
And, therefore, however zealous in work man may
be, so long as he remains a mere link of a natural
chain, so long will he lack the decision to handle the
material which he takes up, and his will fail to decide
concerning the nature of such material; but all the
particular is determined through the connection of
the Whole; and what on the surface may appear as
no more than a link of a chain, on a deeper view is
perceived to reach forth into immensity.

Why does man himself struggle against the acceptance of such a state of things which besets him
with irresistible intrusiveness, and which incessantly
propounds determinism with its old and new grounds
as the only possibility?   Why, indeed, but because
through the tying of man to such a situation unutter-
ably more is lost than willingly allows itself to be

destroyed. There is lost all inner relation to reality through resignation to the dark night of fate; there is lost all inner obligation and, indeed, all ethical character for action through the shifting of action to an imposed necessity, and, consequently, when we reflect on it, what determinism leaves over is nothing more than an empty word; there is lost all present living consciousness, and the present is viewed only as a mere conclusion issuing out of given premises containing nothing in the least original; there is lost all hope of sunnier and nobler days; and all the possibility of inward renewal for peoples and times, as well as for the whole of humanity, fails, and thus life in its march becomes more and more numb and senile; and finally, there is lost the striving to construct our existence, through our own original activity, out of the deep and out of a permanent foundation, and all is simply turned into a piling of a mechanism upon a surface-foundation. Accordingly, life, through its complete resignation to an external necessity, loses all inner movement, all soul, all value; it is now a mere appearance and not an original life to us.

It is no wonder that man strives against all this, that he strains every nerve to resist such a destiny. But it is impossible for him to resist it without a transformation of the whole view of reality and of his own nature. For all attempts to escape to some refuge within the given world of necessity must fail, and such attempts issue from turbid thoughts as determinism itself has shown with convincing power. It is the elevation into a new world alone that can help us; and such a world is not a mere system, but is ever a new and inner governing Whole proceeding out of

activity, and which can become our own characteristic
life of all activity. The Spiritual Life becomes such
a world in so far as it gains a full independence and
engenders out of itself a characteristic reality. The
cosmic "becoming" of the Spiritual Life, however,
surmounts all the capacity of the merely human, and
appears to man as the dawning of an Absolute Life.
This has been a leading thought of the whole of our
investigation. How freedom and necessity in man
may clash and yet stand apart is a question which does
not concern us at this point. Here the main point is
that without the presence of a new world, all possibility
of freedom—all the transformation of existence into
one's own life—breaks in pieces, and, at the same time,
all genuine living present vanishes. The origin of the
longing itself remains a mystery. And yet such a longing moves in mighty waves over humanity and has
brought forth such greatness and nobleness. Thus,
once more, all this is religion, and in it a general
movement of life connects itself together, and with it
something remains which in the final resort nobody
can destroy. If, however, that deepest origin of the
effort of freedom is taken up into our own conviction
and direction of life, then all activity in this direction
can be purified and ennobled, then the individual movements blend themselves more completely together so
that in each individual position the whole man is now
able to step into activity. Many generations of the
past loved to conceive of religion and freedom as set
up pointedly against one another and as irreconcilable
opponents. A deeper meaning, however, here, as
often elsewhere, shows the truth to be quite contrary
to the opinion of particular epochs. Without religion

—religion in the *universal* sense—freedom is a hollow term; no definite freedom can originate without religion, and certainly no religion can originate without freedom.

The movement towards freedom annexes itself to the movement towards equality, and often they walk hand in hand. Experience shows universally an inequality of man; even nature endows individuals unequally; culture brings forth difference after difference the more it develops itself; and this is true, too, of the newer culture with its heightened differentiation of individuals and its technical shaping of activity. The course of history itself drops many differences as having become obsolete; but it brings forth newer and greater differences, and, on the whole, the inequality is continually becoming more marked.

But over against the whole of this current of what actually happens, there arises and asserts itself in a notable manner a longing after equality. Is there imbedded in all this merely the ordinary disposition on a small scale, does nothing commanding endure, and is all drawn down to the ordinary surface-level? This cannot be admitted, for an inequality without the presence of counter-effects to it would endanger most seriously the inner convictions of man, and, indeed, destroy them; it would become an intolerable hardship for that which commands the vicissitudes of life to a lower plane; and it would lead astray to a wayward vanity the very things which ought to have stood on the summit of life. But how are we to overcome such dangers? and how powerless are all abstract conceptions over against them! The equality of all " who carry a human face " will not allow itself to be

established through a mere decree.   It can only come
to a reality and power over against the painful
differences of the standpoint of experience if, on the
one hand, all the differences of men finally vanish and
strictly turn into an infinite greatness; and, on the
other hand, if a common problem is started and
overflows all else which otherwise compromises effort
and achievement.   Nothing other than religion can
verify this.   For the conscious hold upon an Absolute
Life prevents the man from reaching final conclusions
in the differences of the standpoint of experience;
and the opening out of a new task concerning the
whole inner man together with the demands of this
conversion of man press down all remaining activity,
press the whole province of achievement to a lower
level.   This truth appears in that emancipating parable
of Jesus, that of the Talents, and from this source it
flows through the whole broad current of humanity;
it has often run underground, but ever anew runs out
into the light.   Also, out of the consciousness of the
equality of all before God has sprung, upon the
ground of human history, a longing for equality over
against the different situations of men, a longing for
an acknowledgment of the rights of man.   In the
army of Cromwell there originated first of all a
longing after universal and equal political rights; and
it was out of a religious foundation that the proclamation of the rights of man went forth in America.
Thus religion has called forth great movements—
movements which often, partially through the fault
of their representatives, have turned against their own
origin, but not without having to pay the penalty
by falling into shallowness and degenerating into

agitated passions and unveracity. Wherever religion has stood with the fresh energy of youth, it has always brought men nearer together, it has always been the protector of the weak, and always a help to the aspiring soul; it is only where it has become withered and senile that religion is used for the maintenance of private interests and privileges.

(*cc*) *The Aspiration after Eternity.* — At a first glance, man appears throughout as a creation of time; he lives and works in time; the actual affairs of time seem to determine his whole life and being. But in spite of all this, it is false to assert that man belongs entirely to time; the situation, if it were so, would become intolerable to him and would mean an inner devastation. And, on account of this, he undertakes an energetic struggle against the seeming situation; and this struggle forms not a mere episode of his life, but penetrates all culture and spiritual work, for without a trust upon eternal truth, and, indeed, without some kind of eternal life, there is no energy in the effort, no greatness in the character, and no depth in the love. "Love—sincere love and not a merely passing desire—never clings to the perishable, and awakens and kindles itself in the Eternal alone. Never is man able to love himself except when he conceives of himself as an eternal being, and outside this he is unable either to respect or to sanction himself. Still less is he able to love something outside himself unless he raises that something into the eternity of his belief and of his soul, and links it to these" (Fichte).

Thus, there proceeds through the life of humanity an energetic struggle against the dissipation of

things on the mere flux of time. We have seen
repeatedly that all that is termed "history" in a
special human sense carries in itself such a struggle;
and that man, in such a struggle, holds or might hold
with his utmost exertion something inward which
otherwise would be lost on the river of time. The
historical configuration of life and conduct signifies
the building in the midst of time of an order of things
superior to time; this is purely the aspiration after
eternal truth and an all-comprehensive present, which
confers on history an inner movement as well as an
inner connection. And does not the individual strive
in a similar manner in connection with his own self?
Is there a true life without a stepping beyond the
mere transitoriness of the moment, without such a
crystallisation in one's own self as happens in the
formation of character and of spiritual individuality?

Such a superiority to time, and such a power over
against time, can never be brought forth by the
Spiritual Life through merely human means; what is
found in us must stand in connection with an independent world of spirit. Without such a world and its
conscious presence all attempts to rescue ourselves from
the river of time are hopeless, and the man becomes a
mere creature of the day. The inauguration of an
Absolute Life in our domain is, as we have seen, the
kernel of religion; and such a Life in this respect
forms the conclusion of a great movement, whose
reality may be judged as a corroboration of its own
truth. Religion not only forms the ground of, but
also heightens the aspiration after eternity; and finds
this goal more and more through its turn to man's
own nature, and in this, too, discovers an altitude

above mere time. All the great thinkers have been united in proclaiming that all spiritual work of the deeper kind participates in an eternal world; but when a formation of man's nature appears beyond the province of all mere activities, and when an independent starting-point of a true Spiritual Life is recognised in man, then this characteristic spiritual existence must be raised above the transient. The current opinion and, generally, also religion give an insufficient and even incongruous expression to this necessary truth, because they consider as the main fact the duration in time of the natural individuality with all its egoism and limitations. This mode of conceiving things must call forth a progressive contradiction in the particular interest of a religion which has been laid in the forms of the finite and of human nature. But it is one thing to doubt an anthropomorphic immortality; it is quite another thing to deny the spiritual nature of man as a participator in eternity. For such a customary notion means not so much the adumbration of earthly views of the future, as of surrendering all Spiritual Life to bare Time, and along with this to press it down, fritter it away, and inwardly destroy it. Also, the life of man in Time thus becomes a mere appearance and shadow unless there dwells within him a striving towards eternity; and consequently, through a complete binding to Time, all human experience and all human reality which endeavoured to illumine the mere moment sink back into the abyss of nothingness.

Whilst, however, religion clearly encloses an eternal order and allows not merely the acts of men but also their existence to participate in such an order, the thought of eternity gains a great power for life and

character.   Now, all active progress in Time finds its
opposite in a life resting in itself; the movement
of life is not an entrance into Time but a stepping out
of Time.   And thus we are able to understand the
proclamation of a thinker of the Middle Ages, that
man shall become younger every day.

(dd) *The Aspiration after Fellowship and after a
Soul.*—The world of experience shows a co-existence
of elements in nature and in human society, which
move amongst each other in the most varied ways,
which link themselves ever faster, interlace themselves
ever more definitely, and construct an ever-completer
web.   But all relation and intricacy remain linked to
the external performances and effects ; what precedes
what is in the elements themselves, or if anything on
the whole precedes them—this is not the question.
Viewed from this point, then, human connections as
well as the whole of the world become more and more
a well-regulated mechanism into which the individual
life must enter in order to accomplish its own work,
and in order to detach any special movement of the
world-machine.   An inner fellowship, an over-individual experience of men and things from within,
must now appear from this point of view as an absurd
and illicit thought.   And yet such a thought gains a
power over man and engenders an endless movement.
All friendship and love might now participate in the
inner life of another ; and that these possess a soul
behind all external activity is undoubted ; our own
experience of things unlocks the door of art and leads
to the realm of science.   Everywhere we find demands
and movements beyond the external contiguity,
everywhere one's own life with its entrance into the

18

life of another seems to experience an immeasurable
elevation, and to gain supremely a content and a
value. Does not the whole of culture place itself
under the view that over against the world of effects
and counter-effects a province of existence-for-self
arises and opens out into an ever-greater kingdom?

Thus, the fact of a movement towards inwardness
cannot be doubted; but a mighty problem arises along
with it, and also mutually complementary transformations of the view of the world become necessary.
The whole movement is an error and a falsehood if it
possesses no depth of the things and exhausts its own
life in this system of relations. But what is to be
understood by "depth," and how is it reachable?
Reachable it is in no way through the mere agitation
of subjectivity, as the prevalent thought of the present
day would make us believe. When this prevalent
thought of the present states that depth of soul is
reachable through an emancipation from the environment as well as through the transformation of life into
a free and somewhat artistic character, all unbiassed
opinion easily recognises this as an error. Man, in
the mere disposition of his nature as well as in his
mere achievements, is still sufficiently empty and
shallow; he has only changed one superficiality for
another, but in no way has he gained in depth. Have,
then, all the broad developments of external harmony
of to-day, all luxury and self-importance, strengthened
the substance of life, and have they in any kind of
way made man fuller of content and deeper in
experience? In reality subjectivity is not yet by
any means inwardness, and disposition is not by
any means a soul. There is no inwardness of life

possible for us without an inward life of reality;
there is in the individual positions of life no inner life
without the presence of an inner world.   Man could
never strive after an inwardness had he not been
able to disengage himself in some way from niceties
of forms, and to gain a portion in Eternal Life.   And
the facts are such that a genuine inwardness only
develops where great tasks and a great strain
originate, where a struggle for a new being burns
within, and along with it a spiritual self ascends, an
essential formation of the nature results, and in the
throe a personality and spiritual individuality is born.
He who carries not such problems in his own soul
and who seeks not, in all the expansion of work,
before all else to find his own self, can never gain a
depth and soul for himself.   But is all this possible
unless our life stands within a total-life, and unless
we are carried by such?   It is religion, however,
which pleads for the presence of this total-life, and
which brings us to an appropriation of it.   When
religion conceives of the facts as a Whole, the movement towards inwardness will considerably intensify,
and the insufficiency of the ordinary situation will
enter for the first time into consciousness.   Now it is
clearly discovered how alien man usually appears in
the midst of all external relationships, how coercively
the narrowness of natural existence holds him fast,
and how shallow and soulless the life becomes
through all this.   Ever clearer, too, it will become how
the movement of culture itself heightens the danger
in that it differentiates men from each other more
than ever, increases more and more the distance
between them, and rejects more and more the in-

dividuality. Through all this there arises an inner
alienation of man, and a loneliness of soul in the
midst of all the fellowship of work. How otherwise
can the walls of separation be broken down, and how
can the inner experience of one individual draw
nearer to that of another save through the opening
out of a life on the other side of all natural individuality, through a participation in a world which includes
even our own natural world, and, indeed, can include
all worlds? It is only when a fellowship of life and
a mutual understanding have been gained that the
various individualities can further one another in a
positive manner, and, out of the contact, a mutual
restoration can take place.

Thus, in the relationship of man with man, all lies in
the gaining of a common life which encompasses and
binds all together. The problem, however, reaches
beyond this to the relationship of man with his own soul.
In this natural state his deeper being is no less strange
to man than is the deeper being of another; his own
soul is to him closed and inaccessible, and, before any
discovery of spiritual qualities outside himself becomes
possible, he must first of all discover and assimilate
his own deeper being. And he can do this only
through the vivification of a spiritual world which he
makes objective for himself, which gains for him his
own special nature, and which raises him beyond
his natural state. The customary opinion can only
accentuate such a limitation of the characteristic life
through the environing and changeable world, because
such an opinion has no eye for problems of a nature
like this, and looks upon the most difficult as self-
evident, and conceives of the fruit brought forth

through the universal toil of the ages as being nothing
more than a result of the mere moment. Wherever
the problem is discovered, history is seen to furnish
an incontestable proof for the definite connection of
religion and inwardness.   Let us confine ourselves to
the beginnings of Christianity.   What changes have
these early movements brought forth in this respect
compared with rich and beautiful antiquity ! How
much nearer they have brought man to man through
the opening of a corporate world out of belief and
hope as well as a corporate activity of life ; how they
have created the basis for a spiritual art and a spiritual intercourse with nature ; and how they have unlocked man's nature and brought him nearer to his
own soul ! Could Jesus have seen so much in the
little child, could he have explained nature as a symbol
of the Divine without the presence of a kingdom of
inwardness within himself?   And such holds good
for the whole course of the ages : wherever religion—
religion understood in the widest sense, and as a
religion of the spirit—has stepped into the background,
there the inner life has become stunted, if not at once,
yet after a while.   Also, it holds good for the present
day that wherever religion has been awakened out of
the social custom into our own life, it has in the
simplest relationships of life aimed at discovering
more depth than is often to be found in the highest
achievements of culture.   Thus, all gain of a true
inwardness becomes a testimony for religion ; and
thus we see the struggle for religion forming a portion
of the struggle for the soul of life.   To-day, when
the external world forces itself so mightily upon
us, and draws us to itself so coercively, there is

needful, indeed, more than a subjective fortification in ourselves—there is needful the development of an energetic inner life. Shall we give up lightly the indispensable associate in the struggle—religion—as happens too often to-day?

(*ee*) *The Aspiration after Greatness.*—The view of human things shows the individual so small by the side of the whole of humanity, and the view of the world shows humanity so small by the side of a boundless universe. What has been held true from time immemorial in connection with this matter has been brought fully to consciousness only in modern times. Viewing things from the ancient childish level, humanity considered itself as the centre of all; and even with the toning down of such a claim there appeared still a greatness of a human kind, which man saw within the All, and with which he believed himself to have definite intercourse. We have already observed how nature gained a complete independence over against man, how it has drawn him more and more to itself, and how step by step it has honoured him. Through all this his condition and actions seemed entirely to lose significance for the All, so finally man had to seek his happiness and greatness within his own circle. But if he depends on the light which shines from such a corner and not on the light which shines from the inward connections, if he is posited wholly upon his nearest-at-hand existence and develops all out of this, there originates a picture that has no place for inward greatness and original worth. Far too intrusive stands before our eyes the struggle for existence, the stormful hurry of this life, the wild unkempt growth of greed and passion, the

organised and coercive power of general effects, for
us to dwell on and depict.   In a word, we witness an
immeasurable expenditure of life and a vast amount
of work, and yet through it all no corresponding
gain and no meaning of human life either for the
individual or for the Whole.   Such contradiction and
senselessness, and, indeed, nothingness of the whole,
cannot be avoided by man so long as he remains
simply within the clanking of this mechanism, and
so long as he attempts to develop his life merely
from point to point, and allows his whole efforts to be
concentrated upon isolated aspects.   But as soon as
thought and reflection are freed from such a bond and
are set upon a Whole, then there can be no doubt
as to the intolerable hollowness and nothingness of
such an existence.   Such an emancipation and
reflection of the Whole cannot possibly allow itself
to be hindered.

Thus, man will reflect on ways and means of escape
from this abasement ; and to-day an effort in this
direction is visible enough.   But as the effort reveals
itself in the province of a superficial situation, it is
consequently of a kind too little inclined to set the
highest goal in front of itself.   One hopes to push
aside the small and commonplace and to obtain once
more greatness and joy for the nature of man—a state
in which man raises himself into a free condition
above the whole mechanism ; and thus the differences
of individual and individual are brought forth, and
the differences of the individual over against other
individuals and over against the whole of the environment are strengthened.   In such a course of thought
the uncontracted sovereignty of the individual is often

proclaimed, and greatness is sought in the discarding of all external restraints. In this manner the man seems to enjoy what is ordinarily termed personality, but what in reality is only a kind of natural individuality. Such a course of thought has its own right— or, rather, its own semblance of right—only through a strong optimism hardly conceivable in the midst of all the experiences and entanglements of modern life. It has to presuppose man endowed with highly-gifted spiritual potencies and set upon high aims, otherwise it becomes a confirmation of an egoistic greed of life and of all the raw impulses of life; indeed, it will work more towards the sinking than towards the elevation of life. The fundamental mistake consists in this: to affirm in the parts what is denied in the Whole; to wish to retain within the human province of the relationship of man to man a greatness which had been lost in the deeper life and nature of man as a Whole. Such a greatness has been lost wherever man has become a mere piece of a closed-in world, and wherever he has forfeited all inner relations to the whole of reality. Man can retain such a greatness only when there dawns within him a new stage of reality, only when he participates in the Whole of this new world, when he ceases to contract himself upon isolated activities, when there breaks forth from the new life a new being and new self. Then the world and its enterprises can become man's own experience, and then he is able to carry the Whole along with him and to participate in the struggle of worlds, then he has to represent the Whole in the individual parts, and thus becomes through what he does a necessary portion of the

cosmic movement; and it is all this which constitutes
in reality his aspiration after greatness of life.   Indeed,
the more certainly the life possesses such greatness, the
less man cares to speak of it.   Understood thus, the
aspiration after greatness is not conceived mainly as
one difference against another, not as a superior pomp
against the environment, but brings along with it the
deepening of the soul itself and the infinite evolution
of one's own soul.

All this is not possible, as we have already seen,
without the opening of an independent Spiritual Life
in the particular domain of man; and with the truth
of this stands or falls all greatness of life.   It is
religion which binds into one life as a Whole,
and which as a Whole opens out to man; and thus
religion is simply indispensable to the establishment
and evolution of the greatness of life.   Religion raises
out of the otherwise destructive and scattered elements
a simple outline; it gives life the comprehensiveness
of a powerful drama, opens out a great antithesis in
the main direction of life, and at the same time calls
man to a characteristic decision of his own; it makes
the problem of the All become the personal experience
of man and gives him, through the inward presence
of the Absolute Life, a superiority to the world.   The
life is here securely raised above the anxieties of
natural and social existence through the inner task
of moving from a Whole to a Whole.   This becomes
assured only through the formation of a religion
of the Spiritual Life and under the demand for a
complete self-sovereignty.   A religion of obedient
subjection and blind devotion must certainly coerce
man—coerce him more absolutely than any human

power of command, and such a state of things brings
about a stagnation of life in its inmost source. But
why should we as free men bind our conceptions of
religion to the presentations of another, and why
should human disfigurements darken the picture of
religion for us—a picture that arises out of the
necessity of the Spiritual Life, and which has verified
itself sufficiently in universal effects ?

Conclusion.—In all individual points a definite connection of religion with the complete development of
the Spiritual Life was observed. This fact need only
be conceived more clearly in its main lines in order to
become an evidence of religion. Step by step, movements appeared which burst through the world of experience and which, indeed, could not proceed without
coming into sharp contrast with ordinary experience.
But we cannot draw fully such a conclusion as this
without acknowledging that an inversion has taken
place in our conception of reality, and that a new
world has been gained ; and this actually happens in
religion.

Religion appears as something that is not a mere
epiphenomenon of life, but as a necessity that grows
out of man's deeper nature, and which at the start
may not appear more than a clarification of a matter
of fact without whose authority no aspiration after
spirituality could arise. The miraculous originates not
only in any one special situation of life, but penetrates
far more into all Spiritual Life. To him who does
not perceive the miracle in this, to him who does not
see a secret verified and acknowledged in what moves
us daily and hourly, religion appears simply as a superfluous and noxious weed of life. But to him to whom

the secret has unveiled itself, that all movements
of a spiritual kind work towards us, religion is no
more an alien thing, and he sees in it the conclusion
of what the Spiritual Life all along carried within
itself.   Further, to him will the conclusion and its
emergence out of the deep be precious because what
otherwise would remain veiled has come to great
clearness, and what otherwise would remain scattered
has led to unity.   However, through such an elevation
to the level of a principle an inverted order of life has
resulted, working for the elevation of all the earlier
existence.   In this, religion before all else guarantees
the possibility of a spiritual existence, and becomes
the most certain thing within our whole domain
of life; and also, it becomes the presupposition of
all scientific knowledge.   And as religion, through
such a source of the Spiritual Life, results in a constant
elevation above the interests and even above the
whole existence of the merely human kind, and undertakes such an incessant struggle against the small
human modes of life, it is completely protected from
the reproach of the anthropomorphism which a shallow
mode of thought has saddled upon the nature of
religion simply because such a mode of thought has
prevailed for a great length of time.   In a far more
fundamental manner than by any sort of negative
criticism will the delineation of the religion of the
Spiritual Life drive out anthropomorphism.   Indeed,
understood in the right way, religion is the only possible way to antagonise the anthropomorphism which
otherwise clings inseparably to us.

Part III.—The Opposition to Religion

INTRODUCTION

OUR investigation has already reached a certain result. It has been shown that we are more than the mere being of nature; it has been shown that an original kingdom of spirit unfolds in culture; we have seen how religion is able to stand by the side of the individual, and how it has been subjectively appropriated by him. The truth of the other provinces of life does not depend upon how far the individual takes possession of them; science remains science although the individual may discover but little intellectual movement in himself; art remains art although many relate themselves to it in a crude kind of way. But in spite of the superiority of religion to the condition and even the caprice of the individual, we cannot possibly consider the conclusions we have previously reached as final. On the contrary, it must have already surprised us that what we have as yet discovered as religion has nowhere out of its own energy brought forth an historical religion, and has never become the conviction of a great community. Religion must always be able to do something *more* than to produce such results as we have investigated; for unless it does so, it is evi-

284

dently unable to arrive at an entire reality. The object of our immediate investigation is to search for this More. We have gained from the conception of the Spiritual Life the certitude of the fundamental fact of religion; but here the object in view was directed upon the positive achievements, upon the triumphant advance of religion. The opposition which religion had to overcome was left largely in the background. But this opposition cannot always remain there; it must come to more than a partial articulation; it will have to be considered and estimated as a Whole. And in this investigation difficult oppositions and hindrances may appear which will perhaps carry our whole consideration of the subject into a new track and therewith lead to a more original formation of religion than has hitherto met us. Let us, therefore, see how matters stand.

That something sub-spiritual and non-divine exists does not become a stumbling-block and a check to religion, for all this is unavoidable on account of the imperfect stage of the reality we find in the existing world. Religion cannot explain evil—all attempts at explanation within the province of religion are lamentable sophisms—but religion can overcome evil, overcome it through its elevation and triumphant achievement of a representative Divine world. But religion must keep unconditionally to such a progress. Indeed, the less religion presupposes a reason in the nearest-at-hand world, the more vigorously must it further a "becoming" of reason—a progressive spiritualisation of existence through the energy of the efficacious Divine within itself. Such a meaning can be extracted in varied ways according to the different stages of the reality with which we are dealing, but always the higher stages must raise up the lower to themselves; the Spiritual Life must raise nature, the substance of the spirit must exalt the human form of existence; all that represents within the Spiritual Life the unity and the Whole must exalt the ramifications and particularity of life.

The picture, however, that we subsequently expect and must expect is not corroborated by experience. In our domain especially, the new life not only meets individual hindrances, but it thrusts itself in the whole of its effects upon an opposition which seems insurmountable. It attains no independent existence, but remains directed by the energies belonging to the lower level of things; the Divine here is not able to raise to itself the non-divine, but is drawn down to it, and is degraded to a mere means for the aims of the non-divine. Such defencelessness over against a world man has entered into to rule, and such a perversion of his activities of necessity shake his belief in the truth of things. How are such weaknesses compatible with the conception of the Divine, and how can a hemmed-in and powerless life be of a Divine kind? But, also, when the reality of the Divine remains unapproachable as a power superior to the world, its communication to us becomes a matter of ever greater doubt. Of what use is a definite Spiritual Life to us if it is only a knowledge out of the distance, if it is unable to permeate through the hindrances of our existence, but is further drawn into the very same discord from which it ought to free us?

Thus, the turn of life undertaken through religion seems to be drawn right into the entanglement instead of being drawn out of it. There results undeniably in connection with religion a removal from the prior situation, a new starting-point is gained, some kind of movement is brought into a current. But when this movement, after opening out vistas, and after raising desires without being able to fulfil them, is unable to occupy them, it has made the situation rather worse than better. The idea of an independent Spiritual Life has brought forth a new standard which makes much inadequate and intolerable which previously had raised no kind of obstacle; especially do the shallow relationships and the ordinary everyday life which otherwise might have remained neutral now step upon the opposite side and strengthen the opposition; the hindrance turns from the external to the internal: out of the weakness of the Spiritual Life there issues an inner entanglement, and within our own domain there issues a discord. Such a confused situation lands reflection and conviction in the most painful dilemma. Too much exists in the mind to allow of a simple Nay because an actual turn of life has already resulted, and the conflict itself with its bitter pang is engendering a movement. Too much exists to allow of a Yea. Thus, neither the one nor the other is able to win us. And yet the necessity of life drives imperatively to a decision. Will this knot allow of any method of untying? Will it at least notify the direction in which we have to search and to work? Only further actual conclusions and not imaginative suppositions can definitely decide this question; and attention must be directed especially upon it.

First of all, however, the province of the hindrances has to be traversed, and its impressions to be brought to an open judgment, for all disguise or extenuation of the truth would be a wrong as well as a danger to all further progress. Evidently our investigation has entered upon a new stadium. Now, first of all, we saw the sun of a Divine Life rising out of the thick cloud of the initial stages, and enabling us to witness a kingdom of reason in the midst of all hindrances; reflection can follow joyously the extension of this kingdom, and see all the fulness of life and effort drawn to life itself. Now, however, thick clouds arise anew and veil that light so much that it becomes dim and dull—more apt to allow us to discover the cessation of truth than to lead us nearer to it.

Further, our life may be compared to a drama whose climax has been reached in a toilsome kind of way. But a plot has unfolded, and the world seemed to have opened to its victorious advance. Now, however, the counter-play begins and grips so mightily that all the gain is endangered, and, indeed, it threatens to transform all into a loss. Whether the matter remains ultimately in such an entanglement, whether reason is not able to put forth further energies, and through this to remain master of the field—all this must remain open as a possibility, and may present itself as a hope. In the meantime, however, the *advocatus diaboli* has the best case, and may express it bluntly. For all enfeeblement and excuse come from evil. In connection with the particulars of explanation one alone has to be remembered, viz. that in reference to the whole question the matter is not concerned with human happiness but with the reality of a definite Spiritual Life, and with the presence of a higher world within our domain. All this gives the fact a more earnest aspect and the question an incomparably greater urgency than the mere problem of happiness can furnish.

CHAPTER IX

a. The Explanation of the Opposition

1. *The Opposition of Nature*

THE Spiritual Life is unable to desire an independence without imposing specific demands upon nature. The entire restriction of the life of the soul to the natural process shown by experience raised no obstacle prior to the turn towards spirituality. For hitherto the life was a mere means and instrument for the self-preservation of the individual; it would not and could not be a kingdom of its own; it developed no original content, and opened out no new world. At the spiritual stage, however, all this has been evinced. Therefore the turn to spirituality necessarily produces the longing that there should correspond to this independence in the nature of man an independence of existence over against nature; the new aims and the immediate participation in the whole of an infinite and eternal world, existing by itself, demand appropriate forms of life. Indeed, a superiority and sovereignty over nature become here an urgent demand. For if the turn to spirituality signifies truly a penetration by reality to its own essence, the independent progressive Spiritual Life must out of itself illumine the whole domain and draw all to itself; it must use this domain as means to its own ends, and as a stepping-stone to its own level; and it will at least desire in all connections to take the lead. Such a demand emanates not only externally but far more internally. As nature itself with its order and mechanism enters into the very soul of man, the awakened Spiritual Life must verify its independence and superiority over against this; it must rule our actions more and more, and must link all effort to its own career. How could it otherwise effect a revolution of the total reality?

Do the facts of experience show such a " becoming " superiority of the Spiritual Life? They show quite the reverse. The spiritual development of man as well as the natural life of the soul remain tied to the body, and, at the same time, they remain attached to the order of nature; they become and grow with the body. The Spiritual Life, too, waxes and wanes within us. That the body is more to man than a mere tool is clearly proved by so-called mental pathology—which is really brain pathology—which contracts most powerfully the psychic activity and drives man to perverted paths. Death, again, with its extinguishing of the whole existence, appears as a great evil proceeding from the province of nature. For the Spiritual Life sets aims within the individual being which far outrun the short span of existence; activities are initiated and relationships of man to man are formed which involve a longing after a per-manency of duration; the man works with incessant toil for his own cultivation, and attains by his labours a personal standing and a spiritual individuality only to witness all his results destroyed so cruelly.   Over against this, there awakens an ardent longing to burst such limits asunder, and to participate in some way in eternity; thus religion has become in the main the promise of individual immortality. But not only does experience fail to give the least clue to this, it also refuses to affirm that what appears on one hand as indispensable is on the other hand superfluous.   And, further, how often does all spiritual emotion fade in the soul; the spirituality becomes numb and dull, and by gradual stages it almost wholly dies in the lifetime of man.   What has immortality to do with such a spent-out life.   If, however, death forms the natural conclusion, can things stand otherwise in regard to what persists as a spiritual fire for the whole of life, and, indeed, what in its course burns with love ever more strongly and clearly?   Question after question, and riddle after riddle! This, however, is certain, that in our view of the matter the natural process, unconcerned with spiritual values, follows simply its own course; the most glorious spiritual greatness offers no protection against an early death or against collapse brought about by ill-health; although, on the other hand, we often witness spiritual nobodies unhappy and dragging idly along an enfeebled existence.

The experience of peoples and of humanity corresponds to the experiences of individuals.   The aims and values of the Spiritual Life do not seem to exist for the blind mechanism of the natural process; these natural powers know of no difference between good and evil, righteousness and unrighteousness, inward greatness and meanness. Earthquakes and floods as in a play destroy the blossoming Spiritual Life; pestilence and famine produce their effects without any concern for human welfare and spiritual values. Nowhere does nature rise to a higher order as the symbolism of the Middle Ages imagined to have been the case with plants and animals; it merely constructs an enclosed kingdom concerned with itself alone. A mysterious sphinx stands in front of us, incessantly bringing to birth and bringing to death, patiently preparing and rashly destroying, benevolent and pitiless at the same time, its objects quickly befriending one another and quite as rapidly pursuing one another in a relentless struggle; all this verifies the saying that nature is less of a mother than of a step-mother to her children. We find then in nature an incessant impetus towards life; but in all the agitation and movement we find no existence-for-self, no life-for self, and thus no genuine fruits, no meaning, no reason of the whole, but all seems a passionate play without reason and for nothing. It is not, however, without any reason at all: for all the works of nature result in simple, unvarying fundamental forms and in a fast chain of occurrences; they result in law and causality. All this is certainly reason, but as yet only a *formal* reason which is throughout indifferent to the content of the occurrences. Further, the most appalling destruction of life, the occasions of dreadful malformations, the inheritance of painful diseases, follow throughout in accordance with these laws and with the causal order. Of what help to reason, it may be asked, is that which places so much power in the hands of unreason?

Such indifference of nature to all spiritual aims becomes intolerable in religion; and religion, in the straits of necessity, has sought a help in the miraculous which appeared as an evident proof of the sovereignty of spiritual and divine energies above nature. But, notwithstanding all toilsome effort, a secure foundation for such an assertion cannot be found. The scientific conception of nature as well as historical criticism have undermined the belief in miracle, until that belief has become, right down to its main prop, a burden for true faith. How can we now hold up a consolidated inner life over against the insecurity of the external situation! And, further, the mechanism of nature seizes the soul and places all action in an iron band. This mechanism cannot hold us entirely, for how could a Spiritual Life rise up on all that is within us? And also, after such a turn towards the Spiritual Life the immediate consciousness subjugates the mechanism to itself; the spiritual activity must thus have won some kind of place for itself; it is soon pushed out of it, but quickly and strongly it returns to its abode. The Spiritual Life has to be formed out of the Whole, and has to convince us of infinity as well as of eternity. But in the nature of man it disperses itself into the sheer, incessant, changing, and interacting flux of consciousness. True, the Spiritual Life struggles against such a hindrance but does not forge its way through it; it remains pushed into the background and sees itself shut out of the obvious reality as an alien.

Further, the emancipation of spirituality from nature cannot be brought about through the motive-powers of life. However the sensuous impulses may be relegated to a lower level, they reassert themselves with such strength that spiritual activity does not seem able to dispense with their help. How dull would such an activity remain, how uninteresting would all work become, how insipid would all love be, if they were not linked to a natural impulse, and if they did not draw the potency of such an impulse to themselves! Further, the characteristic configuration of the Spiritual Life in different civilisations seems determined before all else by the standard and custom of the natural energy of life. But does not the question concerning the differences of the historical religions resolve itself to this : whether a people hold tenaciously to an affirmation of life and set forth this affirmation in spite of all hindrances as the Semites have done, or whether a people tend to deny and to destroy such an affirmation as is done in Indian religions ?

The natural life stands on a lower level than the instinct of self-preservation ; and, on the other hand, in the domain of the spirit this impulse is censured and repudiated as selfishness. But shall we become free of it, and can we, in the main, be deprived of it? While we have to wrest our existence incessantly out of an alien and indifferent world, can we and dare we put in place of such a world the anxiety for self-preservation? This anxiety grows and refines itself over whole nations and over the whole of human society. How much depends on material welfare and how much it signifies even for the Spiritual Life, is shown with special clearness by the economic movements of the present. But when material things become so much to us, and hold us in so obligatory a manner, what becomes of the elevation to the new world which the Spiritual Life and also religion with all its might long for ?

The total impression on this level can be no other than this: that the Spiritual Life, too, with its awakening to a clear consciousness remains a mere accompanying phenomenon of the natural process. In all its lofty flight the effort cannot disengage itself from a dependence from without ; it remains tied to the energies of nature ; it is drawn down to the service of nature.   This barrier becomes an intolerable contradiction when the presence of the Divine is experienced within the Spiritual Life.   If the Divine is really in the transaction, the Spiritual Life must be able to bring its efforts to fruition.   If it is not able to do this, how can we revere such a Life as Divine ?

2. *The Opposition of Culture*

Certain as it is that the weakness of the spirit over against nature remains a mystery, it would have been intolerable if the man had been unable within his own province to construct a kingdom of reason and to fortify himself against all attacks and doubts.   In fact, a unique human province originates over against nature : this province is culture, through which man prepares a new kind of world.   This new world is culture as it develops itself, through the conclusions of individuals, into an historical life and, through history, into a stream of activity.   We have previously shown that this human culture is not able to bring forth spirituality out of itself, but much rather presupposes it.   But in spite of such a limitation, it must be in the position to construct its basal development out of deep connections, and to co-operate in the construction of a kingdom of reason. This is to be expected and desired of culture. Culture is called to break the contradiction and untruth of the ordinary commonplace life, and to seek for a new order of things. Now, as such a new order is known and acknowledged, culture must victoriously out of its own energy make headway against the old situation; it must free and weld the immanent reason of our existence, and triumphantly drive out all unreason. In the midst of all the unreadiness of our situation the rise of a Divine Power ought to seal fast the superiority of reason and transform the movement of history into a progressive conquest of the spirit.

It is thus we ought to find things, though in reality we find them otherwise; instead of human culture placing itself in the service of definite spirituality, it raises itself as an independent master, treats its own existence and development as the highest of all ends, and consequently cannot very well but reduce the Spiritual Life to a mere means, and set it down on a level where its services seem advantageous to culture. A strong inversion is evident in this procedure. It belongs to the very nature of the Spiritual Life to be independent and self-valued, and this claim it can in no way renounce. Culture, however, need only be viewed a little more closely in its limitations for its inability to discover the Spiritual Life to become evident. In culture there result conclusions of the human mind, a reciprocal contraction of certain individual elements becomes clear, a visible union takes place, which at the same time undertakes spiritual tasks. In this union the individuals advance with their given sentiments, *i.e.* with their prevailing natural impulses and with but little spiritual qualities, with much delight in themselves and with but little love for others. Thus, there results in the union of individuals some kind of binding of spiritual elements, a certain summation of potencies. But such a binding issues only in external achievements and without a just differentiation of the definite and the indefinite. Consequently there easily arises a manifold and complicated web of relations, without, however, an inner Whole; the current of life thus flows not from the internal to the external but from the external to the internal; and whatever awakens in the form of spirituality remains tightly tied to the purely human formation.

All this may be relatively valuable, and throughout indispensable for man, although inner barriers are perceptible enough; and if, in spite of the acknowledgment of these barriers, social culture makes of itself an all-governing end, and directs itself against the independence of an awakened spirituality, difficult entanglements and, indeed, perversions are unavoidable. That social culture in reality is not more than it is, is no detriment or reproach to it; while, however, it can be more than is possible for it otherwise to be through the actual natural state of affairs. It cannot become more so long as it presents its mixture of reason and unreason as *pure* reason, so long as it attributes the rights of absolute spirituality to its conditioned human spirituality. When it acts from such a disposition it seeks to mould all spiritual great-

ness out of itself, it seeks to command all effort out
of its own achievement, and to satisfy all demands
out of its own means; and finally to restrict the
movement to the point where it can reach its own ends.
Hence, there necessarily arises an opposition, and,
indeed, a struggle between a merely human and a
genuine spirituality arises—a struggle which must
work with all persistency because the struggle on the
mere-human side is also led in the name of the spirit.
Such a dissension lies evidently before our eyes if the
all-powerful State or the Church, with its monopoly
of all means of grace, claims also the monopoly
of all Spiritual Life. The struggle spreads itself,
however, beyond all this to the whole domain of
human relations. Everywhere the desire tends not
to raise, free, and transform human existence out of
its level, but to leave it tied to itself and satisfied with
itself, and thus, in spite of all the seeming expansion,
to narrow it inwardly. Utilitarianism and relativism
—two points of view that tend to belittle the Spiritual
Life—become inevitable if spiritual greatness and
connections as well as religion itself are considered
pre-eminently as social organisations. Then, that alone
is termed " good " which is useful to society; that is
termed " true " which finds its acknowledgment in
society; and both are an inner subversion of the
definite meaning of the two concepts without the
discovery of such a subversion. The subversion is so
varied and disfigures life so much that it will prove
of little avail in the main tendencies of life.

Human alliances always develop the Spiritual Life
in a particular fashion; but on this path the Spiritual
Life is not able to stamp itself energetically without

a marked one-sidedness.   But this particular mode of treatment tends towards the greatest stubbornness in its attempt to become a Whole, and it coerces with passionate intolerance all remaining activity. Such contradiction necessarily leads, in course of time, to a reaction ; other ideals arise, progress, and discover their rights, but only to fall quickly into the same narrowness.   Thus we witness an incessant change of ideals, a zigzag movement, without the superior unity of the whole, without the necessary demand of definite spirituality to step forth from the background to take the lead.   We observe such a change of ideals clearly enough ; the course of history shows it openly with impressive clearness ; and, in spite of this, social culture ever anew treats the occasional drift of activity as the only right, the only possible, and the conclusive truth.   In the abstract, we have the clearest consciousness of the relativity of all human and historical achievements ; in the concrete, any suitable time qualifies us to become carriers of absolute truth.   And must not this issue, or is the error avoidable in order to gain character and energy for the problems of time ?

Social culture can do no other than present the achievements in front of us and partially conform to such achievements.   This would be no detriment if such a limitation were acknowledged, and if the inwardness and rights of the life of the soul were preserved.   But such is not the case, because the achievements together with all their consequences as well as the character itself are enclosed within the circle of social culture.   Thus, all life and action are driven from the character to the mere performances ; and this

conduces towards only a stunted growth of all independent inwardness. The direction of all striving for
achievements—the acknowledgment of external results
alone in the life of others—becomes a great danger to
the independence of character; man now finds his
centre of gravity not in himself, but in the social
environment, and the life thus loses the energy and
veracity of original creativeness. He who in the first
place works not for himself but for others, not for the
facts but for the social environment, must, in spite of all
his activity, exclude himself from the depth of things.
The greatest defect here, however, is the inevitable
speedy growth of pretence. Where all the value lies
in the effect an action has on another and on the mere
acknowledgment of another, the semblance of truth
does the same and often better service than truth
itself. And this semblance will confuse the whole
of life, and poison the real soul of man. This
semblance-character of social culture becomes an
intolerable peril when the inmost soul of the Spiritual
Life is in question, as *e.g.* in religion and morality;
so that all penetrating creativeness within these
provinces is a burning protest not only against the
pretence of the special social situation but also of
the social mode of handling such problems. Yet
all protests have altered the social situation but
little.

As the inwardness is in this manner stunted in
its growth, so the individuality is thrust back and
suppressed. Since society supremely values and
nurtures in man what enters into its ordinary arrangement, individuality, discernment, and eminence
are thought lightly of, discounted, and ejected. In-

deed, the more exclusively the social leadership of
life takes the field, the individual quality suffers the
more hindrance ; the more monotonous and mechanical existence becomes, the more must activity itself
grow inwardly coarser. Again, society will give a commonplace and shallow character to its organisations
—a character which often accords but little with the
inexhaustibleness of the individual cases which originate, and which collides sharply with the individual
nature of the particular cases. Thus, for example,
we find in law an incessant conflict between the
general norms and some feature of the individual
fact. But shall we therefore repudiate such norms ?
Or, are we called to abandon life to a complete
subversion and an incalculable arbitrary choice ?

To base life on the level of ordinary everyday
experience is an extremely risky course because the
level of human relationships is a low one, because
such ordinary existence must depend on a movement
which has spent itself and on an energy which is
waning, and these will consequently organise the
life. When the ordinary existence presents itself as a
totality and as a standard of all spirituality, it enters
on a fierce opposition to the development of true
spirituality. The elevated outlook, greatness, and
originality appear to the ordinary existence as useless,
excessive, and inert. Thus all independent spirituality
becomes a disturbance of social equilibrium, and a
reproof against social conclusions. This opposition
of ordinary existence engenders severe conflicts with
tragic issues not only in particular cases, but permeates the whole of historical life, and persists even
when greatness receives external acknowledgment,

since existence drags such greatness down to its own level. And in the central questions, the acknowledgment has been wont to follow only when the greatness was removed far enough back not to disturb the circles thus acknowledging it, indeed far enough to be able, as " classical," to become a weapon against the Spiritual Life struggling upwards in their own time.

Again, in the field of culture there appears the same defect of which nature already makes us painfully aware, the cleavage between *formal* and *intrinsic reason*. Society places all life and action under conjoint forms, and insists, before all else, upon the observance of these forms; and social culture has a decidedly formal character. As against the merely natural level the confusion is here even increased, since *formal reason* steps forth and is acknowledged by society as the carrier of intrinsic truth; the pronouncements of this formal reason claim absolute validity. Now, the most correct observance of all forms of existence offers no guarantee of an intrinsic truth, since fallible and fickle men have to apply those forms. Socrates and Jesus were sentenced in accordance with all the forms of law; and the Inquisition and the trials for witchcraft were quite according to recognised canons. All social modes of life stand in danger of injuring intrinsic truth whilst holding fast to the formal truth. Hence all true friends of morality have so little admiration for the virtue and righteousness of merely civic life; and deep religious natures are so often found in sharp opposition to the basing of religion on forms, dogmas, and rites, towards which the social formation of religion moves.

The more clearly the effort in the Spiritual Life after a genuine being—an aspiration towards the essential development of life—is acknowledged, the more serious must that disfigurement and damage appear. But does a knowledge of this fact make formal reason superfluous, and is not the life without it abandoned to an entire dissolution?

Thus, there appear a multitude of abuses; and common to them all an inner unveracity, a desire to appear more than one can be, the raising of a highly problematic half-reason to absolute reason, an idolatry of the social circle! Such a situation of life must in turn cause a counter-movement, and this must rise in opposition not only to individual sides and regulations but to the whole of this social mode of life. If great spiritual renewals work in such a counter-movement, they can effect an elevation of life. If such counter-movements, on the other hand, be, as is usually the case, mere reactions, all their passionate protestations can be of but little real service. What shapes itself here against a binding of things within the domain of freedom remains so many formless waves of feeling; the individual can indeed appeal to the immediacy of his life and can revel in ever new moods, but the substance of life in this way profits but little. If, similarly, the present seeks to cast off all the burden of history, and seeks to defray the cost of life on its own means alone, no complete freedom is attained. For the aspiration of the movement is, viewed empirically, a testimony to history even when it places itself pointedly over against the immediate past. Such an opposition may well show the defects of social culture, but it is not able to overcome such defects radically. Such opposition with its exaggeration of the individual and the accidents of his lot passes easily into one-sidedness and error, so that the scales of right must turn again to the level of social culture. Thus the pendulum of the movement swings incessantly from one side to the other; ever in turn one side succeeds through exaggeration against the other side, and in the passions of the struggle the best energies consume themselves without having gained anything essential for the main fact. But it is always the conclusion of absolute truth that makes the struggle passionate and overthrows all error.

Thus, social culture is far from being the realisation of a kingdom of reason or even from becoming such by degrees. The greater will be the upheaval—not only in formal speech but in acts —when social culture stands for such a kingdom of reason. There lies in such a worship of humanity a delusion which must issue, in the particular as well as in the general, into vehement opposition and misrepresentation. But even such a mode of life received its characteristic feature from the Spiritual Life, and can never wholly deny its origin. Yet how does this Spiritual Life explain itself now that the lower mode of life draws it into its own web and offers the most persistent opposition to all progressive effort? And even when the Spiritual Life is conceived as a world-power and returns to the Divine, even this conception is drawn into the sphere of doubt. Is not the Spiritual Life able to complete the work begun? But why then was the work begun? Out of what do these hindrances explain

20

themselves — hindrances which, however, do not
originate out of the mere individual, but which carry
a necessity in themselves? Here again we find riddle
after riddle! All the obscurity concerning these questions is, however, intensified on the path of denial.

3. The Opposition within the particular Province of the Spiritual Life

Difficult as the previous entanglements were, they
did not reach to the deepest root of the Spiritual Life.
However much such a life may be confined within
the human circle, it signifies even here, through inner
movements and necessities, a real kind of existence
and-a real efficacy. For how otherwise does the
struggle against bare nature as well as against bare
society explain itself, and how could the injunctions
of both be discovered as insufficient? Again, such an
elevated Spiritual Life not merely encompasses and
permeates our existence as an invisible total atmosphere, but it unites itself as a great Whole in art,
science, morality, etc., and develops a propelling force
within its own province, and works beyond the
individual province in the whole realm of life. Thus
there arises here without a doubt an original sphere
of life. Has this sphere proved superior to the entanglements, and has it resulted in an emancipation
from the hindrance and error which otherwise saddle
human existence?

Such were in fact the thoughts and hopes of ancient
and modern times. All disorder was attributed to
the relationship with the environment; the particular
circle of the Spiritual Life was supposed in this way
to avoid any deformity; spirituality and reason

seemed to have an equally valid greatness. According to this, man need only set himself into spiritual activity in order to place his life in pure reason. It is on this fact that the convictions of all the enthusiasm of culture and all the confessions of enlightenment are persuaded that the development of mental energies carries directly within itself the security of a right usage of things, and is convinced that even when errors arise they will soon correct themselves easily and smoothly.

In connection with the whole course of our investigation quite a contrary picture has presented itself. The entanglements vanish in no manner within the province of the Spiritual Life, but reach within it their fullest expression; the most difficult hindrances and disturbances are not of an unspiritual but of a spiritual kind. That an Absolute Spiritual Life became manifest in the domain of man brings, instead of a smooth solution, far more a sharpening of the opposites, a heightening of the conflict. Indeed, when the disturbance threatens to extend to the fundamental existence itself, when the Spiritual Life is confined within itself, doubt penetrates now into the final depths. How does it stand in reference to the Divine that suffers such an inner disorder to prevail? Or shall we flee to the mode of thought which comes to expression in the noteworthy words: *Nemo contra Deum nisi Deus ipse*?

(a) *The Disruption of the Spiritual Life.*—The Spiritual Life begins in us at individual points and initially constructs further Wholes; it shows the nearest-at-hand view of things as scattered into a multitude of isolated elements. The presence of the Spiritual Life promises an entire revolution of all this. For in it the unity longs for sovereignty; little as the fragmentary elements may be abolished at *one* stroke, yet the Spiritual Life will undertake an energetic struggle against them, and out of a Divine power within the soul it will penetrate into them victoriously; more and more the Spiritual Life must connect all into a Whole and permeate each special province with the spirit of the Whole. We must expect and aspire after all this. But again, the expectation is deceived, again a still greater entanglement grows out of the alleged solution.

True, in all this the idea of a total-life arises, works, and extends itself into the individual provinces. Yet the elements do not bend before this idea, but seek with all their existing rights to draw it down to themselves, and with the help of such an idea of a total-life to raise themselves to the level of all sovereignty. Now it is science, now art, now morality, now historical religion, now practical activity, which make themselves in turn a centre of life, and seek to confine all effort to their own special arena. Consequently there originate varied types of life with their antagonistic movements and their disagreement and the division of fragmentary portions of spirituality amongst themselves. And, indeed, such a procedure seems to issue out of an inner necessity. Thus the Spiritual Life within us seems to belong to no special and clearly marked province beyond the social circle, and does not seem able to gain the energy necessary for high aims without concentrating itself on one aspect of life alone, and expecting all safety through attaining that particular view. Therefore, there is with us no prominent achievement without a strong one-sidedness and also unfairness; all greatness thus works tyrannically and coercively; all effort, with all the glow and passion of its activities, appears, after a just balancing and a reciprocal reservation, as an intolerable dulness. But as all this conflict realises through the idea of an Absolute Life the most important enhancement, the entanglements are still found beyond the existing situation.

The next result is a sharp division of the various movements, a hard conflict on the whole, the transformation of our Spiritual Life into a relentless struggle. And all hope of a reconciling conclusion fails. As each party represents a right which must never be lost, none of the elements of the movement must be destroyed; and thus the victory won by each element carries in its very ascendancy a turn to a lower level; and further, the prospect opens out upon an ebb and flow, upon a fluctuation hither and thither. When, however, the one ever in turn displaces the other, so also do the ideals and the convictions change suddenly into full opposites. Does not the whole thing then become a mere play and caprice? True, the thought of an all-encompassing and all-governing truth is there; but it does not seem able to mould itself without being under the power of the merely individual formations, without serving the ambition of these isolated formations for an absolute monarchy, and without making wider the cleavage which was its very business to overcome.

This assumption, however, to be a Whole in the particular is thought to be atoned for by the individual movements; they will make some amends through

the shaping of the meaning of the true and the false,
the spiritual and the human, freedom and necessity,
which in their original state are entangled in one
another, and which nowhere long to reach pure reason.
Therefore, it is only out of the Whole that the
necessary division of things results; it is only in the
relations of life framed in an inner unity that there
results a transformation into full freedom and original
activism—into an illumination and spiritualisation of
the total existence; it is only out of this that each
province receives definite boundaries within which it
has, in its own way, to represent the Whole and
work for its further development. If, on the other
hand, the individual formations in their exclusiveness
allow the good and the indispensable to flow alongside of the perverse and the problematic, life falls
into the most painful dilemma. What life dare
not miss as a truth cannot possibly be extracted out
of the region of the annexed error; but, however, if
life ignores the error, the truth quickly fades and
vanishes. Therefore life must at the same time
affirm and deny, accept and reject; everywhere truth
disperses into error because the particular rules the
Whole, and forces its own nature on the Whole.

The complete needs Art for its emancipation and
thorough cultivation, for Art makes Truth significant
and joyous at the same time; Art baptizes Truth in
the element of Beauty, but as soon as truth, merely
from the æsthetic side, rules the Whole, it produces
a pleasurable, playful, and hypersensitive mode of
life. Science brings forth a resolute clarification
and consolidation, an ascent of man to a world-
consciousness and to a life which proceeds from the

expansion and truth of things; but science is not able to become the sole mistress without engendering through its merely intellectual culture an excessive self-consciousness of the work of thought, without turning the tasks of life into problems of knowledge, and finally injuring the development of an independent inwardness as well as of the fresh apprehension of the immediate movement. A manly strength and a consolidation of character which the whole being stands in need of originate out of morality; but a specifically moral conduct of life is wont to become hard, stubborn, and self-conscious. Over against this, religion develops more gentleness and more fervour; but to fill the life exclusively with these is likely to lead easily into the danger of turning aside from the work of the world and of revolving simply in one's own passivity, and, finally, of transferring to the Divine the claims which humanity makes upon us— the very qualities by which we are able to know the Divine at all. A counter-effect is produced by the practico-social life with its development of the contact with the environment and with its participation in the energies of the ordinary everyday experience; and this works in the direction of greater security and skill, of fresh courage to face life, and of a joyous self-existence. But as soon as such a mode of life conquers the whole man, it drives him into a fussy activity and into a soulless alienation. Thus each isolated method leads into error as soon as it becomes a Whole to itself; and yet each individual method refuses to give up its claim to become a Whole, and strains every nerve itself to become such a Whole.

Through such a disintegration the conduct of life

produces a characteristic obscurantism which tends to an arrogant contempt of all the provinces except its own, whilst it rejects such a treatment from any other side as an insufferable outrage. The æsthetic mode of thought feels itself superior in the fineness of its sensations and the distinction of its taste; the scientific mode feels its superiority in the expansiveness of its view and the clearness of its insight; the moral mode feels its superiority in the strength of its virtues; the religious mode feels its superiority in the inwardness of its soul-life and its being well-pleasing unto God; the practico-social mode feels its superiority in the secure rule of immediate existence. Each misses the ideals of the rest; and no wonder that each easily defeats the others. Thus, through a variegated colouring we obtain usually a pharisaic self-consciousness; and, along with it, a disfiguration of the Spiritual Life into a factious life which is as unavoidable as it is intolerable.

But how shall the substance of the Spiritual Life conquer if each element strives against the others, and all contend against all, and in the strife destroy their best energy? On account of this, such strife, in the course of history, will increase rather than decrease. For in spite of all the vacillations of individuals, divergencies on the whole increase, and the characteristic development of each particular province takes place at the same time. Modern times especially constitute a significant period through the dissolution of the mediæval mode of culture; but the danger has become ever greater through the development of one-sided formations, through a disintegration of the Spiritual Life and the transformation of our existence into a hopeless struggle. Also, it becomes ever clearer that the entanglement lies far beyond all will and capacity of mere individuals; the individual here appears all along as a child of his age; the waves of his age play with him and carry him far out until he becomes without a will of his own, and merely floats on the current of external circumstances.

The idea of a Spiritual Life cannot prevail against such a discord, but is considered a specially evil defect; and it is driven into stubborn doubt at the moment a Divine power is recognised in the idea of such a comprehensive spiritual life. Then the Divine seems too weak to become the ruler of the human formation of the Spiritual Life; indeed, what is present as a stimulation of the Spiritual Life seems to fall under the power of a lower order, and to heighten the arbitrariness and confusion of that order. How can a Divine Being work thus against His own aims?

(β) *The Disintegration within the Spiritual Life.*— The opposition to the unity of the Spiritual Life reaches even deeper: disintegrations multiply at the very foundation, and produce a dispersal of elements and conflicting formations. Three such disintegrations have already been noticed in our investigation. First of all, our investigation considered the cleft between subject and object — between the individual consciousness and its external world. From the beginning this cleft checks progress towards truth; but it seemed to imply a conclusion concerning the opening of a definite spiritual and essential life within the particular domain of man. For along with the cleft there appears within the

domain of activity a reality; there originates from
within and not from without a world which is
contiguous with the self, but such a world becomes
our very self through the binding of its elements
into a unity. That this new world, first of all,
finds itself in opposition to the old world, and only
gradually subjects it, cannot astonish and terrify
us. This is certainly to be expected in regard to
a movement which arises towards a new direction,
and which slowly yet securely advances over against
the cleft. But when this expectation of overcoming
the cleft is unfulfilled, even the presence of a higher
order of things, so far from lessening the problem,
complicates it. Not only is the idea of unity unable
to draw the being to itself, and mould it out of
itself, but its tendency is to give an edge to the
situation, as each of the two sides—subject and object
—is driven, through its indifference to the unity, to an
attempt to tear the total-life into pieces and to bring
the opposite side entirely under itself. In the one
direction, the peculiar works of man free themselves;
they present themselves as independent powers, they
transform the life of the soul into mere means for
their own necessities, they coerce ever more strongly
all inwardness and mechanise more and more all
existence. But this progressive absorption of the
subject leads in the end towards the overthrow of
man's powers. For the more the activities loosen
themselves from a soul-foundation, the less can they
signify a connection by themselves, and the more
must their own energy and greatness sink until their
inability to inspire the whole of life becomes con-
fessed. Then comes the rotation to the other side:

there results now an inversion of the prior course of work. The subject now raises itself in a titanic manner and disconnects itself to the utmost from the object in order to construct all reality by itself. Its own individual situation becomes its world; the enjoyment of its sensations and the refinement of its dispositions become its life. But if the subject follows exclusively on this path, the reality, internal and external, is more and more dissipated. For the subject is not able to preserve its own unity on account of its growing resignation to a mere sentiment; it falls into purely isolated and incessantly changing positions, and its existence drops more and more into the transient and the shadowy. On the other hand, a great longing will again awaken for the object as an indispensable support for our life, and thus once more the beam of the scale inclines to the other side. This dialectic, in which each side through its isolation and overstrain destroys itself and returns to the other, shows clearly the necessity for *both sides* to instruct each other. But with the acknowledgment of a homogeneousness we do not gain a living unity; all merely individual effort for a Whole fails to free us from the power of a lifeless disunion, as our own times with their vacillation to and fro between soulless technics and a fanciful sentiment show with painful clearness. The presence of an Absolute Life which shall be above the opposites has as yet only intensified the longing for unity without conferring the power to satisfy the longing.

Another vicious cleft from which the Absolute Life should be freed is that between energy and character. Experience from of old has shown how the energy

has often mangled the character and the character the
energy, and how life has entertained a blind natural
impulse on the one hand and a powerless spirituality on the other hand.   Such a situation ought to
correct itself through the presence of an essential and
cultivated spirituality.   For within the province of
such a spirituality there is no definite energy which
does not involve an independent appropriation of
that spiritual world, and, along with this, acquire a
moral character; at the same time, the character
raises itself from a merely passive disposition to an
energetic decision—a decision in which the whole soul
connects itself together.   Thus, through the ennoble-
ment of energy and the strengthening of character an
inner unity is reached, and a new type of life is gained
in which the strong is good and the good is strong.
It is a matter of regret that such a type of life signifies
for us more of a distant ideal than of a present reality.
For not only does the antithesis imply undiminished
energy in the direction mentioned over the whole
breadth of existence, but the attempt at emancipation
seems to it to lie back still deeper in the spiritual.
Also, from an earlier simplicity of mind the idea has
become progressively explicit; so that one of the sides
raises itself above the other as alone of value, and
handles its opposite side as superfluous and even evil.
Thus, on one side, we find the exclusiveness of
spiritual energy—great dæmonic formations which
are completely absorbed in the victorious progress
of their own doings and creations, and treat all else
with supreme indifference ; which are served by the
events of life, and to which fate itself appears to
pay homage, although their course lies on the other

side of good and evil. And thus all moral judgment appears as a subsidiary consideration and even as an unbecoming intrusion. In all this there lies a wantonness which not only leads sooner or later to external ruin, but which also from the outset damages the spiritual character of the achievement. And, over against this cult of mere energy, we find a cult of mere disposition, the self-conceit and self-righteousness of a disposition apart from action, and resting exclusively in itself. Now, what happens within pure inwardness may, in its ultimate valuation, surpass in lustre the most brilliant performance in the moulding of the world. But when a frame of mind has no contact with the entanglements and temptations of the world, when the disposition is not turned into action, when there is no struggle with external things, when man revolves, from the outset, within a fancied superiority of his own mind, then life threatens to sink into inactivity, the weakness of the soul is reckoned as a merit, and in such a numbness and smallness of nature a pharisaic self-complacency arises. And the self-complacency of weakness is even more painful than that of strength. But how will such a disposition become the soul of a great life, and how will the cleft between wishing and achieving be spanned? Once again, we have not found those things together in human life, which, in themselves, require each other.

In corporate life that conflict appears in the discord between culture and morality (especially as represented in religion). Culture, with its development of energy, is apt to treat morality as a subsidiary thing, and to sacrifice it to its own ends; morality develops, over against this, a consciousness of inner superiority without being able, however, to develop a corresponding power. Morality, nevertheless, shows itself energetic enough to reveal the limits of culture, and to check men from finding full satisfaction in it. Thus each tendency is able to break the exclusiveness of the other, but neither is able to reach an exclusive rule. What, however, does the whole of the Spiritual Life gain through such a mutual hindrance?

The third antithesis is that of spiritual substance and psychic existence—an antithesis expressed in the noological and the psychological methods. This antithesis is brought, first of all, to the surface through the idea of the *essential* development of our nature, and only therewith does it become clear that, without the attainment by the Spiritual Life of an independence over against the purely psychic, there is no content of life and no connected spiritual world. But at the same time, the fact becomes apparent that such an elevated Life realises itself only in the form of psychic existence, and that its development proceeds only through the movements and experiences of such a form. Thus, as necessary as a clear separation of each series becomes the constant reciprocity of both. Here, also, the experience of life shows, in the main, a pointed and severe enmity. On the one side, we find misinterpretation of the incomplete state and limitation of human Spiritual Life, a rash seizure of the substance and the fixing of one's self on it; through this, however, a cutting off any further movement, thus causing a repression of all initiative and a premature conclusion as to the

meaning of life.   On the other side, we find the
attempt to gather up fragments of a content and
of a spiritual world out of the constituents of the
immediate psychic life ; and thus we obtain a good
deal of freshness, movement, and variation, but we yet
find also, on account of the inward contradiction of the
facts, a constant wish for more than can ever possibly
be, we find a fraudulent acquisition of the unprovable
and a great danger of shallowness.   Thus the opposition between substance and particular modes of
existence resolves itself into a disorder of the depth
and freedom of the nature ; the depth threatens to
become rigid, and the freedom superficial.   This strife
permeates the whole ramifications of life : no other
opposition drives men into such contending camps,
and none engenders so many parties.   It is thus
to-day in the particular province of Philosophy.   For
what else constitutes the deepest ground and the
strongest energy of the divisions of thinkers but
that one section takes its stand on the necessity of
the Spiritual Life, and that the other takes its stand
on the mere circumstances and experiences of man ?
The struggle between idealism and realism, the *a
priori* and empiricism, metaphysics and psychology—
all originate in the last resort out of the same root.
How can the presence of an Absolute Life be sustained when the movement towards truth itself is
retarded by the strife of parties, and remains determined by such a situation ?

(γ) *The Impotence of Morality.*—After all the
upheaval we have already observed, there remains
the very last means of escape, *i.e.* morality in its
self-subsistence as a kingdom of pure character, as the

decision concerning the complete direction of effort. However few results such a decision may possess from an external point of view, however many hindrances and limits it may meet within the soul itself, there originates with it an original province of life, a full *self-subsistence* of the inwardness of life which all the power of the enemy cannot possess. Here the soul longs for a secure superiority to the world, and gains also the indestructible certainty of a new order of things. Thus, many epochs became the possessors of all this; and later antiquity especially made morality a fast bulwark against all the doubts and toils of life.

All this becomes more conspicuously operative when the turn to religion posits the decision upon the whole of the universe, and when the decision yields itself to the determination of an Absolute Life. True, the problem becomes far greater; but also the confidence of man becomes far more joyous. Indeed, that turn originates from difficult entanglements of a moral kind; and an immediate conquest is not to be expected, but an inward strengthening and a victorious ascent are certainly craved by the soul of man.

Do things stand thus in the reality of our experience? First, so much is certain: religion shows far more the inadequacy than the sufficiency of our actions; concerning the judgment of the moral situation of man the Standard, for example, decides before all else the nature of what we construct, and shows what we ought to construct. Now, religion with its relationship to the Divine reveals such an Absolute Standard; the Divine valuation displaces all merely human estimates of things. While the latter state of things coerces the man within the man, its judgment with all its relativity loses its edge. The ordinary situation of human actions constructs its standard, but what remains behind such a situation condemns the situation ; what advances perceptibly beyond the ordinary situation is praised as being somehow meritorious, and is honoured as a service which is not unconditionally required from man. Over against all this, the Divine valuation of things raises itself and transforms the ordinary valuation, because its claims rest upon absolute perfection. Measured out of the infinite, all the differences of the finite vanish, and there remains only the common boundless expanse of space ; and it is through the recognition of something of this kind that all moral greatness and all moral service of man develop. Thus it has happened everywhere where the religious idea has dawned with full originality, as in the beginnings of Christianity and in the rise of Protestantism. It is only in the weakening of that idea that human valuations gain so much ground as they actually have gained in Catholicism.

The problem becomes acute, however, in the degree in which the spiritual and essential mode of religion longs for a recognition, and in the degree in which the conviction obtains that there stands in question not merely some kind of development in certain directions, but the essential development of the whole of our nature. After this, the revealed inadequacy confronts the whole of our existence ; then all which is termed customary morality appears as a thing which belongs far too much to the mere surface and far too little to the substance of the soul. And

21

when the inadequacy presents itself as the all-sufficient and the all-encompassing, a relentless struggle of genuine morality as against the mere semblance of it becomes inevitable.

Thus, all development of morality under the influence of religion has given a continually lower valuation to customary moral values. That which in worthy achievements attaches itself to bare natural energy must finally crystallise into the non-moral; that which works within the merely particular circle of human society towards the curtailment of selfishness and towards mutual advancement is much too external and is afflicted with far too much pretence to enter into the balance as an absolute valuation. But placed in a " beyond " to the social formation of things, all human morality appears insipid, vacillating, and hollow. It is a virtue out of a defect occasioned by temptations or by the equilibrium of errors; a legality which was never placed on trial; a love which remained true out of mere custom and because it knew nothing different; a belief and trust which never had doubts, and which felt no need to prove anything; a sacrifice which at the same time brought forth much profit. Over against such weaknesses we find the evil power of the passions, and man torn through them from his better judgment, and, indeed, against his better will, and all the remaining fully-recognised excellences driven from his nature as a dream and a shadow. And over all the particular passions we find the egoism, with its loosening of the individual from world-connections, and from its relationship to the infinity of the universe, brought to beggary. This egoism, through its inversion of the world (and so fundamentally different from natural self-preservation), seems to grow not weaker but stronger with the advance of culture; the historical movement may vary its form but it leaves the substance untouched. Such a relegation of effort to the small self becomes intolerable when the turn to his essential nature and its cultivation holds definitely before man a new self in the Spiritual Life; now the hold upon the small and shallow causes a self-alienation of man and a destruction of his own nature. And yet it persists and ever draws the new movement back to itself.

Thus the inadequacy of all human morality becomes quite evident. But what harm can come of this inadequacy if over against it a Divine energy awakes and a superhuman life kindles itself; if such a transition to a " better " then appear more clearly and more convincingly before our eyes ? But in the meantime such obviousness and energy of conviction fail to appear. Not only does religion seem to alter but little the total situation of life, but the entrance of the " higher " works in the first place principally in driving further the contradictions and in the awakening of otherwise slumbering oppositions ; thus the inversion reaches its climax, whilst the " good," even with the recognition of its highest worth, is dismissed, injured, and destroyed. When many thinkers of a rationalistic turn of mind declare it impossible that such an activity, which works against one's own conclusions and which disapproves of a Divine, can be itself Divine, they fail to understand the abyss of human nature and contradict the experiences of humanity. For in human life in general

there is an evil that goes beyond simple self-love—
there are envy and malicious joy over the calamities
of others, hate and jealousy ; and where one's own
welfare is not touched at all, there is an antipathy
towards the Great and the Divine, and a pleasure in
the defacement and destruction of the Good.   Through
this, what is evil assumes a positive form—it becomes
diabolical.   The burlesque figure of a devil has
vanished from our figurative ideas, but it has not
vanished out of human nature.   Further, the
mysterious fact of evil as a positive opposition to the
" Good " has not ceased to occupy the minds of the
deepest thinkers, and in spite of all attempted reconciliation the problem has ever anew broken out ;
it stands clearly before us at the present day not only
through the teachings of Kant and Schopenhauer,
but far more through the specific experience of
modern life itself.

Evil is thus in the highest degree to be understood
as an evidence of freedom, and the conception of
moral wrong will never allow itself to be expelled in
spite of all attempts.   But although moral wrong
gives its edge to evil, it is not responsible for all
the evil.   But what makes the situation of man so
especially painful is the fact that the total arrangement of life—which at least leads man if it does not
force him—becomes a failure even with man's own
activities.   Out of the hand of nature man receives
the charge of a persistent self-preservation which
often drives men against one another, and allows
one to welcome the injury of another on account
of advantage to himself.   Civilised life heightens
these entanglements through its multiplication and

refinement of wants and needs, through its manifold complications and the narrow concentration of men, through its fierce blaze of ambition and lust for gain—all which are deemed necessary for our self-preservation. Thus the release of energy and the restless extension of effort appear self-evident and incontestable; the common atmosphere, the social organisations, etc., are made to suit such a notion. And if we proceed only a step further we find the admission of merely instinctive attitudes into complete self-activity; we find that which occurs in daily life elevated into a principle; and thus the thing which really matters appears as a painful inversion, and falls in for unfriendly criticism. But this criticism grows out of relationships which carry our whole life, and, along with it, our spiritual development!

How shall we disengage ourselves from such a confusion? And what becomes of the presence of the Divine through such an upheaval of morality? In so far as the actual situation has been acknowledged, it has to all appearance less strengthened the reason of our existence than brought the unreason of it to a clear consciousness.

4. *The Darkness of the Human Situation*

Our attention hitherto has been specially directed towards the entanglements in the actions of man; but we have also to estimate his condition and the formation of his capacities. In regard to these latter the matter is not concerned merely with man's subjective happiness but with the Spiritual Life; it deals with the question—whether such a Life through its founda-

tion in an Absolute Being gains the energy to force
its way to the external world and to subject the
universe to its own ends? What leads to the formation of the value of values should certainly be able
also to reign and rule in our circle.

Before all else the desire of man appears in his
effort to reach spirituality through the aid of a power
superior to the world, to reach it especially in a hard
struggle against an alien, dark, and powerful world.
Indeed, the more the threads of the phenomena of
the universe run tangled through one another, the
more indispensable it is to link all human aims to
a power superior to the world; the harder are
the oppositions of the world-environment, the more
urgent is the hope fixed upon a help that is greater
than the world. Such a power is to raise our own
potency out of its insufficiency; it is to prepare a
secure path for our activity through a deep darkness;
and it is to transform the hindrance and opposition
into a conclusive advancement. It must raise man
immeasurably in the inmost of his being and strengthen
him in his courage to face life, so that he may be able
to consider himself an object of the care of an over-
world power and wisdom, and also of eternal love.
Upon the lower levels there may be enough admixture
of self-love and even vanity, but on the higher level
all this vanishes before the unique end of the spiritual
maintenance and elevation of man.

In reality this idea is so indispensable to religion
that an entire renunciation of it has been conceived
as the destruction of religion itself. In any case,
every conception of religion must aim at the
realisation of such an idea. If and how such a

realisation can happen does not concern us at this point of the inquiry ; here the question is not how the attainment of such a realisation reaches the idea of a Providence, but whether the idea seems sufficiently clear over against the condition of the world to win the seeker for itself. It is a bad mistake to mix together the matter-of-fact of experience and the claims of religious belief ; for he who carelessly carries into his nearest view of things what seemed to him from such a view to be self-evident, but what in reality becomes possible only after a great conquest, not only diminishes the expansion of life but also endangers the truth of life.

We must ask, therefore, without any prejudice, whether the surrounding objects allow us to infer a movement of the universe in the direction of spirituality, and whether a superior furtherance of a spiritual striving of man becomes clearly manifest. Doubtless there are numerous examples and modes of life which create the impression of a well-marked directivity ; numberless threads are discovered which bind themselves together and produce a favourable final result ; dangers are averted, and aids, beyond all expectation, are gained. But yet, the impression of the systematic arrangement of things can occasionally produce a result of the blindest gamble of things ; and in order to estimate with any certainty whether any evidence of a higher guidance and love is to be found in the co-operant behaviour of things, more is under consideration than a mere solitary event ; we must be able to know the relationship of actual instances to possible ones ; we must estimate the ratio of the prizes to the blanks ; and all this we are unable to do.

The impression of many opposite kinds of experience associates itself with such a darkness as we find in things around us. For we observe that there remain in man himself, without the needed aids from above, not only much goodwill and many busy activities, which, however, break in pieces before they reach their highest ends; there remain not only much spiritual energy and warm love unrealised—and in other cases much of all this is painfully lacking—but we also discover enchainments of phenomena which seem to lead to the creation of great misery, and which with unmerciful callousness drive man over the brink of an abyss. The faintest hint would have sufficed to hold him back from such a catastrophe, but this is not given, and consequently destruction takes its course. Petty accidents destroy life and happiness; a moment annihilates the most toilsome work. Often, also, we discover a chaotic medley, a sudden overthrow of all potency, a seeming indifference towards all human weal and woe, a blind groping in the dark; we discover gloomy possibilities constantly sweeping as dark clouds over man and occasionally descending as a crashing tempest. But, also, man's own destiny, as it were, plays with him, raising hopes soon to destroy them and preparing energies soon to annihilate them. And in all this we are to view an order of reason and a kingdom of love!

The attitude in which the customary mode of religion places itself in regard to these problems is lamentable, and is unworthy of the seriousness of the whole question. The matter is handled as though it were a legal question in a thoroughly attorney-like fashion.

The cases which seem to present an affirmative answer are recognised gladly as " the finger of God," especially where He seems to strengthen one's own party; but what shows life as suffering and unreason, as stubborn opposition and fruitless toil, is ignored or placed out of the way in a manner we should be ashamed of in connection with human things. Soon one flees to mere possibilities, and holds to the comfortable thought that things will soon turn the balance in an opposite direction, and that what began in pain and sorrow will end in pleasure and bliss. Soon this thought grants the consolation that, in spite of all the misery, it might have been worse; that the agony of suffering leads, after the exhaustion of all the energies, finally into death; and that a devastating calamity has not reached the depth it might have reached—all this is extolled as a grace of God. These assumptions easily satisfy; but does the world constitute a kingdom of reason because it is not the worst of all possible worlds?

If, however, the unreason is far too evident to allow the above conclusion to be accepted, there remains to the official defenders of the Godhead one other exit: suffering is not only apologised for but welcomed as an indispensable means for inner purification and moral cultivation. Now, one must be very undiscerning not to be aware that an order of things whose highest end is reachable only through severe suffering can never be a kingdom of reason. How stands the actual fact of the assertion? Can we say with certainty that suffering reforms man— reforms him in a decisive manner? Or does it not perhaps give another direction to his errors? As the experience of life is raised to the level of an unbiassed reflection, suffering is a shield against evil and pride ; man is able through great tribulation to rouse himself out of the numbness of daily routine, and is able, too, to pitch his courage to a gentle key, as well as to render sincere services to his fellow-men.   But, on the other hand, suffering often works in the direction of deadening and discouraging the powers, especially when it does not come to us in the form of a volcanic catastrophe, but accompanies the whole course of life as a continuous grief and as a cramping pressure.   The mean and common found in the chain of relations, from which the man is not able to withdraw, although he longs to do so with the whole of his soul, confine all aspiration and lower the level of life ; and close to such a level lies a turn to a petty and narrow-minded disposition, to bitterness of heart and jealousy ; indeed, through conditions wholly external, suffering and sorrow can suffocate all spiritual effort.   Thus testifies the immediate impression of experience for the Greeks, to whom happiness and success were held as aids of advancement for the moral education of man.   And the fact that Christianity took up suffering into the inmost soul of man, and made it a point of departure to an entirely new direction of life—a fact which will occupy our attention later—can only indicate a delusive superficiality and a dangerous inversion ; as though suffering, without further ado, through a kind of necessary effect, promoted a spiritual advance and a moral purification.   Then, indeed, the fact would be most simple, so simple that religion itself would become superfluous.   Certainly to all religious conviction the thought is indispensable that somehow at least a reason shall issue out of unreason. As it is presented in the book of Job: " And now men see not the light which is bright in the skies, but the wind passeth and cleanseth them "; but it makes a great difference whether, first of all, doubt is fully tasted, and whether an inner turn of life, through the deepest conviction, is prepared; or whether, through those supposed reasonable counsels of the Godhead, all shall soon be turned into the pure and the clear, and, along with this, all sting shall be plucked out from the serpent's head. As this beautiful colouring tends towards the blunting of the problem, it enters into a constant conflict with the plain meaning of truth. For the meaning of truth can only acknowledge the impression that certainly much in our potencies seems to point beyond ourselves, which, however, allows itself to be understood on the whole as a strong enchainment and a chaotic derangement of events, as an indifferent treading upon weal and woe, as no order of reason for the hopes and fears of man, and as no kingdom of love. And with what other eyes are we able to see things but with our own?

Much certainly remains mysterious; and especially mysterious is the fact that the life of man is not able to follow a directed course. It seems sometimes as if his life and actions were driven by an inexplicable power into a course unwilled by the individual himself; in many instances a strong wave seems to raise the potencies of man and to carry him far past his own capacities; in other instances such a power, with equal energy, seems to work against him, and to allow his choicest undertakings to be cruelly

wrecked. Thus, there has originated from of old
the belief in destiny which, with iron will, prescribes
his course for man, doles out his luck, and to resist
which is to wanton perversely. Spiritual control
is withheld from such a belief all the more because
human self-love disports itself wildly in the idea: if
the belief sometimes flatters the vanity that destiny,
through a supernatural power, raises the individual
beyond others, pettiness and weakness find their
most comfortable refuge in their attempts to impute
their own defects to an irresistible destiny. It is
a noteworthy fact that especially renowned men
of action, whose deeds operated so efficaciously in
a dark world and who brought forth incalculable
results, often lived in the conviction that they were
tools in the hand of an all-powerful destiny. This
belief, invulnerable against all dangers and certain
to lead to the appointed goal, was indispensable
to them in order to possess a joyous courage for
creativeness and for the assured success of their
enterprises. But all the power of such a subjective
conviction falls short of objective proof. Could it
not be that the self-feeling alone was expressed in
such a belief? Were, however, the reality of a
higher power here acknowledged, the mystery of the
whole world would increase rather than lessen. For
why does its solicitude contract itself upon individual cases; and how does it accord with an infinite
good when man is treated as a mere tool, and
recklessly cast aside just as he is about to reach his
longed-for goal? Also, in the lives of great men,
their energy seems to weaken after the culmination
of their work. And does there not remain here an

inexplicable incongruity between the seeming power of reason on its summits and its weakness on the whole? Heroes appear, work, and create; they overcome, as in a play, all opposition; they link their achievements to their further pursuits; thus their achievement enters into the whole and seems to control the destiny of humanity. But has much of reason, on the whole, issued out of all toil and work, and does history exhibit itself as a victorious ascent and a secure advance of definite spirituality? And if this is not the case, what avails all help of the Divine in individual situations? Once more, a half-reason seems to confront us, and the riddlesome appears as an entire unreason. Thus, it happens with us in our search for a guiding thread as it does with those who search for a track in a deep thicket. We seem to have found such a track; it seems to show a way through the labyrinth; it becomes clearer and seems to lead securely to a goal. But soon the track grows narrower, fainter, and vanishes, to reappear; again the imprints become fainter and fainter, until finally the last trace disappears, and all toil has yielded only a delusive hope.

Perhaps, however, the blame of the previous discontent lies on the inquirer; perhaps we have sought in a mistaken direction. If a benevolent providence that orders all for the best is not recognisable, yet there appear perhaps to clearer vision a moral order, an equilibrium of all action and condition, a strong kingdom of strong righteousness. The longing after a requital for righteousness is in no way the result of a petty disposition which desires a reward for the good and a punishment for the evil, or of a jealous calculation which grows anxious lest too little should come to us and too much should go to another. But the thought permits of being raised above the small human mode; and places before itself for its advancement the fact that the spiritual governs and rules the world as a moral order. This is what a Plato and a Kant aspired for.

Thinkers have thus shaped into a Whole and a Spiritual only what inspires peoples and epochs; and the former were rather called to transform the entire concept of reality beyond all experience than to bequeath anything for the intensifying of the demand. In the first place, one hoped to find the entire adjustment ready within the course of each individual life; as experience contradicted this, the vicissitudes of life were drawn into a concept; and consequently righteousness was hoped for in the future experiences of the race as a whole. But such vicissitudes of life engendered new problems without having solved the old ones; and now the thought soars beyond the realm of fear and hope, and passes beyond the limits of this life to seek the atoning righteousness in a future existence. Most peoples satisfy themselves with such a unitary consummation of things, and find in the thought of a judgment day a satisfying conclusion. Others, however, who have not merely thought forward but also backward, and who, with an unbounded imagination, soaring beyond the world, have gone much further and made of the present life an individual link of an immeasurable chain—as, for example, the Indian doctrine has done in its teaching of the transmigration of souls. The doctrine of an unescapable destiny controlling all actions constitutes the centre of religious conviction nowhere more than with the Indians; what is truly man's own seems here to be nothing more than his deeds; through life and death, through rebirth and transformation, the consequences of his deeds return to man from the good and the evil; nowhere is there an evasion or an aversion, nowhere a forgetfulness or a loss. The imagination has never worked more powerfully than in the keen tracings of such views of the universe; and the sway of such a teaching has not failed to exercise a strong effect upon the soul of man. But such systems carry conviction only for believers, to whom the doctrines make possible what is necessary for their souls. But he who does not feel himself in the position of a believer, but of a seeker, can have no choice but to look within his own experience for the essential facts.

Such essential facts do not fail us. A certain moral order, as it is termed, appears already in the natural concatenation of things as well as in the external results of action and in the judgment of the mind on such action. In reality, certain kinds of action exhibit characteristic connections which produce agreeable results, but there are other kinds which produce disagreeable ones; dissipation is less conducive to well-being than a well-regulated life; and an action corresponding to the legal and social ordinances is more favourable to decent living than a contrary kind of action. But how little, after all, is gained from such platitudes! They are valid only for isolated fragments of life; and this kind of adjustment touches merely the visible action, whilst the character remains unaltered. Indeed, the more the life intensifies itself, and the more the moral tasks extend over the whole area of life, the more inadequate will all such adjustments by means of natural results become.

But perhaps there grows with such a development of life as the action engenders in the inwardness of the soul a power of self-judgment, of conscience. Whenever life takes a turn from external effects to an inwardness of soul, it believes itself able to find here an uncorrupted judge of good and evil; the approval of this judge seems to produce joy and power before which all the suffering of life vanishes; its condemnation, on the contrary, causes a torment which reduces the value of the most brilliant external achievements.

Without a doubt we obtain here a primal spiritual phenomenon which only a shallow external mode of thought can lay on one side. Yet the question arises, as to how far this primal phenomenon reaches, and whether it helps to the production of a righteous order of things for the whole of our existence. But the most manifold reflections arise against such a view. First of all, the fact loses its supposed inviolable sublimity because the nearer kind of self-judgment is seen to be under the influence of a strong social environment: many actions have been valued by different peoples and epochs in quite contrary ways; a conscience which, however, as a kind of soft wax, shapes and alters itself with the customs, opinions, and tendencies of men, cannot very well be a true standard for good and evil or enunciate an entire righteousness for human existence.

Further, conscience is dependent in a high degree

on the individual nature of the soul. The reflex which the action throws on the consciousness is of various degrees of strength and accuracy: with one man the reflex may be extremely dull, and may work as an impulsive decision; in another, on the contrary, the reflex pins the man with great energy and will not let him free. Thus, the first man does not trouble over the most grievous wrongs, whilst the second excites and grieves himself over mistakes hardly perceptible. Physical differences of a coarser or of a finer sensibility have a large share in connection with all this; it is the height of the moral development, however, which decides concerning the strength of such a self-judgment. Thus most comes to him who needs it least. In the words of Pascal, " the righteous are wont to consider themselves sinners and the sinners righteous."

Finally, who can deny that conscience underlies the influence of men who have greatly perverted moral values and the aims of life? The words of Goethe, " the goal gives things their glory," hold good also in the particular domain of character. For the evil which we choose arouses us but little when its ill effect is not perceptible, or when it is trimmed into a supposed good through the sequence of circumstances; and thus the most righteous effort towards ourselves, and more still towards others, seems to remain trifling and poor if all success is denied it. Where, however, success in good or evil has been conspicuous, the disposition seems to grow greater and more energetic on the one side or the other. A judge so dependent and corruptible can never bring forth righteousness for the whole of life.

22

All in all, the matter here stands in a similar state to
that in which it stood in reference to previous points we
have considered.   It may well be, that a phenomenon
appears within the human province whose ultimate
meaning reaches back into the super-human.   But in
all the nearer development, the facts come under the
influence of human means and imperfection; we thus
seem to sink back into the same uncertainty out of
which we strove to escape.

If, however, human existence is not able through
its own means to satisfy the longing after righteousness, the moral order cannot be other than of an over-
natural kind: an over-world Will must re-establish
the equilibrium of action and condition which our life
fails to do.   The fact of such an adjustment of things
must become clearly discernible in regard to our
human view of things; and, indeed, it must become
clearly evident even beyond the human view of things
in order to be able to protect our conviction and to
govern our life.   Does it in reality do this?   Who
could confidently answer in the affirmative?   For the
impression of what is immediately present confirms in
no way within our experience the doctrine of a righteous course for the achievements of life; but it shows
far more clearly a great disproportion of things.   Soon
the action has the most serious consequences, and
all these consequences return to the man himself;
causality holds him unmercifully in its grip, and a long-
buried past may rise out of its grave and terrify him
as a ghost.   But, inversely, painfully wrong courses
remain for a long time without any consequences;
but finally these courses deprave the man not only
externally but also internally; they come upon him

as something alien, and disperse and destroy all as
with the ravages of a storm. Thus particular kinds
of foundations upon which life is based come to such
a lawless medley when they oppose the righteous
allotments of destiny. The individual is not an island,
but stands in manifold and often complicated relations;
he is conditioned by the nature of the environment, by
what he does and what he neglects to do in wide and
narrow circles, by family, nation, times, etc. Such a
serious complication here obtains that the consequences
of the action fall often less on the doer than on others;
one individual has often to atone for the wrongs of
others, and one generation for the foolishness of
another; the offence of one drags others into unhappi-
ness and misery; "the fathers have eaten sour grapes,
and the children's teeth are set on edge."

Herewith the threads run into the individual
scenes of life, entangled in one another without
binding themselves into a connected web and without exhibiting a common character. He who seeks
to draw a conclusion concerning the destinies of life
can hardly avoid that of a blind confusion; and
this confusion becomes a strong injustice when so
many differences of an inward kind and character
originate, as they in fact do originate. Such an
impression may call forth passionate protests and
accusations from one direction; in another direction
they may take the form of a disquieting doubt; but
in both cases the indifference of the world opposes
itself against the moral relationships and being
of man, and in direct antagonism to the strongest
activity of most earnest minds. That evil often
not merely hinders and rejects, but even advances

and rewards, and that the good seems continuously to abandon the hoped-for energy for the suppression and overthrow of wrong—all this has become in the particular province of religion a matter of incessant searching of heart and of sorrow. " Behold, I cry out of wrong, but I am not heard : I cry for help, but there is no judgment" (Job). " The righteous perisheth, and no man layeth it to heart ; and godly men are taken away, none considering that the righteous is taken away through wickedness " (Isaiah).

The general custodians of belief and the official representatives of religion have, of course, here as well as elsewhere a comfortable answer at hand. Man, they say, dare not reckon with God, whose decrees far overreach all human knowledge ; also, according to the Divine Standard, no one is free from blame, and, therefore, suffering met not unjustly even him who was righteous among men. How clear all this mystery seems to self-righteous men, who yet make a confession of their impotence ! What do they know of the decrees of God ? And how could they expect from man a suspension of his judgment and a denial of the imperative and urgent impressions which he forms? Certainly, all the moral differences of men vanish in the light of the conception of absolute perfection ; but man is not able to consider his actions in relationship to the Divine as solely his own concern, but also through the connections of these actions with his fellow-men ; he is not able to adjust the vicissitudes and values of life ; and when therefore he can find no righteousness anywhere, religion with its basing of the good in the Divine must heighten the pain and the unrest. And is not the history of religion itself full of the most painful persecution and oppression of the Noble and the Divine? Religion is never able to think lightly of such problems.

Further, injustice limits itself in no way to the relationship of inner and outer, of guilt and conditions, but it strikes its roots into the inward nature itself, it turns into guilt what is in no way so over its whole extent, and what is often hardly a guilt at all. The causation of things and the growing relationship of the individual with the environment through which much unmerited wrong has fallen on the individual enter, as we have seen, into his particular actions; what he designates as his own act is discovered inwardly to be only an inevitable final link in a long chain which reaches far back; indeed, reaches into immensity. All this may not lie entirely outside the fault of the individual himself; but the share of the fault that is not his own is nothing compared with what is reckoned as the guilt of the individual soul itself. The seeming inevitableness of that which, however, works as our own act—the growth of faults through the impervious web of destiny—has from of old occupied the attention of the deeper minds. The problem permeates ancient tragedy, and has ever since attended artistic creativeness to its heights; and that thinkers have not shut out the problem is shown by the words of Schelling: "The greatest conceivable misfortune is to become guilty through destiny without being conscious of any guilt of our own."

It is of great importance to bear in mind that things are not sharply marked off from one another in the web of life, and that good and evil do not

stand here pure and clear over against one another,
as has been pointed out in books on morality and in
edifying discourses.   But in the confused state of the
human situation, one element flows almost imper-
ceptibly into another ; our actions seem often entirely
indifferent to morality, and no danger whatever is
perceived as being present in the sphere of history.
And yet the road can lead, if we follow it further, to
the brink of an abyss ; a catastrophe breaks forth
suddenly ;   the   past   illumines   itself   clearly   and
piercingly, and shows a guilt in what previously
seemed to require no consideration.   The guilt here
often seems to lie more in the omissions than in the
commissions of life.   The unholy thing is avoided
through the calling up of opportune energy and
through the skilful installation of our activity.   We
have not called up the consciousness of the wrong,
but it comes upon us.   But did we know what stood
in question ; and could we measure the consequences
of a hesitation to decide ?   Thus it was upon our
ignorance and inability that the fact returned.   But
did not our action in some kind of way participate
in such an ignorance, and does not the fact, along
with this, again become our own guilt ?   Therefore,
guilt rests not so much upon the individual act as
upon the whole of our being.   But have we ourselves
brought forth this being of ours ?   Has it not de-
volved upon us through the destiny of nature, of the
situation of life, of education, of our times, of our
environment, etc. ?   Is not the fact of our aspiration
after the heights of spiritual development, in order
that we may feel ourselves free, in order that we may
strive after self-activity—is not all this more than the

result of that dowry of a particular existence and destiny? But if we are a mere piece of the world with its causality even when we feel ourselves free, whence comes the feeling of obligation and the consciousness of wrong which burden us often so unbearably? Is there not here imbedded the greatest injustice, that man should have to carry in his breast the pains and sorrows of freedom without being able to possess freedom? If things are otherwise, freedom is, in spite of all hindrance, able to maintain itself, and the whole world is rather to be dashed in pieces than to abandon freedom! But who confers on us the indispensable energy—the energy for the construction of a new kind of world? In the meantime, we remain in the custody of the old world, and experience here perpetually shows the most painful disagreement between the "ought" and the "is." We must act: the necessity of physical and social self-preservation compels us with unrelenting constraint to this. And we act in the region of darkness with a chance of success even there; without our being able to trace the connections and to measure the results, our actions alter the course of things and create a new situation. And yet in this we have fallen under the power of destiny. For the sequence of things may bring forth effects which we had not dreamed of, which contradict directly our own plans, and for which we are not responsible. Through such an inversion of plan and result we may injure where we ought to help, and destroy where we ought to build. When the winds and waves of destiny drive us to entirely other bearings than were present in our minds, what in all of this is man's own work, what of his

own being is in it? Does he steer his own course,
or is he a mere tool in the hands of dark powers?
Thus could the old poet cry out:

> "What then is man, and what not, too, is he?
> The dream of a spirit that ceases to be" (PINDAR);

and with a turn towards the moral problem, a more
recent great poet thus conceives of doubt:

> "Thou leadest man to life's domain,
> Thou countest to him many a blame,
> And then thou leavest him in pain" (GOETHE).

All doubt and sorrow, however, which call forth
such a view of the world and such a situation of man,
must fall with their whole energy on the soul of the
individual after the inauguration of an Absolute Life
within man's domain has immeasurably raised him.
For now he is no longer able to cast off from himself
the problems of the world; now he has immediate
participation in Infinity; now he must discover as
his very own the destiny which the Spiritual Life
experiences within the human province. Indeed, he
sees all his work and being placed under a pointed
contradiction which limits his actions, which renders
his feelings uncertain, and which makes his whole
existence enigmatic.

So far as the Spiritual Life develops itself, the individual gains the unique place where an originality
is able to break forth and to give an incomparable
worth and a secure superiority against all the remainder of his existence. Here alone—if anywhere
in human things—can there be a self-aim and self-
worth. That which pertains to the development of
man's soul—to the working out of his spiritual nature

—must act on the individual and must precede all
other tasks; it must all the more set the individual's
main energy in the direction of this goal because the
path to such a goal is full of toil and beset with
obstacles; and the individual dare not consider
anything which belongs to such a striving as small
and insignificant. For in all this the individual
struggles for something which brings forth with itself
a *world*—an essential world, behind which all the
"goods" of natural things take a secondary place;
here the matter at stake is concerned with the salvation of his own soul, the loss of which cannot be
counterbalanced by the gain of the whole world.
Thus, man's inmost consciousness enables him to discover such a fact as a holy duty; and the human
environment does not fail to support him in this.
Religion and morality strengthen him powerfully
in this task, and all deeper cultivation concerns itself
with the effort of reaching such a goal.

That such an upward movement proceeding from
such an inward obligation clashes with the most
pointed contradictions of the world-mechanism, has
already been shown in our investigation. Such a
mechanism treats all actions, and, indeed, all the
being of the individual with indifference, so that from
the mechanical standpoint they appear as illusory and
unreal. According to the meaning of the external
world, all the inwardness of man appears as an
insignificant point of an immensity whose original
elements become ever more inaccessible the more
science binds its effects into laws, and shows ever
more plainly its extreme callousness towards our
strivings. Human connections give the individual a

higher value: but here, again, the more the complexities multiply, the more exclusively do the achievements of man turn towards merely external aims, and these achievements become accordingly more and more one-sided; what is inwardly going on in man, what issues out of this inwardness, and what has become the stand-point of his soul, become largely subsidiary facts. Also, where all value depends on the achievements, no one is indispensable and no one but can be substituted by someone else—for all this mode of thought there is provision elsewhere for anything and everything; thus the stream of social life flows quickly over the individual with all his sorrows, hopes, and burning aspiration after a self of value. Consequently, on such a level, there remains but the relationship of indi-vidual to individual; if there is anything here which man may hope for, it is to be found as a self-aim and self-value in reciprocal love in the whole of his being, in his drawing nearer to the spirituality of his nature, and in his directing himself towards sympathy, com-prehension, and love. But through such a relation-ship of individual and individual, we meet not only in the province of the accidental but also within the inner situation of the soul, difficulties and infirmi-ties which persist with great obstinacy. What is usually praised as love rests so little upon the whole, the inward, and the essential; it is so entangled with bare natural impulses, and so dependent on external things, and especially so fugitive and transient, that it presents the deeper aspiration of the soul as an illusion far more than it helps that aspiration to obtain its fulfilment. Thus the individual sees his impulses appropriated—impulses worthy in themselves: they become acknowledged, valued, furthered, but are of no help to him in his hard struggle; he cannot, with all his aims, prevent himself from being dealt with by the whole of experience, because he himself must deal with all things from an inward necessity.

What conclusions, however, shall man draw from the fact that the world-mechanism is so indifferent towards him, and also seems so superfluous? From of old—with special energy in Stoicism—the method has been to seek liberation from the world, and to withdraw solely to one's own inwardness, and here to construct an independence against all the environment. In reality, the power to accomplish this lies in the ability of man to fix himself upon his own thoughts alone, and to reject all connections with the world; he can then create a characteristic happiness and a stolid feeling of superiority out of the liberation from all oppression and out of an elevation above the things of the world. But does such a self-affirmation of the individual suffice, and is it able to inspire the whole of life? Is there not, first of all, indispensable in all true effort towards spirituality a reciprocal communication, an exchange of life? Does not the separation of man from things speedily issue in an inner impoverishment? And when man casts a glance at himself, does he not meet difficult entanglements within his own nature; and does he not need for their solution the Other—the Whole? The fundamental fallacy of such an abstraction is to see the problem only in the relation of man to the environment; and if the soul discovers itself as full of entanglements, the insufficiency of such a view is clear.

But what shall man do when the world treats him indifferently, and when he finds no refuge in himself? Shall he, on his own side, acknowledge the negation which the world imposes upon him? Shall he simply abandon himself to that which restrains all effort, which suspends the Life-process, and which expects all safety through death and annihilation? He could do this if the movement of life were his own concern —his own private fact. But he could not do this if within him a Life-process not capable of being exactly defined—the opening out of a higher order of things—is acknowledged. Thus, there is something implanted in him which he dare not rob himself of; he now deals with a problem which he himself has not set, but which, as from a sublime energy, rises within him and refuses to be abandoned. However much of all this is concerned with the renunciation of his own happiness, man is not able to disown his spiritual nature and its tasks. In his nature and its tasks a fact seems committed to him which is of value not only for himself but for the whole; for the vindication of a higher order of things does not seem possible without his activity. Therefore, beyond all the physical oppression of life something metaphysical seems to govern and forbid a simple abandonment. If the fact stands thus, why does not that superior power help man? And why is man placed in a situation where neither success can be expected nor desertion be allowed? Must not such a contradiction destroy all courage for effort and creativeness?

CHAPTER X

b. The Opposition Considered

1. *The Inadequacy of Proposed Remedies*

WE have followed the main directions in which the development of an independent spirituality met with oppositions; evidently the hindrances do not stand separately side by side, but they mutually strengthen one another and raise one another into united action, so that they become an invincible power. The external world seems indifferent and rigid; human society is considered inadequate, and resting less upon truth than upon semblance; the spiritual movement within our own province is weak and full of contradictions; and in destiny there is to be recognised no government either of love or of righteousness; all, with the whole of its energy, extends into the life of the individual. Thus, how can man keep steadfast to his effort after independent spirituality and to a belief in the presence of the Divine?

All attempts which human need has made for its justification have been shattered on the rocks of these hindrances. First of all, all systems of optimism have been shattered. These may point out the

349

evident unreason of our situation and seek another standpoint of valuation, and also may place things in a larger system of relationships. Why could not the contradictions of the world disentangle themselves through such a standpoint into a pure harmony, or why could not what seems as a stubborn hindrance prove itself a means to the awakening and elevation of life? A beautiful prospect, but only a prospect! As we are not able to plant ourselves upon that higher standard, such a solution at the best remains no more than a mere possibility; and compared with the very stark reality of unreason, this possibility is hardly more than a shadow compared with a living body. The main fallacy of this attempt consists in that the fact is conceived as a problem of mere observation. If we were related to the world simply as observers, and if all suffering were nothing other than a displeasure of the observer with what occurs externally, a modification of the standard might effect in all cases a complete change of judgment. But we stand in no manner as mere observers of the world, but through actions and sufferings are drawn into the depth of the world; what we herewith experience is itself a piece of actuality; and this actuality will never allow itself to be placed on one side, or allow itself through any dexterity to be dissipated.

Also, the delusiveness of the hope of finding more pure reason in the movement of culture has been demonstrated in the whole course of our investigation. Indeed, the main point of the entanglement consisted in the fact that difficulties of an essential spirituality in connection with the highest questions made all progress insecure and all results double-edged ; the alleged gain transformed itself lightly into a loss, and what had long seemed certain fell ever anew into doubt and struggle. He who hopes for an essential betterment in the situation from the historical movement has to weave together independent and mere-human, central and peripheral spirituality into one.

Thus the solutions offered leave the facts un-furthered and the problem unsolved ; in the last resort we find ourselves ever thrown back upon the point from which we set out ; and the attempt to switch off from the entanglement makes it reappear in greater clearness.

2. *The Impossibility of a Negation*

If the facts stand thus, the oppositions increase from stage to stage and frustrate all efforts for the welfare of the soul. What then remains but an entire negation ? If the intolerable entanglements do not get resolved in some kind of way, the whole movement towards an independent spirituality is withdrawn, and the conviction of the presence of a Divine within the human province is relinquished. In whatever manner the conviction originated, it seems to prove itself an error by the poverty of its achievement. If the facts really stand thus, nothing must prevent us from drawing courageously and pronouncing honestly the legitimate conclusions. Thus, all that belongs to the turn towards spirituality or which results from it would be rejected as a mere illusion, and would be removed wholly from our life. Although this could not happen at one stroke, the duty of veracity would at least command

an energetic striving towards this end, if, indeed,
after such a breach there should be any place left
for veracity and duty.

The consequences, difficult as they are, should not,
therefore, deter us from a task of this sort. But we
are not quite so sure whether absolute negation really
brings the situation to a correct expression. We
have already seen that a painful contradiction permeates the whole of our existence, that neither the
world nor our own capacity corresponds to the tasks
laid on us and which gain our conviction. Could
the contradiction long for the vehement and stirring
energy which we have already discussed, if such tasks
were imposed on us only externally, and if such an
energy deceived us as a merely transient play of fancy ?
If there develops within the whole of life an earnest,
penetrating conflict, a two-sidedness of life has
become apparent ; there originates now not only
something that hinders, but also *something that is
being hindered*—something whose development fails
to succeed, something that is everywhere denied its
request, but that never allows itself to be explained
away into pure nothingness, or to be blotted out of
life as mere fancy. Pascal was right when he stated :
" *Qui se trouve malheureux de n'être pas roi, si non
un roi dépossédé* "; and were there not imbedded
in human nature an exalted movement superior to
all arbitrary action, the state of our world could
never engender so much agitation, indignation, and
pain. Through what other means do the strangeness
and indifference of soulless nature become grounds
of complaint, than through the fact that we are able
to reflect on a Whole and relate ourselves to higher

aims ?   How could the evanescence of our existence, for example, create a pain unless something Eternal worked in us and withstood the dissolution of things into a mere flux of time ?   Why do the inadequacy and the perversity of the social configuration of Spiritual Life grieve us unless another configuration of life aspires over against the social form, and now relegates all actions and impulses to a lower level ? Could such difficult entanglements be discovered in the inwardness of the Spiritual Life unless in some way a superior order of energy brought about the opposition, and unless we were, in some way, inwardly raised beyond the sphere of conflict ? Why do the flaws in love and righteousness within our circle distress us so acutely unless some precious good suffers injury ?   Finally, how could the individual experience the entanglements of the whole as his own particular life unless he had some-how raised up a new order of things to the level of cosmic significance ?

All this has run as a leading thought through the whole of our exposition ; the hindrances have ap-peared so great because new and greater demands have been made ; so that here we only gather together what, as a matter of fact, manifested itself step by step in the actual condition of things, viz. that the strength of the suffering and the hardness of the contradictions prove themselves to be the best testimony for the depth of our existence, and for the efficacy of a higher energy. A Nay which calls forth so much stir and movement is impossible without a Yea, although such a Yea may be imbedded far in the background of life.

The inward contradiction of absolute pessimism

lies in that it sees but one side of the facts, in that it ends with what falls within the realm of perception only, and in that it does not concede that the impressions, the stirring, and the suffering, however deep and ardent they may be, could occur unless somehow a positive life and striving were being hindered. If all is futile, there arises no kind of disparity; pain is an illusion which easily allows itself to be shaken off. It is an absurdity to bewail the privation or the loss of that the possession of which granted no happiness. Such a contradiction permeates the Indian conviction and feeling respecting life. Here pain originates primarily out of the experience and perception of the instability, transitoriness, and incessant flux of things. But how can the transient be an evil if we, root and branch, belong to the kingdom of flux, and, therefore, lead but the life of a day? If in reality the evanescent can be felt as pain only by a nature intended for the Eternal and thirsting after Eternity, then the strength of pain bears immediate witness to that longing for Eternity. This is the element of truth in the Hellenic thoughts concerning the privative nature of evil—in the conception of evil as a mere hindrance and a robbing of the good—so that, in fact, without some kind of pre-existing good, suffering would have no intensity and pain no depth. But such an optimistic conception erroneously assumed that through the presence of a ready-made kind of good it was able to substantiate the predominant power and authority of the good. But a mistake quite as great is to be found in pessimism, in that, speaking generally, it wipes out all the good because its development in human existence strikes upon difficult entanglements.

Also, the experience of life speaks clearly enough in the same strain. In no manner is the sense of hard suffering wont to drive man to an entire negation. But even when calamities hurl themselves against him, when he is threatened not only from without in all that he loves, but also when he is convulsed to the very depth of his existence, such a situation is able to quicken in him a certain axiomatic consciousness of his relationship to an order of things on the other side of all the conflict, the certainty of the indestructibility of his inner nature, as well as a strength which will enable him to reach his goal. Such a province of hindrance appears then as a stage of reality, as a stage which cannot possibly signify the whole of man's existence. Nothing protects life so effectively from the total abandonment of existence and from a docile resignation to the thought of annihilation as deep suffering, especially suffering and pain in spiritual things—in such things as are here in question. It is not epochs of troubled experiences and difficult entanglements which make humanity err in regard to its higher tasks, but far more epochs of idle pleasures and seeming plenty. Further, over against religion, a strong experience of the unreason of our existence has worked not so much in the weakening as in the strengthening of belief, and such an experience, beyond all capacity of a direct demonstration of the truth, heralds the necessity, the certainty, and the actual presence of a new world. In the midst of the most confirmed doubt—a doubt that cannot be refuted to its very root—the impossibility of a complete negation has become manifest with victorious clearness.

In view of such a train of thought, all the stubborn
hindrances which human existence reveals cannot lead
towards an entire renunciation; that which always
stamps human existence as something petty and inadequate—that which brings to the mind our long
distance from the goals of life—transforms itself into
a testimony for the reality and the altitude of these
goals; thus the greatness of the Spiritual and Divine
clearly appears in the pettiness of the human.

Thus, a depth of things is evident in all hindrance, and such a depth demonstrates the impossibility
of a simple negation.   Also, all the darkness leaves
it beyond question that the Divine emerges, first of
all, not from the outermost boundary of our life, but
through a creativeness and activity in the inmost life
itself.   In the form in which this work of the Divine
appears first, it certainly negates more than it affirms:
there does not result the construction of a kingdom
of pure reason, yet all satisfaction in merely human
things is forbidden; all attempts at a self-revolving
and at an anchorage in the merely human province
are opposed, and an inexorable tribunal is set up
against all self-sufficiency and all self-adulation of
human nature.

This appears clearly in two directions.   On the
one hand, it is seen in the power of logical thought,
in which appears something superior to all human
opinion and inclination, which shows fearlessly the
weal and woe of mere man.   The process goes
forward, is driven and linked solely through its
own necessities; all the attempts of man to draw
such necessities into his own track and to adjust
them to his aims are lamentable failures.   Certain

ideas have appeared, they have won us, they were welcomed by us so far as they have performed for us some service and did not exact too great a sacrifice from us. In such a situation we might, as individuals and classes, have retained such ideas and placed on one side certain uncongenial circumstances; we might have shaped them so that they might fit comfortably into our plans. But however much we might labour and trouble, however much we might attempt to turn the current with all zeal and perseverance, it avails us nothing, because logical ideas will not allow themselves to be bent and turned; a secure superiority over all the contents of time is presented even to weakness and awkwardness when these possess the conclusions of thought and bring them to a clear expression. Thus, we find a secure superiority of thought over all the undertakings of mere man.

A similar conclusion presents itself in the appearance of contradictions in human life. Pointed contradictions may be contained within the bounds of an epoch, and may cause no unrest or disturbance so long as they do not become explicitly recognised. But a moment arrives when this happens; and when it does happen, all the possibilities of repression, enfeeblement, and cheerful accommodation disappear; then the higher assertions develop their full strength, and the opposition to them is unceremoniously ended; happiness, rest, and the earthly welfare of man become secondary things. This has actually occurred in political and social movements.

The encounter between such a progressiveness of logical process and such an irreconcilability of the opposites creates a universal dialectic, which does not move in the precise forms presented by Hegel, but whose mighty power is unmistakable in human life. The Spiritual Life always steps on a special path within the human ground, and the following of this path issues necessarily in a strong one-sidedness, where its very success engenders more and more error. Now, a rejection of this error does not result through any toning down of the assertions that are made, or through the breaking off of points and angles, but through a sudden change into an entirely real—not logical—opposite; after such a change, a new power is conferred on man, and yet he follows his track with the old exclusiveness until the integrity of truth is threatened; and one sudden change after another probably enables the man to take a new direction. Such movements fill the history of the world with their smaller and greater waves; whether a positive progress towards reason is to be found in them, can in no manner be discovered. Viewed externally, the waves seem to run in an aimless ebb and flow. However, it is certain that all ascent and descent, all " becoming " and passing away, lie on the other side of the interests of the individual, and are in no way confused through his wishes and strivings. Such movements never allow man any kind of rest; they never reach a secure foundation; their continuance is always in jeopardy; they destroy ever anew all self-satisfaction through the effects and creations which they produce. Thus spiritual forces rule in man —forces which humiliate him profoundly, and which adjudge him a worth only in so far as he decides to become their own instrument; while, at the same time, in spite of all his brilliant achievements, they destroy him if he attempts to thwart their action.

Along with this superhuman sovereignty of a formal kind, there becomes allied a sovereignty of an intrinsic kind. This results in its characteristic features in morality, in its superiority and, indeed, in its opposition to all purely human aims. So morality must consider the natural mode of man as something distant, alien, and even hostile; it has a kind of natural instinct against itself; it is quickly repressed through the ordinary everyday experience of the human situation, and is easily transformed into a mere semblance. It gains no strong positive power in such a situation. On the other hand, however, an influential authority in negation is unmistakable. But such an authority renders man uneasy and brings clearly before his mind the inadequacy of all his undertakings; it exercises, in the form of conscience, a judgment concerning his actions from which he is not able permanently to withdraw himself; it destroys also satisfaction in the most brilliant achievements of a culture which believes itself able to dispense with such a sovereignty; it avenges itself throughout for all neglect of the consideration that without such a sovereignty all the gains of life, with their tendency towards selfishness and pride, threaten to capsize into peril and loss.

Matters do not stand otherwise with religion. Religion, too, in so far as it has outgrown superstition, has the natural inclination of mere man more against than for it; nature does not transmit a veneration for a "higher" than itself; and even where religion has stood in high external honour, there have been many complaints of the unbelief of mankind. In the average of human conditions, religion has always been more of a semblance than of a reality ; and what religion has performed on such a plane has been full of contradiction. But in spite of all this, religion remains a mighty power in human life and in the universal movements of mankind. For it has brought forth a new standard which makes inadequate all that previously sufficed ; it has shown the evil doings of man and the limitations in his valuation of things ; and, along with this, it is called to create a cleft in the inmost soul itself. That great turn of religion is the raising up of new demands to the level of the Spiritual Life and a blotting out of what had hitherto satisfied man. Thus we find it most of all in the personality and life-work of Jesus. Here we find a human life of the most homely and simple kind, passed in a remote corner of the world, little heeded by his contemporaries, and, after a brief period of blossoming, cruelly put to death. And yet, this life had an energy of spirit which filled it to the brim ; it had a standard which has transformed human existence to its very root ; it has made inadequate what hitherto seemed to bring entire happiness ; it has set limits to all petty natural culture ; it has not only stamped as frivolity all absorption in the mere pleasures of life, but has also reduced the whole prior circle of man to the mere world of sense. Such a valuation holds us fast and refuses to be weakened by us even when all the dogmas and usages of the Church are detected as merely human institutions. That life of Jesus occupies evermore a tribunal over the world ; and the majesty of such an effective bar of judgment supersedes all the development of external power.

Hence, in spite of all the confused state of human things, an elevated Spiritual Life is not merely an object of aspiration and hope, but also works in us in the form of immediacy; first of all, certainly, as a law and a bar of judgment—as a power which forbids in an obligatory manner the conclusion that human effort is no more than the work of mere man, and which sets forth with uncompromising clearness the vanity of all merely human undertakings. Not only in certain directions but in all Spiritual Life such meek and energetic effects appear with mighty power.

Man is incessantly endeavouring to attribute to himself what comes only from the Spiritual Life; he interprets himself as a standard, as public opinion, etc. ; he makes himself judge over good and evil, the true and the false. But when he presents the semblance of truth, he does not present with this judgment the energy of truth ; sooner or later the definite standards of the Spiritual Life make their appearance and demolish the semblance. The Spiritual Life allows itself provisionally to be drawn into the service of human aims ; but it soon disengages itself from the obscurity and humanisation, and demonstrates its independence and superiority.

All this remains full of problems and mysteries ; but in spite of the darkness so much as this is certain, that a superhuman Spiritual Life signifies no illusion. If it rules over us as a sublime power, as law and tribunal, it is and remains a reality founded on a rock—safe against all the waves of negation.

3. *The Necessity of Further Manifestations*

Impossible, however, as an entire abandonment of religion is, the entanglement receives through religion more of another configuration than of a satisfactory solution. For a greater depth of life may be recognised on the other side of the province of the hindrances, and a directive power of a spiritual kind may work within our existence. We are not able, however, to know whence such a power comes; but it is a positive participation in the Spiritual Life and a full awakening of powers planted in the hidden depths of our nature. It is this alone which invests our action with value, and which is able to free our conviction from doubt. Without such a turn we remain permanently in a vacillating, intermediate position: a higher world is perceptible, but in our province it does not seem able so far to overcome the immense oppositions so as to reach a positive development; it has certainly driven out all hope of deriving satisfaction from merely human things, but it has not granted us the compensation of a new life. Thus, we do not see what the goal of our action is, or the Why and the Wherefore of the action. Has the Divine only opened our eyes in order that we may discover its immeasurable distance from us and our own vanishing smallness at the same time? And is then all that we may undertake of no avail; and must not, under such impressions, all human effort be utterly dissipated?

Thus, even with the recognition of that depth of things, and of that sovereignty of the Divine, all still remains in question; and the most painful dilemma ever confronts us, viz. that there is too much reason to pronounce a negation and too little to pronounce an affirmation. *Si deus, unde malum; si non deus, unde bonum?* How can we hope to escape from this dilemma? All the previous facts and reflections do not help us to answer the question; the one hope lies in the fact that the Divine, through some kind of positive effects, may appear in our circle. It is only a further reality that can lead the Yea to a final conquest, and, along with this, rescue our life from the menace of destruction. Therefore, it behoves us to look for this. That man, in the disorder of his life, cried for outward signs and wonders, we can understand without having to do the same ourselves; but we, too remain dependent on a wonder, on an ampler and more pervading Divine, since this alone is able to raise us out of our hitherto-prevailing contradictions, and to guide our life to a path of safety.

Part IV.—Characteristic Religion

INTRODUCTION

Our previous discussion has resulted in a strong aspiration after new realities—after a further manifestation of the Godhead. The counterpart of this developed so powerfully within the domain of man that the life entered into a complete deadlock; there could be no doubt as to the inadequacy of mere man; the Divine, however, revealed itself as law and tribunal, and brought new aims and standards into our life, but it granted not the energy to realise such aims and standards; it allowed the unreason of existence to be disclosed to its very depth, but it did not lead reason to a victory against unreason. Thus, the entanglement seems heightened within us; what grows thence into doubt may not extend to the Divine itself, but man is saturated with it, and, indeed, it robs life of all its significance. Of what avail are all toil and activity if they are not able to assert themselves against such powerful opposition, and if while we divine a new world we yet find the path to such a world closed?

We have already seen that there is only one hope of escaping from such an intolerable situation: the Divine Life and Being must reveal itself still further in the midst of the needs and struggles of our existence; such a new reality alone can prevent an inner collapse of life, and turn doubt and depression into fixity of purpose and joyousness. Does such a turn in actual fact result?

A belief in this runs through humanity; it speaks out of all religions, and has attained an independence over against culture, and has brought forth from the so-called historical and positive religions a characteristic world of thought. For to all religions belonged the desire not so much to assist in obtaining the whole of the Spiritual Life through man's own achievement, as to bring forth something *new*, and to gain the whole soul for this. Over against the chaotic darkness of human existence they created their own kingdom and rescued in this, as in a sheltering ark, the ideals of humanity; this kingdom, however, seemed especially strong through what it possessed in discernment and uniqueness. The historical religions, through such a configuration, appear as an answer to the question which presented itself in our prior investigation—an answer not through ideas and doctrines but through life and act, an answer not of the mere individual but of the corporate experience of humanity. Only the pity is that where we long for a flawless certainty a strife soon breaks out, and that where we desire *one* answer the historical religions offer many and conflicting answers. How is this? Do the various claims destroy one another, and does hope of help disappear at the same time? Or does all the ramification allow a universal truth to break forth—a truth which promises to guard us and to lead us further?

CHAPTER XI

a. The Historical Religions

1. *The Fact of Religions*

Our introduction dealt briefly with the historical religions; but it is our aim now in a more precise manner to conceive of their significance and greatness, and to consider what is problematic in them. That such religions present a unique mode of life over against the ordinary world and ordinary reason, is shown by the mode of their origin. For they do not spring in a calm kind of way from the ordinary work of thought; but appear as an entirely new beginning in great personalities, who, as mediators between the Godhead and the world, announce the will of God to humanity, and establish a closer communion between the Godhead and humanity. The precise content of the message and the mode of communion decide the characteristic nature of the particular religions; for religion may be conceived as a conjoint struggle for goodness, light, and purity as means of protection from evil spirits as in Parseeism; it may be a covenant formed between God and his chosen people, which leads to a stricter fulfilment of the law

or to an alternative retribution as in Judaism; it
may finally be a Kingdom of God which binds all
men to their Heavenly Father in mutual love, and
which, indeed, leads to a union of the Divine and
the human natures as in Christianity. Religion ever
establishes a unique communion of life with God;
it ever allows such a communion to engender a new
reality which will signify not a mere addendum to
the remaining life, but the kernel of the whole. The
conceptions of God, the tasks of life, spiritual greatness and values, shape themselves characteristically
and pre-eminently in accordance with the quality of
the new life. Thus, each religion has its own view of
the universe and its own morality. And it is by virtue
of this individual and underivable characteristic that
religion feels itself mighty and hopes for redemption.

Such an independence and individuality have been
attained by religions especially through the greatness
and energy of their founders. To these founders the
new kingdom was no vague outline and no feeble
hope, but all stood clear in front of them; the
kingdom was so real to their souls and filled them so
exclusively that the whole sensuous world was reduced by them to a semblance and a shadow if they
could not otherwise gain a new value from a superior
power. The new world could attain to such immediacy and impressiveness only because a regal
imagination laboured for a unique picture in the
confused heap of life, and held it up over against all
the confusion, and because it invested this picture with
the clearest outlines and the most vivid colours.
Thus, the new world dawns on humanity with
fascinating power, rousing it out of the sluggishness

of daily routine, binding it through a corporate aim,
raising inspiring ardour through radiant promises and
terrible threats, and effecting achievements otherwise impossible. This prepared road into the kingdom of the invisible, this creation of a new reality
which is no merely serene kind of play but a deep
seriousness, this inversion of worlds which pushes
sensuous existence far away and which prepares a
home for man within the kingdom of faith—all
this is the greatest achievement that has ever been
undertaken and accomplished upon human soil. In
order to accomplish all this, the founders must be
great thinkers; and far more than being thinkers,
they must be great artists ; and far more than being
artists, they must be heroes of action. And, at the
same time, they must be raised above all action to a
secure repose in an Eternal Order, and be possessed
of homely simplicity and a deeply child-like nature
in the midst of all the complications and excitement of world-transforming power. Consequently it
becomes easily conceivable how the estimation of
their adherents raised the founders beyond all human
measurements to a likeness to God, and, indeed, to
an equality with God. Their works seemed to carry
within them Divine energies ; wonders surrounded
their paths; their life and being bridged securely
the gulf between heaven and earth.

It thus became of the greatest importance to
acknowledge these personalities in order to bring life
into a safe track. But the reality founded in God
became at the same time an enormous task for man.
The new life had to be assimilated, to be developed, and
to force its way against a hostile world ; thus man

became a co-worker with God, and his life through this gained immeasurably in value. Out of such an association a corporate circle grew up ; high aims and great hopes united men together and strung their energies to the utmost tension ; in united convictions and in their fundamental experiences men found the help of God entirely certain, and were fully armed against all doubts and temptations.

The rights of what had been discovered as truth in such a new world could not be set aside by general reason. For it was precisely in that which brought *something new* over against such reason that the energy and strength were to be found ; therefore, the *New* must stand upon its own particular kind of proof; and thus it comes to possess an actuality against all reason, and demands for such an actuality a willing acknowledgment in the confiding faith of man. The conception of faith received through this a more definite meaning than is presented in the *universal* delineation of religion. It is not mainly a revelation of God that stands here in question but this special revelation appearing in the midst of history; the Yea bound itself more definitely with a Nay, and the acknowledgment was bound up with an exclusion. Here, the thought of the underivableness of the truth easily became excessive ; so that the contradiction of reason was welcomed as an evidence of the incomparable and superhuman character of the new truth, and a *credo quia absurdum* inspired joy. In any case, one felt certain and joyful in the possession of a truth lying beyond all the complications and superfluous formalities of brooding reason ; this truth

24

alone seemed accessible to man independently of his stage of intellectual development ; men of deep spirits, however, could point to the justification of what they held in the fact that all mediate knowledge in the last resort rests upon something that is evident only in the form of immediacy, and that the final root of reality is to be conceived as an act of freedom which is simply non-derivable.

To such a positiveness of the foundation there corresponds in historical religions a positiveness of content. We have already seen religion, in general, dividing life into a For and an Against, and creating an enormous movement ; and all this in the historical religions experiences a general enhancement. As the affirmation here is more precise and is traced out in an enclosed circle of life, much is pushed out to the opposite side—even much that belongs to the Spiritual Life itself—and thus the tension and struggle must become incomparably harder. But this may signify from the standpoint of historical religion simply a gain, because it will more than anything else lift life out of the idle indifference which forms the worst enemy of all spiritual movement ; it will, too, exercise an energetic counter-effect to all that is small and mean, which otherwise chokes human life ; it will, through such a concentration, consolidate life securely in itself and place it on a foundation which seems simply indestructible.

We have noticed the opposition to religion turning into a doubt whether man, in spite of all his efforts, penetrated in any kind of way to truth ; whether the union of the Divine and the human, which constitutes the kernel of religion, reaches any measure of success. Historical religion overcomes this doubt from its very root and through the whole of its extent. For historical religion causes the Divine to enter into the province of man, and makes the effective communion the soul of all life. Through such a definite union of the Divine and the human, the image and the conception of the Godhead at the same time transform themselves. How could the Godhead be moved by human need; and, on the other hand, how accept the help of man? How could the Godhead bind itself to an inner communion with us unless It left Its celestial abode and dwelt among men? If, thus, the human appears as essentially related to the Divine, or if the human is raised beyond all narrowness and particularity through the descent of the Divine into its nature, the human may assign the highest conceptions of its own circle to the Divine, and thus penetrate beyond the colourless conception of the Godhead to the conception of a living and personal God who is present in the form of immediacy, and with whom the soul can converse as an I with a Thou. If man owes his greatness to the fact alone of a communion with the Divine, then it is not an anthropomorphism which the man holds; but a return is made from the image to a prototype when man, from the best in his own nature, traces out an image of the Godhead.

Through such an approximation of God to man, the union between both could develop far more inwardness—an inwardness which is able to dispense with all relationship to the world, and which is even able to exercise its entire energy in opposition to the world. It is here therefore that the individual

acquires a value, because it is here that the Highest
Nature concerns itself with him; here man may
have intercourse with the Divine as with his best
friend; here originates a religious emotional life—a
piety in conscious opposition to all external forms
and productions.   In such a religious emotional life
there develops a pure life of the Spirit within itself;
here an unassailable refuge from all strife and alarm
is found; here flows a pure stream from which
life is able to refresh itself ever anew with might.
Through their achievements within their own province
the historical religions have worked mightily upon
the whole of life and have implanted in it an
energetic motive for the deepening of the self; wide
circles of the human race have gained an energetic
emotional life through such religions.   As soon as
religion becomes relaxed, the inwardness turns into
insecurity and succumbs to the power of the intrusive
external world.

A union with God so intimate and so fervent
would have precluded all relationship with the world,
and would have made all work for the world so indifferent if the historical religions had not created side
by side with the formation of such inwardness a visible
sphere of life, and had they not united men most
intimately with each other.   And how could these
religions abstain from such a creation, since they were
concerned fully to develop the fellowship of life manifested by them and to maintain such in the midst of a
hostile world?   Thus, there arose communities and
churches governed by religion which presented themselves as the soul and kernel of the whole of life.
In these religion gained a visible presence; here

the Divine seemed to flow intimately into the human. On account of this, such institutions became in the course of their development the main evidences for the truth and power of religion as well as a solid bulwark against doubt. Life was here brought into a safe path; here a sharp distinction between friend and foe was made; here individuals united themselves in a co-operation not only of character but also of work. Man, in the inmost depth of his being, was here united with the fellowship; because nothing other than this fellowship could grant and guarantee a Divine revelation superior to all subjective reflection. Thus, a withdrawal from the fellowship appeared as a falling from truth.

True, difficult entanglements and perhaps, also, contradictions are involved in all this; and these will shortly occupy our attention. But, indubitably, a great fact and a mighty enrichment of human life are to be recognised in the historical religions. Through the concentration which they accomplish and represent, they have conferred upon history incomparably greater intrinsic value, contrast, and movement, things which otherwise threaten to dissolve into sheer unintelligibleness; they have incarnated in flesh and blood; they have gained wide spheres of the human race for spiritual things; and they have raised, in the midst of our world, an over-world of the most mighty power. If, then, every unbiassed mind is compelled to acknowledge here a great and, indeed, a unique phenomenon, it means that a decisive and final turn has resulted for men through their entrance into historical religion. Life can no more come to a deadlock, and doubt can no more harm where God, over against the world, has revealed Himself to man and never ceases to reveal Himself.

2. *The Opposition to Religions*

History bears testimony to the mighty effect of religions, but none the less does it show an incessant counter-effect ; religions, in spite of their development of power, are always objects of gainsaying. Such an opposition has formed an undercurrent wherever religion has stood externally in an entirely secure sovereignty. The constant complaints as to the indifference and the unbelief of its adherents show this. Whenever the relaxation of the social pressure permitted a free articulation, doubt grew quickly into a dangerous power, and threatened religion in the whole of its existence. If Augustine was right in stating that religion, as an historico-social institution, cannot subsist without a strong authority (*sine quodam gravi autoritatis imperio*), he indicated, at the same time, how slightly religion roots itself in the inwardness of man. But it is not mere individuals or even mankind at large, who, from an insipid disposition, raise ever new doubts ; there are also entanglements of an actual kind — hesitations and doubts within the Spiritual Life itself, working for a painful upheaval of the whole.

First of all, it is the plurality of historical religions which produces alienation and uncertainty. Religions themselves have sought to place the facts aside ; indeed, they have kindled a flame of passion against the facts. Through such an opposition to other modes of thought and religion—modes which appeared to the advocates of the " chosen " religion as

a web of human folly, and, indeed, as a deception of
the devil—the greatest energy was awakened and the
most frantic passions were not only tolerated but
commended.   Religions, in their struggle against one
another, have fettered the soul of man to themselves ;
also, within the individual religions such a schism
has heightened work and zeal, and when peace was
brought about, it brought inevitably along with itself
an enervation.   Struggle is the life-element of historical religions ; for it alone seems able to set the
truth in full light, and to carry the energy to its
greatest tension.

But the problems are not solved by the mere
assertion of their solution by religion.   Questions
and doubts do not allow themselves to be banished
out of the world by interdicts and threats.   So long
as man remains within an enclosed social sphere
and brands all that exists outside that sphere as
a monstrous folly, so long is he able unhesitatingly
to consider his own religion as the only true one.
Modern man, however, has outgrown such narrowness ; he surveys the different provinces of culture
and also of the various religions ; an historical mode
of observation compels him to estimate religions in
their connections, to enter deeply into these connections, and to investigate their validity.   The more
he does this, the more uncertain becomes the exclusive
validity of his own religion.   The sincerity of conviction and the passion of belief of the remaining religions
are not less strong and genuine than those of our
own religion ; they, too, rest upon great personalities ;
they have their signs and wonders, and, what is more
significant, their heroes and martyrs ; and they have

also moved individuals to the depth of their souls as well as surged through the history of the world with mighty power. What right have we to interpret these phenomena outside our own sphere as fancy and deception; whilst our own phenomena are of the same nature, and these are considered by us as solid facts and as safe citadels of truth? Could the ideal world and the life-constructions of many millions and whole millenniums originate through bare illusion? What in the face of all this assures us that it is not similar with us; and that our belief, too, has not been revealed from on high but has issued from purely human ruminating? Or shall we estimate ourselves and others by different weights and measures, as the fanaticism of all times has done, but always without the sanction of justice?

But perhaps religions will deal with a proof obtained through a comparison of their most important achievements, and thus seek to demonstrate the characteristic superiority of such achievements over all else. But does that demonstrate their truth, their absolute truth, their Divine truth? The achievements lead into the province of relativities; one achievement may largely overtop all the others; but it remains still an open question whether such an achievement is the final, the highest, and the all-inclusive. Further, the human and historical situation is not a product of religion alone; varied movements run crossways through the situation, so that it is hardly possible to decide whether that which happened within the life-circle of religion happened from religion's own energy, or whether it did not proceed, in a far greater measure, from the more or less gifted nature of peoples, from the characteristic greatness of special personalities, from the favour of external circumstances, etc.

For example, is Christianity indebted to its most important origins and its religious contents alone? Is it not also indebted for the revival and restoration of its youth to its association with highly-gifted peoples, to its coalescence with the rich and beautiful culture of antiquity, and to modern culture?

The questions, however, which most religions set us, lead back to the fundamental problem, as to how far, on the whole, an historical religion can manifest absolute truth; and, also, as to the doubt whether such a religion's concentration of life does not inevitably involve a contraction the disadvantage of which counterbalances all gain, and which may turn all gain into a loss. The proof offered by a positive religion is in its nature of an historical kind; certain events are recorded; a certain spiritual content is announced as a revelation. Even if we admit that there is not the least doubt concerning the events, yet an historical occurrence can never prove of itself that a certain fact is of Divine origin and its content is an ultimate truth; for such a claim can be proved only through the ideas and convictions into which it is brought; and such a conclusion never comes to man from without, but is founded in his own inwardness by the whole of his life. In the historical data it is impossible to recognise the Divine as Divine without antecedent conceptions as to the nature of the Divine, and without the standard implied in such conceptions; for otherwise, religion and magic, faith and superstition, could not be separated from one another.

This train of thought leads necessarily to the point that all the argument from history must rest upon the immediate life itself, and that the intrinsic nature of the truth of all historical facts can be tested by the Spiritual Life alone. Here Lessing's well-known words meet us: "Accidental truths of history can never become the proof of the necessary truths of reason." Though this may carry in its form the antiquated mark of the *Aufklärung*, its kernel contains a truth which it is not so easy to get over as was supposed by the historical positivism of the nineteenth century. True, history at the present day has come to mean incomparably more to us than it used to ; and it may deem such a course of thought as antiquated, and refuse it a place ; but he who is not to fall into a destructive relativism must conceive of history as being encompassed and borne along by an intimate and timeless Spiritual Life which relegates history with all its accumulation to a secondary place. But, also, historical religion is through this withdrawn to a secondary place ; and it can by no means become the ultimate basis of our religious conviction, and by no means can its greatest achievements in the realm of time prove its eternal truth. And if religion is to secure a basis at all, it must secure it in eternal truth.

Doubt, however, does not remain merely in the mode of the foundation ; it also attacks the content of historical religion, and even combats that wherein it seeks its strength—the distinctive, the unique, the super-rational ; and, further, the definite union of the Divine and the human—the kernel of all religion— turns into doubt, and fashions itself into an inner prejudice towards the Divine. The historical religions cannot claim for themselves a definite relationship to the Godhead without having to leave out of account portions of human nature. And yet we occasionally hear to-day people speak of a " God of the Christian," seeking thereby a special strength of belief. Does not this lead to a particularism which lies not very far from the belief of a primitive stage of culture in special national gods? And as to each historical religion every other religion seems false; so here, all religious mode of thought of a more universal kind will appear to such a particularism as unreal and worthless. At the zenith of Hellenism, in men such as Æschylus, Pindar, and Plato, particularism can recognise no genuine religion ; and it will exclude the leaders of modern culture—men such as Leibniz and Kant, Schiller and Goethe. How close lies such a narrowness of belief to the pharisaic self-righteousness of small souls who have never laboured and grieved for the truth! But how is this danger to be avoided if the affirmation of historical religion is considered as the sole source of truth? And who can blame anyone who would rather side with the men in all of whom there was something great—for there is no greatness without independence—even with the unbelievers, than be included in the army of believers?

Further, it is not easy to accept the statement that historical religion inevitably draws the Godhead into the arena of time and thus into variableness. Such could happen if the Godhead, instead of pervading the whole of time with eternal truth, had opened, only at a special moment, its inmost essence, and had in this manner communicated that essence to human nature. To attribute a variability to God

means nothing less than to surrender the absoluteness
of truth; it means no less than to leave the field
to a blind positivism and a destructive relativism.
Augustine, a man wont to think out any thought
he had laid hold of, has in the main tendency
of his conviction—in another direction he is more
rational—maintained that prior to the advent of
Christianity, not only were beliefs concerning
morality different, but morality itself was something
different from what it subsequently became; prior to
Christianity things were allowed which were forbidden
after its advent. This is consistent thinking from
the standpoint of a merely positive religion. But, at
the same time, it shows that such a mode of thinking
even transforms morality into an arbitrary precept,
and therewith inwardly destroys it.

Also, the closer union of man with the Godhead
and the clearer representation of this union which
the historical religions have striven to present are
double-edged, and produce a huge complication.
Indeed, if in that intimacy the human arises too
easily and perpetually to the Deity, not seldom
has the Divine been drawn down into the narrowness and passions of the human situation! But
in the very conception of God there are very
marked difficulties. The idea of personality is
formulated to render comprehensible the incomprehensible, and to bring the representation of the
Godhead nearer to man; but how powerfully does
an anthropomorphism pervade such an idea and
render it extremely dangerous, inasmuch as it so
easily resolves itself into a mere replica of man's own
nature! And does the introduction of religious

relationship which develops on this ground bring with
itself, always and with certainty, a spiritual elevation
—an inner transformation of man ? How often do
we experience immeasurable waves of subjective
feeling ! How often do an egotistic desire after
well-being and a passionate excitement believe themselves justified and even consecrated by religion itself !
Or, again, positive religion through its aspiration after
a reality superior to all brooding reflection — after
a tangible and incontestable reality—is tempted to
establish a sensuous and even a materialistic system of
pictorial ideas, and, indeed, to acclaim with special
zeal what has been left behind by the movement of
the Spiritual Life. Thus, definite religion is measured
by the doctrine of the sacraments which easily degenerate into mere magical charm ; thus, many believe even to-day that Christianity is threatened at
its root if the belief in a reconciliation through the
blood of Christ does not form the core of its nature.
Wherever men insist primarily upon positiveness in
religion, the liability to a relapse into an infra-spiritual
stage lies perilously near. Plotinus had good reason
for giving the warning that man should not sink back
below reason whilst striving to rise above it. The
historical religions certainly represent a justifiable
and even a necessary aspiration when they reconsolidate the tattered life through the inauguration of
a new kingdom which is able to save the harassed soul.
But in that which they offer there seems to be interwoven a higher and a lower, a right and a wrong ; and
they do succeed in finding the line of demarcation.

It fares similarly with the effect of religions upon
the life and actions of man ; these bring him clearer

aims and more dynamic motives; but they also readily bring contractions and coarseness. Life, under the influence of positive religion, gains a strong consolidation; a province of truths is traced out and all doubt disallowed; men, through this, are brought into greater concord and are called to mutual assistance; the direct relation to the Godhead gives a keen zest to all demands and an increasing earnestness to life. But the consolidation turns readily into a rigid fixation, and the reflection turns into a narrow exclusiveness. How often have religions imagined something great to reside in such elements as these, and how often have they rejected everything that lay beyond their own province as something inferior, indifferent, and even dangerous! This attitude does not confine itself to particular points, but enters into the whole. The direct relationship of man to man aims at placing in the foreground, as factors in the formation of life, the rendering of help and love in mutual intercourse and the well-being of the human province. But the relationship to the universe and to the inward expansion of one's own nature which science, art, and culture strive to set forth, is but little thought of. Thus, the governing life easily becomes subjective and merely human; and this soon turns the man to revolve around himself.

Again, within man's own province, that which seems at first a pure gain may readily turn into a loss. Historical religion binds men closer together on the Godward side; it creates more inward fellowship, more mutual understanding, more cohesion of the soul. But such can hardly happen otherwise than at the cost of free movement and of individu-

ality.   Each religion has its own type of life, and
forces this upon its adherents from youth upwards
with mild or strong constraint.   Does not the life
through this become bound and mechanised ?   Does
it not become to many individuals, who bring no inner
movement against it, a mere clinging to the external,
and does it not threaten to become a gross untruth-
fulness—a merely conventional participation in an
imposed order ?   There is an hypocrisy which reaches
beyond the conscious idea into the recesses of the
soul, and which unites itself with the subjective notion
of veracity ; there is an hypocrisy of the nature to
which nothing more easily lends itself than religion.
This is the pharisaism which true religious natures
have to fight against with the whole ardour of their
conviction ; and the sad thing is that such hypocrisy
is no transient appearance of certain times, but seems
to connect itself inseparably with religion.

Historical religion is the strongest mainstay of
morality; but, at the same time, nowhere else are there
such lurking dangers.   Historical religion consolidates
morality through a linkage of it to a Divine Will,
and it strengthens the energy of morality through
the awakening of an indestructible belief in the moral
order of the universe.   But, at the same time, the
founding of morality upon an historical religion draws
morality into a position of great insecurity, from
which it yet refuses to move ; the moral motives are
threatened with defacement, for the winning of Divine
favour becomes now the main motive-power of action.
Thus, a religious morality, through its orientation of
thought towards a " beyond," is apt to injure a joyous
labour and creativeness in the " here and now "—since

with its pictorial ideas of future expectations and confidence in these, it may maintain a passive attitude; it may repress a courageous entrance into reality and exchange it for a mere logical and prudential kind of reality; it disunites and estranges human nature; it produces unutterable bitterness, for which it engages all the qualities of the moral disposition as an aid to its own propaganda, and explains everything existing outside its own circle as unreal and worthless. Do all these questions allow of being placed on one side as an outcome of mere "unbelief," or as a shallow mode of thinking?

All these problems, however, culminate in the transition of religion to the Church. The Church presented itself as indispensable to historical religion, for only through the incorporation of religion in the Church did religion attain a full actuality for man; only in connection with the Church did religion gain the distinct stamp of its characteristic features; only in connection with the Church did religion work for the whole of humanity, and not merely for specially selected minds. But, at the same time, the danger of humanising the Divine is greatly accentuated through the conception of its entrance into the province of man. The Church is not able to exist without a human and temporal element; indeed, the more it develops to a full independence, the more will it bring forth the claims of the human and temporal elements and transfer them to the Divine and Eternal; it will then busy itself mechanically with the Divine, and probably consider quite worldly men as being religious and in communion with the Divine. An inversion of the most deadly kind threatens the Church; it becomes liable, instead of labouring for the presence of the Divine, to clothe a certain kind of the human with a semblance of the Divine, and to confer upon this humanity the qualities of Divine truth and glory; indeed, the Church is able, when it carries such a procedure to its uttermost, to elevate the priesthood above the Divine, and to attribute to it power beyond that of the Godhead. Then the Church is concerned for a veneration of itself and not of the Divine; and this becomes a mere means to the heightening of its own glory. However, through such a transformation, through such a wanton exaggeration of the human to the scale of the Divine, the Church becomes the greatest danger to, as well as the greatest enemy of, religion; for, in fact, nothing has injured religion so much as the Church. But, at the same time, religion did not seem able to obtain for itself a secure foundation and its legitimate effect upon men without a development into a Church. How, then, can we disengage ourselves from the contradiction; and how can we find the line of demarcation between good and evil, between a genuine elevation of man through the Divine and the lowering of the Divine to the human? If such a line of demarcation cannot be found, then a grave doubt concerning the whole of historical religions is bound to arise; and that doubt appears strongest in that religion which bears most clearly the marks of historicity, i.e. in Christianity. Does not historical religion appear as something which must of necessity destroy itself through its own development to excess, thus revealing itself as an untenable contradiction?

25

3. *Impossibility of a Simple Denial of Historical Religion*

What we have already advanced makes it intelligible that historical religions should become a target for the hardest assaults; and, indeed, this has been seen not to come about only from the pettiness of a subjective mode of thought, but also from the numerous interests of the whole province of life. No struggle has kindled more angry passions than this; and none has so pointedly divided men from one another. In earlier times, the attack was wont promptly to issue in a complete denial of religion; religion, to such times, was explained as a mere web of illusions or even as a product of conscious fraud. To-day, the hazardous character of such a sweeping condemnation is clearly perceived. In any case, the capacities, achievements, and sense of truth of mankind fall into entire mistrust if the most powerful energy of the historical development and the most secure anchorage of peoples and times are to sink into an empty illusion. There is not a more deplorable contradiction to be witnessed than, at once, to praise in the highest terms the greatness of human reason, and yet to surrender as unqualified error all that is inmost and holiest in human nature. Only to an absolute pessimism can such a turn give no shock.

Therefore, one seeks to avoid this inconsistency; and, in order to do so, devises a mid-path between truth and error. It is now affirmed that the historical religions were not merely pictorial illusions, but products of the momentary situations of peoples and epochs; such peoples and epochs have, in their re-

ligions, freed themselves from such situations, and
raised themselves beyond them through the aims and
ideals which were involved in their efforts. Thus,
religions, in the form of union of ideals, have a certain
kind of reality, and have undeniably contributed
towards a progressive development of humanity.
But all this has happened, it is said, only within the
human circle and for human ideas; life itself won
nothing which it had not previously carried within
itself and from which it was able to develop. Thus,
the great problem seems smoothly and simply
settled : religion is accorded a right to be approved of ;
and, at the same time, shows that what are exhibited
as differences and even as opposites are but an expression of the characteristics of peoples and times.
The conclusion follows that we shall have to do
with purely relative truths which do not exclude one
another but dwell together on friendly terms.

But, in spite of such alleged superiority, this solution is no more than one of those multicoloured com
promises through whose presence the edge of the
opposites is blunted and the energy of life is depreci-
ated. The deeper conviction of religions has been all
along in its ability to introduce man to something
superhuman and to shield him from inner destruction.
If such a superhuman did not at all originate, man was
only intoxicated with his own creations, and climbed
to the height of his own subjective notions ; thus the
whole of religion appeared to him as a self-deception
of human nature, and although the representatives of
religion were not considered to be conscious deceivers,
yet they were regarded as " deceived deceivers."
Such a view, in fact, alters the situation but little,

so that the same answer which opposed the old
sweeping denial must meet the new one. Without
a doubt, the historical religions have strongly affected
the life of the spirit of man ; they have carried it
into original paths and have brought to it an inward
elevation. They have, on the whole, done this less
directly than indirectly through a transformation of
the entire life. We need only trace back a little the
threads of creativeness in art and in the mental constructions regarding the universe, in morality and the
formation of communities, in order to recognise
everywhere the connection of all this with the effects
and sway of religion. Therefore, the alleged illusory
character of religion extends over the whole of the
Spiritual Life ; and if we follow this path, it will
lead us to the same conclusion as previously—to
the entire bankruptcy of human capacity and to the
extinction of any hope of help from truth. Out of the
attempted obscuring of the problem the imperative
Either-Or ever presents itself. *Either* man is nothing
more than mere man—a ready-made kind of nature by
the side of innumerable other similar natures ; and
then certainly religion falls to the ground : but at the
same time there falls each and every truth—even
scientific truth, for to truth belongs necessarily a validity beyond human opinion and vacillation, *Or* there is
implanted in man more than an isolated, completed
nature, and he is able to take up a struggle against the
petty-human self ; and then religion refuses from the
very outset to be considered as a mere phantom, and
compels us to seek in it the element of truth.

If an unequivocal condemnation of the historical
religions is thus precluded, and if, at the same time,

we can neither recognise different truths existing side by side nor consider any one of the historical religions as absolute truth and all the others as entire error, one possibility remains open: there must result in all historical religions a common further inference of the Spiritual Life; a common fundamental fact must precede all the ramifications and strife. This fundamental fact has to be set forth with the utmost clearness; and from it alone we must undertake a critical valuation of the particular religions, and seek to differentiate that which transcends humanity from that which is merely human. That much of that which is merely human in the small and narrow sense flows into religion and filters into a seeming inseparableness with the Divine is only too evident; indeed, it is this that constitutes the kernel of the problem and the main knot of the matter, that historical religions contain too much that is merely human to be valued as a pure work of God, and yet too much that is Spiritual and Divine to be considered as a mere product of man.

Thus, in connection with the historical religions, we come back to the same question with which we opened this section of our investigation—the question whether, within our life - province, some kind of further development of Spiritual Reality culminates beyond the hitherto-explained situation, and whether the manifestation of a further cosmic depth results. The course of our investigation does not allow such a possibility to be rejected as a matter of course. For we have already seen a spirituality superior to the world dawning within our existence; but such a spirituality developed itself entirely through our work in the world, and remained associated with the advancement of this work. And we have in conse-quence witnessed the growth of inexpressible en-tanglements. Now, could not a spirituality superior to the world make its appearance in relation to man without the intervention of the world ? If this were possible, we might expect a new kind of life, new spiritual contents and values, an entire turn of our position, and, through all this, some kind of conquest over oppositions that have hitherto been all-powerful.

In the meantime, this is no more than a possibility ; whether a reality corresponds to such a possibility, only further experiences can decide, and to these we now turn. But it is important to know that the investigation even at our present stage is not mean-ingless, and is in some degree able to indicate the trend of the path we have to pursue.

CHAPTER XII

b. Signs of a New Depth of Life

WE cannot, according to the whole course of our investigation, offer or expect a further depth of reality from any external conditions; we can search for such a depth nowhere else than in the Life-process itself; we have to explore this depth, and from this point to secure a connection with a new order of things. It is nowhere more necessary than at this point to avoid the mistake of a deep-rooted intellectualism, which first of all constructs a world beyond man and from thence supplies his life with a content; instead of taking possession of such a world and grasping it as a Whole in order then to hazard convictions of the All.

However, the new sought-for depth of life will not probably present itself to us immediately as a Whole; but at the outset will appear in particular manifestations. These manifestations are able, however, to lead further if they reveal themselves on closer inspection as portions of a larger connection; and if, in such an investigation, further avenues open out until at last a *new world* dawns before our eyes.

391

Therefore, we seek before all else to win some kind of tangible point of departure whose original nature announces a new order of things; we seek then to gain, through a gradual ascent, more and more comprehensive values and at last a total-life.

1. *The Idea of Love of One's Enemy*

As a point of departure, we are helped by the fact that upon a certain height of historical life, the thought and demand of love of one's enemy appear not only in Christianity but also in other religions; and, beyond all religions, it has impregnated the general atmosphere of life. Love of enemy seems here as the summit of ethical conduct and as the most certain sign of its completion. Whilst, however, love of enemy was strongly approved, and the infinite aim seemed to raise man beyond himself, the question usually remained unasked whether this exalted virtue was possible within the given situation of man, whether the effort for the virtue sought also related transformations in the whole of our life and being. This question may be lightly put aside if the two dispositions of the soul which we meet in love of enemy are taken up in a faint and slurring kind of way so that no earnest conflict arises. At the point, however, where the claims of love of enemy break forth, things relate themselves otherwise: here an entire turn—a transformation of the prior situation —is discovered. Enmity is no fleeting ill-humour, but an antagonism of the deepest character and of the whole mode of thinking; it is an encounter originating from an objective necessity, since our highly valued goods are seized, reviled, and injured

by another.   And love, moreover, is not that faint-
hearted disposition which begrudges to another his
existence and which allows all blessings to fall on
itself; but is an active and positive demeanour, a
strong joy in the being of another, a furthering and
a raising of its own life through the communion
established with the other.   If things are so, is there
not an irreconcilable opposition between love and
enmity, and is it not an absurdity to will at the same
time to hate truly and to love truly ?

Indeed, the question here lies close at hand—
whether an enfeeblement and slackening of the strife
is desirable for man.   It behoves us, first of all, to
bring forth and to carry forward a Spiritual Reality
over against a hostile or indifferent world.   In order
to accomplish this, the greatest tension of energy and
an untiring struggle are needful ; as this struggle
is for the possession of the highest good, it demands
the whole soul of man—the entire strength of his
affections, the full glow of his feelings.   Plato had
good reason for desiring a " noble passion " in order
to the success of the work of life.   Now, does not
the command to love our enemies threaten to weaken
the earnestness of the matter, to handle good and evil
as equally valid, and to concede willingly the right
of the field of conflict to unreason ?   Thus, unmanly
cowardly compliance and a sentimental weakness are
exalted as highest virtues ; or else the character remains a mere semblance and under the mantle of love
such a passion and hate grow luxuriantly, as witnessed
so often in religious strife.   A depression of the energy
indispensable in the struggle against evil has, from
the beginning, been made a matter of reproach against

Christianity. Thus, we find Plotinus with this reflection concerning the matter: "If we do not struggle, evil men will triumph." Should such weakening of man, so often witnessed in the history of Christianity, be the final word of Christianity? In any case, it was not the final word of Jesus when He launched fierce denunciation against the Pharisees, and when He drove the money-changers out of the Temple.

But how does it stand, then, with love for enemy? Is it really no more than a deceitful semblance—a phantom of an overstrained disposition—and must we conclude in regard to it that a friend is a friend and an enemy is an enemy; and that we are indebted to justice for telling us the latter, and that we should preserve our love for friends alone? It was thus thought at the zenith of Hellenic thought; and so, too, Confucius taught consciously and emphatically. "Someone asked, what shall one think of him who repays injury with kindness? The philosopher replied: If one so acts, with what can kindness be repaid? One must repay hate and injury through justice, and kindness through kindness." That is a clear and honest mode of thinking which corresponds to the natural feelings of man. But it imposes on human life limits which the revolutionary experiences of the inmost soul have to burst asunder. Such a conclusion suffices only if, and when upon the whole, a ready-made world surrounds us; if we develop ourselves in its restricted province, and if there is nothing essential to be transformed or renewed. But such a conclusion becomes an intolerable narrowness when the prior situation contains difficult entanglements, and when only a fundamental renewal can give a value to our life and action.   If such a new order of things makes its appearance, everything which divides and estranges us can be removed ; and upon a new foundation a new fellowship of life can be built which now binds the minds that otherwise strove against one another, so that we are raised above all strife, although many opposed points of view must be retained.   That which otherwise is impossible now becomes possible through a radical renewal of life— through the opening up of a depth which relegates the whole prior life, with all its struggles, to the status of mere superficiality.   If, herewith, the demands of love for enemy emerge from and rest upon genuine love and not upon mere pity, the hope of a new order of things lies close to this foundation, and a yearning for an emancipation from the bounds and barriers of the " given " world arises in human nature.   Does not then the joy itself build such a hope, and does not the very strength of the yearning constitute a testimony that here we are dealing not with a mere phantom but with a new life within the domain of man ?

2. *The Deepening of Love*

The problem of love for enemy is only a section of a more general problem—of the problem whether the direction of our life, in the last resort, belongs to justice or to love.   There was good reason for the old Greek thinkers siding with justice—with justice in the broad sense of an arrangement of all relationships according to individual merit.   Each receives what falls to his share, no less, but no more ; even love has thus to be measured according to the degree of presented love, and all unmerit and all non-limits are excluded. Such an ideal calls for the utmost exertion, for the transmutation of all capacity into efficient activity, and for the construction of an organised kingdom of reason. Such a system of justice had also place for mercy in so far as the harshness of an exact measurement was toned down, and in so far as the over-tension of right was held to become an injury (*summum jus summa injuria*). The idea of justice has pre-eminently brought forth and developed a connected spiritual order, and it is and remains indispensable for the vindication of such an order.

How, then, does it come to be that in spite of so great an achievement justice has not satisfied man? How is it that the movement of universal history has left that ideal of justice behind? The answer is : that such an ideal of justice has been left behind through painful experience and through the persuasion of the inadequacy of man as mere man, and through knowledge of a deep disorder in his own nature. Such experience and knowledge, however, became an urgent need as soon as man ceased to remain within a " given " world, and raised himself beyond all earthly connections to infinity ; and as soon as he measured himself not with his equals but with the ideal of an absolute perfection. The growing depth of life, with its discovery of infinity in man's own nature, requires him to measure himself in this manner. His life does not exhaust itself with the solution of this or that problem, and does not content itself with the attainment of some kind of elevation, but it drives him from within towards the domain of the Whole ; he is now after absolute perfection, and, before all else, after the perfection of a comprehensive life and conduct in the Whole. The setting up of such a goal brings to clearness the entire inadequacy and even the hopelessness of his actual performances and situation. Along with this, the standard of justice becomes intolerably exacting, and the judgment passed upon a man's common behaviour is such as to threaten him with entire repudiation and reprobation. On account of this, man defends himself through energies which have in no way originated out of his egoistic desire of life, but rather from the deeper springs of which he has become conscious, giving to his life a value beyond all price; but he cannot call into being such depth and value from his own energy, and, therefore, he depends on redemption and love for the realisation of his own nature. Thus there springs up, beyond all questions of merit, a burning desire after Infinite Love on the other side of all questions of merit, and after a new order of things beyond all calculation and measurement.

Is such a longing an impertinent fancy, and could it arise and gain such power if some kind of reality did not stand behind it? Also, the relationship of man to man would become cold and soulless if all unmerited and unmeasured love were removed from the soul. But how mysterious is such love! How could it ever have originated out of the selfishness and impurity of the ordinary impulses of man? Man has to be raised out of such a condition and set, from within, in other connections; an energy out of the Whole must become his—an energy which lifts him beyond the initial stage and, indeed, beyond his natural capacity, and which, issuing out of a new life,

brings the seemingly impossible to fruition. This is
especially clear in connection with the great personalities whom human life has to thank for an inner
elevation, and especially in connection with the heroes
of religion. The external situation of life left them
forsaken, and the circumstances of life carried them
but little love ; yet these men were too clear of vision
to disguise the true position of things with idle phrases
about the greatness and progressive development of
mankind. Thus, they have often felt themselves
so lonely within human circles, as the yearning
and fervour with which they fled to the Godhead
reveals. Mahomet was not among the deepest
spirits, but even he brought that feeling to a tender
expression. " In the glare of noonday and in the
stillness of the night the Lord casts him not away,
and the future will be better than the past. Did
He not find him an orphan and has He not given
him a place in His home ? Did He not find him
astray and has He not led him to the right road ?
Did He not find him so poor and has He not made
him so rich ? " But has such a loneliness of these
leading spirits amongst men destroyed their love to
man ? Has not a mighty power of love kindled itself
in the midst of all opposition—a fire that even enveloped drowsy souls, becoming in them a quickening
passion for the welfare of mankind ? Thus, these
men were able to see more in man than lies on the
surface ; they were able to penetrate through all
meanness and failure to a depth of the nature in
which the apparently severed becomes united, and
the seemingly worthless invested with value. But
could such a depth be possible without a new order

of things—without the presence of a Universal Life
in the human soul ?   As these men were constrained to
view humanity in the light of the new order of things
in order to work as they did, it would have been
difficult for them to find, without the energy of that
Universal Life and without an ascent beyond themselves, the stability, the joy, and the inexhaustibleness which their work aspired after and to which their
success itself is a testimony.

Thus has it been on the summits of historical
life, but not on the summits only.   Our life would
lose its deepest soul were it a mere system of effects
and counter-effects ; we should have to estimate all
actions according to what should issue in the form
of a result which corresponds to the thought of
justice.   Our life, as Goethe has often in his marvellous style presented it, would soon slacken and stag-
nate unless it contained much activity which expected
no gratitude and much love which claimed no reciprocal love.   Such a love—selfless and strong at the
same time—may show itself in unpretentious achievements and may raise the inner worth of life beyond
all the exploits on the scroll of universal history.   In
such daily occurrences—seemingly trivial—a mystery
is imbedded and a marvel happens ; what happens
contradicts not only the order of nature but also the
order of the natural life : in so far as what happens
follows justice, it hangs in the air and cannot find
a substantial ground until a new order of things—
a kingdom of creative love — carries and animates
it.   To acknowledge such a superiority of love does
not mean that justice is to be attacked and banished
out of the world, for justice is ever needed in human

relationships for the growth of reason over the whole expanse of life, and for the consolidation of mental and moral things over against bare nature. But a mere acknowledgment of a kingdom of love does not establish its order in the whole of our inner world; for it is not only through hope but also through its own effective presence that love is able to strike its roots into our life and alter its whole complexion, and, at the same time, further the acknowledgment of a new depth of reality.

3. *Self-Maintenance in the Midst of Hindrance and Suffering*

Our earlier consideration of this subject has shown us that in the acknowledgment of an independent spirituality, life presents itself not as a calm ascent but as a hard struggle. With the appearance of spirituality there appeared *something essentially new*, which has to forge its way over against an existing world; collisions are bound to take place, and hindrances and deadlocks are to be expected. But from the first, hope and belief in all this endured, and believed that the Spiritual Life, carried as it is by an Absolute Life, would emerge victoriously from the struggle, and that the hindrance, through the stimulating energy of such hope and belief would ultimately become a help. Now, we have witnessed the opposition gaining such strength and extension within our circle that the whole life is endangered, and the hope of a conquest within our domain is dashed away. Our effort everywhere strikes against stubborn barriers to which it dare not yield on pain of becoming aimless and meaningless. What does the experience of mankind here indicate? It shows us that, amidst such painful hindrances and notwithstanding that hope of success is eclipsed, the Spiritual Life can be maintained and has been maintained by individuals as well as by mankind at large.   Our scientific investigations strike up against insurmountable obstacles; we discover with pain our inability to wrestle with the dark mysteries of existence.   In the effort for a genuine Art we find ourselves far too weak to give adequate form to what shapes itself in the deepest recesses of our soul, to what thirsts after an embodiment, and we fail to aid it towards its longed-for reality.   Thus, we remain incomplete, and, indeed, tattered and torn in our existence—insufficient for, and locked-out from, ourselves.   Must we not become convinced of the impossibility of an essential betterment of the human situation, when we view the results of experience through millenniums, and do we not see the goal recede ever before our reach?   And must not the individual, the more he stands upon an inner connection of his life, recognise life as a mere torso?   It is easily conceivable that human nature, under such a hard and harsh Nay, should lose all the courage of life and should relinquish all activity.   In reality human nature has *not* done this.   True, certain views of the universe and of religion seek an entire negation; but this negation, even if it did not carry within itself a prior affirmation, would soon turn into an affirmation. Buddhism has toned down the unqualified negative of its initial stages, and has transformed itself into some kind of affirmation.   Was this due to the mere stubbornness of the natural impulse, to an ineradi-

26

cable quality in the common craving for life? Hardly, for the affirmation itself has, in the form of spiritual self-preservation, brought so much labour and sorrow upon humanity that it would recommend, rather than a satisfaction of the bare natural desire for happiness, a calm submersion and the dissolution of its own existence. Further, the affirmation has brought forth far too much spiritual movement and newness of life to allow itself to be swept on one side as a mere illusion. Therefore, there must be present in such a need of the life of man something deeper; for man, through some kind of energy, will hold fast to his life and fill it with a confident hope and trust, although these cannot be justified by any view of things as seen on the mere surface.

No great thinker has more truly seen the urgency of these problems and brought them more powerfully to expression than Augustine. Before his eyes the old world sank before a new one had yet emerged; he found himself haunted by the dread of a wholly empty world, and felt all the desolation and contradiction of human existence with the most painful intensity. And yet he held fast to life and withstood the total destruction of his soul. But why? Because the hindrance itself brought him to the consciousness that something greater than it is imbedded in it; because all menace and intimidation made him absolutely certain of something in his nature which could never be lost. This something is of an axiomatic kind—something at first mysterious; but out of the mystery a powerful energy originates and gives birth to a new and higher need of life which, over against the energy of nature, may be termed *metaphysical.* Whence all this if life has exhausted itself in the hitherto-prevailing situation and is not able to realise a further depth for the strengthening and renewal of man? The experience of Augustine is not singular, but is an experience of mankind, an experience of all individuals to whom these problems come to signify their own destiny. It has not been the most troubled times and experiences that allowed doubt to penetrate into the whole of life; but such a calamity has happened far oftener in times of idle superabundant plenty and in the absence of great tasks. The former hard times rather worked in the direction of strengthening and energising human nature. But how could they do this without the hope and even the certainty of a new order of things—an order in direct contradiction to all that life had hitherto brought to them?

4. *The Progressive Development of Inwardness*

According to our exposition, it was essentially necessary for the Spiritual Life to raise the inner life to an independence, to extend it to *a world* which does not merely take rank with other things; but which takes these things, in the whole of their existence, up to itself, and which reveals to them their own nature. The development of the Spiritual Life becomes through this a progressive inwardness of existence. But we have already observed how this inwardness in all its toil strikes against most painful oppositions, so that a danger is here evident, viz. that what we attain as inwardness may be looked upon as an enclosed circle by the side of the great world, and that it may finally resolve itself into bare subjectivity.

But mankind has in no manner surrendered itself to such a disintegration; it has ever sought to
shape the inwardness anew; it has sought to lay
such inwardness deeper in the nature and to give it
a new foundation and a new content. And such
effort seemed to it to be no mere aberration of judgment. At least, we often witness new movements
issuing forth from the hindrances themselves. We
get roughly thrown back upon ourselves by the objects
around us, and we discover with pain stubborn
obstacles. But what we witness and experience in all
this becomes the point of departure for a new kind of
life; the hindrance engenders not merely a sentimental
echo and a timid reflection, but becomes absorbed
into a wider, deeper, and more basal life; it serves
towards a further development of the soul in regard
to all the work of the world. Thus, an inwardness
seems to constitute itself here, which rests purely
within itself—an inwardness which transforms into
a gain what was previously a sheer detriment to
work.

The acknowledgment of such unalloyed inwardness
must change in an essential manner the aspect of life:
what seemed hitherto to be the whole of our world
becomes now a mere segment of it and appears in
comparison with the inwardness as something external;
what hitherto appeared as the total range of our
soul now acknowledges a depth beyond itself. Man
will be the readier to acknowledge this depth because
he sees the inadequacy of the restricted life which was
formerly his, and because he feels his own previous
mode of viewing things as a forbidding destiny
from which he wants somehow to free himself.

But how is this pure inwardness, which brings such great changes and awakens such great hopes, itself to be explained? How could such inwardness be possible unless our life had won further connections than before, and through this had drawn a new content? All this can hardly come to be without a further manifestation of the Whole of Reality.

5. *The Further Development of Morality*

The further inner development of life which here occupies our attention is nowhere more evident than in the problem of morality. Wherever we have had to deal with the problem in the course of our investigation, morality, in our view, has not detached itself from the whole of life and has not shut itself up in a province of its own. Morality has not merely a special task of its own, but it extends over all Spiritual Life; since all through it does not surround man as a natural inheritance but governs him through his own decision and appropriation. We must unconditionally hold to such a universality of morality; in particular the practical social domain—the domain of human intercourse—has no right to claim the moral disposition for itself alone, and to deny it to others, *e.g.* art and science. The antithesis extends over the whole of life, whether the action is governed by the necessities of the Spiritual Life itself, or by the interests of the individual; whether the disposition is that of the person who follows after truth and is affected by no kind of ulterior motive such as pleasure, gain, and renown, or is that of the artist who reflects in his soul how to bring an unborn form to expression—a form as morally valuable as the practical conduct which stands in the service of humanity. Understood so, morality develops itself all the more happily the less it becomes an isolated province separated from all other tasks.

But morality experiences oppositions and entanglements similar to those found in religion. That full devotion to the Spiritual Life is not entirely wanting in morality, yet it acquires but little strength; and the entanglements often hinder spiritual work as well as the character; and, also, the most brilliant results of work do not guarantee a corresponding disposition, for natural impulses penetrate deeply into the very province which purported to lead man beyond nature, and the trivialities of human life hold the human soul in their powerful grip. Thus, in the ordinary surface-life, morality has but little power, and is considered as a quite subsidiary matter. Indeed, it is often considered an irksome and obtrusive disorder—an attempt to impose an unwarranted limitation. But human nature as a whole has not rested on such a denial; it has ever returned to an appreciation of morality; and well it might, because in its abandonment of morality it followed a track which led to an irreparable loss in depth and energy of life. In such upheavals of life, morality has carried itself above the initial formation of things; and has even attained a special province over against the former life. Morality, through the cultivation of pure inwardness over against the work of the world, gains a new task—the task of preserving unconditionally such inwardness and, along with it, the kernel of the life of the soul, and heroically and faithfully to preserve a "soul of the soul" over against immense opposition.

Life, through this, seems for the first time to reach its deepest root; and what takes place here is immeasurably superior to all other work.   Christianity especially supports this conviction; as we find it expressed in such fitting words as that "the gain of the whole world can not counterbalance the loss of the soul, and that with the price of the whole world not one soul can be purchased" (Luther).   So that in the case of conflict with other aims there cannot be the slightest doubt that the autonomous moral task precedes unconditionally all other tasks; "the eye is to be plucked out and the hand is to be cut off" if they endanger the salvation of the soul.   Along with such a high estimate goes a greater rigour in the demands of life.   The necessity for the preservation of that depth of the nature applies not to practice alone, but grips the whole province of the Spiritual Life and there starts a struggle with "the life at ease." Thus, that which had a right in the particular situation must now rest in the Whole; and it is for this reason that a counter-effect is bound to arise.   It is in this connection that conceptions such as responsibility, guilt, conscience, arise—conceptions of a most mysterious character — but which in spite of all their darkness are powers which defy disparagement and rejection and ever reassert themselves; they are powers which, when once they have sprung up with their full energy, bring the whole of life under their sway.   They obviously withstand being driven out of the world of man because the maintenance of a spiritual self-reliance and the possibility of a spiritual self-preservation are indissolubly linked with them. It is easily possible to show that human life, even at the epoch of its most brilliant achievements—as, for instance, in the period of the Renaissance—rapidly fell into inner decay. Thus, that mysterious, uncomfortable, agitating force, is ever indispensable; indeed, life seems to obtain an enduring consolidation and an incomparable worth through it alone. How can all this be explained unless more is present in the whole of our life, and unless further energies rule in us if morality attains the content and the position here claimed for it.

When we review the several points which have hitherto occupied our attention, we discover in all the multiplicity one persistent fact—an advance of life beyond the point of hindrance. And this fact is a pure inwardness from whose growth a further consolidation and a turn of life were to be expected. But, in the meantime, this inwardness is wholly without a reasonable justification for itself; and we have not yet seen how it can gain a characteristic content, and how it can grow into a self-reliant kingdom. And yet there lies here far too much actuality for us to consider the whole as a mere play of fancy. What appears as not easily comprehensible in the life of the individual is found in the whole history of mankind as a great characteristic trait. Here the new mode of life specifically appears in the raising of life beyond all mere culture. At all times there is present in life more than mere civilisation and culture; but in special epochs this More comes into bold relief and to full self-consciousness. There are times when special circumstances bring civilisation and culture to a standstill and even to a retrogression; and yet, in spite of this, such circumstances do not

invest the times with a character of mental and
moral emptiness but develop a noble and worthy life
in another direction.

The epoch when the ancient world suffered dissolution was, measured by its achievements in culture,
to a high degree barren and, indeed, unedifying; but
it was this epoch which for the first time brought
the life of the soul to a full self-reliance within the
human province, and which penetrated beyond all
purely subjective inwardness to an inner world—one
of the greatest transitions in the whole history of the
human race. Thus, we are ever able to draw much
from such men as Plotinus and Augustine; and they
are valued by us as heroes of the spirit although they
damaged more than aided culture. The fact that
they made accessible to man a new world of pure
inwardness signifies more than the most brilliant
performances in the mere work of culture.

Hitherto we have had more questions than answers,
more puzzles than solutions, so that a conclusion at
this stage of our inquiry is impossible. But within
the province of the inner life *an earnest effort is
itself a fact*; and it must, especially when an essential
renewal stands in question, be present in that which
though it flits as a far-away gleam was yet the possession of the soul from the very start of its enterprise.
If it were not present, how could such a distant aim
move us? Pascal's words are valid not for religion
alone: "Thou wouldest not seek me had it not
been that thou hadst already found me." But it behoves us to work out the hidden possession in order
to press on from mere ideas and suggestions to a full
and joyous life.

CHAPTER XIII

c. The Unfolding of a Religion of a Distinctive Kind

1. *Introductory*

Various indications of a new depth have already become evident; they all point to the fact that a further inner life, lying far beneath the surface, reveals itself, and that a reality previously hindered by the entanglements has now been gained. Such a movement could never originate from mere man, but must have originated from the All; it can only originate, according to the whole course of our investigation, because the All-Life is present not only in its unfolding to become a world, but also within us as a Whole in the form of immediacy. That this actually comes about is the vindication of religion as it shapes itself into the *Characteristic* mode; but such a religion allows itself to be certified only by the discovery of a new life—only by an original connection of life in which an actuality manifests itself, and reveals to us our own being along with the whole of reality.

This *New* cannot be of a sudden and unannounced

kind, but must somehow be imbedded in us, or how otherwise could it become our inmost being? But on the first view of it, it appears as something scattered, subsidiary, a mere addendum. But religion accomplishes a transformation of this; it gathers, binds, and brings the scattered elements into a Whole; it turns this Whole into man's own act; it places for the first time the significance of the *New* in a clear light and recognises in it the presence of a *new kind of world*.

Thus, religion is not able to obtain its final depth and inmost unity for the life without differentiating itself from the remaining spiritual life, and constructing for itself a province of its own. Through such a transition to the *Characteristic* mode religion comes into definite contact with the contention of the historical religions, and gains a nearer relationship to them than was possible through the *Universal* mode of religion. Along with the historical religions, religion of a *Characteristic* kind participates in the conviction that man, through a further manifestation of the Divine, has been raised beyond the region of entanglements into a new life; and, moreover, Characteristic religion recognises a gradation of reality through the further development of the Spiritual Life within one's own province; it invests, at the same time, the inner experiences as well as the historical movement with more significance. But in spite of so much similarity between these two modes of religion there remains an essential difference. The new life, according to the Characteristic mode, appears, in so far as we understand it, not as the exclusive possession of a particular historical religion, but as the common aim and the common primary

energy of all religion.   These historical religions are
now regarded not as irreconcilable opponents, but
as co-workers in the great enterprise of the spiritual
redemption of humanity.   This does not mean the
placing of all religions on the same level and the
effacing of their differences ; indeed, the measuring of
them all by one common standard may even accentuate such differences.   But the differences now lie
within something deeper and something common to
them all—they lie within a common striving, and
thus cannot lead to an uncompromising enmity.
That which any one particular religion develops
at all times into a spiritual content does not signify
a subtraction from the truth of all other religions ;
but is seen, when it is brought to the light of the
substance common to all religions, as that which is
able to protect and strengthen together all the
others.   In dealing with the several religions, attention must direct itself especially upon what each religion contributes towards the formation of a religion
of the *Characteristic* kind ; we have to see how *the
one truth* works in spite of the inadequacy of, and
often in opposition to, the scaffolding of doctrines
and institutions.   Thus there has to be raised up in
all religions what in reality is *religious* in them—what
is *substance* and not a merely intellectual expression.

On account of this, religion as well as its treatment
are able thus to gain a broader basis only through the
energetic concentration upon the inner life.   The truth
of religion rests upon facts, or, rather, upon a coherent
actuality of an inward kind.   These facts are to be
discovered nowhere outside the human soul ; and, indeed, the facts are beyond all particular achievements

and those very deposits of life which have hitherto
occupied our attention.   In a far greater degree than
we as yet have observed does man become the
starting-point of a new world.   Through this transition the motives of mere subjectivism and humanism
will become strengthened—motives which are from
the outset only too liable to make their presence felt
in the more special and typical forms of religion,
and which could be more easily obviated in the
Universal mode.   Further, he who recognises in
the complete development of the Spiritual Life
an inner unity and an invisible depth may oppose
the transition to a Characteristic or special type
of religion because this seems to be a relapse into a
mere humanism which places itself over against the
meaning of the rest of the world, and which seems
to exchange the driving energy of movements outside
the individual for a basing of life upon mere self-
preservation.   Does the alleged new kind of world
construct no more than a mere web of human ideas
and interests; and does it not merely spin around
itself at a loss of all connection with definite reality?
Is not the vigorous and assertive freedom of Universal
religion from mere humanisation again lost in the
transition to Characteristic religion?   Doubtless,
much subjectivism and much that is merely human
are imbedded in the historical religions, and threaten
also the Characteristic religion.   Yet, however luxuriantly such a subjectivism may grow on the soil of
ordinary life, it does not exhaust the matter—indeed,
it does not touch its kernel.   In the transition to a
Characteristic kind of religion, as in religion in general,
the motive force is not the self-preservation of man as

mere man, but the maintenance of a Spiritual Life
superior to his interest and his notions—the impossibility of a renunciation of spiritual contents and
values. Thus, there here works a metaphysical and
not a physical impetus of life. And what is hoped
for as *new* is not a fostering and furthering of the
merely human—not a purely epicurean well-being of
a more refined nature—but a new stage of spirituality
which creates out of man something other than what
has hitherto been evolved, which reduces the value of
what has hitherto sufficed as happiness, and which
leads to a goodness which has hitherto been alien
to his life. The historical religions show this quite
clearly. They are not mere mirror-images of human
doings and dealings, but through them man has
scaled spiritual heights; he has learned to see and
to understand himself; he has gained courage and
energy in the struggle against a world and a way
of life that are paltry and merely human. This
has happened, too, within the intellectual province.
Nothing has more clearly set forth the limitation of
the range of human conceptions than the idea of an
Absolute Reality and Life. The demands involved
within the intellectual province have reduced in value,
from their very foundation, the forms of space and
time, and have relegated them to a particular—not
equally valid—mode of existence. And not less have
religions taught us to think of man's moral capa-
bilities; for, judged by the standards which they
have brought forth, the most splendid human
achievements have fallen far short of the needs of
the human soul. It is impossible to assert that
religions, through their representation to man of

the problems of life, have made existence lighter and more agreeable, or that they have flattered his natural longing for happiness. Although much has been taught in religions concerning the next world—far too much which belonged to the merely pictorial ideas of man—yet there has worked herein a demand for an entire transformation of life—a demand which gives an incalculable seriousness to human actions.

This detaching of a spiritual world—a world of independent inwardness—from human doings and dealings operates in all religions, and is able to express itself in so far as religion is conceived by the entire consciousness to be a fact of the Spiritual Life at large and not of mere man, and in so far as the Spiritual Life is itself conceived as an encompassing and an overcoming of the antithesis between subject and object, and as a development and not a mere copy of reality. On such a ground as this, the movement to a Characteristic or special type of religion is secure against the danger of solipsism; and so far as a further development of the Spiritual Life virtually appears, a new kind of a reality wholly active is gained. Everything depends then upon whether such a turn of life happens; and the turn can happen, as life shows, through its own development and through the construction of a new reality.

Nevertheless, the danger of a humanising of religion is considerably increased at this new stage. And further, the more life is pushed back into a mysterious region, the less are we able to bring the spiritual content to an adequate expression; and if man fails here, he becomes satisfied with mere symbols which have incessantly to be referred back to their basal truth in order not to relapse into purely illusory images. In order to be armed against such a danger, it is necessary never to allow the Characteristic or special type of religion to fall outside the *whole* of religion, but to consider it constantly as one side of that whole. The Universal mode of religion must remain at hand if the Characteristic mode is fully to preserve its spiritual character, and is to be protected also from dangers of all kinds. Thus, we come to the relation between these two modes of religion. How precisely this relationship is to be conceived, and what rights it has, are matters for further investigation; for misunderstanding is only too apt to enter here—misunderstanding which our prior consideration has not sufficiently dealt with.

Certainly, there are not two religions but simply one religion; but this one could well have different stages, and such stages might be indispensable to the complete vivification of the whole. Indeed, if we take our stand decisively upon a religion of the Spiritual Life in opposition to a religion of the mere-human kind, the more necessary it is to relate our religion to the whole of the Spiritual Life, or, rather, to bind this Spiritual Life into a Whole, and to acknowledge it in its independence. But now we discover the hindrances upon which the development of the Spiritual Life has struck. These hindrances made us seek for a new stage of life; and, through this, religion receives a definite meaning, and must now commend itself through definite achievements as a Characteristic religion. All this connects itself again with the Universal mode, and thus obtains a secure footing against all embarrassments. Upon the ground of history there has never been presented a Universal religion of a self-reliant kind; but a Universal religious mode of thought has rapidly fallen into decay as soon as it gave up all connection with the Characteristic mode of religion.   But, at the same time, the Universal mode maintains an independent importance in so far as in it the elevation of man to spirituality becomes clearly and strongly apparent—an elevation which also belongs to the Characteristic or special mode.   The Universal mode has to bring movements and experiences into a current out of which issues the transition to the Characteristic mode; for without the undertaking of a struggle against the world as a whole, the longing after a new order of things acquires no personal truth.   How unsympathetic, for instance, is the officious confession of the inability of human reason made by people who have never undertaken any struggle in order to possess genuine knowledge, and who are unaware of the pain and renunciation involved in such a struggle. How unsympathetic are those who depict the nature of man as totally depraved, and pronounce him as corrupt from the beginning because he is by no means equal to his spiritual tasks, and, indeed, has often stood in direct opposition to such tasks.

But the Characteristic mode also requires a constant relation to Universal religion as a counteraction against a threatening narrowness. Through every turn into the particular, Characteristic or Specific religion must retain an influence upon the whole of life, and the total-task must remain present at each particular point, and must be furthered by it.

27

Otherwise Characteristic religion becomes in itself a mere escape from the exigencies of existence, and for the remainder of life it becomes a numb and gloomy narrowness. Indeed, such aloofness may endanger the spiritual character of religion; since by it religion may completely lose all definite content, and may finally degenerate into the mere agitation of empty emotion.

Our affirmation of the growth of Characteristic religion from the Universal pretends in no way to be an account of the historical course of religion with peoples and individuals. In regard to such a development, positive religion aims at fixing the starting-point; and it is only later that a general mode of thinking develops itself and exercises a criticism on the traditional material—a criticism which appears first of all as mainly negative but which finally leads back to a positive valuation of things. Then only we reach the ground of philosophic discussion; and now the double-sidedness of religion becomes recognisable within its totality.

Understood thus, both modes must remain permanently side by side, and refer reciprocally to each other. Through this, the whole of religion gains an incessant movement, and this movement is of great advantage as a security against the finality of dogmatism. At the same time, however, such a movement gives free play for the special characteristics of individuals and of epochs. In the whole of religion, indeed, the Universal and the Characteristic modes work together; but their relationship can shape itself in various ways, and here the one, and there the other, stands in the foreground; thus, either the greatness

and energy of the Spiritual Life occupy thought;
or, first and foremost, the hindrances are felt, and a
further manifestation of the Divine is desired as the
only possible means of salvation. The leading religious personalities present us with very varying combinations. How great, for instance, is the difference
between Luther and Zwingli in spite of all the affinity
of their ideas! Probably none of these personalities
developed both sides of religion more energetically
than Augustine; and even he was able to adjust both
sides only in an imperfect degree.

Thus, a view opens out over much movement
and a rich manifold, and also upon oppositions and
struggles; but nowhere more than in religion does
the struggle itself demonstrate, through its stirring
of all the energies, the power of the Whole and the
necessity of striving.

We have now endeavoured to find an assured
place for Characteristic religion; and our next object
is to reach nearer to its content.

2. *The New Life-Process*

(a) *The Main Thesis.*—The assertion of Characteristic religion consists in the fact that a pure self-
subsistence of the Spiritual Life within the human
soul, as a communication of an Absolute Inner Life,
involves a claim in which man reads his true nature
and shapes his life accordingly; and involves the
hope that he will gain an entire superiority to all
conflicts and hindrances. As a self-subsistence of
the Spiritual Life, the inwardness here in question
cannot signify a special province by the side of
reality: it must signify the most essential nature—

the inmost depth—of reality.   And, at the same time,
this inwardness is not mere subjectivity, but has to
unlock a new content ; and such an achievement can
in no way be the work of any individual point of
the nature, but must originate from the whole of
the Spiritual Life.   This precisely is the conviction
of Characteristic or Specific religion that such an
inwardness becomes a pure self-existence through its
development not merely by means of the world but
also in opposition to the world, and that it brings
help to man in his troubles—troubles which otherwise
threaten to make him succumb under his burden ;
through the creation not merely of individual processes
of life but of a new unity of life in man, life is
freed from the deadlock which otherwise attends it
and is brought into a fresh current.   How all this
happens with man is now to be considered more
closely.

The point of departure is to be found in the fact
that the problem originates beyond all particular
achievements of man, and also beyond the whole intellectual explanation of achievements ; it is a problem
concerning what man is in the whole of his soul—in
the whole of his character.   In all this, Life appears
solely concerned with itself—with its own situation—and in no way to reach beyond itself ; and
yet in what life does or leaves undone in such a
seclusion seems to lie the decision concerning its work,
concerning its success or failure.   Expressions to represent such a fact do not here altogether fail us :
we speak of moral character, moral personality, etc.,
but we do so at the risk of narrowing and coarsening
from the very outset what stands here in question.

What happens here is mysterious enough. Life here forges its way beyond the work of the world to a persistency and duration in itself, to a new kind of being; but in all this it is at the outset split up into so many isolated appearances, and it falls so easily into mere subjectivity. But some kind of unity seems apparent at the beginning, though it is not able to overcome the hindrance, and succeeds in bringing forth none but poor results. The whole is as though nebulous or veiled; and how it is possible from such vague motives to gain a foothold over against the entire world-order or even to set up a new world over against the old is absolutely incomprehensible. And here Characteristic religion steps in with its fundamental assertion that a "becoming" independence of pure inwardness and the unfolding of a new unity of life result; but this is shown to happen not through the energy of these qualities themselves but through the communication of the inmost nature of things—from the pure self-subsistence of reality. Certainly that communication is no mechanical instillation, but must awaken the energy of the soul itself; but such an energy does not appear as a natural possession but as a gift and a grace. What is always fundamental in religion seems in this special position to be assuredly so : that the vivification of the Whole at this particular position is not able to be effected without man's own decision and appropriation, and that this in turn includes in itself an act of the Whole.

That a new life of pure inwardness is not found in advance and does not depend upon particular effects, while yet man himself brings it forth and, in the inmost of his life, makes it the bearer and the cause of all, and that through this he gains a new kind of reality — all this is conceived by Characteristic religion as a fact and a miracle for the defence of which it is ready to take up with confidence a struggle against the whole of the remaining world. For this new centre alone is able to confer stability upon the fluctuating material of the rest of life; for nowhere is life more entirely itself than at this centre, and nothing is able to destroy what appears to it here as a certainty. But this holds good only in so far as the movement belongs to the Spiritual Life itself, and does not fall from it into subjectivity ; and the main business of religion is to secure its being the former. When this conviction lodges itself in the soul, the cosmic character of the Spiritual Life reaches a new stage, so that the new unity of life has to be viewed as the accomplishment of the one essential development which fixes the decisive character of the Spiritual Life.

Such a turn invests religion with a sovereignty over the whole of life. Henceforth man gains out of the relationship to God not only some kind of promotion for his life, but he gains also a self-reliant life and nature over against the world and in the midst of the most serious upheavals and the threat of destruction. In this new life the self-subsistence of infinity becomes his own, and opens out to him the final depth of reality. Thus the establishment of the relationship to the Absolute Life as the exclusive ground of spiritual self-conservation must far precede all remaining tasks; and these tasks may not detain man, for this relationship now demands recognition unconditionally and exclusively as self-sufficient. And thus we find on the summits of religion the claim raised that all things are to be loved not for their own sake, but for the sake of God from whose energy they proceed ; and consequently they are always relegated to a secondary place through such a mediation, all things thus acquiring value only in so far as they are founded in God and are filled with His Life. All devotion to anything but God now appears as a robbing of God ; all belief in one's own capability to perform anything as culpable pride (*superbia*). If thus God effects all in all and yet remains in Himself, no aim can lie outside Himself; and consequently the conviction develops that all happens for the glory of God (*propter majorem dei gloriam*). It was by no means a gloomy fanaticism that thought thus, as is often imagined by shallow opinion ; even a Kant in the expression of his ethical mode of thought did not so regard it. "They who place the aim of creation in the glory of God (setting it forth in no anthropomorphic way) have probably hit upon the best expression." It was in fact the anthropomorphic expression which made such a thought appear hard and crass ; but such a thought becomes indispensable with the recognition of the pure self-subsistence of reality and of the redemption of life solely through the communication of such a reality.

This demand, however, cannot develop its whole potency of meaning unless there is recognised with scrupulous precision the wide difference between, and even the entire opposition of, the ordinary human situation and the deeper task in hand, and unless the problem of life is immeasurably heightened. The new

standard causes all which proceeds from natural impulse
and from a satisfaction in one's own powers to appear
as insufficient ; and, indeed, all now appears as a contradiction in the light of the higher order of things.
It is not only this or that particular act or tendency,
but the whole habit of clinging to natural existence—
the existence of a mere creature—which stamps this
mode of thought as an insurrection against God and
as an apostasy from God. Amongst thinkers on this
subject Augustine appears prominently. Through
him notably there resulted the elevation and emancipation of the ethical task by this raising of the problem into the Whole, along with the demand for
a completely new nature ; but none the less he recognised also great dangers that lie on this path. Herewith the demand increases not only its content but
also its urgency. For the contradiction extends not
against something that is apart from us but against
the most intimate object of thought—against the
Absolute Life that is the basis of our inmost being,
and consequently against our own being itself. The
contradiction runs against not merely an impersonal
law, but against the world-power immediately present
as a whole. Thus evil appears as a personal outrage
—a grievous wrong and a contempt of the highest
good ; it shapes itself into sin and guilt, and it weighs
upon the soul of man with incomparably greater
heaviness ; it sets the soul in agitation and fills it with
alarm. Religions have often expressed all this in too
anthropomorphic a manner and have distorted it
almost to morbidness ; but despite the imperfection
of the formal statement the fundamental fact of an
inner rift in life and of an imperative responsibility

glimmer through it all plainly enough. This fact
may long lie latent in the consciousness of the
individual and of humanity; it may be put out of
sight by a shallow and idle mode of thought, but it
breaks forth ever anew against the opinions and
inclinations of men; and as soon as this happens it
speedily re-establishes itself as the dominant factor of
the whole life.

It is evident that man's own energy is unable
to save him from such a discord. If a rescue is
possible, Divine power and grace must do the work.
That such power and grace really accomplish this,
is the fundamental conviction of religion. Religion
doubtless is unable to appeal, in proof, to any completed work; for usually it is just those personalities
who felt themselves entirely certain of a new life who
have felt with painful intensity an opposition to such
a new life within their own nature. But the experience of the conflict was at the same time an
elevation above the conflict; and in this elevation
they grasped the immediate presence of a Higher
Power. The new life was further strengthened within
them through this convulsion; its origin in God now
became more clearly manifest; suffering and guilt
not only revealed their deepest root in our being
but they led to the point where a lofty " becoming "
—indeed a new " becoming "—through a Higher
Power shone forth in the seeming collapse of man.
In all the unreadiness and darkness of the human
circle a firm belief and a sure confidence asserted
that what was begun by such a Power can never be
lost; so that it was a trust in God which gave man
once more a belief in himself.

The effort to root these movements and experiences of the soul, with all their clash and their dialect, in the inmost nature—this resurrection of the nature out of its destruction, this progressive certainty of conviction in spite of the most stubborn doubt—succeeds but imperfectly; the facts tend to become more obscure and, indeed, the more complicated becomes the apparatus of thought which was set up for the elucidation of the facts. It is sufficient for religion that in man an independent point of departure, though in direct contradiction to the whole of his psychic life, has been assured and is maintained. Herewith there results not only a rearrangement but also an *inversion* of life; and it is this which becomes the fundamental fact which soon transforms itself into an immeasurable task. Fact and task together testify to the presence of a new order of things in the soul; and there originates, too, a new centre of life. But the man must not, as is often the case, mistake particular aspects and proceedings for the *whole* of life, and especially must he not extol feverish emotions which disappear as rapidly as they originate. Whenever religion is developed out of the Spiritual Life, a new stage of the Spiritual Life, not to be confused with the branching out of psychic activities, is required; the reflex of such a new stage may be observed in the immediate psychic life, but never allows itself to be attributed to the psychic life. Kant severely, but not without reason, termed " the will to feel such an immediate influence of the Divine a self-contradictory presumption." There easily develops a disposition to luxuriate in professed religious feelings which falls entirely

outside the realm of truth, and which involves a
good deal which helps to reduce religion to the level
of a merely subjective fancy.

Religion is best able to lay aside like this a reproach when it brings with itself a new kind of being,
and along with this a secure consolidation of the whole
life. The spiritual concentration found in religion
with its development of a pure self-subsistence of
the Spiritual Life and not of the mere subject—this
gaining of a new stage of life—is lost to him who
holds fast to the naïve, one might say, Ptolemaic
mode of thought—a mode of thought which believes
that certainty can proceed from the external alone,
and which seeks to prove the inward by the outward. The historical development of humanity, and
especially the inner movement of modern times, have
resulted in an inversion of the old conviction in solid
material existence, and have shown more and more
that all reality is known only to our inner experience ;
and that there is no kind of stability possible for us
unless there is a more unassailable point in our own
life. If this were not so, then absolute Phenomenalism would be right in resolving both the inner and outer
world into a mere stream of appearances. Now, the
main concern and the main achievement of religion
are to offer a foothold above the vacillation of things,
and to lead life to its most original sources. This
conviction is the most certain thing of all to the
Standard of the Spiritual Life, and it is that alone
which gives certainty to everything else. That much
controversy exists concerning it does not alter the
fact itself but our relationship to the fact. Such a
central life is not perceptible right in front of us, but

we have to climb through our own movements and experience to the point where it becomes accessible and convincing. And in connection with this fact there are various stages observable. To him who busies himself entirely with the external world and who does not reach some kind of unfolding of an inner life, the whole question of religion appears as futile ; and consequently he will possess only an anthropomorphic interpretation of the external world, and will endeavour to lay even that on one side. But he who while recognising a complex of the inner life yet sees in it only a succession of individual activities obscuring all else, or a mere background of life, and takes his stand towards life from such a point of view, may admit the validity of religion as one province by the side of other provinces ; but such a conception of religion will not acquire an imperative energy and will not become the governing principle of his life. It is only to him who fastens the inward aspects into a Whole, and, along with this, measures the whole of his potencies by the whole of the demand, that a radical change of life will carry him to the point where the presence of an Infinite Life breaks forth and where the appropriation of such an Infinite Life for the first time affords an indestructible foundation which all the contradictions of the remaining world can only strengthen. Thus there lies in the relation-ship of religion to man a more than subjective—a more than personal—element. Religion can produce this element only by recognising it as something that enters vitally into the life and not by conceiving of it as something only far off. But if life relates itself in a fundamentally different manner to morality, art,

and even science in so far as these unite into a Whole,
is it not then characteristic of religion that it combines
the personal judgment into a Whole ?

In any case, the questions of the acknowledgment
of religion by the individual and of its truth within
the Spiritual Life should not be confused with one
another.   The judgment concerning the latter
question, which constitutes the main fact, depends
upon the question whether Characteristic religion truly
brings a further development of the life of the spirit,
whether it leads to contents and values which lie far
above all the subjective reflections and arbitrary
actions of men.   This question will be dealt with
more fully, and its ramifications followed out.   But
before we turn to it, we have to notice the idea of
God which issues from Characteristic religion, and to
determine its essential and specific formation.

(β) *The Idea of God and the Relationship to God.*—
Characteristic or Specific religion draws its idea of
God from the Life-process ; it cannot expect as did
the older and more child-like mode of thought the
idea to come from an external revelation ; it cannot gain the idea from free speculative conceptions
whose shadowy creations are unable to move or to
take a warm interest in anything.   But in the Life-
process itself such a significant culmination cannot
take place unless the idea of God discloses further
characteristics for man.   But there appears here the
paradoxical character which belongs to religion
everywhere, and more particularly to Characteristic
religion.   In the apprehension of mankind the intimacy which the idea of God gains through its further
inclusion in life is the most striking thing.   The

Highest Power has not only taken into account human needs, but this Power has had communication with man, is present within his soul, has become his own life and nature, as well as his self-subsistence over against the order of the world. Here love is raised up into an image of the Godhead—love as a self-communication and as essential elevation of the nature, and as an expression of inmost fellowship. Since the whole of the Divine Life is here most intimately present, the relationship of Whole to Whole creates a new unity of life and, through the constant relationship, preserves and develops itself; there originates a mutual intercourse of the soul and God as between an I and a Thou; and the thought concerning the Godhead is not able to become really powerful unless it endeavours to be a living and operative unity. Consequently, there culminates here a movement away from the colourless conception of the Godhead to that of a living and personal God. The idea of the personality of God, which appears inadequate as soon as it is detached from the Life-process of religion and appears in a doctrinal form, is, when found *within* the Life-process, entirely obvious and indispensable. One may be clearly aware of the symbolic character of the idea; and yet, at the same time, grasp in it an incontestable intrinsic truth which he knows to be far above all mere anthropomorphism. For it is not that a merely human greatness has been transferred to the Divine, but that it is a return to the source of a Divine Life and its mutual communication with man. All this is not an argument of man concerning God, because the Divine must be apprehended through the Divine within us. All opposition to the

idea of the Divine personality is ultimately explained
by the fact that an energetic religious Life-process is
wanting—a Life-process which entertains the question
not so much from without as from within.   Whenever
such a Life-process is found, there is found simultaneously, often in overt contradiction to the formal
doctrinal statement, an element of belief in such a
Divine Personality.

But this intimacy is only one aspect of the idea of
God ; and the danger of falling into a merely human
mode of conception is avoided if the further removal
of God from immediate existence is simultaneously
acknowledged.   Characteristic religion brings forth a
new content only in so far as it penetrates beyond the
effects of Divine activity in the universe to a self-
subsistence, and recognises in this a new depth of
reality superior to all other formative action.   This
can only happen through a loosening from the bonds
of the world and an elevation above all the conceptions of the world ; thus there appears here something
simply not found in the world—a transcendent
summit, a mysterious sublimity.   If this sublimity
superior to the world secures an abode in the soul,
and, indeed, becomes the inmost and most intimate
of our being, and enables us to participate in the self-
subsistence of infinity, it opens up within us a fathomless depth which relegates to a subsidiary place the
existence that lies nearest to our hands, and it makes
us a problem to ourselves—a problem which transforms the whole of life—whilst it enables us to
understand and to handle as a mere phase and
appearance what at first appeared to be its whole life.
Thus it is the same religion which opens out from

God to man and simultaneously opens itself out in man himself and becomes to him a great mystery. Therefore, in the idea of God the intimate and the ultimate must both be present if religion is to reach its full development and to avoid the dangers which everywhere threaten it. Thus the Godhead appears, on the one hand, at an infinite height and distance above man, so that man, to his great sorrow, discovers his own littleness ; and, on the other, the Divine appears as most intimate and as the dearest possession, so that man is raised thereby to immeasurable greatness. The fact that both tendencies interlace in one Life-process, that they do not follow one the other but work together, that the unity is present in the manifold and the ultimate present in the intimate, starts an endless movement within the life, and enables it ever to renew its youth ; life is thus carried beyond all limitation and forbids all self-sufficient conclusions. The contrast of the finite and the infinite, of the unreal and the perfect, which was already developed by religion of a Universal kind, and which was recognised as the secret of all sublimity, becomes for the first time an immediate personal experience of the whole man.

A closer relationship to the vicissitudes of life corresponds to the richer content of the idea of God. The fact that the new life is disclosed to man not as something at hand but as a counter-action to, and as the overcoming of, an unreason otherwise insuperable within its own domain, shows the idea of God in a quite different relationship to suffering and unreason than has hitherto appeared. The manifestation of the Divine in Universal religion also

occurred through an incessant struggle with a resisting
environment.   But there the opposition seemed to lie
mainly in the external situation, and a decisive ascent
beyond it was confidently expected.   But later the
view of reality appeared a still more gloomy one, and
our Spiritual Life showed itself involved in the entanglement to its very root, so that help was to be
found only through the communication of an entirely
new life by means of a Power above the world.   Now
that Power has turned towards us and has had a care
for our misery by raising us to itself.   Can this come
about unless such a Power is itself affected by that
suffering, and unless it enters into the very sphere of
suffering?   Is there a genuine help obtained where
an inward participation—a common experience—is
wanting?   The doctrine of a suffering God arose
from such a train of thought—a God who took our
misery upon Himself in order to free us entirely from
it.   This doctrine is an irrefragable evidence of a
deep feeling ; but, through its turn to a doctrinal
form, it strikes a decidedly wrong note.   It is true
that religion must insist on the intimacy—the closest
intimacy—of the Divine presence precisely in suffering ;
but to attribute the very suffering to God Himself,
and especially to press such a great mystery into
formulated doctrine, leads to anthropomorphic and
even mythological ideas of an intolerable kind.   Since
such a course of thought does not set suffering in the
final cause, it devises gradations in God ; it develops
the idea of a reconciliation and substitution, and it
feels itself warranted in striving to express the impotence of man and his entire dependence on love
and grace.   This is a fundamental subversion of and

28

a direct injury to religion inasmuch as it does not carry the efficacy to its final root—to God Himself, and inasmuch as it will not allow that any success can be achieved through man's efforts. Further, in the religious province a reciprocal action of the Divine and the human takes place ; the intimate relationship to God suffers injury when redemption is sought through mediation; indeed, the notion that God does not help us through His own will and power, but needs first of all His own feeling of pity to be roused, is an outrage on God and a violation of the fundamental idea of religion—of the intimate presence of infinite love and grace. Also, in spite of his guilt and in the midst of his guilt God must be near to man. Dare we for this reason ascribe guilt to God? All dogmatic formulation of such fundamental truths of religion inevitably becomes a rationalism and a treatment of the problem by means of human relationships and according to human standards. Such a rationalism would have injured religion far more than it has already done were not life itself raised beyond all the conflict of ideas through the inner abiding energy of the Divine. It is sufficient for the religious consciousness to experience the nearness of God in human suffering and His help in the raising of life out of suffering into a new life beyond all the insufficiency of reason. Indeed, the more intuitively this necessary truth is grasped, the less does it assume the character of a doctrinal speculation, and the more purely and energetically is it able to work.

The facts regarding the relation of the Absolute Life to history are similar to those regarding suffering. History also gains a far greater significance in the

Life-process of Characteristic religion. For it is only through experiences, shocks, and transformations of the soul that the life that is not of this world unlocks itself to us ; such a life appears as a higher stage which postulates a higher still beyond itself, and gains its energy from such a source. In reality there originates a "history of the soul" only in connection with Characteristic religion, and a place in the literature of the world was first gained for such a history by the Confessions of Augustine. But because the movement presents itself to man as a succession, and because grades of revelation contrast with each other, yet, to place an historical process or even an inward change in God is again to judge from human analogy, and to measure God by human standards. But this is done if we conceive love in God as having only begun at a certain point of time, or under an appeasement of an alleged wrath, or if that love could reach its consummation only through the efficacy of certain conditions. It is a mistake to attempt to reach a greater intimacy with God through projecting forth human notions of His image.

Even in its simple ultimate root religion, as a union of the new nature of man with God and as a participation of his being in an Absolute Life, places the whole of life under a new aspect, and causes an entire revolution of the being. Also, the union with the Divine brings a complete calm under the vicissitudes of life ; nowhere but in relationship with God can this be gained. The Infinite Power and Love that has grounded a new spontaneous nature in man over against a dark and hostile world, will conserve such a new nature and its spiritual nucleus.

and shelter it against all perils and assaults, so that
life as the bearer of Life Eternal can never be wholly
lost in the stream of time. Thus we obtain in this
connection an essential portion of religion with its
belief in immortality—the conviction of the indestructibility of that spiritual unity of life in man, which is
the work of God. And it is from such a conception
that the conviction of the eternity of the Divine Life
proceeds—a conviction which gives man a confidence
in the preservation in some way of the spiritual
nucleus of his nature though not of his natural individuality; and upon that conception is grounded the
inward conviction "that what can not pass away for
God can not pass away for itself either. But God is
Lord of the living and the dead" (Augustine). The
train of thought of religion here is: that where the
greater is certain there can be no doubt about the
less. Religion holds as certain and conclusive that
this new inner foundation is the greatest thing of all
and the wonder of wonders, because it carries within
itself the power and certainty of the overcoming of
the old world and the creation of a new one; it is on
account of this that religion longs for the conviction
of the whole man, and brands the refusal of it as
pettiness and unbelief. The world may therefore
remain to the external view as it appeared before—a
kingdom of opposition and darkness; its hindrances
within and without may seem to nullify everything
else; they may contract and even seemingly destroy
man and his spiritual potencies ; all his acts may seem
fruitless and vain, and his whole existence may seem
to sink into nothingness and worthlessness.   Yet
through the entrance of the new life and a new world

everything is transformed from within, and the clearness of the light appears all the more by contrast with all the depth of the darkness.   Indeed, in the midst of all the mysteries of existence, hope and conviction and certainty will consolidate our experience, so that ultimately evil itself must serve the development of the good.   " This is the spiritual power which reigns and rules in the midst of enemies, and is powerful in the midst of all oppression.   And this is nothing other than that strength is perfected in weakness, and that in all things I can gain life eternal, so that cross and death are compelled to serve and to contribute towards my salvation" (Luther).

(γ) *The Verification of Religion through the Progressive Development of Life.*—Religion, like all things original and axiomatic, can establish its truth not through a reduction to general conceptions, but only through its development and effects.   And in order to do this, its effects take place in the conditions and content of life and not merely in the reflection and frame of mind on the subject; it brings forth not merely isolated stimulations but a thoroughgoing further development.   That such is the case in Characteristic religion we shall seek to show; but we have first to show how the indications of a new depth—a matter which has previously occupied us — now grow clear and integrate themselves; secondly, how the movements of life, begun in Universal religion, are now carried further; and thirdly, how from such a further development new characteristic traits enter into the entire life.

(*aa*) *Elucidation and Integration of Life.* — A yearning aspiration after a self-reliant inwardness

grows over against the work of the world and all
culture and in the midst of all the confusion of life.
But such an inwardness needs a new fundamental
relation to life—it needs an inner world superior to
all subjective reflection. Religion, and religion alone,
is able to grant this through the manifestation of an
absolute self-subsistence ; and it is here alone that the
reality integrates itself into a Whole and works as a
Whole towards each individual ; here man is delivered
from the psychic isolation into which he must otherwise fall, in proportion as the movement of culture
dissolves the sensuous connections of life and separates
individuals ever farther from each other. Religion, in
the experience of universal history, has proved itself
indispensable for the gaining of an inner connection
of life, for the deepening of life in itself, for overcoming all the alienation in one's own nature, for
drawing to one's self and vivifying what hitherto had
appeared as a mere environment. It has disclosed
man to himself, and has revealed to him, through the
presence of an absolute self-subsistence, a kingdom of
pure inwardness ; and it is in religion that man first
finds his own inwardness and an inward relationship
to the world. This comes to expression in innumerable examples. How, for instance, did the religious
movement, prior to and after the Christian era, turn
the ideal world of classical culture into a thing of soul
and inwardness ! How definitely connected in the
writings of Plotinus is the foundation of character with
the turn to religion ; and how much did Augustine
enhance the soul's moods and the musical strains of
the Latin tongue ! Also, an intimate relationship to
environing nature and an emotional mutual intercourse

with it come into realisation only through the conviction of the inner presence of an Absolute Life.
German people pride themselves since Fichte on the
possession of a certain characteristic disposition [*Gemüt*],
as a faculty specially developed amongst them; and
who else has given the expression such a characteristic
sense as the mystics who created such a "tendency"
from the intimate relationship to the Eternal Being?
The inwardness of the soul, which is the inheritance
of our language, was gained and has unfolded itself
in close connection with religion. And it is not only
at its advent alone that the inwardness needs religion;
if there exist no cosmic inwardness and if we acquire
no participation in it, the inner life manifestly loses
its root, its energy, and its truth. Thus we often
find to-day an empty subjectivity usurping the rights
of inwardness; men clutch eagerly at the mere letter
and semblance of things whilst the reality is threatening to vanish entirely.

Together with the progressive autonomy of inwardness goes the ascendancy of morality, and the one is
inseparable from the other. True inwardness grows
only where life connects itself into a Whole; and in
order to do this, it needs the subject's own elevating
deed. Such a deed is not easily wrought; it has to
be wrestled for and formed; and here is the point
where an energetic, manly and healthy inwardness
differentiates itself from the weak, effeminate and
morbid disposition of romanticism. Contrariwise,
there is no genuine morality which does not aim at
a whole of the inwardness and does not strive for
a new being. But religion alone ensures such a mode
because it opens out a new life from cosmic connec-

tions, and makes the question of the redemption of
the soul the kernel of all effort. True, morality has
often claimed for itself an absolute value outside
religion and often in opposition to religion : the Stoic
habit of thought has persisted through the centuries
as a permanent type of this mind. But such a
morality loosed from religion is deficient, as in connections, so also in a living content and a secure
foundation ; man here will easily overestimate his own
capacity, isolate himself, and thus fall into hollowness.
The single point is not able of itself to lead any life
out of the Whole, if such a life is not communicated
to it from the All. As soon as the moral problem has
exercised itself upon the whole of life, and as soon as
herewith not only the greatness but also the pettiness
of man become evident, the union with religion
becomes inevitable; it is in such a union alone that
the moral life integrates itself into a Whole and is
able to justify its claims to priority, which otherwise
would appear as dictatorial and arbitrary ; it is in this
way alone that the pride and harshness of moralism
can be held at bay—qualities which have provoked
many assaults on morality. True, an act—an act
encompassing the whole nature—has to carry our
Spiritual Life, but this act is itself more than a subjective flight : it is the appropriation of a new life,
and appears, in the midst of all its activity, as being
carried and even engendered by the Spiritual Life.

Life persists in the midst of painful hindrances
and ever finds new courage for its ascent. In all
this we have already recognised a difficult problem—
even a mystery. For a merely instinctive clinging to
life would not discover the energy for a new develop-

ment, and all subjective agitation would quickly grow
weary in face of the hardness of the opposition. That
positive impetus of life is able to obtain an illumination and a justification from religion—an illumination,
because here a new life superior to the entanglements of human existence is really mediated; a
justification, because this new life is freed from all
that, in the self-conservation, was lower instinct or
narrow selfishness. For it is not mere man but the
conservation of the Divine Life which now governs
all the effort ; and the struggle is not for a finite being
but for the presence of an Infinite Life. We hear
over and again religion reproached for lessening the
energy of life and even for breaking the courage of
life. But such a statement holds valid only for
special times of degeneration of religion, or for an
external view of the matter, to which the inner life
remains a sealed book. Nothing in fact so much
as religion has sustained man in painful tribulations
from within and without, and filled him with a joyous
courage of life. For man is now transplanted from
the effect to the cause, from the periphery to the
centre; and here Infinite Life with its perfection
becomes his own life. No doubt, as we have
long realised, the entire energy of affirmation is here
intensified through the thoroughness of the negation. But how can men with any pretension to
alertness overlook the Yea which stands behind
the Nay ?

We saw the claims of love and a shaping of life
from out of love persisting in the midst of all the
hardness of human relations ; but love itself found
no secure " ground," and the movement towards

it, restricted to itself, threatened to end in empty sentimentality or mere pompous talk; and often enough such talk has to conceal a lack of substance and truth. New contents of life in which man shall acquire a value and shall grow beyond his former self are absolutely necessary; if such is to happen over against the whole condition of the world, there is need for new beginnings, a new world, an infinite power and love, which communicate of their fulness to man, which free him from oppression, and which make him capable of genuine love. In this connection the exercise of such a love is able to become a testimony to its Divine origin: " that we forgive our neighbour makes us certain that God has forgiven us " (Luther). Only that a real transformation of life has to take place herewith, and not simply a higher estimation of what has remained unchanged; else we sink back into the subjective and anthropomorphic which will prevent us, until we overcome them, from taking a single step forward in religion. The expression " Infinite Love " contains something pictorial and human which can easily lead into error. But the mere approximateness, indeed, the inadequacy of the expression does not matter so long as we hold fast to the truth that, beyond all nature and culture, a new being is bestowed on man from the relationship and in the relationship to the Absolute Life —a being whose most adequate expression is that genuine love.

Such a founding of love in the Absolute Life will shield it from the effeminacy and lightness which it so easily assumes amongst human relations; it will detach humanity from the external appearances to which it tends to cling, and will unite it with the kernel of man's being and, at the same time, will avoid all the false idealisations which inevitably lead to grave disappointments. Thus, secure against defacement and certain of a new spiritual content, love will work as a powerful motive towards the shaping of human relationships from the foundation according to the valuation which is the due of man as a member of that new life. Love will undertake a manly struggle not only against what oppresses and defaces it from the outside, but still more against what threatens to destroy it inwardly. Thus, love of one's enemy can now mean more than a mere demand or a mere phase, because the new life is able to found an inner fellowship which certainly does not simply abolish the opposition and struggle (indeed, it may not abolish them), but which raises man beyond them and enables him to work against them.

Thus religion unites into a Whole movements otherwise isolated; it gives a firm foothold to things otherwise insecure; it illumines the darkness which otherwise enwraps such movements. Now for the first time what previously appeared more *beside* us than *in* us becomes our own act—our own being; an inversion results and along with it an immense elevation of life, because we step out of the effect into the cause, and, moreover, gain as our own an infinite life and creativeness of pure inwardness, and, indeed, find our true self in it. But all this comes about only in so far as religion opens out in fact a new content—a new stage of the Spiritual Life— not from a mere tendency of life based upon some indeterminate over-world and "beyond." It is essential to the religion of the Spiritual Life that it should continually forge its way ever and ever into a content which raises man beyond his initial situation and not merely stirs him to movements within his unaltered condition. True, even the religion of the Spiritual Life is unable to detach itself from the human form of life; but it makes an immense difference whether it accepts such a form as valid without any more ado, or whether it deals with such a form as a mere receptacle—an entirely inadequate receptacle—of a rising Spiritual Life within us.

(*bb*) *The Further Development of the Movements of Life.* — We have seen religion, even in its Universal mode, initiating the most effectual movements of life. But these movements undergo the most varied hindrances within the human domain; they threaten to come to an entire deadlock if the potency of religion does not strengthen itself, if it is not able, at least, to carry through that which aspires after a Whole. And how this becomes really possible through the manifestation of an absolute inner life will now be briefly explained.

An effort after Infinity belongs to the very essence of religion; but the world of man withstands such an effort in a harsh and hard manner. Struggling man finds himself not only hemmed in from without; but from within also he is fettered by the particularity of his own nature; and its own psychic potency is doled out to it by destiny generally parsimoniously enough. How can he escape from such a barrier, and how can he make the whole of life his own real life?

He is able to accomplish this only at a new level
where the pure self-subsistence of reality communicates itself to him, and awakens within him a new
life. In this life of pure inwardness, he grasps the
whole of Infinity as his own possession, and his life
is raised above all the barriers that have hitherto
thwarted him. This is done first in an inwardness of
the soul; but yet it does not arise out of a purely
subjective imagination, but out of the energy of a new
cosmic order—out of an All-life subsisting in itself.
If, thus, our life anchors itself at the central point
of Infinity, it will be able to hold fast to such an
Infinity in the midst of all hindrances.

The problem of freedom is closely connected
with the problem of infinity. Life had to insist
upon some kind of freedom; for without freedom,
as already noticed, there is no originality, no personal
life, and no genuine present moment. Religion,
however, became the best champion of freedom
because it manifested an original life out of the
Whole over against the concatenations of nature
and destiny. But such a life of the whole of our
existence does not forge its way right through the
hindrances, but falls, in its inner woof, right under
the power of the concatenations; and, thus, without
a new start, freedom must succumb to destiny.
Life gains such a new start at the new stage of
life which Characteristic religion inaugurates. For
here new beginnings are gained over against one's
prior psychic potency; and in this domain of pure
inwardness even that is not lost which does not
succeed in translating itself into visible work and
achievement. This does not mean that a faint dis-

position, in the form of a merely subjective emotion, suffices—little enough is gained in that way—but that the presence of an Absolute Life creates an activity springing from pure inwardness, and creates herewith a new province of life removed from the hindrances of the world. Through the consolidation of this province of life the law of natural causality is not annihilated, but still exercises a power over the very soul of man. But it has lost its old monopoly; man is now able to withstand its effete power of binding and restricting; he is able to set his life in its inmost depth upon his own act and upon an original creativeness, and, along with this, to drive out the old strange elements, and thus to bridge the chasm which otherwise lies between himself and his own soul.

All Spiritual Life is here a struggle against the flux of time—an ascent to eternal and immortal truth. Because religion raises things into a Whole and a Principle, it executes an inversion of man's first view of things. But we have already seen how man's effort after truth fell under the power of time and change, and how this called forth the most difficult entanglements and a painful anxiety, so that ever anew the transient presents itself in the garb and with the claims of eternal truth. There is no certain overcoming of time and no consolidating of the eternal through the ordinary every-day existence, or even through the surface-aspect of spiritual things. This achievement is possible only through a new order which reduces our whole world to a particular kind or aspect of reality. In this new order life may gain a timeless character, and may transform itself in its inmost depth into a pure self-subsistence with a persistence within its own essence. Characteristic religion inaugurates from the side of an absolute self-subsistence an emancipation from time ; it brings calm and consolidation into life ; hence it works beyond one's own circle for the maintenance and strengthening of the whole effort after timeless truth. Wherever religion has acquired full energy and independence, it has scorned being dismissed on the current of time or being shut up within the region of fluctuating human fortune ; rather has it held up a standard against the movements of time, and such movements have had to justify themselves before it ; it has worked for the differentiation of the transient from the permanent, and of pretentious culture from spirituality. But if religion itself falls into the entanglement, it finds no help in the precarious pro-ducts of time, but in an energetic consciousness of the eternal within its own being—in a revivification of its indestructible source and spring ; and it is this power alone, which supports religion in the midst of the movements of time, and which can be considered as possessing value. Thus, religion has held aloft the idea of eternity present in human life ; it has estab-lished an abode for life in itself in the midst of all the fever of work, and has founded a secure rest in the midst of all movement ; along with this it has given existence a depth, and has maintained a constancy of life against the vacillations of time.

The aspiration after greatness is, as we have already seen, no mere outcome of vain, overweening pride and self-mirroring. Man has to think greatly of himself and of his potency when he pursues his own task in spite of his apparent lonesomeness in an endless world, and has to forge his way through enormous oppositions. Religion gave to such an aspiration a solid justification and a secure support; and since it revealed the presence of an Absolute Life in man it calls him to pursue this life and to transform its entire infinity into his own possession. But man could not succeed in drawing his whole domain into this infinite life; the oppositions threaten to overpower him, and crippling doubt presses him down into littleness. In order to get beyond this, religion must establish a new depth of life; and it accomplishes this through the turn to Absolute self-subsistence, and, further, through the ensuing union of human and Divine life. Man is here removed into the centre of reality; here he has to reach decisions concerning the Whole; here the success of the Whole is tied to his decision in so far as the vivification cannot occur at this particular spot without his own deed, and this deed has to carry farther the movement of the world. Thus the deed has gained a cosmic character and cannot possibly be deemed trivial. Rather, as against the inner forming and building of reality proceeding here, does all that the external view of things exhibits, all that the history of the world shows in sensuous results, in catastrophes and colossal effects, become merely secondary. Everything has now a true value only in so far as it furthers that development; and for the best minds the more or less consistently valid environment is a coming and going, a rising and falling, a collecting and scattering, of human things. Thus, we have here also the inversion of life and of values which is characteristic of religion.

Characteristic religion, in all this, brings the stagnant life into a current. It does this not so much in that it breaks down the opposition, as in that it raises the life throughout above the domain of the opposition; it does it through the production of a new characteristic domain; but, as the longing for this ideal proceeded from out the Whole of life, so also will its satisfaction re-act upon the Whole and strengthen the Whole.

(cc) *Peculiar Effects of Characteristic Religion.*— Our previous exposition noticed the fact that Characteristic religion not merely carries on the previous process, but also brings forth something *new*, and we have now to lay hold of some of the peculiar developments of this New. And here again there is nothing astonishing to be expected—nothing that was formerly alien to us; but it is to be expected that phenomena which up to this stage were dispersed, and through the dispersion remained without any effect within the Whole, now connect themselves together, and, along with this, gain a new significance and reveal a further development of the Whole. Religion thus appears as the power which teaches man, through a discovery of the relations and a transposition into the creative " grounds," to see the facts as a Whole and to grasp them as his own. Its action, viewed externally, may seem to emerge only on the horizon of life and to evade all precise description. Viewed inwardly, it accomplishes an inversion of life by pushing all that surrounds man with manifold abundance and limited form to a secondary place, and by causing a new kind of life to arise, which appears over against the prior life as the fundamental depth, and which transforms the entire aspect of reality.

29

Religion generally comprehends reality as a
development or expression of a complete life; but it
makes a great difference whether such a complete life
appears as effective in the concatenation of the Whole
and as mediated through this to the individual parts,
or whether it appears as immediately present in the
part, and as directly related to the part.   The former
view predominates in Universal religion, and the
latter in Characteristic or Specific religion.   The manifestation of the immediate presence of the Whole
places the individual in possession of a new light,
by teaching him to understand such light as an expression of infinity—as the point where an original
and self-subsisting life bursts forth.   Through this a
mode of reflection arises which is the direct opposite
of the exact scientific mode with its all-pervading
connection and its deduction of each element from out
of the series to which it belongs; the new mode cannot
hope to eject or to replace this scientific mode, but it
is able to maintain over against it its independence and
its own rights.   For there results through this a more
intuitive and æsthetic insight which cannot possibly be
abandoned in our consideration of the whole meaning
of the universe.   The individual receives here an
immense enhancement because the fact is grasped as
an intimate verification of an inner life of the All—
as an expression of Divine glory; man in his individuality gains along with this a self-subsistence, a
self value, an inner infinity, and all this becomes an
object of pure insight and of a disinterested de-
votedness.   Here Art has its pre-eminent task and
develops, through the solution it offers, a new and
more inward relationship to the world; "it does not

raise nature and it does not make it more majestic
than it really is, but it raises human nature to see its
own glory and the glory of the world—it helps to
see right through the confusion of the external"
(Runeberg).   Art will thus see and honour the Divine
not merely in what is charming and harmonious, but
also in what is mighty and awful.   Would not such
an inner vivification of nature—such an inner reflected
light of the spiritual from out of nature—be an unreality, and could it therewith unlock such an immeasurable fulness of individuality, if the reality had no
self-subsistence and no inner depth ?   All art becomes
an evidence of such a depth.   But such an insight into
the infinite—such an intimate apprehension of the
infinite in the particular point—reaches beyond all art
into the whole of life ; for without this, life could never
become a pure self-life and never attain to a full present.

Just as with that transition, reflection is raised
above mere causality, so also is action raised above
merely utilitarian levels and above the whole
mechanism of ordinary life.   It is only through
the gain of an inner infinity that action is relieved
of the necessity to be ever on the look-out for new
tasks beyond the position attained at the moment, but
can rest in itself, return from all movements into itself without falling into an idle lethargy.   Herewith
there opens out a sphere of inner peace—the calm of
a Sabbath rest in the midst of all the tumult and
struggle of the ordinary surface-world.   Such an experience is either an empty delusion and, if so, we are
the entire slaves of a restless and senseless world-
work, or there is such a thing as a self-subsistence
of reality which becomes man's own possession.

The manifestation of such self-subsistence as is represented by religion works in another direction: it invests life with a greater simplicity and child-likeness than is possible through social relations. For where infinity is placed over against the individual, the individual's dependence upon infinity, his relationship to infinity, and his security therein are now perceived. And there can be no more suitable symbol to express this than the life of a little child with the simplicity of its feelings, its full dependence on others, its unconditional trust, its certain expectation of help as a matter of course. Life here appears as a relief from a painful entanglement, and yet there results something more than a mere relief—there results an inner renewal, the manifestation of an otherwise locked-up depth. Religions pre-eminently have brought such a spirit to development, and in none is this more conspicuously true than in that of Jesus. The reformers of education, too, have had the persuasion that nowhere is man more himself and nearer to the source of life than during the tender age of childhood, and hence that from such a source a rejuvenation of the whole life can proceed. Such a conviction penetrates the life-work of Froebel; and Pestalozzi chose the dispositions that permeate child-life as the most secure point of departure for the cultivation of religion. We quote once more his words: " The amazement of the sage in viewing the depth of creation and his search in the abyss for the Creator are not the education of humanity for the production of this faith. In the abyss of creation the investigator loses himself, and in its waters he can only drift about aimlessly far away from the source

of a fathomless sea." " Innocence and purity, an unalloyed human feeling of gratitude and love, are the
source of faith.   In the pure child-like disposition of
mankind the hope of eternal life wells up, and the
pure faith of mankind in God is not experienced in
its energy without such a hope."

These various traits are evidently developments
of one single life.   Such a life resists being
fastened to adjusted conceptions, and can attain some
representation only through metaphors and parables.
Yet notwithstanding this, it does not lose its power
and reality ; and in it alone is man able to gain a
secure foothold and a pure self--subsistence without
which his whole life must break in pieces.   Thus,
there culminates here something indispensable and
urgent ; but, at the same time, human life seems
most unstable — poised between different orders
of the world, and moved within itself by sharp
opposites.   But the movement itself is the most
valid testimony that the whole is no mere fancy ;
and religion will increase this assurance because it
turns the matter entirely into an individual concern,
and lets the world-problems be experienced by man
directly.   But religion must reflect with the greatest
possible zeal as to how to differentiate clearly between the new life-content and all the mere subjectivity which seems to accompany the new life as
a shadow, but is utterly unable to produce it out
of its own capacity.

(dd) *Retrospect.*—To derive the proof of religion
from the experience of the Life-process is a method
in no way new.   For from of old the quickening of a
new life has been the main achievement of religion and

the most convincing proof of its truth. The new life
won the soul and inclined it towards the instruction
imparted and not *vice versa*. The more, however,
religions have turned into Church organisations, the
more have they developed their doctrines into an
enclosed system; and the more have they deemed an
acknowledgment of this system as the main end, and
have been apt to treat life as a secondary, and doctrine
as the primary, thing. It is difficult to avoid such a
course within human conditions; but it involves so
many dangers and engenders so many abuses that a
counter-action is ever necessary and ever important—a
counter-effect that will raise life out of any and every
merely opportune manifestation to the level of a
principle. Such a turning of religion into doctrinal
conceptions easily brings it into a condition of
inertness and cripples man's own activity, because
religion is thus conceived as something ready-made
which stands with unconditional authority in front
of him; whereas if religion is referred to life, it
appears far more as a progressive co-operative work,
and set as a task from without. But life has to
struggle gradually for its content, and work out such
a content with increasing clearness; it must ever
ascend, ever draw reality more and more into itself
and grow along with it. And, further, the setting of
religion in doctrinal ideas can result only in its definite
connection with the ephemeral situation of culture;
thus there is found in religion a temporal and problematic element which easily treats itself as the main
fact; and the severe treatment which this main fact
experiences through the advance of culture turns
easily into an assault upon religion, and causes it to

appear far more insecure than it really is. Religion steps thus into immense entanglements because it is not able to carry on the struggle from the point where it is truly strong.

This and other abuses have for centuries pressed men to put life, which in reality has ever been the decisive factor, first also in the consciousness and activity of mankind, and to work out its implications with all possible clearness. The Reformation and Pietism acted thus; Pascal and Schleiermacher did the same; and the present day demands such an achievement with special insistence. But at the same time, history shows the great danger and entanglement connected with such an effort. The turn to life which shall energise the whole degenerates easily into mere subjectivity, and this is certainly unable to give religion either a secure foundation or an original content; and consequently an evaporation and a dissolution of religion become unavoidable. It is necessary then to raise life beyond its ordinary vagueness, to discover within it inner connections, and, indeed, the source of a reality; and, further, to release life from merely isolated aspects and to invest it with a self-reliance as well as with a cosmic character. We have already sought to show this through the turn to the Spiritual Life and its clear differentiation from the empirical psychic life with its "given" existence; and our whole investigation stands or falls with the acknowledgment of the Spiritual Life. We in modern times have long given up the attempt to found religion upon an investigation of the world, because the world itself has become far too much of a problem for us; and consequently we flee to man as our starting-point in the development of life. But man in his empirical existence is far too petty and confined to be able through his own potencies to set up against the boundless universe a new and elevated world ; and thus religion threatens to become a mere emanation from subjective human craving and fancy, and its entire world threatens to sink down to a dream-world. No amount of shrewdness or acumen can prevent this issue if man is no more than the first impressions show him to be, if there is not present within him a really-subsisting All-Life which enables him more and more to bring about an inversion of his natural existence. This, however, is a question of fact and not of argument ; therefore our main investigation directed itself to the tracing of such facts. Because we became persuaded that things were so, we gained the standpoint of spiritual experience over against a merely psychological standpoint. For the latter standpoint is concerned with purely psychic processes, and in the province of religion especially it occupies itself with the conditions of the stimulation of will and feeling, which are not able to prove anything beyond themselves. The spiritual experience, on the contrary, has to do with life's contents and with the construction of reality ; it need not trouble itself concerning the connections of the world except in a subsidiary manner, because it stands in the midst of such connections, and without these it cannot possibly exist. Man never succeeds in reaching the Divine unless the Divine works and is acknowledged in his own life ; what is omitted here in the first step is never again recovered, and becomes more and more impossible as life proceeds on its merely natural

course. If, however, the standpoint of spiritual experience is gained, then religion succeeds in attaining
entire certainty and immediacy ; then the struggles in
which it was involved turn into a similar result, and
its own inner movements become a testimony to the
reality of the new world which it represents.

3. *The Moulding of the Religious Life*

Even he who views in a friendly manner the
religion of Spiritual Life may still be in doubt as
to whether such a life be not too far removed from
the ordinary situations of experience, and whether it
be anything more than a kingdom of mere schemes
and shadows, which surrounds him. Consequently,
religion appears as something which is able to originate a powerful movement, but its effects are
restricted to specially endowed minds, and cannot
possibly work upon the whole of mankind. Such
universal effects, however, are unconditionally necessary to religion, for it lowers its own proper value
whenever it limits itself within any prescribed circle.
Thus, it becomes necessary to prove what a religion
of Spiritual Life is able to accomplish in this respect,
and to show further that it is able to satisfy fully
the inevitable demands made upon it. This problem
is divided into two parts, which present themselves in
turn : What significance does a religion of Spiritual
Life give to society, history, and the individual life
of the soul ? And, closely connected with this question, Is religion able to value sufficiently the evolution
which has occurred within these provinces, and which
has rendered explicit the difficulties which each of
these sides presents ?

(a) *The Religious Community*

(*aa*) *General Considerations.*—We have already noticed the fact that Universal religion hoped to satisfy man through spiritual activity itself, and without the presence of any special organisation; whilst Characteristic religion drove man imperatively to such an organisation. For that cosmic depth and its new life, which religion revealed over against the impulses and passions incident to the natural and social order of things, could never have brought about the necessary independence if conceived as the work of the mere individual; and neither could it bring itself to an increased energy and clearness or convert and elevate mankind in any comprehensive way. It is not here simply a question of the mere trimming of a life already existing, or of some kind of betterment of an existing situation of life, but of a radical transformation which leads into something *essentially new.* Even religion of Spiritual Life does not merely place man in some kind of relation to the Godhead, but it grants him a genuine nature out of the Divine Life, and this cannot possibly happen without a break with traditional aims and standards; and, further, religion of the Spiritual Life discovers a specially difficult problem in bringing the *new world* to an immediate presence and effective result within the soul. Here, the *necessity* of a religious organisation becomes realised as a conception required in order to unite currents otherwise distinct, in order to gather together elements otherwise scattered, and in order to uphold a persistent duration over against the fleeting moments. But when religion of Spiritual Life, proceeding from that inversion and conversion of life which have taken place, carries such experiences distinctly further, it necessarily discovers with great clearness the confusion of the situation. Indeed, in relation to the problem of a common formation of religion, it finds itself in the midst of motives of a conflicting kind. On the one hand, Spiritual Life can be to religion no other than a world of invisible greatness and goodness, an entrance to which is granted only to an inwardness of the soul. In order to reach such a world, each individual must unfold his own nature by means of an original energy ; for as a mere participation in a visible organisation religion can never become an independent factor in the individual soul, and such a participation would present religion as something external and alien. Thus, the formation of the relations of the religious community and of the individual soul with the religion of the Spiritual Life as represented by the historical development of Roman Catholicism is an impossibility ; for where the individual has value only as a link in the whole, and, indeed, in a visible, organisation, the result is bound to lead into an entire mechanising of the individual. On the other hand, the inwardness which stands in question in connection with Spiritual Life, and which is not an idea of the mere individual, concerns itself rather with the gaining of an inner world and of the presence of a cosmic life within the soul. But such a new world would remain only a vague outline if there were not granted to it some kind of thorough cultivation— some kind of substantial formation. The individual by himself is unable, however, to reach such a state save in connection with the co-operative work of an organisation. The individual cannot, from the standpoint of ordinary experience, distinguish the nature of Spiritual Life as something which, from the outset, points in the direction of the True and the Good. In order to see the true nature of Spiritual Life, an inner transformation is essential—an elevation to the level of spiritual energy—so as to construct a spiritual world. A movement in such a direction is present in the soul of each individual, but the point of greatest significance is whether such a movement fully declares itself and reaches further in the direction of its goal; and in order to attain this it is necessary that a society should transplant the individual into a characteristic sphere of life, that it should surround him with a spiritual atmosphere, and that it should present before him the movements and experiences implicit in the long and toilsome works of humanity. And, further, besides and beyond such an educative discipline, the incorporation of life in a solid society is indispensable in order to vindicate the cosmic character of Spiritual Life and its construction of reality, and in order to prevent it from sinking into a merely subjective impulse.

That such an incorporation carries great dangers along with itself is now evident from our consideration of the historical religions. We have already noticed how Churches may enter into strained relations not merely with individuals but with Spiritual Life in general, and, indeed, with religion itself. And, further, religion of Spiritual Life itself is bound to be affected in consequence of such confusions in its

root of pure inwardness as well as in the whole of
the development of its cosmic character. But little
as the historical religions are willing to change, the
changes of time ever bring forth new situations which
they are compelled to face ; and religion of Spiritual
Life affords a specially suitable ground to work over
against them. It does this in so far as a present
" becoming " of a total-life enters into each single
situation, and, accordingly, raises itself above the
opposition of a hierarchical formation of society on
the one hand, and a merely associative formation on
the other. In the one case, the individual is treated as
subsidiary ; in the other, the whole is so treated. It
does thus, further, in that it differentiates between an
essential foundation of life and its human form of
existence, and contends that the former is deep below
the flux of time, whilst the latter may be considered
as obtaining its existence within the flux ; it does this
inasmuch as its presentation of life—not of the animal
life, but of the Spiritual Life which constructs its
reality—regards the movement as inner immediacy,
and sets such a movement within its proper current,
judges all the diversified achievement by means of a
governing unity, and resolves all the mixed elements
into simple characteristic features.

Over against such gains, however, religion of
Spiritual Life has undergone great strain through
the fact that in the transition to a Characteristic or
Specific mode it opens up a new depth of life and sets
forth a new view of the world, both of which facts
carry within themselves something unique and incomparable—something which passes beyond the world
of work, and even beyond the world of mental and

spiritual activity.   But, at the same time, it cannot be
denied that, as in the shaping of life in its diverse forms,
so here in the further development of life, this further
development remains tied to the ways and means of
the ordinary situation, so that it only becomes explicit
through the help of that which stirs within the depth
of the soul.   Along with this, it is contended that the
new depth of life can never find an exact explanation
because a gulf permanently remains between goal and
achievement ; and all explanations of this depth of life
are, in the last resort, no more than metaphors which
point beyond themselves.   No danger need arise from
such disparity between will and capacity so long as
life and its efforts retain their full originality, and
hinders the mere means from injuring the main basis.
But as soon as life and effort grow weary and recede
into the background the danger becomes inevitable,
and then immediately difficult entanglements arise.

Further, the incorporation of life in a community
engenders dangers in so far as it seeks its justification in
the special situation of its epoch or its day, while at the
same time it carries the characteristics of the old situation into the new one.   The course of time brings forth
new situations, and it now becomes uncertain whether
the established institution suffices for such new situations—whether men find within it the expression of
their deepest convictions.   Up to a certain point, and
in a limited degree, an adjustment may be found in
the fact that the old possession has within itself the
power to develop, in the " long run " and unobserved,
in the direction of a *new* mode of thought.   Such a
new tendency often exercises great influence, even
when the mind believes the old to be entirely un-

changed. But definite limits are set to such a mode
of adjustment. Between what the old situation offers
and what the inwardness of the religious life desires
there is discovered a deep cleft and, indeed, a direct
opposition; so that a friendly understanding between
the two modes becomes impossible, and a break with
the old may become an obligatory necessity. No
human conception of the Divine is more than a
symbol, and any further development of the conception does not pass beyond a symbol; but the symbol
to which we cling must be the highest conceivable
one we are able to bring forth: otherwise, the symbol
does not present us with the fact which it is destined
to serve; and when it fails to do this, the human and
the Divine fall apart. If this occurs, solicitude for
the Divine becomes a holy obligation and the merely
human conception is driven out. This occurred in
the early stages of Christianity; it occurred at the
time of the Reformation; it occurs in our own day.
But such a necessity may be harsh and painful because it deals with things which we revere as holy.

Finally, the Spiritual Life becomes incorporated
only in so far as it proceeds from a unity, and interprets
itself within the main individual activities which
present themselves to it. Thought, Feeling, and
Will need special development in order that each
may obtain satisfaction. This aspect of the matter
again in its turn involves the danger of laying the
basis of life in partial provinces, so that one takes pre-
cedence of the others and consequently produces a
one-sided life. In order to withstand this, the partial,
isolated provinces must be constantly drawn into a
Whole superior to themselves, and, at the same time,

their own peculiar rights must be accorded to them.
A religion of Spiritual Life is especially destined to
work for the realisation of such a goal.

(*bb*) *The Consolidation of a Universe of Thought.*—
First of all, the religious organisation has to transmit
to the individual a consolidated and basal world of
thought.   The fact that to-day wide circles are
resolutely set against all dogmatic systems does in
no manner detract from the rights of such a demand.
For such adverse attitude arises mainly on account
of the fact that the traditional dogmas in no manner
coincide fully with the present-day demands of the
religious life, and hence touch man in an alien manner ;
but this defect of the present situation should in no
way obscure the necessity of a definite statement of
religious thought.   Religion, without such a statement, may easily turn into a mere heightening of
vague feelings.   Such a religious world of thought
must certainly be conceived in its main characteristics, and be marked off clearly from all other tasks.
This has to be done in connection both with its
content and its form.   Theories *about* the universe
in its partial relations do not construct the content ;
but the content is realised through an understanding
and building up of a reality—of a Divine Life—
and especially of the relationships of God and man
which become here evident.   Religion of Spiritual
Life must especially take its stand upon the acknowledgment that the world of religious thought has to
be considered as not proceeding from man to God,
but from God to man.   How this comes to be may,
in the beginning, appear quite enigmatic.   Religion,
however, presents its truths in the form of a Whole

only in so far as it shapes itself into a society, not
as a problem existing in the flux of things, not as
subjected to the seeking, brooding, and doubting of
individuals, but as an actuality firm as the rock and
founded in itself.   Such an actuality comes to the
individual as a holy proclamation, as a revelation of
a new depth which provides him with a support,
and which is in no need of the individual's consent
for its stability.   Without reverence before a sublime truth, no religion is possible.   And yet, on the
other hand, no external constraint can possibly impose religious truth upon man.   Hence there arise
distressing confusions, and these appear throughout
the whole history of religion.

The confusions which arise in connection with the
content and form of a world of religious thought
need not, however, discourage a religion of Spiritual
Life.   Such a religion, by means of its conception
and development of the fundamental fact of a
Spiritual Life superior to the world and penetrating
through the world, possesses an independent sphere
of thought which illumines and vivifies in a specific
manner the whole of reality.   This world of thought
roots itself firmly in the fundamental fact of this
Spiritual Life; it receives, however, an inner movement and history by means of which it ascends
through struggles from a basal spirituality right up
to a conquest.   All this carries within itself the
great experiences of mankind—experiences which
can become *individual* experiences.   Each individual
invests each grade of the ascent with his own
specific reality and with the work of the world;
but all the manifold coalesces into a *total-view*, and

30

gives, from this standpoint, a distinctive character
to all the material. A distinctive character of this
world of religious thought is its sharp contrasts. On
the one hand, we find the depreciation of the *old*
life—the insufficiency of all that hitherto satisfied
man ; and, on the other hand, we discover the holding
forth of a *new* life, and, indeed, a transplanting into
another kind of life which is incomparably higher
than anything which the old standards presented.
When religion of Spiritual Life brings forth such
fundamental truths to man as superior and incontestable facts, it presents these in no way in a tyrannical
and coercive manner, and in no way does it deprive
him of proofs of the validity of the new. For such
a fact is the power which raises man for the first
time to a spiritual essence, and which brings him to
himself. Through this assimilation he is able to
experience, in a form of immediacy, a greater and
further evolution of his own life ; and through such
proofs of the spirit and of the new energy, he is
strengthened in the conviction of the truth of all
this. Where the fact of a new life stands in question,
it is only the evolution of life itself which can
constitute the really valid proof. If, however, there
works in us a sublime truth, and if such a truth
becomes more and more our own life and actions,
we are securely raised above the antithesis of external
authority and subjective desire, and are reshaping
our conception of reality in a fundamental manner.
Consequently, the individual now outgrows the confines of sensuous ideas and the conclusions which
issue from them, and he will also protect religion
from the intrusion of magical elements. Religion

can now acknowledge the historical movements of the world—movements which have shifted reality from the sensuous to the spiritual; and it can, further, succeed in concluding that true reality does not lie by the side of, but within the Spiritual Life. Religion lies in its own consolidation, its deepening of a self-subsistence, its heralding of a new reality, and in its grip of a totality of an essential reality in the process of each individual act. By means of such a development, a religion of Spiritual Life can well develop a common world of thought, which surrounds individuals and binds them together.

(cc) *The Organisation of Activity.*—In connection with activity within the religious world, union with an organised society must not be wanting. This activity is characteristically shaped throughout in purport and motive, so that religion, in its specific and distinctive character, makes the Divine Love the origin and vehicle of all that happens in connection with human life. Further, an independent life, conscious of, and persisting in the midst of, all hindrances is maintained; and this is altogether the work of such an independent life. According to this fact, human activity turns its attention pre-eminently upon God; and is an evidence of an inward and joyous gratitude for salvation out of difficult circumstances and for an elevation to a holy life. Everything here that originates in love rests upon the love of God and has to recreate itself continually from such a source. " We love God and our neighbour out of the same love; but we love God for His own sake, but ourselves and our neighbour for the sake of God "(Augustine). The strong stimulation of the soul, which such a love brings with itself, engenders a powerful longing to set the character in action and to pour forth into all actions the joy which penetrates one's own nature. "There flows out of faith a love and joy in the Lord, and out of love a joyous and free spirit to serve our neighbour out of one's own free will regardless of gratitude or ingratitude, praise or blame, loss or gain" (Luther).

Lofty as such a disposition is, and much as it is able to accomplish, it is not without dangers. Such a longing as that spoken of, with its limitless views, may yet fall into impetuosity and pride; and, also, individuals can become very much divided until ultimately all fulness of energy may pass into barren emptiness. Consequently, such a longing needs organisation and control—a linking of the stormy passions in useful points, a relation and a union of individuals. What else could undertake such a task as that of the organisation of religious co-operation save that which is represented by the Church? Such a co-operation was exercised by the Christian community of the first century, in which hardly anything is so wonderfully noteworthy as the trend of religious enthusiasm towards the fruitful work of daily life.

But as is usually the case within the province of religion, one danger can hardly be avoided without our passing into another; and it is so here. The religious society links its enthusiasm with the fact that it stimulates the man; that it demonstrates his disposition as being consecrated to God, by means of specifically religious works; that it separates a particular province of the Divine from the remainder of life, and attributes any ultimate value to such a province alone. Much inwardness of feeling as well as much self-sacrificing activity has issued from such a point of view. But such a movement leads easily, and, indeed, unavoidably, into a depreciation of the remaining tasks of life ; and, in particular, we consider our relation to the human world as something subsidiary, and the simple duties of the hour are relegated to a secondary place. Further, such a transition, together with its emphasis on the " dead level " life, threatens to engender a highly strung self-consciousness which inflates itself into a pharisaical pride. Thus religion may become an enemy of morality ; and when the Church draws the religious life of the community entirely to itself and makes itself the main fact, the aims of the Church may quite easily appear superior to the aims of morality, and the imperatives of morality may thus be robbed of their august authority.

It is, therefore, quite intelligible that wherever the religious life has dawned with original power it has forbidden the sundering of specifically religious work from its connection with the soul ; it has extended the inner experience and elevation of life to the whole domain of life ; and the religious morality, vivified and deepened, has been made the main fact. Such a truth echoes in the teaching of Jesus ; and it is the main service of the Reformation that it freed man from being monopolised by specifically religious activity and placed the true service of God within the whole of life ; and, at the same time, as soon as the power of spirituality is granted him, man is freed from the mechanistic necessity into which otherwise he unavoidably falls.

The rejection of a specific type of sanctity alters as
well the position of the religious society, which may
seem upon the first view to take up an independent
task.   It may appear further that, with the abandonment of the relation of activity to God, human
welfare becomes the sole end, and that herewith a
narrow utilitarianism holds the field, which, in its
anxiety concerning the conditions of life, lets the
inner life escape.   That the fact is otherwise becomes
indisputable as soon as we recognise in man's nature
a great problem and a spiritual depth.   For then it
cannot possibly satisfy him merely to shape his natural
and social existence; but it becomes now a *necessity*
for him to develop a *new world* within himself and to
transport himself, from the very depth of his nature,
into such a world.   When this happens, the anxiety
for the real welfare of men is incomparably more than
a heightening of the social welfare.   Activity does
not now exhaust itself in certain particular work done
for individuals, but it becomes necessary to transform
the whole of the prior situation; and in order to
accomplish this the co-operation of all provinces of
Spiritual Life as well as of Art and Science is required.   The task is not so much to satisfy man as
he now is, but to make of him something essentially
different from what he is—indeed, to raise him into
a *new world*.   Thus the religious motive is able to
find its full satisfaction in its work on men; and,
consequently, the " Holy " need not separate itself
from life, but finds its own depth in such work.
The saying is true without qualification that " one
must seek God among men."

In such a turn towards man, in such a union of

morality and religion, there is needful a focussing of
energies in order to constitute a solid society.   This
need arises especially out of the situation in which
activity, in its attempt to pass from the world of
ordinary experience to a world of genuine spirituality,
discovers itself.   In this attempt activity meets with
the hardest resistance, and has incessantly to struggle.
Indeed, activity appears here as if dispersed and
scattered; and unless all the particular energies are
concentrated together, all the possibilities disappear
—possibilities which would otherwise bring independent spirituality to realisation and effect within the
human circle.

All this is necessary for every age, but it is specially
necessary for the present day.   The present age finds
itself in the particular situation in which it actually is
on account of the fact that spiritual activity, as found
in the convictions of men, is more and more detached
from a solid foundation, and is treated as an evidence
of a capacity merely human.   A great intensification
of human activity during the nineteenth century is
evident; and a further heightening of the self-consciousness of mankind is also conceivable.   But all
distinctive capacity in man roots itself in the last
resort in the spirituality immanent within him.   If
that spirituality be darkened—if that depth of the
nature be denied and man be placed entirely upon
his immediate existence—this is nothing other than a
struggle of man against what gives him his peculiar
greatness and which raises him above the animal level;
and the more such a struggle succeeds the more must
it lead to self-destruction and bring the spiritual content of life into rapid decay.   The presence of such a

danger is fully realised by the most earnest minds of our day ; and along with such a realisation there is found the aspiration after a powerful counter-effect. Such a counter-effect can only result through a focussing of energies ; and this, in its turn, needs the help of religion, in order that the depth and the energy may be attained which further this mighty movement. Thus, the problem of religious organisation at the present day is in no manner either solved or obsolete ; and the fact that religion can in no manner be trusted to the whim or caprice of the mere individual, in the midst of the embroilment and storms of the present, certifies that a religious organisation is as needful as ever in order to maintain Spiritual Life. A religion of Spiritual Life, however, is able to connect all the diversity of effort upon the one great task, viz. to hold upon human soil an independent spirituality superior to the world over against a culture merely human and against all merely human manipulations of Spiritual Life.

(*dd*) *Religious Worship.*—Neither in knowledge nor in active life does religion reach its highest summit, but such a summit is found rather in the immediate union of the soul with God—in the apprehension of the Divine in the immediate present. It is here alone that the religious life separates itself from all other ends—here it rests within itself, and carries blessedness within itself. The words of Hegel concerning this summit of religion hold true: " The streams of Lethe, out of which the soul quenches its thirst, flow within this region of the religion of the spirit : here all pain is drowned, and the soul transforms the hardness and darkness of Time into a vision, and interprets all things in the light of Eternity." Other words of Hegel's point in the same direction : " The contemplation of the Eternal and a life concentrated upon the Eternal must be present in order to possess not what is useful but what is holy."

Such a vision of the Divine falls entirely within the very inwardness of the soul ; but this inwardness needs a support for its own development in order to be a match for and to overcome the confusing and diverting impressions of a very different kind of world, as well as in order to raise itself above the precarious- ness of individual disposition. Thus the meaning of a society with its system of religious worship be- comes manifest ; for it is such a system alone that is able to create a permanent spiritual atmosphere, to bring forth persistent effects, to bring a new world to an intuitive nearness to the individual, and to transplant the soul within such a world. Within such a society, the supersensuous world can come to expression only through the help of sensuous means ; it comes to a pure expression by means of æsthetic re- finement ; and especially has it to embody the double aspect of the religious life—on the one hand, the wide interval between man and his religious ideal and his painful quest for it ; and, on the other hand, the immediate nearness and felicity of the Divine Life. Herewith arises a danger in that the sensuous does not remain satisfied with being a mere means, but succeeds in attaining an independence of its own ; and thus instead of pointing beyond itself it fortifies itself within its own content. Thus a cult easily passes, on the one hand, into a state of mere pleasure and into an Epicurean luxury of soft feelings; and, on the other hand, the sensuous may, through such a turn, draw the æsthetic refinement down to itself, and thus rob the elevated Divine Life of its rights. When this occurs, the sensuous hinders instead of leading to what is beyond itself. Indeed, while such a state of things can obtain between man and God, the thing appears to men of deeper spirituality as a detestable idolatry which ought to be wiped out. At different periods in human history, all that intertwined between the soul and its God has called forth the fierce opposition of many earnest souls and the necessity of its removal. Consequently, it is of the greatest importance that the symbol which expresses the Divine to man should be the highest conceivable one. And if the movement of the ages proceeds from outwards inward, from the sensuous to the soul, earlier forms of worship may very well become untenable, and new ones have to be sought. On the other hand, the main element in the power which a cult exercises over the mind consists in its tradition, its venerableness, its constancy, and its seeming immutability. It is necessary, therefore, to be on our guard, lest whilst gaining what is valuable for the individual situation, the whole should be destroyed. But a change of symbol proves unavailing if, in the common conviction of mankind, the symbol and the truth which it serves contradict each other. All counsels of expediency attempted in such a situation only retard the advancement of truth. Great problems of this nature stand before us at the present day, because a revival of religion will never come about without giving to cult its full rights.

(*ee*) *Retrospect and Conclusion.*—When the religious organisation relegates its manifestation to several provinces, these provinces must necessarily remain in constant interchange amongst one another, and proceed uniformly in their development; for any disproportionate growth of any one side endangers the development of the whole. A disproportionate growth of the content of thought threatens to bring the religious society to the status of a mere intellectual community; and a one-sided development of activity leads to eager and even excessive occupation, and thus injures the self-subsistence of life; whilst an excessive development of a cult reduces the life of the soul into a dreamy submersion under a soft sentimentalism.

Further, for the aid of Church organisation, the demand that the Characteristic or Specific formation of religion should remain in constant union with the Universal formation is of special significance, because otherwise the organisation can readily take on an intolerable narrowness; for the cosmic character of religion may suffer great injury in the personal experience of a " specific " kind of piety. But also, Universal religion is indispensable in order to establish and to preserve the right of the religious society and the movements of civilisation and culture, for Universal religion has here to play a mediating part. The religious society cannot seclude itself from that influence which civilisation and culture exercise upon the whole of life; but it cannot possibly follow out and bring into its service all the ramifications of civilisation and culture. How far such ramifications are qualified to enter is a question which must be answered by religion out of its own resources; and it is religion in the Universal sense which is able to bring forth their testimonials. Also, the religious society must bridge over both these provinces of religion, for it is only by doing this that it gains sufficient breadth to afford enough work for the different modes of feeling and thought, as well as the possibility to overcome any limits of particular spheres of thought and to bind the whole of mankind to itself. Such work will become more and more necessary in the future. When, in the past, the spheres of civilisation and culture stood side by side without any connection, and without reciprocal understanding of each other, different religions and religious organisations could originate and raise no stumbling-blocks. At present, however, we witness Spiritual Life everywhere pressing towards a unity which will encircle the whole of mankind, and men becoming more and more united in a co-operative activity. And, if this is the case, the disruption and jealousy caused by different religions will become a grave defect. He who doubts whether any one of the historical religions, as it is at present constituted, will bring all other religions into subserviency to itself, has to strive after an encircling unity—a unity which does not confine itself within any particular sphere of civilisation and culture, but which is able to include the whole of mankind. This means that neither can mere general doctrines be raised up from the manifold content found in the religions of the world, nor that the different religions can be mashed together into one religion. It means that it is necessary, in the midst of all the particularity, to emphasise the *essentials* of human life—the *substantial*

facts and experiences—and to strive for an understanding of these. Beyond all individual religions,
the religion of mankind must take its stand. We
here discover ourselves in a situation similar to that
of late antiquity. Now as then the spheres of history
and of life extend beyond each of the different religions—religions which, in the first place, belonged
to special nations. The movement here will not
reach its goal until a religion and a religious community take unto themselves many of the elements
of other religions, and, at the same time, rise
victoriously above them all. Christianity did this
in late antiquity and triumphed. If it is to triumph
in the struggle of the present, it will have to bring
about important transformations within itself; and,
therefore, it will have to ally itself more definitely
with the whole Spiritual Life.

(β) *The Relation to History.*—The whole course of
our investigation has shown the definite connection
of religion and history. We have seen that history,
as a spiritual experience, becomes possible only
through a return upon a spiritual order; we have
also seen that religion, with its revelation of different
grades within life and of a movement involved in it,
heightens in a most important manner the significance
of history; and, indeed, that, through its acceptation
of a movement within the nucleus of life, it makes
history in the full sense of the term possible. The
experiences of epochs and times corroborate all this.
For such experiences show that antiquity, although
it possessed greatness and glory, treated Spiritual Life
as an enclosed and final quantity or value; it granted
the Spiritual Life no inner ascent, and consequently

it knew no history in the sense here employed. These experiences show further that the present itself, with all its effort to interpret the past, and with its high estimation of the doctrine of evolution, threatens to overthrow history in the sense of an inner personal experience, and to transform all phenomena into a process merely natural. And, at the same time, the present alienation from religion and from the deeps of life carries within itself the danger of losing a history of the soul, of reducing life in an immeasurable degree, and of rendering spiritual creativeness more and more impossible. The late Professor William James in his excellent work—*The Varieties of Religious Experience*—notices the fact that there are so few autobiographies found outside Christian literature — so few confessions purely spiritual. Does not such a fact indicate that Christianity is especially fitted to grant to the soul of man a history, and that individuals have to become aware in an ever greater degree of what obtains within the depth of their own souls? It is not necessary, however, to open here the further discussion of the relation of religion and history; here it must suffice to consider how far religion can become its own history, and how, in particular, a religion of Spiritual Life relates itself to this problem.

The more a religion of Spiritual Life unfolds its specific nature, the more inclined it will be to approach history as one means of support for itself. For the experiences upon which such a religion is founded do not appear with equal clearness from moment to moment. It can well be believed by the individual that earlier times offered stimulations

and opened avenues by means of which the religious
life reached a summit otherwise unattainable. Such
summits are generally found where urgent problems
of the universal and most important situation and
great personalities meet each other. Wherever this
has occurred, human life has been imperatively roused
out of its lethargy, and thus spiritual creativeness
found a way out of the ordinary vagueness of life into
a clearer and more consolidated moulding of religion.
Thus it is quite intelligible that the historical religions
reached and held fast to such summits, and have consequently made such summits permanent standards
for all religious manifestations.

Whatever else history means to a religion of
Spiritual Life (and we shall soon refer to this
question), it is impossible for such a religion to be
based, in a most fundamental sense, upon history,
or for it to bind itself entirely to any particular
historical achievement. As all other truth, so the
truth of religion is superior to Time, and has to come
to birth ever anew in an original manner. Even if
a particular epoch presses far forward towards the
vivification and appropriation of the truth of religion,
still the epoch has not engendered but only conceived
in a better manner the Eternal and Original necessary
for all epochs; so that the definite effect of any epoch
is to be seen in the fact that the entrance to the
Divine is made easier for us, and not in that such an
epoch should bind us entirely to itself. What alone
is of religious value in history is that which transmutes itself into the immediate life of man; and it
is the duty of the historical situation scrupulously
to prove how far it responds to this test. Religion

develops its spiritual character not so much from the materials of history as *within* history; and in this respect the meaning of all genuine history is something quite other than a mere past.   History can thus bring advancement only to what knows how to verify its independence over against it, and how to free the Eternal content of past times from the mere form of Time.   Where an ability to do this is wanting, there speedily arises a disposition to set life in an alien past, and to dive more and more into such a past.   In all this renunciation one's own self and its needs are forgotten; until finally a life is led which has more of an alien than of its own content within itself. Further, a religion of Spiritual Life discovers, in its exclusive attachment to a special historical epoch, the abuses which such an attachment produces—the sundering of mankind into different groups, so that what is holy to one group appears to another as a mere error, and, if not, indeed, as a detestable mimicry.   The struggle here of each against each, in accordance with a consistent mode of thought, is unavoidable; and the roughest group has the greater logic on its side.

When history, however, takes a secondary place to that of a religion of Spiritual Life, it need not on that account be worthless or easily dispensed with. The disparagement of history may be attributed to the period of the *Aufklärung*; but this period had certain preconceptions concerning history which a religion of Spiritual Life cannot possibly share with it.   The *Aufklärung* made the individual alone the bearer of life, and believed that reason was so firmly laid, and so ready for use, as to develop into the needful situation through its own inherent power alone : there is no need for the life of the individual to be thus drawn into history, and no need for the support of history.   But the facts present themselves quite otherwise whenever man discovers himself by means of the aspiration after reason and spirituality, whenever he climbs to the height of his own nature— and he can climb to such a height only through the inauguration of a new reality and the importation of a new current of life, which seizes and raises him. Whenever Spiritual Life is not a mere clarification of ideas, but brings forth an unfolding and renewal of life, then the historical religions signify to us not merely views of the universe or theoretical inter- pretations of reality, but we see and revere in them potent focussing points of Spiritual Life, which lead to hidden depths, and which not merely give pictures of life, but develop further man's deeper nature.

Thus has Christianity not so much brought forth new conceptions of God and the world, or framed in good order a special kind of life, as that it has transformed the fundamental process of life as well as our relation to reality.   True, new conceptions have been formulated, but they possess right and energy only so far as they spring from such a fundamental process.   When we bring such a world-constituting life into the inwardness of the soul, and allow it to work in the most immediate and intimate manner upon ourselves, all this certainly cannot absolve us from our own work in life, but it can lighten our burdens, it can help us in the efforts to strengthen our energies, to overcome the accidental in the par-

31

ticular situations in which we are placed, and to succeed in entering the spiritual current of life.

Life calls life into being: this fact holds good also in this respect.

Another aspect of great importance, and to be borne in mind, is the fact that genuine Spiritual Life, with its construction of its own reality, does not grow from the "dead-level" life of the hour, but usually finds itself in opposition to it. For such an ordinary every-day life aims at pursuing spiritual tasks only in a secondary manner and in the service of non-spiritual ends; whilst all tasks have to be handled as one's own object or end in order to find the necessary energy and a pure moulding of life. On the summits of the historical movements of the world there has issued a power beyond the limits of ordinary life: in great personalities and great epochs the spiritual gains an independence, and out of these the spiritual is held up as a *necessity* over against the pettiness and triviality of daily occurrences. Thus a blending of Spiritual Life with history is able to lead personal effort to higher motives, and to awaken what, as a spiritual movement, is implicit in our own nature.

Hence, a religion of Spiritual Life is fully able to appreciate great personalities, and also clearly to understand that they mean more for religion than what is to be found in any other province. For here it is clear, before all else, that such personalities bring forth not merely a More of the ordinary, common-place situation, but a More of something *essentially new*. It was given to these creative spirits to free entirely the Divine from what is merely human, and to hold forth the Divine in the clearest manner as a *world* immeasurably superior to man, as well as to allow this to work upon themselves with quickening energy. The result of this was the raising of life into greatness and sublimity; it meant the suppression of ordinary existence with all its aims, as well as the fading of the most brilliant achievements in the light of the glory of the *new world*. All this happens not through new doctrines, but through the creation of a *new life*—through the development of a characteristic, spiritual type of soul which enables man to vivify the best within himself; and without this aid life easily tends to shade off into a merely shadowy existence. Hence, such great personalities were not merely sages and teachers; they did not merely point out a path for others, but, in the midst of innumerable difficulties, they paved the way and compelled others to enter into their own movement.

The construction of a new reality over against the ordinary, commonplace mode of life, which originates in such personalities, persists through succeeding generations, and creates a new history over against what is ordinarily termed "the history of the world"; and such a new history means for them the main reality. This belongs especially to the epochs of the formative influences of the great religions. In such epochs wide circles were stirred by spiritual movements; they were raised above the pettiness of the interests of daily life, and brought into a sure tendency of life. And such influences do not die away when an epoch vanishes, but are capable of being carried further, in a stimulating and urgent manner, by virtue of the unity of spirit which embraces all epochs. Ever afresh, such influences enable us to bring nearer to ourselves the tasks, conclusions, and renewals towards which our spiritual nature directs us. All particular, isolated achievements, in the last resort, combine in order to lead to an independent and mobile Spiritual Life, to a culminating effort, and to its own realisation within the human world. We perceive, in all the multiplicity of elements, a pervading enterprise—an enterprise with which we ourselves are called to co-operate. And it makes a great difference whether we isolate such an enterprise or bring it into connection with the most important historical work of the world. By means of the discovery of the *soul* of history even the particular details are seen to be no mere succession of events, but they focus into a Whole or Totality of life, and into a Present superior to Time—a Whole that while it carries within itself the characteristic experiences, oppositions, and hindrances, carries also its victories. Within this realm, the effort corresponds to our aspiration after *spiritual* self-conservation; and thus we are able to penetrate right through the epochs of the past, and consequently turn what is *far* in an *external* sense into what is *near* in an *internal* sense. But we must not for a moment forget that history introduces us to nothing in a merely mechanical manner; it introduces us to things only according to the amount of spiritual energy within it which it is able to carry further; it does not establish something entirely new, but develops further what is already imbedded within itself. If that be so, such a furtherance, in spite of the vastness and difficulties of the facts, cannot be too highly valued. Within such a movement, religion, in particular, raises itself ever higher

above merely human existence, and develops more and
more a spiritual content; more and more does it leave
behind the sensuous and places within Spiritual Life
the actually real necessary for itself. What, however, epochs achieve, each individual, within his own
situation, must achieve afresh for himself.

Reflection might set its face against such conclusions, and ask whether the individual succeeds in
giving its full rights to the historical development—
to what has been at all times fruitful in its effects
upon man. We in no manner deny this effectiveness
of history; for nothing gives religion a more intimate
influence over the human soul than the intuitive representation of an individual kind, as such representation
has proceeded from personalities, juncture of events,
and environment. It is in such a manner alone that
the external and shadowy character, which otherwise
clings to religious presentations, is overcome, and that
the whole man is brought into a current. Within
this province, which is able to introduce a new world
to us, the particular presentation of such a world is no
mere model for us, but a living, actual proof which,
with its interweaving of the visible and the invisible,
speaks more urgently to man than all intellectual reflections of a general kind. By this means especially,
at many times in the history of the world, distant
epochs have furnished support—support more sure
than that of the sensuous environment. Thus, that
distant land which records the life, work, and death
of the Saviour has become a spiritual home; and the
personalities that surrounded him have become types
of human character which have genuinely accompanied
the life and efforts of the centuries. Through a

real union with all this, one's own life receives a transfiguring light and an inner elevation.

Is it necessary to abandon all this because radical transformations have taken place, because a new situation has been created in regard to history—a situation which does not allow us any longer to take the old naïve relation to history—and because we are not able to ignore the interval between ourselves and the past? To abandon the meaning of history would be justifiable if it were not possible to differentiate between the spiritual presentation witnessed in history and the particular events in time which belong to it. We are compelled to differentiate clearly the fundamental content of life from the special development which issues as the result of the situation of men and times. History can remain of value to us although we are removed from it, because it has brought to expression, in a specially energetic manner, a spiritual content, and, indeed, a *type* of life. This spiritual content also makes the individual experience valuable and venerable: we are now able to discern what separates and what unites us. We must then realise that the temporal elements of history, with their immediate contribution to our particular activities, must not dominate us; and still we must recognise and preserve the rights and freedom of the living present. We are able to discover the differentiation, in regard to earlier times, between the spiritual content and the human presentations of that content; we find alongside of a positive relation to the spiritual content a freedom of criticism. And this, for instance, we discover to-day in regard to primitive Christianity. Not only its view of the universe, but also the stormy mode of its feelings, are inwardly far removed from us.   And yet, at the same time, we are able, in viewing its struggles for an inner renewal of life, for an ethical stirring of human exist- ence, for the coming of the Kingdom of God among men, to transplant ourselves within it with the whole of our soul ; and out of the enlivening, directing, and elevating energy, which proceeded from it, we can win ever fresh gains for ourselves.   Thus a religion of Spiritual Life cannot possibly abandon definite union with history, nor yet need it abandon itself to history. True, such a religion is bound to see in history some- thing other than what the customary and far too passive mode of conceiving history describes—as that which has to graduate and differentiate events—but, nevertheless, it discovers the possibility of thinking highly of the past and, at the same time, of drawing sustenance for its own advancement, as well as of preserving the independence of its own proper life in the present.

(γ) *The Soul-Life of the Individual.*—Little as religion proceeds from the mere individual, still the soul of the individual constitutes the sanctuary where it has specially to verify itself; for neither ideas of the world or of God nor social achievements are able to bring any reparation for a failure of immediacy and inwardness within the soul.   But, at the same time, it becomes evident from our consideration of this matter that an inner religious life can originate only by means of a direct intercourse between God and the soul.   Now, in regard to this, on the one hand, human nature seems too weak and fleeting to enter into such a relationship ; and, on the other hand, God seems to encompass all as an encircling world-power, while yet too remote from all human modes to be able to make Himself accessible to man in the same manner as man communicates with his brother-man. Such was the conviction of a thinker so great as Aristotle—the interval between God and man was in his view too vast to establish friendship between them; and, throughout the centuries, the conviction has been expressed again and again. Now, the gulf could not in fact be bridged if man signified nothing other than a mere nature existing by the side of many other natures— as an entity that could not, in any essential manner, step beyond mere Nature. But it is the fundamental conviction of every religion that man *does* this, and becomes, on account of his relation to God, a being with a nature of a characteristic and surpassing kind; and religion of Spiritual Life is able to grant a firm foundation for such a conviction. For such a religion differentiates sharply between the mere order of Nature as it exists in him and what reveals him as a member of an independent Spiritual Life. As such a being he is able to become the possessor of spiritual energy, to experience intimately the self-subsistence of reality as his *own existence*, and to co-operate towards the development of this. As certainly as religion understands this new creation as a work of God, so certainly must it assert an inner relationship of man with God. All this is not for man a subsidiary fact, which obtains in some remaining corner of his nature; but in this relationship he gains a genuine nature for the first time; the Life-process is here an effort and a struggle of man after a true self. It is only when we discover such a self in the union with

God that the life, realised as entirely issuing from such a union, possesses the fullest warmth and inwardness; and, indeed, it is this experience which becomes the root of all that may further develop within ourselves.

Further, by means of such a conception of Spiritual Life as is here represented, God is understood not as mere intelligence or mere energy, but as a *deed* that is the ground and impregnation of the world, and as a source of all activity. We have already noticed how the conception of personality, though only a symbol, yet offers the best symbol for all this. Not only are we able to, but we must, maintain a union of such a penetrating *deed* with the human soul awakened to spirituality. We have seen why a clear consciousness of the insufficiency of all conceptual delineations need not in any way lessen the energy and truth of such experiences; it need not prevent a mutual intercourse as of an I with a Thou. The fact that man is here concerned, not in the first place with this or that particular good, but pre-eminently with his own spiritual being, can invest such intercourse with more energy and depth than the natural individual seeks, by the aid of religion, for the satisfaction of his desire for happiness. It is here beyond the possibility of doubt that, however much man concerns himself in regard to his origin and passing, all his activities and effects are in the last resort dependent upon the Godhead; that he, also, is called to a decision of his own soul; and that the moulding of his relation to God depends upon himself as well as upon God. Thus all relationship is double-sided, so that what man does or leaves undone makes a difference in the relationship.

We are fully aware of the sharp protest which a pantheistic mode of thinking raises against such an acknowledgment of a religious feeling of the soul as a degradation of God into Time and humanisation, and as a break in the iron law of causality which from Eternity has encircled the universe. We mean, however, that in such statements an extra-religious view of the universe is transferred into religion in a highly dogmatic sense, and that consequently the independence of religion is completely sundered. It is essential to religion—and upon such a fact it must unhesitatingly stand—that our world in its spiritual content is still in a state of confusion; that far-reaching meanings are to be met within it, and important changes which still await culmination. How such facts agree with other views of reality of an entirely different kind is a question by itself; but concerning the right of the *independent* view of religion, however, such a right cannot possibly be abandoned. And it is only he who fails to see any original revelation of Spiritual Life who contests these claims on the part of religion.

Therefore, we decisively defend the possibility of a religious life of the soul over against all the prejudice of our day. How such a life of the soul stands in relation to reality, and how this reality unfolds itself, are questions which belong no longer to Philosophy. " The theory leads as far as the road and its direction ; the intuition, however, is a fact which belongs to those who *see* " (Plotinus).

4. *The Religious Elucidation of Reality*

After this cursory glance at the formation of religion, we have now to consider its effects upon

the total view of reality.   We shall consider suc-
cessively the Spiritual Life, the world, and the
position of man.   Religion passes beyond the general
conceptions of Idealism in so far as it presents not
only the superiority of the Spiritual Life, but, also, in
so far as it brings a new opening in the midst of all
hindrances and over against all the confusion.   A self-
subsistent reality with its new world is not developed
in a calm and calculating manner from the environing,
" given " existence, but it results only through a new
enthronement.   Religion does not place man from
the outset within the element of reason, but he needs
the help of religion in order to be set within such an
element.   So that it is not possible for religion to
hold forth the New over against the prior life without also fixing every element into a Whole, and,
further, engendering a movement from a Whole to
a Whole.   At the same time, life verifies itself by
means of its spiritual character as no blind fact to
which we belong willingly or unwillingly ; but it
becomes a problem to us ; it calls forth our own
co-operation, and claims from us a thorough transition.
Along with this, religion, over against all the confusion of civilisation and culture, and all the multiplicity of their effects, traces out simple outlines of
life, and presents before all else a common task.   Such
a raising of a simple fundamental form of life gives
religion especially the power of being understood by
all men and of working with equal energy upon all.
Indeed, the more complicated the progress of the ages
is made to appear in the light of the civilisation and
culture of our times, the more necessary does a counter-
effect towards simplicity and concentration become.

Who can deny that we have a need for such qualities to-day? Also, over against the whole of civilisation and culture, religion has a special work to accomplish. Civilisation and culture become ever more perfect and attain an ever fuller control over life, according as life emerges out of its vagueness of general ideas, takes its own tendency, and places the manifold variety of activities within an all-embracing synthesis. But necessary as such a transition to individuality is, still it has inner limits, and suffices not for any great length of time for the total content of life which wells up ever afresh. And, further, the most brilliant civilisations exhaust themselves and waste their own vital energies; and mankind ever again comes to a point where it is in peril of falling into emptiness, and, in fact, would have so fallen had it not been for the presence of a greater depth—of a more original source of life—which had persisted; and it is from such a life that mankind once again is able to refresh itself and to brace itself for new undertakings. Religion more than anything else presents such a source of life.

Thus religion brings far more movement into life. But this movement does not consist in the haste and unrest of an aimless quest—it is not the puzzling and doubting of mental reflection. For religion is called forth only through the appearance of a *new actuality* —only through the inauguration of a new relation with the living root of all reality. Therefore the movement recognises within itself a fixed aim and a secure support; and beyond the sphere of quest there exists, as the inmost axis of life, one of the possessions which remain superior to all merely human effort.

As the aspiration after such a new life arises out of the insufficiency of the old life, the consciousness of such insufficiency increases still more : one of the main effects of religion is to set forth the contrasts of life with entire energy and clearness, to set the person against all satisfaction in immediate existence, and uncompromisingly to drive such satisfaction out of life.   As religion compels man to measure according to the Standard of the *new life*, it makes him discover the insufficiency of all that which human existence offers to the soul and to love : the righteousness of civic life becomes for him a caricature when it presents itself as anything more than a stage to a further realisation of things ; the indifference of the visible order of the world meets him now in an incomparably more difficult manner as over against spiritual values—so do the fleetingness and illusiveness of all human love and the inner abandonment of Spiritual Life in an untransparent world.   In regard to all this, the leading religious spirits have been at one in the conviction that religion, with its elevation of the Standard and its deepening of the feelings, does not make pain lighter but heavier.   " The more of a Christian one is, the more is he susceptible to pain and death " (Luther).

Greater, certainly, appears also what religion achieves, over against situations of life not only inadequate but also intolerable—the elevation to an independent spirituality with all its contents and values, the holiness of a security in Infinite Love, the peace beyond the world found in union with the ultimate grounds of things.

Now religion sharpens the antithesis between the

Divine and what is exterior to the Divine, not in order to *end* with such a result; but even here it seeks, with great decisiveness, that the Divine should enter and rule within our own circle, that It should break down all opposition, and reach its goal without any further deviation. Such a contrast is, therefore, no mere fact for calm contemplation, but it calls us to the most diligent effort. Religion is the sworn enemy of all attempts to solve the problem of the universe by means of dovetailing and interpreting the appearances of things; it demands victory over what is ungodly and anti-godlike through deed and work and not through ideas and words.

But, at the same time, experience leaves no room for doubt that the effort fails to issue in complete conquest. In no case is the opposition wholly overcome, or even brought to a vanishing point, but it asserts itself and breaks forth ever afresh; indeed, while it obtains nourishment from the Good and Divine, man draws it into the circle of his personal interests and distorts all through his passions, so that in the development of religion much that is unedifying and, indeed, disastrous has been brought forth. Nowhere more than in this respect are the words of Kant corroborated: "All, even the most elevated, diminishes under the hands of man when he turns the idea of what is elevated to his own use."

When, however, religion makes the opposition not less but greater, it may seem as if the whole movement called forth what will only prove futile, and that the mighty effort will lead to no goal in particular. But such a view is simply an external one. For the fundamental conviction of religion is based on the fact that in the struggle the inner life itself develops further and further, that it raises itself more and more securely above the line of battle, that it connects itself ever stronger into a Whole and becomes more certain of a connection with an order of existence above the world.   In the midst of all opposition, the inner growth of life proceeds, and the joyous consciousness of an unassailable possession strengthens itself. The arena of struggle does not signify for religion the whole world, for religion holds forth, over against such an arena, a kingdom of peace and perfection, and is able, by means of a further completion of life, to extract from the struggle and imperfection of our existence some kind of meaning. Though the movement within us may not lead to a final terminus, and though we may remain tied by a thousand threads to a world to which the final conviction of our life feels itself superior, still a deepening of the Life-process is realised a working out of all the problems involved and a progressive elevation of our destiny. In sum, our life certainly appears not only as insufficiently equipped for its task, but in the course of its progress it seems ever more unprepared ; as when, for instance, historical reflection can discover hardly a greater difference between antiquity and modern times than that the former believed the most weighty questions to be so near solution, whilst to the latter the goal recedes farther and farther away.   But is not such a heightening of the problem a growth of life ?   And is it certain that the world of our human experience constitutes a ready-made Whole and explains itself fully as such ?   Could not the meaning of our world be that the problems are only to be clearly worked out, that the energies are only in a state of preparation and juxtaposition, and that opposites succeed in revealing their several natures? If so, our life would in no manner be a mere hope and trust in a Beyond, for it would see that the Divine is *now* present, and that already we are in the midst of the movement. If so, all would appear more as a beginning than as a culmination—as something resembling the first act and exposition of a drama; concerning the final conclusion religion does not entertain the slightest doubt. We may, within our domain, never reach the final conclusion; but what we do within it is not lost. Luther was of this conviction when he said: "We are not it yet, but we shall be it; it is not yet done and has not yet happened, but it is, however, on the move and in full swing; it is not the goal, but the road; all is not aglow and sparkling, but all is being cleansed."

This view of life, opened out by religion, exercises, however, the strongest influence upon the conception of our situation within the All and our relation to the All. For this, in fact, places the foundation of religion within the Spiritual Life—within the self-subsistence of reality—so that the life developed out of this does not constitute a special circle by the side of the remaining reality, but signifies its own depth of reality. Further, the experiences of religion apply an essential standard of measurement to the whole view of the universe. Religion is not able, of course, to develop out of itself the whole view of the universe, and place it under such a point of view, because the other provinces of life, as, for instance, art and science, contain specific experiences which possess an inde-

pendence over against the independence of religion,
and which can be understood only within the whole
of Spiritual Life.   But as religion concerns itself
with the fundamental conditions of the life of the
spirit, its experiences have great significance for the
fundamental constructions of the whole.   The following aspects must especially be referred to.   Religion
begins with a *real fact*, which absolutely refuses to
resolve itself further, and whose independence and
originality would neutralise every attempt at such a
resolution into lower terms.

Herein lies the failure of all attempts to engender
the proof of reality through general constructions,
deductions, etc.   In so far as these proofs have any
validity at all, religion is affirmed.   But the real fact
which religion represents is not an external, existing
thing at all which, only through its effects, comes into
contact with us, but which in its own nature remains
locked from us.   Religion is a fact of a *being-for-self*
or *self-subsistence* within which we place ourselves,
and which we are able to make a possession of in our
own life, and which, therefore, is able to unlock itself
fully to us.   Thus we accept a Positivism not of a
naturalistic, but of a spiritualistic kind—a Positivism
which can hope to reach the depth of reality, and not
merely remain upon the mere relations of things.
Therefore, religion must strengthen the confidence
of man in his spiritual capability and in his courage
for truth.   For Spiritual Life—in its nature a cosmic
development and constructor of reality—is not the
appearance of a depth found beneath itself, but is the
depth itself—it is an original life founded in itself.
This requires the rejection of all phenomenalism

32

—of all completion within a world of mere appearance. Again, religion alone brings to a clear expression the painful resistance which the evolution of a Spiritual and Divine World finds in the world of our ordinary experience. Religion cannot explain the resistance : all attempts at explanation have only succeeded in shifting the resistance to another position or laid it further back. Consequently, religion reveals a distressing breach—a rough discontinuity—in our existence ; it makes it impossible for us to consider our existence as a single, continuous web, or to resolve the whole content of our experience into rational factors. The affirmation which proceeds from the conclusions of the resistance is of a kind other than that which lies within the underivative of a cosmically-founded fact. The latter is capable of illuminating itself, and of transforming itself in one's own life, whilst this is impossible by means of the affirmation brought forth through a knowledge of the resistance ; and consequently the inconsistency of the world is enveloped in deep darkness. But the fundamental fact we have mentioned remains superior to the deep darkness, and, at the same time, it forms the light which illumines the darkness. Therefore, religion can, and, indeed, must plead for this final conviction, and contend, over against all doubts, that we do not belong, in the last resort, to an alien and impervious world ; but that the depth of our nature enables us to reach a union with the final grounds of things, and sets us within an element of entire truth. All this announces a refusal of all agnosticism and relativism. As religion would break into pieces were it not convinced that it brings forth final truth, it

can, therefore, verify to man a joyous assurance in
the midst of all. And, at the same time, religion
will make it clear that such an assurance is gained
only through scaling to the summit of our own
nature, and that it has to direct an unceasing battle
with the impressions nearest to our hands.

For the closer determination of reality, however,
religion furnishes not so much definite doctrines as
certain fundamental convictions—certain main tendencies—which the interpretation has to follow.
The Yea which it announces, in the form of a life
superior to the world and penetrating the world,
carries decisive negations within itself. Religion
opposes the naturalism which lowers all Spiritual
Life to a mere testimony or accompanying phenomenon of the world of sense impressions; it opposes
a pantheism which believes itself able to transform
all the contradictions of the world by means of
a mere alteration of its point of view; it works
against a despairing pessimism which possesses no
power of resistance to the oppositions. The mode
of thought characteristic of religion must work
energetically in the direction of conceiving the world
—a world constantly in flux yet constituting a Whole
—as a stage of struggle and decision; it must
further assert the potentiality for elevation of existing
energies—the possibility of the manifestation of an
original life. As the conception of original creativeness is throughout indispensable to religion, it will
work over the whole breadth of reality in order to
recognise and strengthen such a conception. And,
again, as we have already seen that religion views
our circle of existence, not as the whole of reality, but

as an element of the comprehensive whole, it will resist altogether a dogmatic conclusion concerning *this* world, and generally promote all which raises life as well as thought into breadth and freedom and originality.

The effect of religion upon the individual and upon mankind has occupied us so constantly throughout the whole course of our investigation that it needs no further elucidation. Here it is only remarked that religion can and must work in order to raise mankind above the opposition of its bent upon the world on the one hand, and upon human society on the other, as well as to overcome the opposition of a one-sided *theoretical* and of a one-sided *practical* conduct of life. History reveals much movement hither and thither, from one mode to the other; and, also, different peoples, in accordance with their several distinctive traits and experiences, separate themselves far from one another. Man flees to the universe in order to gain some greatness and stability over against the pettiness and vacillation of daily life, and in order to link his life to an elevated and immutable pole. Soon, however, his inability to do this becomes evident—his inability to dive into the heart of the universe and to participate in its life; the effort fails to reach beyond general conceptions and forms, and the discovery of the emptiness and coldness of all this drives him back to the human circle which grants him more immediacy and warmth, and which gives more fruitful, essential reality to his life. But the more he limits himself within this circle the more human life as a whole loses its great relations; the more all capacity for an inner elevation of man, as well as a counter-action to all petty-human modes, vanish, the more exclusively will these modes govern all human life and effort. And man, as a mere individual, as well as the contraction of life upon his welfare—be that welfare of individuals or of masses—become finally to the man himself an intolerable narrowness, threatening in the midst of immense activity to rob his life of all meaning and value.

Religion is specially called to work against a merely cosmic and a merely social conduct of life because it recognises in man himself the presence of an All-life as the vehicle of the Spiritual World, while, at the same time, it takes hold of the All-life itself in a warmer and more intimate manner. The opposition does not entirely vanish at one stroke, but we do not fall entirely into it : a standpoint is discovered where life is superior to the opposition, and where it is able to work against it. This is, indeed, especially the effect of religion—that it does not simply remove the various oppositions, but that it rises above them, and thereby makes the whole of life more mobile and more deep.

5. *Faith and Doubt: The Denial of Religion*

Religion has to prove its rights not only against certain propositions but against a deeply-rooted mode of thinking. By this we mean, first of all, that naïve fixed mode of thinking with its intellectual outlook on the world—a mode of thinking which conceives that the truth can be determined independently of life, and that life can afterwards be led to it. This is the case only in connection with the relationship to a

world existing outside ourselves; but, if it is necessary
to conceive of the whole of reality only as something
external to ourselves, then religion stands condemned. But it is not only religion but also the
whole of the ascending Spiritual Life which insists
upon an inner relationship to things; and herewith
the whole of life comes to the foreground, and
determines also the particular mode of thinking—its
direction and formation—in accordance with its own
qualities. If religion thus leads into a characteristic
conception of faith, such a life in the first place rests
upon a characteristic life—upon a life in the special
spiritual sense—which carries within itself a reality,
and which develops it out of itself. Religion is not a
communication of secrets from a higher world, but
the inauguration of an unworldly life; and it is with
the acknowledgment and assimilation of such a life
that faith has to do; it has to do with an appropriation
which carries a synthesis and an ascent of man's own
nature as well as an advancement and a lofty elevation within itself. The new life brings forth with
itself a new conception of reality, but faith all along
proceeds to such a reality through life alone; and it
is only in the obscuring of this connection and finally
in its dissolution that faith becomes a mere assertion
concerning things on the other side of this world,
and consequently succumbs inevitably to the criticism
of knowledge; whilst faith as a power of life precedes
knowledge, and it is only out of faith that knowledge
becomes possible. Such a faith is not only of a
stirring and progressive, but also of a welding and
defensive, nature. Then an unbroken decision for a
new life and its appropriation in a Whole becomes

a matter of significance, and life maintains itself against a hostile or indifferent world; it holds itself fast to invisible facts against the hard opposition of visible existence, and to general ideas over against all the failures of the nearest-at-hand achievements.

If faith carries within itself so much movement and struggle, it is not surprising if the matter does not run smoothly, if hindrances and deadlocks interpose themselves, if faith and doubt set themselves against one another, and if the soul is set in a painful dilemma. Doubt, in these connections, does not appear as something monstrous and atrocious, though it would so appear if a perfect circle of ideas presented itself to man and demanded his assent as a bounden duty. For where it is necessary to lay hold on a new life and to bring to consummation an inward transformation, then a personal experience and testing are needed. But no proof is definite which clings from the beginning to the final result, and places on one side all possibility of an antithesis. The opposite possibility must be thought out and lived through if the Yea is to possess full energy and genuineness. Thus doubt becomes a necessary, if also an uncomfortable, companion of religion; it is indispensable for the conservation of the full freshness and originality of religion—for the freeing of religion from conventional forms and phrases which would lead the mighty current into well-ordered channels but which readily cause it to be lost in the sands.

The history of religion presents us with a corroboration of this estimate. For it shows only a mediocre kind of the religious life as being unassailable by any doubt—a life inclined to a pharisaic superiority;

and to such a life the stern suppression of all doubt or even of any problem seemed necessary for the consolidation of its own belief. But on the contrary, many creative spirits—for instance, Augustine and Luther—had much trouble with doubt. This was so, not because their impetus towards religion was less strong, but because, by means of the greater strength of such an impetus, they saw through the inadequacy of all the props which give the feeling of certainty to the average man, and because they longed for something essentially secure, intimately present, and free from every human error, in order to posit their life upon it and in order to defy even death itself. It was only through the possession of such a goal that these leaders could become other than they had previously been; but the realisation of such a goal claimed the greatest toil and a fearless analysis of doubt. And even with all this, no complete rest was gained. What was as steadfast as a rock in the depth of the soul, experienced temptations ever anew from a surrounding world which never allowed the soul a rest. So that the certitude constitutes no idle possession, but has ever anew to be struggled for and ever anew has to wrestle with doubt. "I believe, Lord; help Thou mine unbelief": this is the best expression of the situation of the soul which finds itself in such struggles.

To bring forth palpable signs and wonders to the aid of threatened belief was a very natural and congenial thought to a naïve frame of mind. But on closer reflection, the observation renders this situation precarious, because now external miracles have withdrawn entirely from the heights of spiritual creativeness—from the inner miracle of the Spiritual Life and from the intimate presence of a Divine World. The founders of religion have themselves protested against a craving after such sensuous signs. "Go thither and hush up about your good works, and make a clean breast before the people of the sins you have committed, for that is the true miracle." These were the words of the Buddha; and Mahomet would perform no wonders, but looked upon the great works of God in nature and in the human soul as the true signs and wonders which man is called to believe in. How did Jesus blame those who craved for wonders and who had mixed up his life's work with signs and wonders? "An evil and adulterous generation seeketh after a sign; and there shall no sign be given to it but the sign of Jonah the prophet." This is no other than the sign of spiritual power and of a Divine message and greatness.

Again, there is a mid-level of religion where miracle seems indispensable in order to give faith the certainty from without which it is not able to obtain from within; thus will one, like Thomas, see and feel before one believes. Great crises and upheavals, however, have ever returned to the inner wonder of the spirit of man The Reformation was attested by no external signs and wonders, and yet it found the energy to forge its way against an old and great existing world and its possessions, to renew life, and to fortifiy religious certitude. And so it was with Savonarola in the dark days prior to his violent end—days which chronicle a touching insight into the secret of confidence and joy. Where did he finally find these? He found them not in external

signs and wonders such as lay near to him in the
environment or through tradition ; he found them in
the inward presence of a life-elevating Divine Spirit
that makes something better out of man, and whose
communication can thus be no mere illusion.

Doubt is far more an uncomfortable companion than
an enemy of religion.　Doubt always bears witness
to a strong interest, anxiety, and labour in the cause ;
it acknowledges the problem, it discovers the difficulty
and even the impossibility of an easy solution.　It is
quite otherwise with the complete denial of religion—
with the attempt to drive religion entirely out of life.
But even this can appear monstrous to no one to whom
the entanglements of the question have become evident and who fully measures the wide distance between
our world and the picture which religion demands.
But the question arises, whether these entanglements
can be overcome, and whether new realities—original
facts—stand over against them.　We sought to show
that this is the case through the discovery of an
autonomous depth of life—through the tracing of an
intimate relationship of man to a cosmic and absolute
life ; we ventured to assert the need of a struggle
with all things which, after the inauguration of the
new life, become externals and a mere environment,
and also to assert the necessity for carrying forth such
a struggle to a victorious issue.　Herewith we are fully
conscious of the fact that the new life carries within
itself assertions which are in no way self-evident, and
concerning which much uncertainty and discord can
arise.　But then the struggle is pushed back further
into life ; it does not concern an interpretation of a
" given " world but the production and content of

reality itself; it is not a concern of the mere intellect but of the whole man; it is a struggle of life
against life.   Let us inquire what possibilities are
here in question, and what aspects of life oppose
religion.

First of all, it is necessary to raise life to the height
of an essentially self - subsisting spirituality, and
to gain a new domain—a new place for spiritual
experience; it is here necessary to experience the
Nay and the Yea and to bring them to a right
relationship, and finally raise all to an undivided
and encompassing life.   The main proof of religion
lies always in the Whole of the life developed out
of religion.   This Whole must draw to itself the
entire area of existence; it must sift and winnow,
connect and raise; it must conduct things to their
own truth; it must initiate a powerful movement
which, through its own content and its progressive
victorious superiority, demonstrates its own truth.
Here it is not a doctrine which man has merely
to accept and follow that leads him to religion, but
a life held in front of him and brought near to him;
it is for this he is called, for it is this alone which
grants him the right relationship to reality, and
enables him to dive into the depth of his own nature.
Through this the idea of reality is transformed,
extended, and deepened.   The elevation of the
level of reality, the inner ascent of life in a manner
superior to all capacity of the mere individual, the
growth and creativeness — all these are the main
proof which religion is able to bring forth.   The
fact that religion, with its willing and creating,
stands in no isolation but finds itself in the centre

of life, that it furthers the whole and not merely isolated sides, and that it leads to its own truth— all this belongs essentially to this main proof. As with all things original and axiomatic, this new life is positively demonstrated through its own development and not through a deduction from some other premises: it carries its most effective energy of conviction in the strength and clearness of its own development; it never allows itself to be forced from without, but only to be stimulated from within, and it cannot possibly convince and gain us where such a stimulation finds no kind of responsive spirit.

An indirect proof, however, can be found in the fact that without the connection and elevation of life represented by religion, all that life possesses as any kind of content becomes insecure and unstable. We need only retrace backwards the stages of ascent in order to become aware that with the surrender of religion a decay of life sets in, which eats more and more into its essentials, and finally destroys its deepest foundation. When religion thus decays, a conquest of unreason takes its place, and pessimism becomes the uncontested lord of the field. As a final conclusion, however, such a pessimism must become rigid, embittered, and barren; the whole life sees itself threatened by it with stagnation—indeed, with destruction. An urgent natural impulse withstands this pessimism, and a tenacious clinging to existence to some extent softens it. One wishes somehow to retain life, but is not able to do this without emphasising the brighter sides of existence and placing the darker sides in the background; hence we find an approach to optimism without a crossing over to optimism. Thus we witness in our own day an affirmation of life gaining ground over against an intolerable growing pessimism ; the ground is gained not so much through an inner elevation of life as through men's resistance to an entire denial. But a solid support is in no way granted through such a resistance. Such a resistance either contains but little basal affirmation of life in face of the conflicting impressions of experience, and consequently sinks into superficiality and unveracity ; or these contradictory impressions gain the upper hand and then destroy all synthesis of life and annihilate all self-reliant spirituality. Thus, life loses all spiritual character, and renounces all ideality when it turns aside the inner advance of the movement and its conclusion from the realm of religion. It appears clear in connection with all this, that the matter does not deal with a special province of life, but with the preservation of the whole of life, and that the denial of religion leads inevitably to an inner dissolution of the whole of life.

The so-called immanent idealism with its deceptive, intermediate formations has become a special danger to man and to religion. Such a system dazzles man in that it claims that the reason of reality and the meaning of life descend upon him without much labour, in a form of immediacy. Such an intermediate product springs from a flaw in the energy of life, and is bound to increase such a flaw ; but notwithstanding its clanging phrases it is never able to discover this flaw, and it injures the truth of life. It is not only in the realm of science but also in religion that the words of

Bacon hold valid, that truth proceeds out of mistakes rather than out of chaos. The atheist is not the most dangerous enemy of religion.

The Spiritual Life which attains full clearness in religion constantly remains in difficult opposition to the environing world, and an overcoming of this opposition is not to be found in the ordinary capacity of man. This opposition must and will move and stir ever anew head and heart, and will ever strike out new doubts. The decision lies finally in the question whether for man the external world or a spring of life within himself is *the main fact*, whether the centre of gravity of reality is found without or within. *It is a struggle for the governing centre of life.* If the inner life attains to no independence and is not led as a Whole, the contradictions of the environing world appear insurmountable, and man must decline religion as an impossibility. But if the inner life reaches such an independence, and if man finds within the Spiritual Life simultaneously a new world and his own genuine self, the gravest misgivings will not be able to overthrow the certainty of this fundamental fact. Thus, this fundamental fact remains as the first and foremost, and uplifts itself far above the contradictions of the whole external world, so that the aspect of world has to accommodate itself to this fact and not this fact to that aspect. True, even after such a decision the contradiction does not simply vanish, but as holiness retains the background of suffering, so certainty will preserve its "one thing needful" as the background of doubt. But the contradiction is now removed from the centre to the periphery of life; it can therefore only touch us from without, and is not able to overthrow what is within; it will now not so much weaken as strengthen the certainty, because it calls life to a perpetual renewal and brings to fruition the greatness of the conquest.

Part V.—Christianity and the Present

INTRODUCTORY REMARKS CONCERNING HISTORICAL AND ABSOLUTE RELIGION

IF we now open the question concerning the relation of Christianity to our own day, another character is given to our investigation, and new difficulties are raised. Hitherto we have striven to come to an understanding with all who acknowledge fully the significance of the religious problem, but now we enter into a domain where divergence of opinion is hardly to be avoided. For scientific reflections alone are not able to decide concerning the material within this domain, because characteristics of the work of life, individual impressions and experiences, fall into the balance. Thus much which appeared to us as a main tendency is separated from us through this further problem. But in spite of this we dare not abandon our further investigation. Closely connected with the investigation concerning the intrinsic truth of religion lies a frank pronouncement concerning the situation of our day, for it is such a pronouncement which is able to set forth the essential character of our general conviction. That which refuses to be immersed in mere Time has yet to verify itself in Time. May we as friends, in the midst of all our differences, hold fast to what binds us together in the totality of our convictions.

How we understand the relation of the historical religions, and amongst them of Christianity, to absolute religion, has been shown in the whole course of our investigation. As certainly as there is but one sole truth, there can be but one absolute religion, and this religion in no way coincides entirely with any one of the historical religions. For they all conceive of the Divine under the conditions of the human situation; originating and growing in particular epochs, they have all to pay their tribute to the characteristics and culture of such epochs. But what is problematic and transient in such particularity need not prevent the action of a truth superior to time. If we acknowledge as the one essential of religions that they manifest and represent a Divine Life, such a Life in its inmost foundation is superior to its external configuration and activity, and thus it is able to withstand all the changes of time, and to maintain in spite of all its curtailment through the human situation an eternal truth. It is then necessary to differentiate such a *Substance* of religion from its *Existential-form*; it is necessary to examine how far religion harbours and represents such a fundamental life which runs through all ages and nations, and which raises them beyond the merely human situation. That a religion confesses itself to be an historical religion does not mean that it is to be considered as the final and completed truth, but that it is accepted as a standpoint where there exists the closest possible contact with truth, and where we are able to take possession of it.

33

The historical religions are not the truth itself, but appearances of the truth and pathways to the truth; and it is only where the Divine and the human become confused that men can fail to perceive this limitation in the historical religions.

If from the standpoint of religion a critical investigation of historical religions becomes needful, critical investigation is nowhere more difficult than within this domain. Conflicting considerations here specially antagonise each other. Now the historical religions may aspire after and deserve a great veneration because of their actual achievements. They are not mere systems of doctrine, but a concentration and development of life; they have traced out ideals not through some bold flight of thought, but by rooting such ideals even in the stony ground of the life of humanity; they have worked not merely for a period and upon select minds, but have operated along the whole vista of the ages for the welfare of humanity; they carry within themselves, through their close contact with human reality, great experiences, and have gained an actuality which maintains itself through its own centre of gravity, because religion from the outset deals not so much with the theoretical treatment of the world, as with a content of life which will secure for us a spiritual existence. Thus Hegel's words concerning a preponderatingly critical relationship to the State hold even more valid in the domain of religion. "The State is no work of art; it stands within the world, and thus within the spheres of arbitrary action, of accidents, and of errors; and evil conduct is able to disfigure it on many sides. But even the ugliest person, the criminal, the invalid, and the cripple, are yet living beings: and this affirmation—Life—exists in spite of all its flaws, and it is with this affirmation that we have to do." Where the treatment of religion does not succeed in reaching this affirmative character, where religion is simply cavilled at, and no attempt is made to enter into its totality and its inwardness, such a carping criticism may attain a cheap popularity, but it has absolutely no relevancy to the subject-matter.

This is one side of the matter. But there remains another side, and it, too, has its rights. The historical religions may not be satisfied with their actual facts alone; they raise the claim of being the truth—the final truth, which is superior to all else. Now, nothing—not even the most colossal achievement of an historical kind—is able to furnish the proof of such a truth, for such a proof is only to be found from a standpoint *above* Time and from the very nature of the Spiritual Life and its fundamental relationship to reality. Thus an intimate and immediate life has to stand over against every historical achievement, measure it, and test it. In fact there exists in all times, and especially in such times when historical religion has been in a state of indisputable sovereignty, an internal tension between tradition and immediate life, and the assimilation of the presented material is ever a remodelling and an adjustment. But so long as this adjustment was not too difficult to accomplish, no cleft was felt, and consequently the historical religion could appear to be in entire possession of the truth. When, however, important transformations of universal life heighten the tension, a point is at last reached where men feel especially its distance from their own ideas and efforts, and where, consequently, the attitude to such an historical religion becomes predominantly critical and negative. The differences which thus originate may be twofold. Either life outgrows the content of the historical religion, and therefore great revolutions of an inward character become inevitable; or all the transformations in the existential-form leave so much of the Substance untouched that the changes in the external form can still be connected with the inward nucleus, and thus in the midst of all the disarrangement the continuity of the historical religion can be preserved. Indeed, the transformation in the existential-form may even help towards a purer and more energetic effect of the Substance, and thus the seeming upheaval and destruction may prove itself finally to be a development and deepening of the Substance.

All this has now to be applied in reference to Christianity. It is necessary to ask the question, how deeply Christianity is affected by the undeniable transformations of culture and human life, whether it is able to assert and maintain itself victoriously over against such culture and life, and what such an assertion demands in the way of new activities.

CHAPTER XIV

a. THE ETERNAL IN CHRISTIANITY

1. *The Nucleus beyond all Loss.*

OUR investigation as a whole leaves no doubt as to our position in regard to Christianity. A double aspect has been already fully noticed. On the one hand, Christianity in the nature of its Substance appears as the highest embodiment of absolute religion ; and, on the other hand, a fundamental revision of its traditional form of existence has become absolutely necessary. It has already appeared to us that we are not able to develop what proves itself as absolute religion without a constant reference to Christianity. Christianity has already appeared to us from its inmost essence as the religion of religions, and, simultaneously, as being certain of a permanent duration. But the Eternal in Christianity finds itself not only railed in and interlaced, but also welded with seemingly inseparable elements which bear the imprint of a special age, and which we dare not bind to ourselves—an age which is so distant from us and which in so many ways has been outgrown. It is now necessary to present a connected view of the twofold aspects, to mark clearly the boundaries between them, and to show the necessity of not allowing the religious problem to remain in a state of stagnation. If we bring together the results of our main discussion and the historical conditions of Christianity, we shall see how they illumine one another reciprocally, how they strengthen one another, and, also, how they diverge from one another. This will enable us to understand where the boundary between the temporal and the Eternal lies; and this in its turn will carry to clearer expression the manner in which Christianity has to be shaped in the future.

Christianity is a religion of redemption and not a religion of law. Herein lies the acknowledgment of a pointed contrast between a factual and an urgent situation; herein lies the assertion of the inability, out of one's own energy, to reach the longed-for summit through a general kind of improvement of the prior situation; and herein lies the demand of a transformation and elevation through an intimate entrance of the Divine. Does the general experience of the Spiritual Life corroborate this assertion? It does. For we have already seen how the Spiritual Life is unable to find its necessary self-reliance in the world of ordinary experience; we have seen a breach between genuine spirituality and the world taking place; and we have seen how the effects of all this carry a new world within themselves. In spiritual things every pathway open to man leads to a Yea through a Nay; and all toil is in vain without an inner elevation through the energy of an Absolute Life. This happens in connection with the whole of the Spiritual Life as soon as it aspires to climb from merely decora-

tive culture to genuine truth, and this Spiritual Life
gains strength even through the very effort itself;
it is only the inauguration of a new stage of reality
that is able here to prevent a shipwreck of all toilsome
work.   This new stage places the threatened overthrow of human life, the impotence of mere man, and
the presence of an elevated world, far more intuitively
and urgently before man's eyes.   Thus, the religion
of redemption only brings to a fuller expression and
more tangible configuration what is present as a
demand and a fact throughout the whole of life.

The religions of redemption which are found alongside of Christianity are esoteric Brahmanism and
Buddhism.   But the difference between the latter
and Christianity occupied our attention at the com-
mencement of our investigation, and has appeared
all the greater during its course.   Now it becomes
quite clear how wide an interval lies between a predominantly intellectual religion of redemption and
a predominantly ethical one, and how differently
life shapes itself in each.   In the former mode an
emancipation from semblance becomes necessary ;
in the latter mode an overcoming of evil is the one
thing needful.   In the former, the very basis of the
world seems evil ; in the latter, it is the subversion
of this basis which seems evil.   In the former, the
instincts of life are to be entirely eradicated ; in the
latter, on the contrary, they are to be ennobled or
rather to be transformed.   In the former, no higher
world of a positive kind dawns on man, so that life
finally reaches a seemingly valid point of arrest, whilst
upon Christian ground life ever anew ascends beyond
itself.

In Christianity suffering has its bitterness chiefly as a perversion of an original good, so that a Yea is able to work in the midst of all unreason, and a hope of a final conquest is able to become the possession of the soul in the midst of the seeming collapse of the world. But an elevation into a new world is even here not an entire casting off of the old world. For that elevation does not succeed at the outset in reaching the inmost secret—the centre of life. The old world with its darkness and suffering, its alarm and its error, persists in the whole breadth of existence. There arises thus a striking dialectic of life. What man possesses in this existence has to be won and even often abandoned. Thus, an overflowing joy and a deep pain, a serene security of the inner being and a drifting of existence before all the storms of life; a steadfast conviction and a brooding doubt, a participation in the perfection of Absolute Life and a persistence of human pettiness meet as opposites in the one and same life. If life is ever to rise, it has to take upon itself, in a genuine manner, its own acts, and not be satisfied with a merely sentimental disposition; it has to enter into an incessant tension and movement; it has to be driven to ever further self-deepening; and it has to take up its experiences in all their extent, to live through them, and to taste all their sweets and bitterness. Thus there arises energy without defiance, gentleness without weakness; indeed, the deepest feeling and the most joyous activity sustain and interlace one another. Such an inner tension and movement, as we have already observed, are indispensable for the ascent of the Spiritual Life under human conditions, and Christianity only develops here in a special direction what is struggling upwards from the whole of life and is pressing towards a configuration.

All religions proclaim and require morality. But this of itself signifies in no manner that freedom and deed constitute the source of their ideal world, or that the nucleus of the Spiritual Life is of an ethical nature. What constitutes the decisive characteristic of Christianity is the fact that it roots the whole world in freedom, and that it refuses altogether the reducing of the Spiritual Life to a natural or mental process. But, at the same time, Christianity steps into painful entanglements without and within. Without, a rigid kingdom of mechanism which enters into the soul and overpowers spiritual activity withstands the attempts after a transformation into freedom, into a soul, and into love. The impression of a blind indifferent actuality is here so powerful against all inner greatness and goodness that an *external* view of things deems it hopeless to overcome the opposition. At the same time, entanglements of an inward kind threaten to bring the movement towards freedom and personality under the ban of the trivial and merely human, and to rob these qualities of their cosmic character ; and the threat goes so far as to coerce all inward aspiration under an all-powerful destiny. Therefore, there arises a painful and hazardous enterprise when the struggle is taken up against such oppositions within and without ; but Christianity has found the courage and the faith for this titanic struggle, for it has become convinced that this is the only means for the spiritual preservation of human life and for the gaining of a meaning and value. At the same time, the inmost nucleus of life must withold its assent to all rationalistic deductions, and yet it has to remain in the midst of opposites. Christianity is the most ultra-rational of all religions, because it is the richest and deepest of them all.

It was a main point in our investigation to show that the Spiritual Life is not a manifestation of mere man but of an independent reality, and that, through a communication of this reality, it grants a new and cosmic nature to man. What religion so fully meets such demands as that which makes the Kingdom of God its central idea, and which promises to help the individual not only in a " given " world, but to guide him to a new world? And this new world is contiguous with human life not only from the external; it also becomes one's own world from within and as a Whole; and as each particular point in life has now to be decided by reference to the Whole, and, indeed, has to carry the Whole within itself, life gains a task which cannot be measured and a greatness superior to that of the world

The union of the human and the Divine constitutes the nucleus of all genuine religion, and it is the manner in which this union is conceived that constitutes the main characteristics of the particular religions. Christianity has pursued this problem to its final depths, since it not only effects particular relations of the Divine and the human, but presents a full union of the two natures, and has courageously maintained the indestructibility of the Divine in the midst of all the perversions of the human situation. Not all the crippling of this idea through unhappy dogmatic formulations can obscure the fact that the religious form presents here a truth which is the indispensable presupposition of every effort after truth, and without which our life loses all possibility of a durable support.

A warm love towards all humanity runs through Christianity; it longs to redeem every individual; it gives man a value beyond all special achievements and on the other side of all mental and moral deeds; it has been the first to bring the pure inwardness of the soul to a clear expression. But it has also, through the linking of the human to a Divine and Eternal Order, raised life beyond all that is trivial and merely human with its civic ordinances and social interests. He who, with the best intention, views Christianity as a mere means for the betterment of the social situation, draws it from the heights of its nature, and deprives it of the main constituent of its greatness— the emancipation from the petty-human within the depths of the human itself. It is essentially the nature of Christianity that it transplants man into a new world over against the world that is nearest to our hands; it has planted the fundamental conviction of Platonism of the existence of an Eternal Order over against the world of Time amongst a great portion of the human race, and has given a mighty impetus to all effort. But it has, though it separated the Eternal from Time, brought it back again into Time, and through this presence of the Eternal it has, for the first time, proposed to mankind and to each individual a fundamental inner renewal, and through this has inaugurated a genuine history.

In order to render the Life-process of Christianity characteristic and significant two different elements have to be taken into account—a conception of the Spiritual Life and a valuation of the actual world-situation. A hard contradiction and an immense movement issue from the contact of the two elements : that which from within is real and necessary, is set back and rejected by the reality that lies on the surface nearest to our hands. Thus, life finds itself within a powerful coil, and a great decision becomes urgent. Shall the new world which arises from within and which, viewed inwardly, appears the most certain thing of all, gain our energy and disposition in spite of the contradiction of the whole remaining world ? Or shall we merely accept the fulness of the external world and allow the suppression of our inwardness to take place? There is here no middle course. Christianity has decided for the first alternative; but it is important to bear in mind that Christianity presents no ready-made conclusion, but that it brings forth an inexhaustible movement. Christianity is great before all else in that it takes up the experiences and the opposites of life in their widest extent, and fastens them together into a Whole; it is great in stirrings, struggles, and trans-formations; it appears above all else as a powerful current of life which indeed does not flow into vagueness ; but over against all attempts to make it deviate from its course it adheres to its main tendency. The whole of the Spiritual Life and the total trend of human things point in the same direction. Thus, Christianity is not a special phenomenon by the side of other similar phenomena, but is the main struggle for the soul of man. It has within the domain of religion, and, along with this, in the deepest configura-

tion of life, brought forth to an historical realisation
what genuine spirituality according to its total nature
must demand as indispensable.

Thus, there is no need of a breach with Christianity ;
it can be to us what an historical religion pre-eminently
is meant to be—a sure pathway to truth, an awakener
of immediate and intimate life, a vivid representation
and realisation of an Eternal Order which all the
changes of Time cannot possess and cannot destroy.

2. *The Maintenance of this Nucleus against the Changes of Time*

Let us now consider somewhat more closely how
this Christian cardinal type of life retains its truth
over against civilisation and culture.   We limit ourselves to the consideration of the chief changes effected
in the world of ideas.   Our assertion proceeds from
the fact that these changes undoubtedly enter into a
sharp conflict with the traditional existential-form of
Christianity ; but the Substance of Christianity is not
able to free itself from antiquated forms and gain a
purer and more energetic development without much
trouble and toil.   The mighty expansion which the
whole of modern times has brought forth need not
become hostile to Christianity.   Such an expansion
can be assimilated by Christianity, and through the
contact Christianity can even be strengthened, provided it turns to the depth of its own nature, fortifies
itself with this Substance of Christianity, and simultaneously finds the courage for new creativeness.

(a) *The Further Development over against Nature.*
—The most tangible result of modern investigation
has been the immense extension of the natural world

and the shrinkage of the earthly circle to a minute littleness. The sharp point of modern investigation has undoubtedly turned against the Church-form of Christianity in so far as the latter considers the earth as the centre of the universe, and in so far as it makes our actions decide the destiny of the All. To give the earth such a significance, in spite of all the transformations of modern thought, has been attempted by an apologetic-at-any-price; but all manipulations of possibilities and subterfuges are of no avail against the natural impression of the altered position of our earthly circle. All such manipulations belong to a geocentric and anthropocentric mode of thought of the past. But when the new mode of thought enters deeply into the realm of traditional ideas and feelings, does it destroy the spiritual substance of Christianity, and does it refute the conviction of the superiority of the soul of man? It does this in no manner. For why should the expansion of things limit itself to nature? Why should not the spiritual as well penetrate and encompass the world? Indeed, the spiritual must do this if it is conceded that the web of relations of particular energies observed in nature does not constitute the final depth of reality, but that this depth is to be sought in such subsistence-by-themselves of things, as the Spiritual Life alone offers. It may be that we, upon this earth, are able to apprehend but a small segment of this life, but in such a segment the cosmic character of the Spiritual Life is unmistakable. The fact is not to be overlooked that, in any comparison with the outward extension of nature, the inward transformations more than hold the balance. For a progressive intensifying of the Life-process has made ever more clear the fact that nature is not the final reality it was conceived to be by an older mode of scientific thought, but that it signifies only a human vista of reality. The Theory of Knowledge which has brought to a clear consciousness the limitations of this vista on account of our bodily organisation is only an expression of the inner growth of the Life-process beyond mere nature. Nature, which at the outset entirely surrounded and captivated man, has become more and more a mere environment to him. If man in such an inwardness of the Life-process has gained an Archimedean point, all the palpableness of sensuous impressions is unable to endanger the priority of spirit. The earthly circle, however, not-withstanding all its contraction, does not lose its significance when it appears as an abode where cosmic problems are struggled for, and where a segment of reality is raised to a higher stage. Over against Infinity man appears petty, but he becomes great through the cosmic life and its turn to spirit, which develops also within himself.

Nature has not only extended externally; it has also altered inwardly. It has revealed itself as a connected causal web under simple laws; it has thus obtained an independence through which it dismisses every alien influence as an impertinent intruder. Along with this, all dependence of nature upon the Spiritual Life seems for the moment to cease, and especially all sensuous miracle is placed on one side as a break in the order of nature.

Such a rejection of miracle is directed against all religions, for in all religions miracle is "the dearest child of faith." But nowhere is the rejection of

miracle more pointedly directed than it is towards
Christianity which, with its doctrine of the bodily
resurrection of Jesus, has planted miracle in the very
nucleus of religious belief.   This doctrine not only
constituted the basis of the convictions of the apostles,
but it has remained a main portion of the teaching
of the Church up to the present day.   To touch this
subject may appear dangerous even to men who
otherwise willingly follow the newer mode of thinking.   For must it not alienate and even wound our
feelings to resolve into a mere semblance an event
which has been at the foundation of the belief of
millenniums, and which has been of help to innumerable souls?   Also, all the insufficiency and contradictions of the historical records leave untouched
the fact that the apostles were entirely convinced
of that bodily resurrection, and that this conviction
alone explains the sudden change from entire despair
to the joyous certainty which culminated within their
souls in those dark and critical days.

On the other hand, the opposite reasons retain a
mighty force, when once the exact conception of
nature has been adopted and once an historical
criticism has developed.   To place a miracle in that
one situation would now not merely mean an occasional exception; it would mean an overthrow of the
total order of nature, as this has been set forth
through the fundamental work of modern investigation
and through an incalculable fulness of experiences.
What would justify such a breach with the total mode
of reality must appear to us with overwhelming, indisputable clearness.   Has the traditional occurrence
this degree of certainty, and cannot it be explained

in any other way? Who is able to assert this with entire assurance? If the superiority of the Divine was, on this particular occasion, to be proclaimed in a palpable manner, why did all this happen for the small circle of believers alone, and why did it not happen to others? There seems, however, to have been necessary a certain state of the souls of the disciples to make them see what they thought they saw; but in all this there is found a psychic and subjective factor in operation—a factor whose potency is very difficult to define and to mark its boundaries. It would have been a fact of a wonderful nature if the souls of the disciples, from within, became suddenly and without intermediary convinced of the continuation of the life and the presence of the Master: all this would have been no sensuous miracle —no break in the course of nature. But we have to bear in mind how times of strong religious agitation and convulsion are so little qualified to judge concerning external phenomena, and how easily a psychic state solidifies into a supposed percept! Within and without Christianity there are numerous examples of the sensuous appearance of a dead person being considered to be fully authenticated by the narrower circle of friends. Savonarola appeared more than a hundred times after his death, but always to those whose hearts clung to him; and to fifteen nuns of the convent of St Lucia he gave the consecrated wafer through the opening in their *grille*. (*Cf.* Hase, *Savonarola*, 2nd ed., pp. 99 and foll.)

We can, indeed, while rejecting such analogous instances, still assert the uniqueness and inexplicableness of the events at the death of Jesus. In face

34

of all the obscurity of the facts, no interpretation is pressed by us as being universally valid. But on one point perfect clearness ought to reign—as to what such supposed events can and may mean for our own life and faith. The bodily resurrection is an historical, or asserted as an historical fact. Such a fact is either capable of proof or incapable of it. If it is capable, it can be proved to everyone—even to the greatest unbeliever, and its acknowledgment needs no personal disposition. If it is not capable of proof, or at least of sufficient proof, religion can never make belief in it a duty. Even in connection with any point less critical and less difficult than the one here in question, religion does not compel us to accept as proved what in reality has not been proved. Otherwise expressed : the acknowledgment of an historical fact is a matter of knowledge and not of faith. Faith has as its object what is of a timeless nature—what is able to be immediately present to each individual and able to manifest its own elevating energy ; faith, in fact, carries within itself an inner movement and a courageous ascent of the spirit of man. If an historical fact is put in the place of this object of faith, faith is externalised, and reduces religion to a stage which has been passed by the most important movements of the world ; and thus religion becomes entangled in an insoluble contradiction with the whole of the rest of life. If, then, the belief in the bodily resurrection of Jesus threatens to break up the whole of Christianity, wherein does faith in the truth of Christianity obtain its final root ? Are the new contents of life, which affirm an emancipation from all the ordinary powers of our petty human nature, and which proclaim a new world of love and grace, to be explained as mere illusions if they are not guaranteed to one by a tangible proof of a bodily resurrection? If, in the manner of the Middle Ages, we make the reality of the spiritual dependent upon a sensuous embodiment, we shall acquire the pertinacity of what is termed historical belief, but through this, we confess our unbelief in the all-presence of the Spiritual and Divine Life; and consequently we have parted company with the religion of the spirit and of personality and have sunk back into a religion of signs and wonders. Men certainly do not intend to do this, and yet they allow the confusion which is caused through the mixing up of history and faith to remain—a confusion which has brought so many entanglements upon humanity. We have already quoted the words of Fichte where he pointed out that the emphasis on the historical has resulted in considering subsidiary facts as of equal validity with the main facts, and even at the expense of the main facts, thus coercing the main facts and tormenting the conscience.

Religion, which has already shown so much energy, will ultimately find the energy to subsist without sensuous signs and wonders. It discovers the true wonder in the Spiritual Life itself, which, with its cosmic creativeness and its deepening of itself, demands as well as manifests the presence of the Absolute Life. Nature, through its abandonment of sensuous miracle, is in no way surrendered to mere mechanism; and the denial of a break in its order does not mean a breaking off of all relationship with spirit. Mechanism itself has presuppositions

which it is not able to explain and which point
beyond it, as for instance, the laws of nature, reciprocal
effects, the ascent of types and of animate life out of
seemingly diffused and undirected disturbances.   And
without giving straight-away a religious significance
to all this, yet a depth of reality is here unmistakable ;
and that the whole of nature finally serves the whole
of spirit is held fast by religion in spite of the impossibility of a detailed application.   But the main fact for
religion remains in the wonder of the Spirit and the
wonder in the Spirit ; and in the most decisive manner
religion must reject whatsoever threatens to weaken
the significance of this wonder and its consolidating
and elevating energy.

Not less sharply does modern natural science collide
with traditional Christianity in the theory of evolution.   The fact that the world has at the present day
entered into the current of scientific investigation,
that its elements participate in this movement, that
out of the supposed co-existence of types a succession
of types has been shown, and that especially the
organic kingdom has climbed from simple beginnings,
through a long ascent to its present height — all
this certainly contradicts not less irreconcilably the
traditional doctrine of creation and the whole notion
of the bringing of things into existence through
a will " beyond," as the newer astronomy contradicts the old geocentric mode of thinking.   It is
only certain forms of the evolutionary theory, and in
no way all its forms, which signify a danger to the
substance of religion.   If the interpretation of the
universe from the evolutionary point of view signifies
that the whole content of the universe has proceeded

without the operation of any effective law from within, but solely through chance collisions of elements, so that all the higher is simply a product of the lower, and so that all claim to independence loses its value, then certainly a victory of mechanism and materialism has been won in each and every religion.   If evolution, however, signifies rather this—if it signifies that the attainment of the higher stages became possible only after having passed through the lower stages ; that in each stage the Whole brings forth a new beginning, and that consequently all movement has the foundation of a timeless order, and its advancement happens within Time but not from Time, then evolution can in no manner injure the substance of religion.   If things are thus, there is a growth in the depth of reality as well as in the living presence of a higher order.

Indeed, we observe in natural science itself an inner law of a timeless kind restraining more and more the mere mechanism of a " becoming " induced through external adaptation to environment, restraining the lawless flux of forms and the predominance of a blind chaos of natural selection. Religion is not able, however, to base its convictions upon the currents of natural investigation, and there is no need for it to do so, because the dawning of the Spiritual Life itself is a proof to it of a new stage over against all nature, and of the growth of a further new stage within the Spiritual Life itself.   Thus the Higher is not a mere More and a mechanical result of the lower, but within this Higher an immediate proof of Absolute Life is imbedded.   Evolution is then a testimony not against but for religion.

No unbiassed mind is able to deny a " becoming" within nature and spirit. Reason is for us no ready-made thing; within our own circle it has to be wrestled for, and the wrestling needs both the movement of external things and an activity on our own part. But the question which separates minds is: whether reason is a mere effect of a "becoming," or whether it can be an effect without at the same time being a principle—whether the universe must not be grounded upon reason in order to engender reason at all. He who occupies the former standpoint draws reality down to its lowest stages and is able to see no more in all the rest than a construction of that lower. But wherever characteristic features and independence are accorded to the Higher, wherever it stands clearly before us in all its fulness and depth, there reason is recognised as a principle in the midst of all its "becoming," and there the evolutionary theory and religion can and must walk together hand in hand.

(β) *The Further Development over against History and Culture.*—Changes in human life and actions threaten Christianity still more directly than the changes in our view of nature. Here, again, our investigation leads to the result that an irreconcilable collision originates not so much in connection with the real facts of the movements of life and actions as in connection with certain problematic tendencies which pertain to these facts, and which grow in seeming inseparableness along with them. All that is true and genuine in these movements of life and actions can be accepted by Christianity; but Christianity can accept anything only in so far as it differentiates clearly between the Eternal Substance and the temporal existential-form, and only so far as it strives after a *new* existential-form which corresponds to the demands of the situation reached by the labours of the ages.

First of all, an opposition to religion arises on account of the rise of an historical view and treatment of existence. This view and treatment bring all things into a flux and reveal an incessant change. To draw religion—the work of God—into the current of Time and to adjust its permanent character to the changes of the human situation, means to destroy it at its very foundation. A religion based upon mere Time— accepted with the possibility of a notice to quit—is no religion. Christianity, however, has welded together with special energy not only a fundamental body of doctrines and organisations, but also a characteristic content of life—a content which is to defy all the changes of time.

This is the first glimpse of the opposition, but we shall see that it does not retain all this harshness. First of all, human life refuses to surrender itself entirely into this flux. Modern times, in their first fresh impression of the movement of things, saw only the bright side of the change—they saw only the greater freedom, the rich manifoldness of things, etc. But we are just beginning to discover difficult drawbacks in connection with the facts—the instability of all results, the speedy toppling over of all standards and values, the dissolution of life into mere moments which drive and dislodge each other. More and more we lose an inward connection of life ; we become the sport of an ever-changing kaleidoscopic situation, and are in danger of becoming engulfed into nothingness. In the presence of such a catastrophe we are

no longer able to speak of a history, and least of all
of a history of a spiritual kind.   For some kind of a
persisting factor is present in all history; and in
history of a spiritual kind there is present an inner
representation of the past, a view of the whole course
a stepping out of the stream of time, and a transition to a timeless contemplation *sub specie æterni.*
If life ascends towards such an eternity, it ascends of
necessity towards religion, which calls for a return to
final depths, calls for the illumination of the fundamental relationship of man to the All, calls for the
setting forth of the abiding tasks and experiences of
life, calls for the union of our life with the Absolute
Life, and above all else claims to become the
custodian of Eternity.   If religion is anything at all,
it is that which gives man a secure foundation, and
which measures his undertakings by means of lofty
norms and standards.   If thus a longing after Eternity
arises through the fresh experience and deep feeling
of the vanity of all the mere life of time, the turn to
religion will gain full energy and veracity.

But is religion able to satisfy the aspiration after
Eternity without having to suppress all movement
and without having to arrest the full flow of the
current of life?   The aspiration is not satisfied if the
traditional existential-form signifies its final essence.
The mode of thinking which conceived eternal truth
only as it presented itself in time (of course this is
an indispensable element of religion), and also which
believed in the possibility of man reaching it at one
stroke, has become untenable.   This mode of thinking
corresponded to the old view of truth which has been
replaced by another view.   According to the old

view, the truth appeared so intimately related to man that a courageous exercise of energy seemed able immediately to reach it at one stroke, and then an alleged durable truth was set forth which had only to be guarded in a true and heroic manner. Thus, it was believed at the height of Greek development that scientific knowledge could accomplish this for once and for all; and men believed themselves able to trace out a political constitution valid for all times. Corresponding to this, it was held that religion could be brought into an inviolable and durable situation in the same manner. But it is characteristic of modern times, on the contrary, that a wider division between the truth of the Spiritual Life and the immediate situation of man has taken place; so that now, if an Eternal is not to be lost, man has to labour in the depth of his being, and it is only after a toilsome struggle that the Eternal can be gained and can become the true possession of man. The Eternal, in itself certain and firm, is to us an incessant task. Christianity is able to take over this latter view only when it differentiates an Existential-form characteristic of, and appropriate to, a certain age from the timeless Substance which is effective in all ages; only when it works out the characteristic Life-process and its new reality founded in God, and only when it plainly exalts this Life-process through thought and feeling above all merely human formations of doctrines and works. Then Christianity will give its full rights to the Eternal as well as to the temporal, and the necessary contact between the two will lead to no injurious narrowness.

The transition towards history and culture not only

brought forth more mobility; it also raised man to greater self-activity and led to the awakening of slumbering energies within him. Life, through such experiences, is immeasurably raised, and man gains power not only over nature but also over his own particular relationships and over his own soul: he has now undertaken the construction of a kingdom of reason on a great scale. Such a life, through its possession of reality, has made all things far richer in content than could ever have been the case in the times when man stood impotent over against the darkness of the world, and expected, through tarrying and hoping, his entire welfare from a power beyond. Now, does not such a self-consciousness of human potency involve a strong protest against all religions, and especially against a mode of Christianity which proclaims the vanity of mere man with such special emphasis? A clash is here quite evident; and the question is, whether the necessities of life itself do not tend to level down this distinction, and whether, indeed, religion does not go out half way to meet the desire for levelling it down.

It is undoubtedly true that through the development of modern culture far more has resulted from man's capacities than was formerly the case, but it is doubtful whether it is the energy of the mere individual which has brought all this forth; it is doubtful whether, in the very process of this development, nothing besides the merely human was at work. We have already noticed that Spiritual Life does not proceed from historico-social relations. In so far as civilisation and culture are no more than products of such relations they are, notwithstanding all their claims for being able to form a higher stage of things, afflicted with the curse of pretence and unveracity. Indeed, the further they progress, the more do they remove from their true basis, and thus become artificial and empty, and fall into the petty and the common.

Whatsoever is genuine in civilisation and culture rests upon the fact that a superhuman Spiritual Life with its cosmic creativeness is operative within them. Through such a connection with the Spiritual Life all that is great in man, so far from being given by nature, really originates from a deeper basis, and must rest permanently upon this basis. When it does this, the very sense of power will involve a consciousness of entire dependence on this basis and, at the same time, a denial of all merely natural individuality. Civilisation and culture will not then think lightly of religion, and will not attempt to push it back ; but they will invoke it for their own preservation and purification, and for the elevation of man beyond the region of the petty-human. All merely secular culture will now be seen through as a mere farce ; since man has realised that genuine culture has not merely to develop extant powers but has to form a new being—an idea which helps to develop an ascent from mere time to a timeless order, and from mere man to a world-embracing spirituality.

Religion, however, is able to correspond to such a " call " of culture and civilisation only if it grasps its own task in a great and free sense. Religion must not assume that the work is done by the Divine in some external manner, thus reducing life to a merely passive level, but far rather has it to plant itself in the centre of the highest activity, while it must never forget that such a creative activity is fundamentally different from the merely natural development of energy. And, over against culture and civilisation, religion must at all times assert its rights to prove and to winnow; for it is religion—the power which draws upon the deepest source of life—which takes to itself the whole of man and offers a fixed standard for all his undertakings. Religion, instead of being carried on the face of the changing currents of civilisation and culture, must provide through its timeless truth a secure foothold for the remainder of life. It must cavil less at the transient and particular in the domains of knowledge and life, and rather undertake to test their whole meaning; it has to hold fast to the fact that all civilisation and culture are only phenomena of the Spiritual Life and not the Spiritual Life itself, and that consequently these exhibit only a few of the many possibilities and phases of things which have changed in the past and will continue to change in the future. Religion is thus unable to measure and to pass judgment on things without holding up definite aims before civilisation and culture, but it will accomplish this task less directly than indirectly: it will accomplish it through the working out of the further development of the total-life which connects and encompasses all the provinces of knowledge and life with itself. It is through this reciprocal relationship that civilisation and culture can assert their independence and freedom of movement.

In this reciprocity then religion has not only to give but also to take. For the fundamental condition on which religion finds its secure superiority comes to a full effect in man when it finds an appropriate existential-form; and man is not able to find this form without the aid of civilisation and culture. Thus, we may hope that such change as that which to-day urges culture and civilisation to oppose religion may finally serve the main aims of religion, so that a common spiritual world may span the provinces of both religion and culture and civilisation.

This homogeneousness of both has to be worked out over against the traditional forms not only of culture but also of religion. Religion must not bring forth simply that which lies by the side of the rest of life—merely handling its one-sided content alongside of other contents which it deems as not belonging to itself and which it treats indifferently. Religion must never consider itself as an isolated province but as the characteristic depth of the totality of life ; and it must consider that its full energy and intimate knowledge are to be reached on this pathway alone. Through such an insight, religion will neither be anxious to win the individual to some kind of a mere assent to truth nor to lead individuals to some ready-made spiritual world ; but it will far more constantly attempt to build up and hold forth a Whole of the Spiritual Life within the human domain over against the immense hindrances and perversions of an indifferent and hostile world. We need a religion of the total Spiritual Life and not one of the mere individual or one of the sum-total of any number of individuals; we need as our own that religion which has set forth more expressively than any other religion the central conception of the Kingdom of God. But here it is necessary to purify further the traditional form if that which from of old has worked as an ideal and a demand is to find its effective accomplishment and to become the entire possession of man.

(γ) *The Further Development over against the Changes of the Spiritual Life in Man.*—The most important movements of the day have brought about great changes within the province of the Spiritual Life. But the fact is nowhere more evident than in the changes which have taken place in connection with the traditional existential-form of Christianity; but, rightly understood and carried further, these changes promise to develop the inmost essence of Christianity, and to extend it as the religion of universal life. This matter deals especially with the three points in the analysis and the emancipation of the Spiritual Life: its progressive superiority to sensuous nature, to mere history, and to the form of life that is petty and merely human. This emancipation and expansion of the Spiritual Life are no ready-made results which fall upon each individual in his smug situation, but are movements and invitations of a spiritual kind and from which no individual, who is to maintain human power and creativeness on the heights of the most important movements of life, dare withdraw himself; for these movements of the Spiritual Life present a standard beyond all the arbitrary actions of individuals and beyond all the vacillations of the moment.

1. The Spiritual Life has, upon the ground of modern times, succeeded in obtaining an independence over against sensuous existence in all its forms. It has succeeded in obtaining this through

a more energetic excitation and exertion of self-activity—an activity which does not tolerate a passive immersion of man into the environment, but which precedes and measures the material that is presented to it from without, and even weaves the meaning of the fundamental construction of the world from within. On account of this, the sensuous is no longer able to remain an essentially integral part of the mental construction, but signifies now only a valuable helper and even an essential means of representing the meaning of the mental construction. Sensuous nature extends to the domain of religion : we find this first in the senile character of waning antiquity as well as in the simple-minded way in which the middle ages made the sensuous an essential part of religion. But to the greater activity of awakened modern times, such a mixing of external signs with the inner life has become something magical and an intolerable hindrance to freedom. This mingling of the sensuous and the spiritual is represented in the main by Roman Catholicism, and it is largely to this that the strength of Catholicism in former times was due ; but since the initiation of the movement towards greater self-activity and purer spirituality of humanity, the situation suitable to former times has given way to an inward and higher stage of life. But Protestantism also, which has protested against the magic of Catholicism, has by no means excluded it ; it holds sensuous miracle in high estimation ; it preserves a sacramental mode in all its tendencies, and this shows itself in its doctrine of salvation through the " blood " of Christ. The sacraments are products of an age of deep weariness and

spiritual twilight: Divine energies were to proceed
towards man; but it was imagined that these energies
needed sensuous signs which, however, conceived as
necessary pledges of the truth of Divine energies, became more than sensuous. In order to hide the contradiction imbedded in this, a dim twilight time
and a dreamy disposition of life are necessary, and these
are needed further in order to obtain a foothold and
conviction in the midst of the darkness of the situation.
The fresher life of modern times has scattered this
twilight and has reduced an alleged piety to magic.
The residuum of such magic which has remained
in Protestantism works all the more vaguely, the
more it fails to understand the life of our day.

Many have found and do find to-day a subjective support in such magic, and its removal
may appear to such minds a disaster. But it is
necessary for modern man to bear in mind—and this
truth is of the very essence of Christianity—that when
Christianity entered into the arena of time as a religion of pure spirituality, magic was merely ancillary
to it and was not inseparably connected with it.
Certainly such magic ought not to disappear before
some equivalent appears. The equivalent is at hand:
it is the further development of the Spiritual Life
itself; and this development can take place through
a turn of life to a level beyond all externals—a turn
towards itself and towards a complete activity—and
through the winning of an unassailable reality by
means of a development of a basal and durable life
and being. If the sensuous is not in this manner
replaced by the self-consolidation of the Spiritual
Life, every kind of spirituality tends to decline, so

that the Middle Ages was right in insisting that something besides the sensuous was needful. But the sensuous, through its removal from the centre of life, becomes in no way superfluous and subordinate for the stimulation of man. Indeed, the more religion deepens itself by means of the whole of the Spiritual Life, the more it drives the external into a distance; the less religion is able to grasp the idea, the more necessary becomes the pictorial, and the more religion needs the help of imagination and art. But this indispensable means does not signify the reality itself and will not coalesce with it.

2. The progressive superiority of the Spiritual Life to bare history has occupied our attention so much that it is not necessary here to do more than remind ourselves of our previous conclusions. The fact that we as children of modern times posit all the offerings of history upon our own day and adjust them from such a situation comes into conflict with the traditional form of Christianity. Catholicism is not, on the whole, troubled with this entanglement, because to it past and present join themselves intimately in the manner of the Middle Ages, and also because the differences of the generations are obliterated. To Protestantism, on the contrary, the distinction between past and present was made, and an alleged yet conscientious return to the former became essential: it attempted to carry life back to a special epoch— the beginnings of Christianity—and to shape it in accordance with this epoch. Yet Protestantism discovered that it was still more essential to base religion within one's own life and personal experience; but the attempt to carry both elements—the experience

35

of the personal life and its binding to an historical factor—has miscarried; and this fact is realised to-day, and must soon become intolerable. Catholicism has here decidedly the logic on its side when it makes the Church and its past the guarantor of its truth; while Protestantism, through allowing matters of learned investigation and of an historical nature to decide concerning the meaning of life and the salvation of the soul, has entered into grave danger. If Protestantism is to remain true to its main idea, it must subjugate history to personal life, and this means a radical transformation of the traditional material.

The present day often shows an uncertain oscillation of the religious life between history and the present, between authority and personal conviction; one hopes to help the personal conviction through a retreat to the past, and thus the rich content of history is supposed to procure an intuitive content for life as well as for religion. We resign ourselves, through such a turn, to the impressions of unique epochs and personalities; we transport and submerge ourselves in these so far as to forget ourselves; we seek to understand such epochs and personalities as they really were, and the intuitive presentation of such pictures seems to us a great gain in truth. But this historical and relative truth is not the eternal and absolute truth upon which religion must ever insist. The interweaving of these two things is not far removed from the German mode of conceiving life, and contains the danger of substituting merely imitative feeling for genuine feeling, many truths for the one truth, mere knowledge for life. Let us give

the highest honour to history in its right place, but
let us energetically oppose the enervating influence
of a purely "historical school."

We are in entire unison with the spirit of Christianity when we place history and its results in a
secondary place. It is true that the assertion of the
entrance of the Divine into Time made by Christianity has heightened immensely the significance of
history, and, indeed, has for the first time made
history in a spiritual sense possible. But Christianity
has never made the temporal life the main fact, and
has never turned the nature of man into a predominantly historical nature. For all that happens within
time has here a worth only in so far as it develops
what is eternal and in what it executes for the eternal.
Thus it views and values not eternity by means of
time, but time by means of eternity ; and thus it
finds present within history a greatness : it is a greatness because it is an emancipation from history—a
realisation of an eternal order. Herein is involved
the demand that the contemplation of infinity must
ever remain superior to all, so that Christianity establishes an irreconcilable opposition to any form of
evolution or of purely historical interpretation. The
more energetic working out of its eternal character—
the aspiration after a present superior to time—is therefore no defection from Christianity. We have in our
previous investigation become convinced of the fact
that such a movement is not a relapse into the
Enlightenment, and that history as a subsidiary
element retains great value. We have already seen
that a "here and now" superior to time must somehow through religion become the main standard of

life, and that history will further us in our efforts only in so far as we encompass and govern it with an independent life.

3. The third aspect of the emancipation of the Spiritual Life is that of emancipating it from a merely human form of existence. We have already observed how the modern work of civilisation and culture with its expansive tendency has broken through the merely human form of existence, and we have noticed how it entered upon an energetic struggle for the driving out of that which is merely human in the narrow sense of the word. Throughout the whole development of modern times, the Spiritual Life has removed itself from a merely subjective inactivity and from resting upon a merely human opinion; it has engendered characteristic contents and necessities, laws and methods; it has resolved itself into an independent world and has made man a mere tool and means for its development. Modern development finds its most tangible expression in the linking of the Spiritual Life with a unique and seemingly free-moving thought-process. We have observed how this thought-process pointedly opposed not only Religion and Christianity, but also how it reduced morality to a merely subjective and subsidiary phenomenon, and how it undertook to disintegrate all personal life, all independent self-subsistence, and all ideals favourable to the creation of spiritual energy.

Now, through such a critical situation, constituted by a hopeless entanglement, the emancipation of the Spiritual Life becomes a great problem. But the reason for this opposition is highly problematic, though we venture to say that it is a mistake—a colossal mistake. We have already seen in this book, and the same idea has been more fully developed in other works of the author, that the transformation of the Spiritual Life into an impersonal thought-process destroys it to its very foundation. This method of treating the Spiritual Life issues in its self-distortion, whilst at the same time its content evaporates more and more and the whole life is transformed into a kingdom of abstract values which slip through our hands as soon as they are grasped and subjected to a closer examination. If, however, the idea of an emancipation of the Spiritual Life frees itself from such an abstract process, and if it possesses the further insight that the Spiritual Life, in order to become a full reality, must become a self-subsistence and must, through a persistent self-development, encompass all activity, *then* this movement of thought need not go against Christianity, but can quite well serve for the furtherance of Christianity, whilst simultaneously it brings the Spiritual Life and man into a secure relationship. It is true that in Christianity a high estimate of man and a strong love for man are found. But these do not issue out of man as a merely natural being; they do not fortify him in his merely human self-assertion, but they see him in the light of a new world and inaugurate for him a new life founded in God; so that this estimation and love rest, if not upon the reality itself, yet upon the possibility of an essential transformation of the nature of man. Throughout genuine Christianity everywhere there is operative a yearning after a new man and after a new kingdom of peace and love.

The detailed elaboration, however, which this aspiration found in earlier ages is not able entirely to satisfy our age. Life in those ages, notwithstanding its efforts after what is noble, remained too much within the domain of human frailty and did not sufficiently distinguish the new spiritual contents developed by the relationship to God, from the subjective form of their appropriation by the soul. Such an idea of God to the modern mode of thinking appears too much as a mere idealisation of man, and the religious life too much as an intercourse of person with person, and consequently as too emotional and anthropomorphic. Pantheism, on the contrary, has insisted upon conceptions of the universe and has opposed energetically the religious tendency to dwell on the sickness of the soul, and on account of this has gained a good deal of sympathy in modern times; but we can no more go back to it, notwithstanding the warmth of its definite ideas, than to the Ptolemaic conception of the universe.

But we hear it asked, does not a danger arise to religion through such a Pantheistic conception? Is there not a certain affirmation and strengthening of man essential for religion, and does not there belong to religion a certain anthropomorphism? In any case, the view of God as well as of religion has become more nebulous, the more it has attempted to drive everything human out of religion. We step thus into the dilemma: that the human is too small for us, and that with the renunciation of the human, religion threatens to break in pieces.

Such a dilemma is to be evaded only through an inner analysis of the human—through a sharp differentiation of the spiritual contents from the subjective inclinations. The whole of our investigation has been directed towards demonstrating that such an analysis is not only possible but even necessary, and that without it there is neither religion nor, speaking generally, truth. Our investigation has sought also to show that not only did particular contents develop side by side, but also that they connected themselves together into an authentic Whole and produced an essentially new being, which we aspired after by means of our " ever-becoming" personality. Herewith the man gains a cosmic nature within his own province, so that he is now able in religion and everywhere else to take up a struggle against the petty-human; he is now able to make, if not with ease, yet with great effort, a searching analysis of his own nature. The problem for him remains no longer in his own relationship with the external world, but lies within the domain of his own soul.

Difficult tasks arise along with all this. As modern investigation transforms the immediate picture of nature which appeared to an older mode of thought as the reality itself into a mere phenomenon, and as it passes from the phenomenon to the meaning of this phenomenon in consciousness, we, too, have to pass from the surface-possession of human existence and have to work out the spiritual substance which lies beneath this. The supposed facts then transform themselves into tasks, but within the tasks themselves facts are imbedded which promise to bring us nearer to truth. It is from such a standing-ground as this that religion can hold man fast to his spiritual nature, and struggle vigorously against anthropomorphism. Thus

all objects and qualities have to be changed within consciousness; conceptions such as personality, morality,
etc., have to be carried beyond the meaning that lies
nearest to our hands as human beings, and all merely
subjective inwardness has to give way to an essential
inwardness; in fact, there is now everywhere a remodelling of all into the great, the fully active, and
the cosmic. Consequently, much that previously
appeared as the reality itself is now reduced to a
mere finger-post; but what we thus lose as a surface-
possession is more than compensated for in the gain
of a depth in our nature. Indeed, the more we fortify
ourselves through such a spiritual substance and feel
that the kernel of our life lies beyond that which is
petty and merely human, the more truly we are able
to employ and value such metaphors and symbols of
the Divine. For then we know that they are indispensable means for the furtherance of the soul, and
at the same time we find in them not the reality
itself, but a symbol of reality.

If we consider how much is involved in such a
change in the position of the Spiritual Life, and if
we also present before our view what transformations,
civilisation, culture, history, and natural science carry
within themselves, we see clearly the critical situation
in which religion is placed, because these surface-
changes are not of the essence of religion. Through
the mighty expansion and the fissures which these
changes bring about, the old immediacy and intimacy
of the soul have become lost, and religion has now
receded into the distance, and is in danger of vanishing more and more. The derangement of things
which such changes cause occurs not only in con-

nection with their own facts and material and against their old forms, but the effect proceeds into the very character and feelings of man and into his religion. And yet, when we examine the matter more closely, we find that such changes cause not so much a breach with Christianity as with its traditional form, and that they seek to bring about a fundamental renewal of Christianity. For when we penetrate beyond the motives and dispositions of men to their spiritual basis, all the changes fail to contradict what is essential to Christianity; but they even promise to assist this essential element in its new, freer, and more energetic development. But we have to bear in mind that all this will not descend upon us like a shower of rain, but will have to be brought forth through immense labour and toil. It becomes necessary to replace that which must pass away, and to reconsolidate the essentials which are threatened. All this cannot come about save through an energetic concentration and deepening of the Spiritual Life, through a struggle regardless of all consequences, against the superficiality of time and through a vivification and integration of all that points in the right direction. We now turn to the elucidation of this statement.

CHAPTER XV

b. The Transient in Christianity and the
Necessity of a Renewal of Christianity

1. *The Removal from Past Forms*

We were not able to plead for the substance of
Christianity, without, at the same time, emphasising
strongly the temporal character of the traditional
existential-form. This existential-form took shape
under the influence of a highly characteristic epoch,
and since that epoch fundamental transformations have
taken place in human life and activity. The fourth
and the fifth centuries, in which the conclusions of
the existential-form of Christianity were dogmatically
formulated, were in the whole of their nature times of
spiritual stagnation; they could further Christianity
only through the aid of the very antiquity with which
primitive Christianity had had to wrestle. Thus, the
doctrines and worship of Christianity during the
earlier centuries developed under the strongest influence of Greek thought, and its organisation was
largely influenced by the Roman spirit. At a later
period came the dissemination of Christianity amongst
a people imbued for the first time with aspirations;

then followed the mistakes and finally the decay of
the ideals of these peoples; and later the rise of a
new civilisation and culture brought forth a new
standpoint for viewing the world as well as a new
kind of life; and all this could not proceed on its
course without bringing about changes in the whole
situation of man as well as in the whole of Christianity—without revaluing old values and engendering new demands out of new situations. We have
already sufficiently protested against subjugating
religion to the ordinary changes of history as well
as abandoning it to the limitation of the elements of
time. But where transformations in the world of
thought reach back into the whole of life, and where
these transformations find the soul something other
than it was supposed to be, and where they are
required to bring forth a different view of man and
the world, then religion is not able to withdraw from
such transformations without injury and without
even the danger of being supplanted at the very
core of life. Such transformations against the conclusions of the fourth and the fifth centuries did
in fact result. Thus religion had to speak in a
new way to a new man; for it dare not ever deal
with this New in an uncandid fashion and offer
portions of it as a mere embroidery of life, but it has
always to pronounce openly concerning this New and
take its stand independently upon it, if the religious
life in its totality is not to suffer in energy and
veracity.

The greatness of the change, and the necessity of a
remodelling become most obvious if we compare the
configuration of the world of religious thought at

the spiritual zenith of ancient Christianity—as for example in Augustine—with the configuration which is demanded after the experiences of the millenniums. By these experiences we do not mean the fleeting fancies of many of our contemporaries, which have little enough to recommend them, but we mean the experiences which have issued through the most important and universal results of the Spiritual Life through the centuries; and this inheritance no one, in the long run, can deny. Augustine holds out before us in three main points a characteristic configuration of religion. In his writings the manifestation of the Divine stands in direct opposition to the development of human energy, and this doctrine conceived of and revered the Divine all the more, the deeper it lowered human nature and the more it divested man of all independence. And further, according to this view, religion seemed to be real and true only in so far as it gained a visible embodiment; thus the kingdom of God had its embodiment in the Church; all activity of a religious nature had its embodiment in tangible achievements which were in no way a mere semblance but were essential parts of the reality. Finally, the whole of culture was placed in the immediate service of religion and its doctrines; all scientific, artistic, and political activities were admissible and of value only in so far as they discharged themselves into religion and corroborated its truth. And thus was obtained a thoroughly religious, but not a universal, system of life.

The relation of the spiritual to the sensuous is investigated from these three points of view, and this relation shows how deeply the claims of the heightened self-activity of the Spiritual Life affect the configuration of religion. But we have to bear in mind that the sharp conflict between an older and a newer mode of thinking allows no compromise, but imperatively demands a decision. These two tendencies of thought contradict each other; the inseparable blending of the sensuous with the spiritual signifies to the old tendency an unconditional necessity in order to reach the entire reality of the spiritual; but the newer tendency considers this as a drawing of the spiritual down to a lower level. The newer tendency must desire to drive the sensuous out of the centre of life, whilst the older tendency feels itself obliged here to assert and to consolidate the sensuous. What is to one a rock of offence is to the other a necessary demand.

Further, in regard to the relation of the Divine and the human, we are inhibited from holding fast to the old mode. To Augustine belongs the merit of having formulated with full clearness the fundamental Christian thought of the nothingness of mere man, and also of having severed morality from all mere nature; for with him all greatness in man was a work of Divine grace. But in dealing with one side of the question he allowed the other side, in accordance with the disposition of an enfeebled and despondent time, to become blunted—that is, the side of the restrengthening of man through his union with God and the transformation of his life into self-activity through the new relations. Grace and freedom, corresponding to that conception of the relationship of the Divine and the human, appeared to Augustine as irreconcilable opponents; a welling-up of freedom out of grace remained alien to his dualistic mode of thinking. That Augustine does, on the other hand, assign to man an activity of his own, and that this activity often seems even to contain the main decision of life, we are well aware; but we are also aware that all this is in direct contradiction to his fundamental tendency, and that it is rather a superficial concession to the claims of practice than a deepened conception of Christianity.

This conception of Augustine was bound to result in giving religion a character of passivity, of drowsy devotion, and of blind obedience; it engendered a disposition and even a passion for worshipping its object on account of the security it promises; it threatened to take all backbone out of life and to transform it into mere sentimentality, weakness, and dejection. Also the senile character of Augustine's time has here penetrated deep into religion itself. At later periods in the history of the western world protests did not fail to arise. Especially do we find in the inauguration of the Reformation a glowing aspiration after a manly, joyous, and world-renewing Christianity. But even these new beginnings did not succeed in coming to a full development, and infinitely much remains to be done in the future if world-denial and world-renewal effects are to find an entire equilibrium within Christianity, and if freedom and grace are to settle the dispute between them, and are to unite for the construction of a new reality.

Also, the relation of religion to civilisation and culture needs a remodelling. Because all the provinces of life, in the view of Augustine, had simply to serve religion, all that existed and worked from its own

energy lost its value, and the renunciation of all
objective interests to a subjective state of the soul
threatened to destroy all civilisation and culture.
And, further, religion through its isolation lost all
living content; and when religion degenerated into
a highly abstract conception, it had as an alternative only the return to anthropomorphism. The
Middle Ages gave a higher value to the work of
culture and civilisation through Scholasticism, which
looked upon civilisation and culture as possessing a
certain independence, and assigned to religion only
the work of guiding the totality of things. But
Scholasticism did not carry things to a true settlement—culture was narrowed and religion was still
largely under the influence of an alien mass of
thought. The Reformation accomplished a severer
severance in favour of the independence of religion,
but even here the danger of making religion too
much of an isolated province became quite evident;
religion thus tended to lose its cosmic character, so
that the results of knowledge had but little influence
on life and were considered to be of a secular character. Although religion and science have different starting - points and have each appropriated
opposite poles of the total-life, yet their entire severance would mean the rending of life in an intolerable
manner.

Thus, we stand face to face with new tasks; we
are obliged to do something more than merely carry
further the past: we are to seek for new and independent beginnings. A merely pietistic view of life
has become too narrow for us; but, on the other
hand, the superficiality of a culture devoid of religion

becomes more and more evident. Consequently, an understanding within the domain of a wider synthesis has become necessary. We have already seen how the Spiritual Life, in the sense we conceived it, offers a basis for such an explanation. But this Spiritual Life is not a restful bond of union, which man has merely to accept; it is not the establishment of an equilibrium of life for once and for all. The point of departure and the drift of the movement of the Spiritual Life are fundamentally different from this old conception, and all attempts to weaken this difference threaten to lower the energy as well as the truth of life. The Spiritual Life, if it would remain healthy and fresh, must, founded though our being is in the Absolute Life and Eternal Truth, remain in constant movement. That the truth is to us at once a fact and a task signifies an essential divergence from the older mode of thinking.

Thus, there appears all along a great opposition between the old and traditional types of life and the newer types for which we seek. And it is of no avail to veil this difference between the old and the new Christianity, or to endeavour to make the old and the new flow together in what can be no more than a seeming coalescence. And further, it is not sufficient merely to allow the New to assert itself, and merely to interpret the Old. He who attempts to give equal rights to both is in danger of doing injustice to both; he is in danger of raising the claims of the Old to become crystallised through the centuries without any change although it has no longer the same meaning for the convictions of an increasing number of minds; he is in danger, through the attempt to amalgamate both, of doing injustice to the New, whose development is retarded through placing a millstone around its neck, whilst it needs all its energy in order to re-set its truth, in order to overcome the present-day situation of painful un-readiness, and in order to help in the bringing forth of a new phase of eternal truth.

How great and irreconcilable the opposition is, appears most clearly in the different positions which the Founder of historical Christianity occupies in the Old and in the New. This question we are dis-cussing is in so far the kernel of the whole matter, since we here decide concerning the manner of the relationship of the human and the Divine, which re-lationship forms the fundamental truth of the whole of Christianity. For nothing differentiates Chris-tianity from other religions so much as the fact that in Christianity the union of mankind and God is not determined in an external manner through commands and achievements; but that it results from within through the growth of an entirely new and essential life founded in God and through the summons to man, in the midst of an antagonistic world, to a participa-tion in the perfection and blessedness, in the infinity and eternity of Absolute Being. The old conception presents this union of the natures of the Divine and the human in a supernatural, ontologic-metaphysical manner. The Founder of Christianity is thus simul-taneously truly God and truly man; only at this one life does the miracle of the entrance of the Divine into the human appear accomplished; it is only through the mediation of the Divine in this one situation and the relationship of man to the situation, that a union

36

with God is inaugurated for the rest of mankind. Thus the whole truth and certainty of this union is stated to lie in the fact that in the personality of the Founder it was not merely the energy of the Godhead which was efficacious, but that the Founder himself was of a Divine Nature—was himself God in the fullest meaning of the term. In this connection, every attempt to weaken the Godhead of Christ meant a lessening of the substance of religion, and all similarity between Christ and God had to give way to the strict identity of the two. Thus the more metaphysically conceived and also the more identical with God Christ became, the greater seemed his religion to be and the securer seemed the foundation of its Divine truth. But, however, the entire union of the Godhead and humanity in *one* person has become in no way through its dogmatic enunciation a living reality for the religious life, for the history of Christianity shows here a pronounced dualism. People have not so much revered Christ at the same time as God and as man, but rather they have revered him alternately now as God, now as man, according to the manner in which the dogmatic conception brought out the one side, and the practico-ethical conception brought out the other side. And the contradiction is in reality irreconcilable. The dogmatic conception views the Founder as a man who is at the same time God; who as God possesses absolute truth, and who from such a height leads a human existence; who lays on one side his sovereign rank only for a time; who participates in the cares and quests, the struggles and doubts which constitute not only the most painful but also the greatest conceivable sufferings in human life. Even to the suffering that was preordained by a Divine decree to bring forth the most beneficial results and, indeed, to bring a change in the destiny of the world—even to this the sting which makes suffering genuine is wanting: the seeming end of his life through his death, the doubts, whether all the hard struggles, the bitter pain are not in vain—all these disappear if the dogmatic conception is correct. He who had no need to overcome such a doubt, had not more but less laid upon him than is laid upon us other men, and such an one's conquest cannot bring consolation to others. And when traditional Christianity fails to discover any contradiction in that, on the one hand, it grieves from the depth of its soul over the human sufferings of this Personality, and, on the other hand, reveres this Personality as a God superior to all human anxieties and needs, we are reminded, although they are separated by an infinite interval, of the words of Xenophanes so specially concerned for the unity and eternity of the Divine Nature. When the Eleatics interrogated him whether they should sacrifice to Leucothea and also bewail her, he replied, " Bewail her not if you consider her a goddess; sacrifice not to her if you consider her human."

But the new conception dare not renounce the union of the human and the Divine. The renunciation would be an abandonment not only of religion, but of any and every truth. Yet the new mode dare not restrict the union to any one individual event in history, and place everything else in a state of dependency upon that one event; it has much more to permeate, connect, and elevate all events of a spiritual kind; it has to bring forth a world-encompassing and continuous deed which can become the intimate experience of every individual.

This involves also a severe clash of the new view with the traditional idea of mediation, which Christianity connects with the main idea of redemption. According to the traditional view, redemption does not proceed directly from the Absolute Life and Being that lies in what is beyond man's own energy, but a mid-link is forged between the Divine and the human, and half of it belongs to each side; both sides are brought into a definite connection which could be found in no other way. The power which this idea has exercised over the soul is shown from its origin and through its whole history. It was late Greek antiquity that fled towards it and clung to it. The presuppositions of the idea are quite evident. Deeply conscious of the opposites of our existence, especially of spirit and matter, man sought to elevate the Divine above the sordid mechanism of the world, and to conceive of it as much as possible on the other side of this world; and consequently the Divine appears incapable of coming into direct contact with man. But if, at the same time, there becomes operative in man a glowing aspiration after an emancipation from the hard exigencies and unreason of the world as well as after some kind of participation in the Godhead, and if simultaneously the consciousness of his own impotence is developed, what remains except the hope of intermediate powers that finally integrate themselves into one personality? We are able to understand how such a conception offered a means of support to human frailty, how it seemed to make access to the Divine easier, and how it gave an intimacy to the idea of redemption. And yet there is imbedded in the doctrine of mediation a crass anthropomorphism which religion cannot possibly endure for ever, and the presuppositions of which must fall to the ground as soon as an energetic feeling of life and a firmer faith have bridged the deep cleft between the Divine and the human which ruled there. Then it is bound to become clear that the doctrine is not able to bring forth a gain on one side without bringing a great loss on the other side. For it injures the *direct* relationship with the Divine; as it removes this relationship farther away from man, it lowers the Divine love and grace upon which in the last resort all depends; as it deposits such love and grace in their entirety at one particular point, it falls into anthropomorphism; as it contracts the union of the human and the Divine to one special situation, it thus inevitably draws down the Divine into the existence-form of man. The main fact, however, is that, as with all other life and being, so also that of religion cannot have more than one centre; either God or Christ stands in the centre, and the one consequently represses the other. Concerning the decision, there cannot be the least doubt: the fact is clear in the soul-struggles of the great religious personalities, that in a decisive act of the soul the doctrinal idea of mediation recedes into the background, and a direct relationship with God becomes a fact of immediacy and intimacy. And the idea of mediation glides easily into a further

mediation.   Has not the figure of Christ receded
in Catholicism, and does not the figure of Mary
constitute the centre of the religious emotional
life ?

Such a conviction does not exclude the fact that a
man is able to be a great help to men in their upward
path towards God; nor the fact that the human
personality who pre-eminently brought eternal truth
to the plane of Time and through this inaugurated a
new epoch remains permanently present in the picture
of the spiritual world, and is able permanently to
exercise a mighty power upon the soul.   Such a
personality as Jesus is not the mere bearer of doctrines
or of a special frame of mind, but is a convincing fact
and proof of the Divine Life, a proof at which new
life can be kindled ever anew.   The fact is at the
same time the source of a movement which cannot
be estimated ; it is from this source that a great
yearning has been implanted within the human breast
—a longing for a new life of love and peace, of purity
and simplicity.   Such a life with its incomparable
nature and its mysterious depths does not exhaust
itself through historical effects, but humanity can
from hence ever return afresh to its inmost essence,
and can strengthen itself ever anew through the
certainty of a new, pure and spiritual world over
against the meaningless aspects of nature and over
against the vulgar mechanism of a culture merely
human.

But all this is far removed from any idea of mediation, and also from the setting of a human personality in Divine power and worship.   And if we have
thus to protest against the position accorded to Jesus

by the traditional form of Christianity, so that we
have to part company with a Christo-centric configuration on account of the breach with the old mode of
thinking, yet we cling to an essential content and a
metaphysical depth in the human image of Jesus, and
seek in this the sole standard of the religious life.
One had good ground for doing this so long as Jesus
Christ in his humanity was considered as very God,
as the second person in the Trinity. But where this
belief has been abandoned, the exclusive linking of
life to Jesus becomes an inadmissible contraction and
diminution of religion. Also, the pathway to the
facts must not be substituted for the facts themselves,
and must not bring the metaphysical and eternal
in religion into obscurity. The Christianity which
occupies itself solely with Jesus, and which to many
to-day seems an exit from all entanglements, is not
yet a match for the mighty problems, and does not
carry within itself the energy to overcome the world.

Thus, we witness the most pointed antagonism
between the traditional and a new aspiring Christianity. All along the line, the two conceptions do
not appear as a More or a Less between which some
kind of a Mean can be found, but they appear in their
main tendencies as opposites. The breadth which
the one desires is held by the other to be only a
vapoury sentiment; the consolidation upon which
the one insists is held by the other to be no more
than a semblance and a humanisation; the doctrine
of mediation which signifies to the one an indispensable entrance to the Godhead, appears to the other
as a diminution of the Divine and as a weakening of
the fundamental process of religion.

In the midst of such antagonism and such an actual cleft, what can now signify a clinging to an appearance of unity? The old mode is right when it complains that the traditional values are buried under new and strange phenomena and meanings; the old view fears an injury to the substance of Christianity from such a new interpretation, and calls up and stands upon a tradition from century to century in order to hold fast the pure and true configuration of Christianity gained once and for all. The new mode desires clear divisions of the material whenever it feels itself the representative of truth, and when it feels called upon to set forth truth with the whole of its energy. It feels that it is only through an entire independence it can overcome all the prior hesitation of halting in front of a problem; it feels that it is able to progress from a more negative to a more positive construction; it feels that it is able to test the experience of human nature, and that through a struggle with the opposites it is able inwardly to grow. Thus, as things now stand, the competitors consume their best energy in disputes against each other; through the one questioning the rights and wrongs of the other, the subject-matter itself is not furthered, and, more than all, the confused state of things hinders veracity, and without such veracity the present crisis in religion cannot be overcome.

This new disunion will not be able for any great length of time to keep religion in the background. Indeed, this fact is even now becoming visible. Religious questions occupy and govern more and more the minds of men; they kindle the passions and call to battle.   They do this at present, it is true, more from without, and not always in a desirable manner, but an inward change is apparent and in actual process.   Old and seemingly-settled questions arise anew and show that all the transformations of life have not entirely broken their power.   Such a light in the direction of religion drives out with mighty power that gloomy twilight which is the abode of halfness and obscurity, and such a light brings the concealed contradiction to a clear consciousness and makes it intolerable.   It is out of an honourable adjustment of the Old and the New, however, that the effort after a reconstruction of Christian truth must issue—a reconstruction of the universal validity of the Spiritual Life, which already wells up as a mighty aspiration in the hearts of many who hunger and thirst after truth and eternity, but whose deep craving is no longer satisfied by the old forms.   How long shall religion be looked upon merely as a step-child of that which suppresses conscience and conviction ?   How long are we to search for eternal truth upon an obsolete road ?   That things are not easy and comfortable on the *new* road is easily seen, and it is to this fact we now pass.

2. *The Necessity of a New Mode of Christianity*

When we aspire after a new form of Christianity, and simultaneously deem necessary a breach with tradition, we are not in any way blind to the danger and difficulty of the problem.   The traditional form has for centuries held together a large portion of humanity ; it has given life and conviction a fixed direction, as well as a foothold and confidence to an

innumerable multitude of souls, and it has been the
means of interesting the widest circles in spiritual
tasks.   All this is already evident as something great
beyond measure when we compare it with the small
spiritual activity brought forth by the ordinary life
of men and with the instability of the Spiritual Life
within the mere-human circle.   In reflecting on all
this, a breach with the traditional form of religion
may appear as an upheaval of morality as well as of
intellectual connections.   In a word, this may appear
as an endangering of all that lifted man beyond his
small self and beyond mere nature.   In reality, there
exist here grave dangers, and a great risk is unmistakable.   Such a breach is justified only if it is
desired on account of a spiritual necessity of man's
nature, superior to all human considerations and
reflections.   And this will be the case in the province
of religion when it is perceived that the old form of
religion is unable to solve our own religious problems,
and when simultaneously our own interest in religion
has turned into an aspiration and effort after an inner
renewal.   That this is actually the case to-day has
been the leading thought of the whole of our investigation, and we need here do no more than bring
this thought to its final connection and conclusion.

Religion has its nucleus in eternal truths—in truths
which, once they are grasped, cannot be overthrown
by any transformation of the work of the world.   But
such truths want to produce effects upon man, and,
in order to do this, they must enter into his sphere,
and their existential-form must correspond to the
universal situation of spiritual evolution.   Within
this universal situation, as we have already observed,

not only slight re-arrangements but deep and radical transformations have already occurred against the old mode of Christianity, and these transformations are not merely in contact with the periphery but reach into the very centre of life itself. A mere change of views concerning the external would stir only slightly, but something infinitely more occurs when simultaneously the Life-process and the whole mode of thinking transform themselves, when man becomes something other than he was before, when his fundamental relationship to reality is changed, and when the whole domain of his life is reshaped. For as certainly as religion does not stand merely by the side of but *within* life, quite as certain is it that it relates itself to such transformations. The thought-world of the old form has become far too narrow and anthropomorphic; its opposition to reason—an opposition which was formerly considered to be the doing of man alone—has spread in our time over the whole religious world, and such a conception has increased immeasurably the obscurity of reality and has given rise to an increased difficulty in discovering what religion really means. In its earlier stages, this old thought-world presented a picture of the greatness and goodness of the All; and thus religion appeared as the relationship of man to a nature incomparably higher than himself, but still a nature in analogy with his own nature. But now the world of nature has drawn man to itself; he becomes now a mere drop in the sea unless he recognises the dawning of a new and essential reality within his spiritual nature. Thus, what appeared as his secure possession turns

now into a difficult problem ; he now undertakes a
task—the task how to penetrate from his ordinary
surface-situation to the spiritual depth of life.   Consequently a religion of the Spiritual Life must stand out
in bold relief from that of mere man, for the latter
aspect of religion threatens more and more to become
a mere mythology.   Therewith all conceptions of
Divine things become inadequate ; much that was
previously held valid as entire truth has now become
a mere symbol from which it is necessary to move
further and further away.   But, at the same time, the
spiritual contents gain an independence, and exercise
a transforming energy on man ; life raises itself now
through religion from the subjective to the substantial,
and subsists more and more upon a real transformation of its own being.   All along we stand here face
to face with new tasks, and we can never hope to
come nearer their solution unless the altered situation
is fully acknowledged and unless a struggle from
such an altered situation is undertaken.

The old mode of religion holds off from such an
acknowledgment of the altered situation ; it allows
only some isolated elements to fall upon itself—
results which have now become incontestable.   It
accepts now, for instance, the Copernican view of
the universe, but it had to be dragged to accept it ;
it does not posit itself willingly even now within
the whole meaning of the conception, but stands
mistrustful and on the defensive over against it, so
that it cannot loyally adjust itself on the side of the
Yea or the Nay of that and other movements.   Consequently it cannot seize the fruit offered by such
movements to religion.

The consequence of this leads to a constant and insufferable frittering away of life. Culture more and more pushes back the old mode of religion, and through this enters into an increasingly secular and soulless mode. Religion thus becomes more and more of an isolated province, and the channel between it and knowledge widens; thus its distance from men becomes ever greater until the mental efforts and ascents of humanity become indifferent to it. This indifference is the greatest enemy to religion, and is in reality more dangerous than all the assaults of doubt. And yet this indifference cannot be avoided if religion is severed from the whole of life. The indifference, indeed, will strike its roots ever deeper until religion once more gains a fixed connection with the whole of life.

The older mode of religion, in the midst of all these hindrances, exercises still a powerful effect, and in so far as positive achievements are concerned, it is still far ahead of the new mode. But these effects confine themselves to particular provinces: the totality of spiritual work and the main current of life are no longer dominated by the older mode; it is not so much a universal as a particular mode, as "all who call themselves Christians" are only too apt to let us know. The fact that great masses of the people cling to the older mode does not at all prove that they have come to any kind of conscious decision concerning the differences of the Old and the New, but only proves that they have not as yet come into contact with the problems and doubts of the age— that these problems have not as yet entered into their consciousness. But these problems and doubts are the very things which render the position of religion insecure. For sooner or later a contact with them is bound to come. The question is, will people then be true to the old customs and practices ?

In fact, religion is able to exhibit its entitled position when it holds the full heights of the Spiritual Life, and through this proves itself necessary and fruit-bearing ; and also when, in regard to the movements of life, it draws the " kinsman " within these movements and drives out the " old enemy." But as the old form cannot lend itself in any great degree to such a task, it needs a new existential-form ; it becomes necessary before all else—in the very interest of religion itself— to free the Eternal within itself from its temporal forms, and the spiritual substance from human notions. We discover in the old mode too much that is languid and alien. Men have become tired of its form and also of its language ; and it does not any longer issue forth from a rapturous energy and youthful freshness of the whole of our own life, as it always does when the entire truth and effects of religion are at work. Now, as we have to live our own life and carry our own destiny, shall we reject the aid of our indispensable helper on the road of life—religion ? There are no such things as restorations either in religion or elsewhere ; nor will the Spiritual Life ever return to the old forms. It thus behoves us to pay heed to what is ahead of us and to strive to reach it.

But, indispensable as the effort after a new existential-form is, yet there can be no doubt as to the immense difficulty of the task if we do not conceive it in a wrong or petty manner. The first requirement is, that in the transformation of the *form of existence* nothing of the genuine *substance* should be lost, but that the new *form of existence* should succeed in giving this substance purer, more energetic, and more universal effects.   This is possible, however, only if the problem of the adjustment of religion and culture is not understood as in any way synonymous with the relaxation of religion with increasing knowledge, and, on the other hand, is not desirous of an absolute adjustment of both. The solution will come when religion enters into the relationship as an independent power and with all its independent content—when it is not merely measured by culture, but when it, in its turn, measures, judges, rejects, and selects.   All this is necessary for religion when face to face with modern culture, because modern culture is not of a simple and obvious nature. It comprises movements, experiences, and unfoldings of the Spiritual Life from which it cannot for ever withdraw itself; but such a culture also carries within itself temporal and human tendencies of a highly problematic character—tendencies which contradict most pointedly the dominant trend of religion and even of Christianity.   Modern culture as it expresses itself in human formulations—with its material joy in, and its ready affirmations of, life, with its repression and even displacement of ethical greatness, with its abandonment of eternity for the doctrine of evolution—is not only at variance with this or that existential-form of religion but with each and all religions.   He, therefore, who makes such a culture a standard for measuring religion has there and then decided against religion.   But for him to whom religion has become a serious concern a struggle against such tendencies of culture has become inevitable, and he must forge his way with all the energy at his command to the fundamental differentiation of the elements of spiritual truth and of the human errors found within the whole situation of culture.

Hence all definite movements for a renewal of religion must be differentiated clearly from the movements which are found within the domain of culture. Unless this be done, we may hold fast to a kind of religion which inevitably degenerates into great superficiality. In an age of religious crisis, such as we witness to-day, the superficial is always the most obvious remedy and the loudest in its claims; it is able to hide its own poverty of life under the colours of freedom; it has on its side the half-educated and, even more, the over-educated to whom negations are so pleasing and smugness is so welcome. This is also true of those movements that attempt to shape religion in harmony with what is termed " the spirit of the age "—shape it in harmony with all that bubbles from the playful fountains of time—and that avoid every genuine Nay and look upon every sharp collision as a disturbance of a " life at ease in Zion." Even to-day any movement be it ever so perverted and hostile to genuine religion will find so-called " liberal-minded " people who feel themselves the true messengers of the times when they declare that their message can be made to fit excellently with religion and even with Christianity, and that it is here alone the meaning of both can be found. It is necessary over against such an unworthy adjustment of the times to hold forth the superiority and the trenchancy of the timeless truth; it is necessary to uphold the independence of religion over against a superficiality of knowledge and to exercise an alert criticism on the claims of culture from the standpoint of religion. Those who are unable any longer to cling to the Old constitute two main classes. The one class feels the need for no more than a minimum of religion, whilst the other class strives to obtain a maximum. The former places itself under the contents of time, whilst the latter attempts to raise itself above time; the former feels itself already in possession of all essentials, whilst the latter sees itself as only just entering on an infinite quest. The sincerity of life and the progress of the religious movement can be furthered only when the two classes are differentiated more clearly one from the other than has hitherto been the case.

He who envisages the religious problem in its varied difficulties is unable to deny that religion has lost unspeakably much through the upheaval of the old form; and, further, he sees the need of making good such a loss. But such an urgent result can come about only through a strengthening of the *substance* of religion—through the energetic working out of its fundamental characteristics, and through the undaunted assertion of all that raises religion above the mere level of time. Religion is thus raised to the level of the metaphysical and transcendental which frighten so much the ordinary man of the present. The contradictions of human life must be fully acknowledged if ever a true effort for overcoming them is to be set in motion. The *Either-Or* which runs through the whole of life must stand clearly in front of us, and we must take a decisive stand within the situation. A thorough-going clarification of the

37

entangled situation and a separation of spirits according to their fundamental convictions are the first
requisites for the turn towards a better state of
things. And then comes the need of building up
and creating, of collecting and penetrating, of select-
ing and possessing, a new reality. But all this is not
possible without a deepening of the total Life-process—without an energetic self-recollection of the
Spiritual Life and a stepping beyond the situation of
the times. Our whole investigation rests upon the
conviction that the religious problem is not to be
handled apart from, but within, the totality of
life; it rests upon the actual phenomenon of the
Spiritual Life and the characteristic way in which it
is to be conceived; it rests upon the fact that this
Spiritual Life binds itself into a Whole, and upon
the acknowledgment of an essential and independent
reality within it which becomes the fixed standard and
great task of religion. The necessary conditions for
a renewal of religion are solely the elevation and the
energetic development of the Spiritual Life. It is
in this alone that a sufficient compensation for the
loss of the Old can be found, and it is here alone
that the new mode can overcome the opposition
directed against it from the side of the old mode.

The old mode often misses a sufficiency of actuality
in the New; the New seems to the Old to lack
the certainty that man in religion is raised above
himself by means of a superior power, and is also
led to a new life. This complaint is valid in regard
to all attempts to found religion upon mere psychology,
for when such attempts are made it is either the intellectual or the emotional side of the nature—either

ideas and concepts, or judgments of value and feelings —which takes the lead. Through any of these, man may be able to revolve within his own circle, but he is never able to come out of his subjectivity, and the energy of truth can never invest his psychic state or his partial and one-sided qualities with an absolute value. But it is quite otherwise when the Spiritual Life in its independence is acknowledged, and when it is understood as the presence of a *new kind of world*. Through this the total outlook of life becomes changed, so that it is not now necessary that man should be guided to this new world by means of some isolated portion of his nature. The man now possesses energy of a spiritual nature to be a participator in such a new world; his need now is to develop such a cosmic life within his own consciousness and all that it includes. Thus, the fundamental fact and proof of all lies in the *totality of the Spiritual Life itself*, and all remaining facts and proofs have to be connected with this one fundamental fact. The result then is that religion is raised above all mere subjectivity.

Again, the new mode complains of the " abstract-ness " found in the indeterminate concepts of the old mode, and states that such an " abstractness " does not help towards full religious effectiveness. Much is to be said in support of this complaint of the new mode; but it is not in its favour that it often does not attempt to discover the nature of religion within the characteristic formation of Spiritual Life. It is in so doing that the concrete-ness of religion lies, and not in copious and learned disquisitions concerning doctrines and organisations

—disquisitions which may concede that some kind of needed nucleus lies beneath all this though it is imbedded in great obscurity.   How is it, if no more than this were needed, that Catholicism, with its colossal machinery, often fails to manifest with sufficient clearness and energy what is new and world-renovating in Christianity ?   The characteristic and the concrete in religion can be brought forth, however, by the New through an exclusive concentration upon *the spiritual content* ; and once this Yea has become the conviction of the new mode, it can pronounce judgment on any Nay it likes.   It is characteristic of religion before all else that it constitutes the ethical formation of the Spiritual Life, its foundation in freedom and deed, its demand for a new kind of existence, and *its creation of a world subsisting within itself.*   This signifies incomparably more than a mere fulfilment of moral rules within a given earthly organisation ; it contains the most unique and decisive assertions and denials ; it withstands the alleged sovereign claims of all intellectual and æsthetic formations of life ; it withstands the immersion of our life into an environing world and into a blind destiny.   But notwithstanding all such characteristics, ethical idealism is only the presupposition of religion and not religion itself.   A turn to religion results only through the problems and conflicts which originate from this foundation through a deep convulsion of the nature of man ; and when this has happened, the elevation and transformation become religion.   It is obvious that all this, through its reciprocal relations, exhibits an entirely new and characteristic type of life ; and it is this type with its facts and tasks, its developments and conquests—as our whole investigation has attempted to prove—which constitutes the genuine concreteness of the Spiritual Life upon which we take our stand.

It may appear at the first glance as though the new mode does not place the problem of moral wrong so exclusively in the foreground as it is placed by the old mode; and this assertion appears to the old mode as a sign of a laxer mode of thinking. This may be true concerning a number of the forms of the New, but it is not true of all. The New is able to acknowledge in the fullest possible manner that nothing reveals the depth of life so much as the discovery of an ethical conflict within human nature. And it is this fact which gives the religious problem a compelling power. But the acknowledgment of this inner conflict has to pass beneath the level of conscious mental reflection and shallow delineation, because such a procedure blunts the real facts and glides easily into unveracity. Thus, the conceptions of freedom and moral guilt must be viewed in a wider sense than the old mode has yet done. We cannot agree with the old mode that all evil is to be traced back to the deeds of man or that sin brought death for the first time into our world. We must hold fast to freedom, but at the same time we must not deny the fact of the mighty power of a dark destiny. This problem has to be placed in the very front of the old mode, and it has to be shown that the problem has mysterious depths. The problem will thus be handled in a more circumspect, more tender, and less anthropomorphic manner than has been the case with the past Protestantism of the

Church; and notwithstanding the change, earnestness concerning the facts will preserve everything essential from being lost.

The New then may live in the full persuasion that nothing of the energy and depth of religion need be lost upon its path. And it will certainly realise that it is only at the beginning of the road and still far remote from any kind of terminus. How the course of things will shape themselves in the distant future lies for us enwrapped in deep darkness. For manifold factors are operating at the present day which are creating some of the elements of that distant future. These factors are the fortunes and experiences of humanity, of great personalities, and of the characteristic and most important universal elements of the times. But we need not trouble our minds concerning the contour of that distant future. There is in the present more than enough for us to do. The activism of the present, taken in its deepest sense, has work enough under its very eyes to trace the outlines of a new ideal world in the midst of a perverse generation and the midst of immense confusions. The great task to-day is to carve out deeply and clearly the main bearings of life—bearings where all efforts can co-operate and where the deepest spirit of man can find its greatest energy. Even if all this be only of a preparatory kind, preparation itself is part of the complete work, and no one, at bottom, can know at what stage the preliminaries shade off into the work itself.

· CHAPTER XVI

c. THE SITUATION AND DEMANDS OF THE PRESENT

GREAT as are the difficulties of a new configuration of religion, they must not discourage us from entering upon the task, for behind this task an urgent need of the times calls us to the work—a need which rises ever to the surface. We live in an age of opulence and of movement—an age which no one dare brand as paltry, and which, with all its activities, capacity for work, and its overflowing life, should never be assimilated too closely to the stagnation of waning antiquity. But it is an age afflicted with a colossal contradiction. It is wonderfully great in its mastery of, and achievements within, the environing world, but, on the other hand, it is deplorably poor and insecure in regard to the problems of the inner life and the inner world. Such a contradiction cannot be tolerated forever. As surely as this will be overcome, so surely will religion once more step forth as *the fact* of facts, and prepare for itself an appropriate configuration of the essential and universal elements of life and existence.

There is no need for us here to demonstrate the power of man over the world : it is evident to all. Most evident are the gains over nature through science and technics; and also the conditions of human relations have become incomparably clearer and more tractable. We understand how to unravel the skein of the past and how to weave a meaning out of its isolated threads, and how to differentiate the subjective clothing of things from their essential aspects. Further, we observe in the corporate life of men the immense growth of the power of administration and organisation, and through all this we are able to satisfy our wants and needs in an incomparably securer and easier way than at any other period in the history of our world. In all this, man has become more and more the master of things. But all this potency has fixed limitations. The potency is confined to what the capacities of man are able to extract from the external world, but it does not reach to that which exists within his own soul, and does not lead to the growth and the blossoming of an inner world. And consequently life in the midst of all its achievements continues to rest upon the external, and man has to consider himself ever as something of an alien in the midst of it all if he is ever to exercise real power and to exhibit his genuine superiority over the world.

Whilst the effort and the energy are so strongly drawn towards the external, the inner life—the heritage of long millenniums—has become afflicted with a grave anxiety and insecurity. But this inner life is too deeply implanted and rooted in human nature through the work of the millenniums to be ever

shaken off as an alien thing or to be considered in
any light-hearted manner.   It holds us fast and raises
its claims; it forbids us to find satisfaction in all
the things of sense and time.   But in the midst of
all the contradictions the inner life is unable by itself
to reach a clear and effectual content, nor will it
ever reach it by looking externally.   We remain
therefore on the inward side as poor in the midst of
all the external plenty which surrounds us as if we
were not the possessors of it at all.

We discover this poverty "in the inward parts"
in a stronger and more painful way if we do not
wrap our inward exigency with historical tradition,
if we do not call upon antiquity or upon the beginnings of modern times to come to our immediate
assistance, and if we cease to look to the traditional
form of religion for the deepening of life and for consolidation.   In fact, the situation of mankind has
altered so much through the work and experience of
modern times that the older mode of thinking cannot
possibly satisfy our life in its entirety.   We may feel
great interest in much that is contained in the old
mode and allow ourselves to be carried along with
it, but a point arrives where a parting of the ways
takes place for ever.   In reality, we cannot approach
certain aspects of the Old without simultaneously
moving away from other aspects; we cannot affirm
certain aspects of history without at the same time
having to deny other aspects.   Therefore, if we
take the whole of any historical occurrence as our
guide, there cannot be at work more than half of our
energy and character; we shall thus turn hither and
thither in the most unsteady manner; and amidst all

the chaos of the contradictory impressions we shall
fall at last into dulness and weariness.

What remains? The immediate present moment
remains. And if this present moment possesses not
as yet a connected inner world, still it possesses the
free spontaneous feeling and the natural individuality
of the individual. But can these become the standard
of a new life? It is certain that from this source
much can be quickened and energised, raise and turn
itself, affirm and deny, devote itself energetically in
divers ways to vista beyond vista and task beyond
task. But notwithstanding such a possession life still
remains under the ban of the accidental and the
superficial; it has not yet possessed the genuine substance and the durable truth. Indeed, the farther
life travels on this road without these essentials for
its journey, the more it falls into strange situations,
mistakes, and eccentricities. And thus there issues
that shallow situation of which we are all aware, and
which we need only briefly refer to here.

The basing of life upon subjectivity and natural
individuality causes inner divisions of the human
race; it causes a frittering away of the life of the
soul of the whole and the soul of each individual. It
was the main service of traditional religion that it
raised up and presented a complete task and final aim
for humanity; the individual was introduced to the
life of the fellowship; he received from this source
light and guidance; each individual experienced intimately the fate of the whole, and so could always
escape from the fleetingness of his own individual
conclusions to this; it is in this total-life of the
fellowship that the individual finds support and

consolation, motive and enhancement, norm and standard. And, further, men were thus held closely together; the common task and the daily burden of each and all was understood by each and all; they laboured and suffered together, and they loved and hated together. Here was a source of spiritual energy and of ethical character which no proclamation of mere doctrine and no appeal of mere emotion could ever replace.

It is a loss which cannot be estimated when such an inner fellowship and, along with it, a life out of the Whole decay. It is a loss when each individual plants himself upon the particularity of his natural individuality, and when an exaggerated individualism is developed without any reservation or counterpoise. If this calamity happens, all the energies which in the fellowship worked together now work against one another. The result is an intellectual and moral disintegration; men understand one another less and less, live less and less for one another, and more and more rarely are they to be found shoulder to shoulder. Can we deny that mankind tends to divide itself more and more into opposites and parties, and that the colossal associations in the domains of material work oppose the independence of the inner life?

It is a strange life which issues out of such an unregulated development of subjectivity and natural individuality. Man in all this is most busy with himself, observes himself, mirrors and reflects upon his own states; he ruminates and broods more and more over himself, seeks to refine his small artistic soul and to free himself from all the deeper concerns of life and

existence.   Thus, life is posited more and more upon
mere reflection and is turned towards whims and
delusions ; it loses all its *naïveté*—all simple innocence
and inner necessities.   But herewith it enters into a
track where mind and soul are neither well nor sick,
and where prejudice has for its company artificiality
and eccentricity.

The elevation of natural individuality to the status
of a guide of life has as its result the shaping of life
in a puny, piecemeal, irregular, and curious fashion.
Paradoxes and commonplaces now present themselves
as excellences, but they never lead to even a mediocre independence, although the man is in urgent
need of greatness and independence in order to compare his life with such trivial things and in order to
be raised above them.   The individual has here no
inner world beyond himself, so that he cannot measure
himself and cannot obtain fulfilment for his life.
What remains for him but to return towards the
external world and seek there a flimsy greatness
by means of a "brilliant career" and often at the
cost of an overstrain ?

Through the mere convergence of these individual
currents of life, no life on a great scale can ever issue.
A chaos of conflicting movements, contrary hindrances and weaknesses, sudden rising and abrupt falling, no main governing principle which differentiates
between good and evil and between the real and the
apparent, no energetic counter-effect to the petty
and the common on the highways of human life,
and, instead of an energetic spirituality, a refining of
the sensuous right up to a decadent sensuality—all
this appears.   All culture which possesses no sub-

stance, notwithstanding all its aspiration after reality and notwithstanding all the excitement of its subjectivity, possesses no soul, and in the whirl of fleeting appearances obscures the great *Either-Or*. The words of Pestalozzi are even more applicable to our day than for his own: "Light and darkness have always been in our world, but most of the light and darkness stood out more distinctly marked in days of yore — in the dark days themselves — and were clearer and more real to the eyes of men. Darkness was then recognised by the seer fully as darkness. But to-day the darkness has become light and the light darkness."

In such a critical time as ours, which meets the life of humanity everywhere, this truth of Pestalozzi becomes particularly plain if we compare the universal weakness of the inner life with the colossal capacity of a scientific, technical, and practical kind. We are occupying ourselves very diligently in a scientific, historical, and reflective way with Philosophy, but we possess no Philosophy of our own — no philosophical creativeness of an independent kind. We occupy ourselves incessantly with history, and have carried the results of technics to a marvellous height; but we lack all along the meaning of history as a totality, and are not able to cross the bridge from the past to the present. Our literature sets forth particular aspects of the soul; but it does not seize and hold together man in the totality of his being—it does not strike its root into the depth of man's nature. Our art works diligently and aspires zealously after truth; but it does not succeed in bringing the chaos of the times to its own track. We deal more than ever to-day with education; but we possess no single and simple ideal. We trouble incessantly for the betterment of political and social relations; but we come to a painful halt wherever the final aims and the highest happiness of man are at stake. Everywhere we witness the absence of a self-reliant Spiritual Life which would be superior to the wealth of the conflicting impressions, and which would bring the universal situation of the present into a connected and simple expression. Our day is also full of inner problems, and we have not grown strong enough to attack them; we sink back ever anew down to the petty-human level and fail to reach a genuine content of life—fail to reach consolidation and greatness.

All this will be hidden from view so long as man is content to remain entirely in such a world of impulse and mechanism and only hurries breathlessly along from one small point to another. But once he steps out of such a situation and strikes out on a new path of the Whole, he will certainly discover the painful nature of the situation. He will discover the situation to be that of incessant toil and work with few pure gains, of fascinating achievements in isolated things but with only a trivial value for the totality of life, of a highly complicated apparatus of civilisation and culture but of no living soul in the Whole, of burning impulses of the fleeting moment but of no creativeness, eternal values, or eternal hopes. Why all this labour and toil if the whole thing has no meaning but falls back at last into nothingness?

But one needs only to grasp clearly the crisis of such a culture in order to raise himself above all

concern about the future. The limits of such negations and shallowness have been set: there comes
a point where man within his own being and life
discovers their destructive energy, and when this
happens the counter-effect is not far away. Man
now takes up the struggle on behalf of his threatened
spiritual existence; he grips the inner connections
of his being once again—connections in which his
deepest being has its foundation—and from such a
source new energies will flow and strengthen him
towards producing a culture which signifies once
more an independent inner world, and which is able
to allow their true valuation to all the relationships
of his life. We really stand to-day on the verge of
an aspiration after an essential culture—a culture
of the whole man—after an inwardness which corresponds to the most important meanings of the
Spiritual Life. Notwithstanding the tangle and the
poignant regrets of the initial stages, the aspiration
will become stronger and stronger; it needs but an
energetic concentration of effort as well as a definite
focussing of energies in order that the movement
may proceed on its upward course—beyond the
realm of the petty circle and into a region beyond
all earthly bounds. The possibilities of life are not
yet exhausted: new avenues and tasks open out
whenever we discover the courage of creativeness
and the right point of attack, but it is imperative
that we should possess the conviction and that the
conviction should possess us that reality has a depth
beyond the *natural* man, and that we can gain entrance to such a depth.

But a movement towards a more essential and

soul-stirring culture—to a progressive superiority of
a complete life beyond all individual activities—cannot
arise without bringing the problem of religion once
more to the foreground.   Our life is not able to find
its bearings within this deep or to gather its treasures
into a Whole unless it realises how many acute
opposites it carries within itself.   Either Life will be
torn in pieces by these opposites or it must somehow
be raised above them all.   It is the latter alone that
can bring about a fundamental transformation of our
first and shallow view of the universe as well as the
inauguration of a new reality.   It is this which
religion announces to man and promises to bring to
his soul in its dire need.   Man has emerged out of
the darkness of nature and remains afflicted with the
afflictions of nature, yet at the same time, with his
appearance upon the earth the darkness begins to
illumine, and "nature kindles within him a light"
(Schopenhauer); he who is a mere speck on the
face of a boundless expanse can yet aspire to a
participation in the whole of Infinity; he who
stands in the midst of the flux of time yet possesses an aspiration after infinite truth; he who
forms but a mere piece of nature, at the same time,
constructs a new world within the Spiritual Life
over against nature; he who finds himself hemmed
in by contradictions of all kinds, which immediate
existence in no way can solve, yet struggles after a
further depth of reality and after the "narrow gate"
which opens into religion.   Through and beyond all
the particular problems of life and the world, it behoves us to raise the Spiritual Life to a level of full
independence, to make it at the same time superior

to man as an individual and to bring it back into
his soul. When this comes to be, there is also a
transformation of his inmost being, and for the first
time he becomes capable of genuine greatness.

The aspiration after a new culture carries thus
within itself in an immediate and intimate manner
the aspiration after a rejuvenation of religion. Religion and culture will thus instruct each other.
Without religion the inwardness cannot become a
self-reliant province and cannot rise above the external world; without a connection with the whole
of life and also with culture, religion loses its characteristic spiritual content and threatens to sink into
a merely subjective disposition. Consequently the
deficiency or the curtailment of one is also an injury
to the other.

These final conclusions strengthen the aspiration
after a religion of the Spiritual Life, which has run
through the whole of our investigation. Such a
religion is in no way new, and Christianity has
proclaimed it and clung to it from the very beginning. But it has been so interwoven with traditional
forms which are now so commonly detected as
pictorial ideas of epochs and times. Earlier times
could allow the essence and the form to flow inseparably together without discovering any incongruity in the fusion. But the time for this has
irrevocably passed away. The human which once
seemed to bring the Spiritual and Divine so near
to man has now become a burden and a hindrance to him. A keener analysis, a more independent development of the Spiritual and Divine, and
along with this, the truth of religion, fail to obtain

38

their full effects if religion is looked upon as
merely something to protect individuals, instead of
as that which furthers the whole of humanity—as
that which is not merely a succour in times of
trouble and sorrow but also as that which guarantees
an enhancement in work and creativeness.   The
situation is difficult and full of dangers, and few
in the meantime is the number of those who grasp
it in a deep and free sense, and who yet are determined to penetrate victoriously into it, so that the
inner necessities of the Spiritual Life may awaken
within the soul of man.   Whatever new tasks and
difficulties lie in the lap of the future, to-day it
behoves us before all else to proceed a step upward
in the direction of the summits and to draw new
energies and depths of the Spiritual Life into the
domain of man ; for it is effort of this kind which
will prevent the coming of an " old age " upon humanity and will breathe into its soul the gift of Eternal
Youth.

INDEX

Absolute and Historical Religion, 517 ff.

Absolute Life : its conception, 193, 208.

Activity demanded in religion, 400 ff., 403, 405, 558 ff.

Antithetic character of the Religious Life, 242 ff., 520 ff.

Art : as an overcoming of an interior opposition and in connection with religion, 133 ff., 450 ff.

Augustine, 41, 374, 380, 402, 409, 424, 435, 436, 467, 504, 556, 557, 558.

Autonomous Life and Autonomies, 152, 153, 204, 205.

Bacon, 510.

Being, and the formation of Being, 161, 162, 422.

Biological conception of life : its peculiarity and danger, 27, 51, 52.

Bodily resurrection of Jesus : no object of faith, 528, 529.

Buddha, 519.

Catholicism (Roman), 543, 545, 580.

Changes and crises in historical movements, 357, 358.

Characteristic (or Specific) Religion : its conception, 410 ff. ; its detailed development, 419 ff. ; its relation to Universal Religion, 410 ff. ; its relation to the historical religions, 410 ff.

Childlikeness : its connection with religion, 452.

Christian religion : its peculiarity, 7, 517 ff., 524, 525 ff. ; its eternal substance, 517 ff. ; its temporal forms, 554 ff. ; its union of the Divine and the human, 206, 522 ff. ; effect of its beginnings, 277 ; its mediæval form, 41 ff., 194 ; its maintenance as over against the changes in the views concerning Nature, 525 ff. ; as over against history and culture, 534 ff. ; as over against the changes within the Spiritual Life itself, 542 ff.

Christian State and Christian Science : the right and wrong in these conceptions, 467 ff.

Church, the : demands concerning its formation, 467 ff. ; its organisation of activity, 467 ff. ; its cult, 472 ff.

Cognition : its complications, 100 ff. ; its conditions, 148.

Concreteness in religion : how to be understood, 579.

Confucius, 394.

God, the idea of, 181, 208 ff.,
371 ff., 429 ff. ; its twofold
interpretation in ecclesiastical Christianity, 210 ff.
Godhead and God, 429 ff.
Goethe, 54, 133, 140, 151, 215,
337, 344.
Good, the, and the useful, 124 ff.
Greatness, the longing for : its
connection with religion,
278, 290 ff., 447.
Greek manner of thinking and
view of life, 101, 105, 233,
263, 537.

Habit : limits of its efficiency,
125 ff.
Hegel, 37, 80, 149, 472, 514.
Higher, the, and the lower :
their opposite explanations,
284 ff., 554 ff.
Historical criticism : its origin
and effect, 32 ff. ; historical
religions, 6 ff., 366 ff.
Historical school : refusal of, 546,
547.
Historico - social culture and
civilisation : its incapacity
to produce the Spiritual
Life, 50, 68 ff., 142, 538 ;
is interpretable in two
different ways, 318 ; its opposition to religion, 296 ff.
History : conditions for a history
of a spiritual kind, 55 ff. ;
its relation to religion, 28 ff.,
434 ff.; its significance within religion, 477 ff. ; limits
of its efficacy in the domain
of the spiritual life, 113 ff.,
176 ; history of the soul
introduced by religion, 434,
435.

Idealism and Realism : they can
be conjoined, 178 ff.

Idealistic and Realistic Culture
and Civilisation in modern
times, 43 ff.
Ideals : their peculiar action,
200 ff. ; their constant
change, 300 ff.
Imagination : its operation within religion, 8, 367, 368.
Immanent Idealism : refusal of,
509.
Immortality, 216, 272, 291 ff.,
435.
Impersonal character of the
process of civilisation and
culture in modern times,
36.
Indian religions, 11 ff., 519.
Indirect proof furnished by universal history, 258.
Individual, the : as interlaced
with the environment, 338
ff. ; in relation to society,
300 ff. ; treated by fate as
though of no value, 347 ff.
Infinite Love, 441.
Infinity : the aspiration after,
261 ff., 445.
Intellectualism : conditions for
overcoming it, 181 ff. ; its
insufficiency, 74, 232.
Intolerance, the : of religion,
248.
Inwardness : discrimination between subjective and sub-
stantial inwardness, 67 ff.,
150 ff., 274, 426, 437 ff. ;
strengthened by religion,
437 ff.

James, William, 478.
Jesus : His personality, 16 ff.,
360, 505, 562, 563 ; His
position within the Christian
faith, 16 ff., 560 ff.
Judaism, 367.
Justice and love, 395 ff.

PRINTED BY NEILL AND CO., LTD., EDINBURGH.

A CATALOGUE OF
WILLIAMS & NORGATE'S
PUBLICATIONS

ADDIS (W. E., M.A.). Hebrew Religion to the Establish-
ment of Judaism under Ezra. Crown 8vo. cloth. 4s. 6d. net.
See Crown Theological Library, p. 36.

AINSWORTH DAVIS (J. R.) and H. J. FLEURE, B.Sc.
Patella (the Common Limpet). With 4 Plates. 2s. 6d. net.
See Liverpool Marine Biology Committee Memoirs, p. 42.

ALLIN (Rev. THOS.). Universalism asserted as the Hope
of the Gospel on the Authority of Reason, the Fathers, and Holy
Scripture. With a Preface by Edna Lyall, and a Letter from Canon
Wilberforce. Crown 8vo, cloth. 2s. 6d. net.

ALVIELLA (Count GOBLET D'). Lectures on the Origin
and the Growth of the Conception of God, as Illustrated by Anthropology and History. Translated by the Rev. P. H. Wicksteed.
Hibbert Lectures, 1891. Cloth, Library Edition, 10s. 6d. Popular
Edition, 3s. 6d.

ANDREWS (CHARLES M'LEAN, Ph.D., L.H.D.). The
Colonial Period. F'cap. 8vo, cloth. 2s. 6d. net.

ANGLICAN LIBERALISM. By Twelve Churchmen. Rev.
Hubert Handley, Prof. F. C. Burkitt, M.A., D.D., Rev. J. R.
Wilkinson, M.A., Rev. C. R. Shaw Stewart, M.A., Rev. Hastings
Rashdall, D.Litt., D.C.L., Prof. Percy Gardner, D.Litt., LL.D.,
Sir C. T. Dyke Acland, Rev. A. J. Carlyle, M.A., Rev. H. G. Woods,
D.D., Rev. A. A. Caldcott, D.Litt., D.D., Rev. W. D. Morrison,
LL.D., Rev. A. L. Lilley, M.A. Crown 8vo, cloth. 4s. 6d. net.

ARNOLD (JAMES LORING, Ph.D.). The Motor and the
Dynamo. 8vo, pages vi + 178. With 166 Figures. 6s. 6d. net.

ASHWORTH (J. H., D.Sc.). Arenicola (the Lug-Worm).
With 8 Plates. 4s. 6d. net. *See* Liverpool Marine Biology Committee Memoirs, p. 42.

AVEBURY (Lord, D.C.L., F.R.S.). Prehistoric Times, as
Illustrated by Ancient Remains and the Manners and Customs
of Modern Savages. Seventh Edition, completely revised by the
author just prior to his decease, and containing much new material
and many new Illustrations of important recent discoveries. Large
demy 8vo, cloth. With 3 Illustrations in colour and nearly 300
other Illustrations. 10s. 6d. net.

BACON (Professor B. W., LL.D., D.D.). The Making of the
New Testament. F'cap. 8vo, cloth, 1s. net; leather, 2s. 6d. net.
Forming Vol. 56 in the Home University Library; for list, *see* p. 39.

BACON (ROGER), the "Opus Majus" of. Edited, with Introduction and Analytical Table, by John Henry Bridges, Fellow of Royal College of Physicians, sometime Fellow of Oriel College. Complete in 3 vols., 31s. 6d.; Vol. III. sold separately, 7s. 6d.

BAILEY (JOHN, M.A.). Dr Johnson and his Circle. F'cap. 8vo, cloth, 1s. net; leather, 2s. 6d. Forming Vol. 64 in Home University Library; for list, see p. 39.

BALSILLIE (DAVID, M.A.). An Examination of Professor Bergson's Philosophy. Crown 8vo, cloth. 5s. net.

BARRETT (Sir W. F., F.R.S.). Psychical Research. F'cap. 8vo, cloth, 1s. net; leather, 2s. 6d. net. Forming Vol. 28 in the Home University Library; for list, see p. 39.

BARRY (WILLIAM, D.D.). The Papacy and Modern Times (1303-1870). F'cap. 8vo, cloth, 1s. net; leather, 2s. 6d. net. Forming Vol. 14 in the Home University Library; for list, see p. 39.

BAUR (F. C.). Church History of the First Three Centuries. Translated from the Third German Edition. Edited by Rev. Allan Menzies. 2 vols. 8vo, cloth. 12s.

—— **Paul, the Apostle of Jesus Christ, his Life and Work,** his Epistles and Doctrine. A Contribution to a Critical History of Primitive Christianity. Edited by Rev. Allan Menzies. 2nd Edition. 2 vols. 8vo, cloth. 12s.

BAYLEY (HAROLD). The Lost Language of Symbolism. With above 1400 Symbols. 2 vols. Medium 8vo, cloth. 25s. net.

BEARD (Rev. Dr C.). Lectures on the Reformation of the Sixteenth Century in its Relation to Modern Thought and Knowledge. Hibbert Lectures, 1883. 8vo, cloth. 10s. 6d. Cheap Edition. 3rd Edition, 3s. 6d.

—— **The Universal Christ, and other Sermons.** Crown 8vo, cloth. 7s. 6d.

BEGBIE (HAROLD). See "Character and Life," p. 5.

BELLOC (HILAIRE, M.A.). The French Revolution. (With Maps.) F'cap. 8vo, cloth, 1s. net; leather, 2s. 6d. net. Forming Vol. 3 in the Home University Library; for list, see p. 39.

—— **Warfare in England.** (With Maps.) F'cap. 8vo, cloth, 1s. net; leather, 2s. 6d. net. Vol. 51 in the Home University Library; for list, see p. 39.

BENEDICT (F. E., Ph.D.). Elementary Organic Analysis. Small 8vo. Pages vi + 82. 15 Illustrations. 4s. 6d. net.

BENNETT (E. N., M.A.). Problems of Village Life. F'cap. 8vo, cloth, 1s. net; leather, 2s. 6d. net. Forming Vol. 81 in the Home University Library; for list, see p. 39.

BERGEY (D. G.). Handbook of Practical Hygiene. Small 8vo. Pages v + 164. 6s. 6d. net.

BEVAN (Rev. J. O., M.A., F.G.S.). The Genesis and Evolu- tion of the Individual Soul scientifically Treated. Including also Problems relating to Science and Immortality. Crown 8vo, cloth. 2s. 6d. net.

BIBLE. Translated by Samuel Sharpe, being a Revision of the Authorised English Version. 6th Edition of the Old, 10th Edition of the New Testament. 8vo, roan. 5s.

BILTZ (HENRY). The Practical Methods of determining Molecular Weights. Translated by Jones. Small 8vo. Pages viii + 245. 44 Illustrations. 8s. 6d. net.

BLACKBURN (HELEN). Women's Suffrage. A Record of the Women's Suffrage Movement in the British Isles, with a Biographical Sketch of Miss Becker. With portraits. Crown 8vo, cloth. 6s.

BOÏELLE (JAS.). French Composition through Lord Macaulay's English. Edited, with Notes, Hints, and Introduction, by the late James Boïelle, B.A. (Univ. Gall.), Officier d'Académie, Senior French Master, Dulwich College, etc., etc. Crown 8vo, cloth. Vol. I. Frederick the Great. 3s. Vol. II. Warren Hastings. 3s. Vol. III. Lord Clive. 3s.

—— *See* Victor Hugo, " Les Misérables " and " Notre Dame."

BOLTON. History of the Thermometer. 12mo. 96 pages. 6 Illustrations. 4s. 6d. net.

BOUSSET (Prof. WILHELM). Jesus. Trans. by Janet Penrose Trevelyan, and ed. by Rev. W. D. Morrison, LL.D. Cr. 8vo. 3s. 6d. net. Forming Vol. 14 in the Cr. Theological Library ; *see* p. 36.

BOUTROUX (EMILE). Education and Ethics. Authorised Translation by Fred. Rothwell. Crown 8vo, cloth. 5s. net.

BRADLEY (A. G.). Canada. F'cap. 8vo, cloth, 1s. net ; leather, 2s. 6d. net. Forming Vol. 34 in the Home University Library ; *see* list, p. 39.

BRAILSFORD (H. N.). Shelley, Godwin, and their Circle. F'cap. 8vo, cloth, 1s. net ; leather, 2s. 6d. net. Forming Vol. 77 in the Home University Library ; for list, *see* p. 39.

BRAUNS (Dr REINHARD). The Mineral Kingdom. The author is the well-known Professor of Mineralogy in the University of Bonn. Translated with additions by L. J. Spencer, M.A., F.G.S., Assistant in the Mineral Department of the British Museum. In demy 4to, comprising 91 full-page plates beautifully executed in colours, 73 of which are chromo-lithographs, 18 photographic reproductions, and 275 figures in the text. Bound in half-morocco. £2, 16s. net.

BREMOND (HENRI). The Mystery of Newman. With Introduction by the late Rev. George Tyrrell, M.A. Medium 8vo, cloth. 10s. 6d. net.

BREWSTER (H. B.). The Theories of Anarchy and of Law. A Midnight Debate. Crown 8vo, parchment. 5s.

—— **The Prison.** A Dialogue. Crown 8vo, parchment. 5s.

—— **The Statuette and the Background.** Cr. 8vo, parchment. 4s.

BREWSTER (Prof. W. T.), Editor of the Home University Library ; for list, *see* p. 39.

—— **The Writing of English.** F'cap. 8vo, cloth, 1s. net ; leather, 2s. 6d. net. Forming Vol. 73 in Home University Library ; for list, *see* p. 39.

BRIDGES (JOHN HENRY, M.B., F.R.C.P.). **The life and** Work of Roger Bacon. Being an Introduction to the *Opus Majus.* Edited with Additional Notes and Tables by H. Gordon Jones, F.I.C., F.C.S.

BRUCE (ALEX., M.A., M.D., F.R.C.P.E.). **A Topographical** Atlas of the Spinal Cord. F'cap. folio, half-leather. £2, 2s. net.

BRUCE (Dr W. S., F.R.S.E.). **Polar Exploration.** (With Maps.) F'cap. 8vo, cloth, 1s. net; leather, 2s. 6d. net. Forming Vol. 8 in the Home University Library; for list, *see* p. 39.

BURKITT (Prof. F. C.). **Euphemia and the Goth.** With the Acts of Martyrdom of the Confessors of Edessa. 21s. net. *See* Text and Translation Society, p. 43.

BURY (Prof. J. B., Litt.D.). **A History of Freedom of** Thought. F'cap. 8vo, 1s. net; leather, 2s. 6d. net. Forming Vol. 74 in Home University Library; for list, *see* p. 39.

CAMERON(FRANK K.). **The Soil Solution: the Nutrient** Medium for Plant Growth. 8vo, cloth. 3 illustrations. 6s. 6d. net.

CAMPBELL (Rev. COLIN, D.D.). **The First Three Gospels** in Greek. Arranged in parallel columns. 2nd Edition, Revised. Crown 8vo, cloth. 3s. 6d. net.

CARPENTER (Rt. Rev. W. BOYD). **Some Pages of My** Life. By the present Canon of Westminster and late Bishop of Ripon. With portrait of the author as frontispiece, and other interesting portraits. Medium 8vo, cloth, gilt top. 15s. net.

—— **The Spiritual Message of Dante.** With illus. Cloth. 5s. net.

CARPENTER (Prof. J. E., LL.D.). **Comparative Religion.** F'cap. 8vo, cloth, 1s. net; leather, 2s. 6d. net. Forming Vol. 68 in Home University Library; for list, *see* p. 39.

CARTWRIGHT (Captain) and His Labrador Journal. Edited by Charles Wendell Townsend, M.D. With an Introduction by Dr Wilfred T. Grenfell. With Illustrations from old engravings, photographs and a map. Crown 8vo, cloth. 5s. net.

CATALOGUE DE LA BIBLIOTHEQUE DE L'IN-STITUT NOBEL NORVEGIEN. 250 pp. Sewed, 10s. net.

CECIL (Lord HUGH, M.A., M.P.). **Conservatism.** F'cap. 8vo, cloth, 1s. net; leather, 2s. 6d. net. Forming Vol. 11 in the Home University Library; for list, *see* p. 39.

CHADWICK (HERBERT CLIFTON). **Antedon.** With 7 Plates. 2s. 6d. net. *See* Liverpool Marine Biology Memoirs, p. 42.

—— **Echinus.** With 5 Plates. Price 2s. net. *See* Liverpool Marine Biology Memoirs, p. 42.

CHANNING'S COMPLETE WORKS. Including "The Perfect Life," with a Memoir. Centennial Ed. 4to Ed. Cloth. 7s. 6d.

CHAPMAN (Prof. S. J., M.A.). **Elements of Political** Economy. F'cap. 8vo, cloth, 1s. net; leather, 2s. 6d. net. Forming Vol. 59 in the Home University Library; for list, *see* p. 39.

CHARACTER AND LIFE: A Symposium. By Dr Alfred Russel Wallace, John A. Hobson, Harold Begbie, Walter Crane, and the late Dr Emil Reich. Arranged by Percy L. Parker, Editor of "Public Opinion." Crown 8vo, cloth. 3s. 6d. net.

CHESTERTON (G. K.). The Victorian Age in Literature. F'cap. 8vo, cloth, 1s. net; leather, 2s. 6d. net. Forming Vol. 70 in Home University Library; for list, *see* p. 39.

CHEYNE (Rev. T. K., D.Litt., D.D.). Bible Problems and the New Material for their Solution. A Plea for Thoroughness of Investigation, addressed to Churchmen and Scholars. Crown 8vo. 4s. 6d. net. *See* Crown Theological Library, p. 36.

CHILD AND RELIGION, THE. Essays. By Prof. Henry Jones, M.A., LL.D., University of Glasgow ; C. F. G. Masterman, M.A.; Prof. George T. Ladd, D.D., LL.D. ; Rev. F. R. Tennant, M.A., B.Sc.; Rev. J. Cynddylan Jones, D.D. ; Rev. Canon Hensley Henson, M.A. ; Rev. Robert F. Horton, M.A., D.D. ; Rev. G. Hill, M.A., D.D.; Rev. J. J. Thornton; Rev. Rabbi A. A. Green; Prof. Joseph Agar Beet, D.D. Edited by Thomas Stephens, B.A. Crown 8vo. 5s. net. *See* Crown Theological Library, p. 36.

CLARKE (CHARLES BARON, F.R.S.). Illustrations of Cyperaceæ. Royal 8vo, cloth. 12s. 6d. net.

COFFEY (GEORGE). Guide to the Celtic Antiquities of the Christian Period preserved in the National Museum, Dublin. Second Edition, with 19 Plates and 114 illustrations. Sewed, 2s. net ; cloth, 3s. net.

—— **New Grange (Brugh na Boinne) and other Incised** Tumuli in Ireland. With 9 Plates and 95 Illustrations. Cloth, 6s. net.

COIT (STANTON, Ph.D.). National Idealism and a State Church. Demy 8vo, cloth. 7s. 6d. net.

—— **National Idealism and the Book of Common Prayer.** An Essay in Re-Interpretation and Revision. Demy 8vo, cloth. 10s. 6d. net.

COLBY (ALBERT LADD). Reinforced Concrete in Europe. Demy 8vo, cloth. 14s. 6d. net.

COLE (FRANK J.), and JAMES JOHNSTONE. Pleuro- nectes. With 11 Plates. 7s. net. *See* Liverpool Marine Biology Memoirs, p. 42.

COLLINS (F. H.). An Epitome of Synthetic Philosophy. With a Preface by Herbert Spencer. 5th Edition. The Synthetic Philosophy Completed. 8vo, cloth. Reduced to 5s. net.

COMMON PRAYER FOR CHRISTIAN WORSHIP : In Ten Services for Morning and Evening. 32mo, cloth, 1s. 6d.; 8vo, cloth, 3s. ; with Anthems, 4s.

CONNOLLY (DOM. R. H.), and H. W. CODRINGTON. Two Commentaries on the Jacobite Liturgy. See Text and Translation Society, p. 43.

CONYBEARE (F. C., M.A.). The Ring of Pope Xystus: a collection of Aphorisms and Short Sayings in use among Christian Communities in the Second Century. Beautifully printed on hand-made paper. 4s. 6d. net.

—— Edited by. **An Ancient Armenian Version of the Apoca-** lypse of St John: also the Armenian Texts of Cyril of Alexandria, Scholia de Incarnatione, and Epistle to Theodosius upon Easter. *See* Text and Translation Society, p. 43.

CORNILL (Prof. CARL). The Introduction to the Canoni- cal Books of the Old Testament. Demy 8vo, cloth. 10s. 6d. net. *See* Theological Translation Library, p. 44.

CRANE (WALTER), contributor to "Character and Life," *see* p. 5.

CREIGHTON (Mrs). Missions: their Rise and Develop- ment. F'cap. 8vo, cloth, 1s. net; leather, 2s. 6d. net. Forming Vol. 60 in the Home University Library; for list, *see* p. 39.

CREIGHTON (CHAS., M.D.). Cancer and other Tumours of the Breast. Researches showing their true seat and cause. The Author was sometime Demonstrator of Anatomy, Cambridge Medical School, and is the author of "Bovine Tuberculosis in Man," etc. With 24 Lithographic Plates containing 138 figures from the Author's drawings. Royal 8vo, cloth. 12s. 6d. net.

—— **Contributions to the Physiological Theory of Tuber-** culosis. Royal 8vo, cloth. 12s. 6d. net.

CUSSANS (MARGARET, B.Sc.). Gammarus. With 4 Plates. 2s. net. *See* Liverpool Marine Biology Memoirs, p. 43.

DAKIN (W. J., M.Sc.). Pecton. With 9 Plates. 4s. 6d. net. *See* Liverpool Marine Biology Memoirs, p. 43.

DARBISHIRE (OTTO V.). Chondrus. With 7 Plates. 2s. 6d. net. *See* Liverpool Marine Biology Memoirs, p. 42.

DAUDET (A.). Contes Militaires. 2s. 6d. *See* Army Series, p. 35.

DAVENPORT (CHARLES BENEDICT). Heredity in relation to Eugenics. The Author is Director, Department of Experimental Evolution, Cold Spring Harbour, Long Island, N.Y.; Secretary of the Eugenics Section American Breeders' Association. With Diagrams and Coloured Plate. Demy 8vo, cloth. 8s. 6d. net.

DAVIDS (Mrs RHYS, M.A.). Buddhism. F'cap. 8vo, cloth, 1s. net; leather, 2s. 6d. net. Forming Vol. 47 in the Home University Library; for list, *see* p. 39.

DAVIDS (T. W. RHYS). Lectures on Some Points in the History of Indian Buddhism. The Hibbert Lectures, 1881. 2nd Ed. Demy 8vo, cloth. Library Ed., 10s. 6d. Cheap Ed., 3s. 6d.

DAVIS (H. W. C., M.A.). Mediæval Europe. (With Maps.) F'cap. 8vo, cloth, 1s. net; leather, 2s. 6d. net. Forming Vol. 13 in the Home University Library; for list, *see* p. 39.

DELBOS (L.). Nautical Terms in English and French and French and English. With Notes and Tables. For the use of Naval Officers and Naval Cadets. By Leon Delbos, M.A. 4th Edition, with additional Plates. Cloth. 7s. 6d. net.

—— **The Student's Graduated French Reader.** Remodelled and rewritten. Edited, with Notes and a Complete Vocabulary. First Year—Part I. Anecdotes, Tales, and Exercises. Part II. Tales, Historical Pieces, and Exercises. 1s. 6d. each.

DELITZSCH (Dr FRIEDRICH). Babel and Bible. Authorised Translation. Edited, by Rev. C. H. W. Johns. 4s. 6d. net. See Crown Theological Library, p. 36.

DEWALL (JOHANNES V.). Auf Verlornem Posten and Nazzarena Danti. 3s. See Army Series, p. 35.

DIBBLEE (G. BINNEY). The Newspaper. F'cap. 8vo, cloth, 1s. net; leather, 2s. 6d. net. Forming Vol. 69 in the Home University Library; for list, see p. 39.

DICKSON (H. N., D.Sc.). Climate and Weather. F'cap. 8vo, cloth, 1s. net; leather, 2s. 6d. net. Forming Vol. 36 in the Home University Library; for list, see p. 39.

DIGGLE (Rt. Rev. J. W., D.D.) The Foundations of Duty or, Man's Duty to God, His Fellowmen, and Himself. Crown 8vo, cloth, 3s. 6d. net.

DILLMANN (A.). Ethiopic Grammar. Trans. from C. Bezold's Second German Edition. By Rev. J. A. Crichton, D.D. With Index of Passages, Philological Tables, etc. 1 vol., royal 8vo. 25s. net.

DÎPAVAMSA (THE): A Buddhist Historical Record in the Pali Language. Edited, with an English Translation, by Dr H. Oldenberg. 8vo, cloth. 21s.

DOBSCHÜTZ (ERNST VON, D.D.). Christian Life in the Primitive Church. The Author is Professor of New Testament Theology in the University of Strassburg. Translated by Rev. G. Bremner, and edited by the Rev. W. D. Morrison, LL.D. Demy 8vo, cloth. 10s. 6d. See Theological Translation Library, New Series, p. 44.

DOLE (CHARLES F.). The Ethics of Progress, or the Theory and the Practice by which Civilisation proceeds. Small demy 8vo, cloth. 6s. net.

DRUMMOND (Dr JAMES, LL.D.). Philo Judæus; or, The Jewish Alexandrian Philosophy in its Development and Completion. 2 vols. 8vo, cloth. 21s.

—— **Via, Veritas, Vita.** Lectures on Christianity in its most Simple and Intelligible Form. Hibbert Lectures, 1894. Demy 8vo. Library Edition, 10s. 6d. Cheap Edition, 3s. 6d.

DUNCAN (DAVID, LL.D.). The Life and Letters of Herbert Spencer. With 17 Illustrations. Cheap Re-issue. 6s. net.

EMERY (F. B., M.A.). Elementary Chemistry. With numerous Illustrations. 8s. 6d. net.

ENGELHARDT (V.).   The Electrolysis of Water.   8vo.
Pages x + 140. 90 Illustrations. 5s. net.

ENGLAND AND GERMANY. By Leaders of Public Opinion
in both Empires, among whom may be mentioned :—Rt. Hon.
Arthur J. Balfour, Viscount Haldane of Cloan, Rt. Hon. A. Bonar
Law, Baron Alfred von Rothschild, Rt. Hon. Herbert Samuel,
Sir Rufus Isaacs, Norman Angell, J. Ramsay MacDonald, M.P.,
J. A. Spender, Excell. Karl Galster, Ernst Basserman, Professor Dr
Riesser, Baron Wilhelm von Pechmann, Professor Wilhelm Wundt,
Dr Walther Rathenau, August Thyssen, sen., His Excellency
Dr Adolf Wermuth, Excell. von Holleben, etc. With Portraits.
Stiff Wrapper. 1s. net.

ERSKINE (Prof. J.) and Prof. W. P. TRENT. Great
Writers of America. F'cap. 8vo, cloth, 1s. net ; leather, 2s. 6d. net.
Forming Vol. 52 in the Home University Library ; for list, *see* p. 39.

EUCKEN (Dr RUDOLF, Jena). Knowledge and Life. Cloth,
5s. net. *See* Crown Theological Library, p. 36.

—— Present Day Ethics and their Relation to the Spiritual
Life. Cloth. 3s. net. *See* Crown Theological Library, p. 37.

—— The Life of the Spirit. An Introduction to Philosophy.
Fourth Impression. 8vo, cloth. 4s. 6d. net. *See* Crown
Theological Library, p. 36.

—— The Truth of Religion. Translated from the latest revised
German edition by Rev. W. Tudor Jones, Ph.D., with a special
preface by the Author. Second Edition. Demy 8vo, cloth.
12s. 6d. net. *See* Theological Translation Library, New Series, p. 44.

EUGÈNE-FASNACHT (G.). Eugène's Student's Comparative Grammar of the French Language, with an Historical Sketch of
the Formation of French. The Author was for many years French
Master, Westminster School. For the use of Public Schools.
With Exercises. 23rd Edition, thoroughly revised. Square crown
8vo, cloth, 5s. ; or separately, Grammar, 3s. ; Exercises, 2s. 6d.

—— French Method. Elementary French Lessons preparatory to the
same Author's Grammar. 18th Edition. Cloth. 1s. 6d.

EVANS (GEORGE). An Essay on Assyriology. With 4to
Tables of Assyrian Inscriptions. 8vo, cloth. 5s.

EWALD'S (Dr H.) Commentary on the Prophets of the
Old Testament. Translated by the Rev. J. F. Smith. [Vol. I.
General Introduction, Yoel, Amos, Hosea, and Zakharya 9–11.
Vol. II. Yesaya, Obadya, and Mikah. Vol. III. Nahûm,
Ssephanya, Habaqqûq, Zakhârya, Yéremya. Vol. IV. Hezekiel,
Yesaya xl.–lxvi. Vol. V. Haggai, Zakharya, Malaki, Jona, Baruc,
Daniel, Appendix and Index.] 5 vols. 8vo, cloth. 30s. *See*
Theological Translation Library, Old Series, p. 45.

—— Commentary on the Psalms. Translated by the Rev. E.
Johnson, M.A. 2 vols. 8vo, cloth. 12s.

—— Commentary on the Book of Job, with Translation. Trans.
from the German by the Rev. J. Frederick Smith. 8vo, cloth. 6s.

FAGUET (Prof. EMILE, of the French Academy). Initiation into Philosophy. Translated by Sir Home Gordon, Bart. Crown 8vo, cloth. 2s. 6d. net.
—— **Initiation into Literature.** Translated by Sir Home Gordon, Bart. Cloth. 3s. 6d. net.

FARMER (Prof. J. B.). Plant Life. (Illustrated.) F'cap. 8vo, cloth, 1s. net; leather, 2s. 6d. net. Forming Vol. 72 in Home University Library; for list, *see* p. 39.

FARNELL (L. R., D.Litt.). The Evolution of Religion: an Anthropological Study. Crown 8vo, cloth. 4s. 6d. net. *See* Crown Theological Library, p. 36.
—— **The Higher Aspects of Greek Religion.** Lectures delivered in Oxford and London. Being Vol. 1 of New Series of Hibbert Lectures. Demy 8vo, cloth. 6s. net. *See* Hibbert Lectures, p. 38.

FARQUHARSON (Rt. Hon. ROBERT, LL.D.). The House of Commons from Within, and other Reminiscences. Med. 8vo. With Portrait by J. S. Sargent, R.A., never before published. 7s. 6d. net.

FARRIE (HUGH). Highways and Byways in Literature. A volume of original Studies. Demy 8vo, cloth. 5s. net.

FINDLAY (Prof. J. J., M.A., Ph.D.). The School. An Introduction to the Study of Education. F'cap. 8vo, cloth, 1s. net; leather, 2s. 6d. net. Forming Vol. 38 in the Home University Library; for list, *see* p. 39.

FISCHER (Prof. EMIL, of Berlin University). Introduction to the Preparation of Organic Compounds. Translated with the Author's sanction from the new German edition by R. V. Stanford, B.Sc., Ph.D. With figures in the text. Crown 8vo, cloth. 4s. net.

FISHER (HERBERT, M.A., F.B.A., LL.D.), Editor, Home University Library; for list, *see* p. 39.
—— **Napoleon.** (With Maps.) F'cap. 8vo, cloth, 1s. net; leather, 2s. 6d. net. Forming Vol. 61 in Home University Library; for list, *see* p. 39.

FOUR GOSPELS (THE) AS HISTORICAL RECORDS. 8vo, cloth. 15s.

FOWLER (W. WARDE, M.A.). Rome. F'cap. 8vo, cloth, 1s. net; leather, 2s. 6d. net. Forming Vol. 42 in the Home University Library; for list, *see* p. 40.

FOX (FRANK), Author of "Ramparts of Empire," etc. Problems of the Pacific. Demy 8vo, cloth. With Map. 7s. 6d. net.

FRAPS (G. S., Ph.D.). Principles of Agricultural Chemistry. 8vo. Pages x + 140. 90 Illustrations. 17s. net.

FRY (The Rt. Hon. Sir EDWARD, G.C.B., etc.). Some In- timations of Immortality. From the Physical and Psychical Nature of Man. Royal 8vo, sewed. 1s. net.

GAMBLE (Prof. F. W., D.Sc., F.R.S.). The Animal World. With Introduction by Sir Oliver Lodge. Many Illustrations. F'cap. 8vo, cloth, 1s. net; leather, 2s. 6d. net. Forming Vol. 19 in the Home University Library; for list, *see* p. 39.

GARDNER (Prof. PERCY, D.Litt., F.B.A., Oxford). **Modernity** and the Churches. 4s. 6d. net. *See* Crown Theological Library, p. 36.

—— **The Religious Experience of St Paul.** Crown 8vo, cloth. 5s. net. *See* Crown Theological Library, p. 36.

GELDART (W. M., M.A., B.C.L.). **Elements of English Law.** F'cap. 8vo, cloth, 1s. net; leather, 2s. 6d. net. Forming Vol. 30 in the Home University Library; for list, *see* p. 39.

GIBBS (PHILIP). The Eighth Year. The Dangerous Year of Marriage. Crown 8vo, cloth. 2s. net.

GIBSON (R. J. H.) and **HELEN P. AULD,** B.Sc. **Codium.** With 3 Plates. Price 1s. 6d. net. *See* Liverpool Marine Biology Memoirs, p. 42.

GILES (H. A., LL.D.). **The Civilisation of China.** By the well-known Professor of Chinese in the University of Cambridge. F'cap. 8vo, cloth, 1s. net; leather, 2s. 6d. net. Forming Vol. 25 in the Home University Library; for list, *see* p. 40.

GILL (CHARLES). The Book of Enoch the Prophet. Trans. from an Ethiopic MS. in the Bodleian Library, by the late Richard Laurence, LL.D., Archbishop of Cashel. The Text corrected from his latest Notes by Charles Gill. Re-issue, 8vo, cloth. 5s.

GILMAN (A. F.). A Laboratory Outline for Determinations in Quantitative Chemical Analysis. 88 pp. Cloth, 4s. net.

GIVEN (JOHN L.). Making a Newspaper. Cloth, above 300 pages. 6s. net.

GOMME (Sir LAURENCE L., F.S.A.). **London.** With number of Plates and other Illustrations. 7s. 6d. net.

GOOCH (G. P., M.A.). **The History of our Time, 1885-1913.** F'cap. 8vo, cloth, 1s. net; leather, 2s. 6d. net. Forming Vol. 23 in the Home University Library; for list, *see* p. 39.

GOULD (F. J.). Noble Pages from German History. Crown 8vo, cloth. Illustrated. 1s. 6d. net.

GRAVELY (F. H., M.Sc.). **Polychaet Larvae.** With 4 plates· 2s. 6d. net. *See* Liverpool Marine Biology Committee Memoirs, p. 42.

GRAY (Rev. H. B., D.D.). **The Public Schools and the** Empire. A plea for higher education in citizenship. Cloth. 6s. net.

GREEN (Rt. Rev. A. V., D.D., Bishop of Ballarat). **The** Ephesian Canonical Writings : Being the Moorhouse Lectures for 1910. Crown 8vo, cloth. 5s. net.

GREEN (Mrs J. R.). Irish Nationality. F'cap. 8vo, cloth, 1s. net; leather, 2s. 6d. net. Forming Vol. 6 in the Home University Library; for list, *see* p. 39.

GREGORY (Prof. J. W., F.R.S.). **The Making of the Earth.** (With 38 Maps and Figures.) F'cap. 8vo, cloth, 1s. net; leather, 2s. 6d. net. Forming Vol. 53 in the Home University Library; for list, *see* p. 41.

GRIEBEN'S ENGLISH GUIDES. Practical and handy ; size, suitable for the pocket, 6¼ + 4¼, and bound in cloth.

Switzerland. A practical guide with seven Maps. Cloth. 3s. net.

Norway and Copenhagen. With six Maps. Cloth. 3s. net.

Ostend and other Belgium Watering Places. With two Maps. Cloth. 1s. 6d. net.

Lakes of Northern Italy. With Maps. Cloth. 3s. net.

The Rhine. With Maps. Cloth. 3s. net.

North Sea Watering Places. Cloth. 3s. net.

Belgium. With Maps. Cloth. 3s. net.

Brussels and Antwerp. With Maps. Cloth. 1s. 6d. net.

Holland. With Maps. Cloth. 3s. net.

The Riviera. With Maps. Cloth. 3s. net.

Winter Sports in Switzerland. A practical guide for those visiting Switzerland in the winter. With Map. Cloth. 3s. net.

Dresden and Environs. With Maps. Cloth. 1s. 6d. net.

Munich and Environs. With Maps. Cloth. 1s. 6d. net.

Nuremburg and Rothenburg on the Tauber. With 2 Maps. 1s. 6d. net.

The Dolomites. With 3 Maps. 3s. net.

Naples and Capri. With 7 Maps and 3 Ground Plans. 1s.6d.net.

GUILD (F. N.). The Mineralogy of Arizona. Pp. 104. Illustrated. 4s. 6d. net.

GUPPY (H. B., M.B., F.R.S.E.). Studies in Seeds and Fruits. An Investigation with the Balance. Demy 8vo, cloth, nearly 600 pp. 15s. net.

GWYNN (Prof. John, D.D.). Remnants of the Later Syriac Versions of the Bible. 21s. net. *See* Text and Translation Society, p. 43.

HAERING (Prof. THEODOR). Ethics of the Christian Life. Translated by Rev. J. S. Hill, B.D., and edited by Rev. W. D. Morrison. Demy 8vo, cloth. 10s. 6d. net. *See* Theological Translation Library, New Series, p. 45.

HALLIGAN (JAMES EDWARD). Soil Fertility and Ferti- lisers. Author is Chemist in charge Louisiana State Experiment Station. With Illustrations and Tables. Demy 8vo, cloth. 14s. 6d. net.

—— **Fertility and Fertiliser Hints.** 8vo. Pages viii + 156. 12 Figures. 5s. 6d. net.

—— **Elementary Treatise on Stock Feeds and Feeding.** 8vo, cloth. 10s. 6d. net.

HANNAY (DAVID). The Navy and Sea Power. F'cap. 8vo, cloth, 1s. net ; leather, 2s. 6d. net. Forming Vol. 66 in Home University Library ; for list, *see* p. 39.

HANTZSCH (A.). Elements of Stereochemistry. Translated by Wolf. 12mo. Pages viii + 206. 26 Figures. 6s. 6d. net.

HARDY.   Elements of Analytical Geometry.   8vo.   Pages iv + 365.   163 Figures.   8s. 6d. net.

—— Infinitesimals and Limits.   Sm. 12mo, paper.   22 pp.   6 Figs. 1s. net.

HARNACK (ADOLF, D.D.).   The Acts of the Apostles. Being Vol. III. of Dr Harnack's New Testament Studies.   Crown 8vo, cloth.   5s. net.   Vol. 26 in the Crown Theological Library; for list, *see* p. 36.

—— Bible Reading in the Early Church.   Forming Vol. V. of New Testament Studies.   5s. net.   *See* Crown Theological Library, p. 37.

—— The Constitution and Law of the Church in the First Two Centuries.   Crown 8vo, cloth.   5s. net.   Vol. 31 in the Crown Theological Library, p. 37.

—— The Date of the Acts and of the Synoptic Gospels.   Cr. 8vo, cloth.   5s. net.   Forming Vol. IV. in Dr Harnack's New Testament Studies, and Vol. 33 in the Crown Theological Library, p. 37.

—— History of Dogma.   Translated from the Third German Edition. Edited by the late Rev. Prof. A. B. Bruce, D.D.   7 vols. 8vo, cloth, each 10s. 6d. ; half-leather, suitable for presentation, 12s. 6d. *See* Theological Translation Library, New Series, p. 44.

—— Letter to the "Preussische Jahrbücher" on the German Emperor's Criticism of Prof. Delitzsch's Lectures on "Babel and Bible." Translated into English by Thomas Bailey Saunders.   6d. net.

—— Luke, the Physician.   Translated by the Rev. J. R. Wilkinson, M.A.   Being Vol. I. of Dr Harnack's New Testament Studies. Crown 8vo, cloth.   5s. net.   *See* Crown Theological Library, p. 37.

—— The Mission and Expansion of Christianity in the First Three Centuries.   Second, revised and much enlarged Edition. 25s. net.   Forming Vols. 19 and 20 in Theological Translation Library, New Series ; *see* p. 44.

—— Monasticism : Its Ideals and History ; and The Confessions of St Augustine.   Two Lectures.   Translated into English by E. E. Kellet, M.A., and F. H. Marseille, Ph.D.   Crown 8vo, cloth.   3s. 6d. net.   Forming Vol. 28 in the Crown Theological Library, p. 37.

—— The Sayings of Jesus.   Being Vol. II. of Dr Harnack's New Testament Studies.   Crown 8vo, cloth.   5s. net.   Forming Vol. 23 in the Crown Theological Library, p. 37.

—— What is Christianity?   Translated by Thomas Bailey Saunders. Third and Revised Edition.   Crown 8vo.   4s. 6d. net.   Forming Vol. 5 in the Crown Theological Library, p. 36.

—— and Prof. W. HERRMANN, of Marburg.   Essays on the Social Gospel.   Crown 8vo, cloth.   4s. net.   Forming Vol. 18 in the Crown Theological Library, p. 36.

HARNACK (AXEL).   Introduction to the Elements of the Differential and Integral Calculus.   From the German.   Royal 8vo, cloth.   10s. 6d.

HARRIS (Prof. D. FRASER). Nerves. F'cap. 8vo, cloth, 1s. net; leather, 2s. 6d. net. Forming Vol. 79 in the Home University Library; for list, see p. 39.

HARRISON (JANE, LL.D., D. Litt.). Ancient Art and Ritual. F'cap. 8vo, cloth, 1s. net; leather, 2s. 6d. net. Forming Vol. 75 in Home University Library; for list, see p. 39.

HART (EDWARD, Ph.D.). Chemistry for Beginners. Sm. 12mo. Vol. I. **Inorganic.** Pages viii + 188. 55 Illustrations and 2 Plates. 4th Edition. 4s. 6d. net. Vol. II. **Organic.** Pages iv + 98. 11 Illustrations. 2s. net. Vol. III. **Experiments.** Separately. 60 pages. 1s. net.

—— **Second Year Chemistry.** Sm. 12mo. 165 pp. 31 Illus. 5s. net.

HARTLAND (EDWIN SYDNEY, F.S.A.). Ritual and Belief. Studies in the History of Religion. Demy 8vo, cloth. 10s. 6d. net.

HATCH (Rev. Dr). Lectures on the Influence of Greek Ideas and Usages upon the Christian Church. Edited by Dr Fairbairn. Hibbert Lectures, 1888. 3rd Edition. 8vo, cloth. 10s. 6d. Cheap Edition, 3s. 6d.

HAUSRATH (Prof. A.). History of the New Testament Times. The Time of the Apostles. Translated by Leonard Huxley. With a Preface by Mrs Humphry Ward. 4 vols. 8vo, cloth. 42s. (Uniform with the Theological Translation Library, Old Series.)

—— **History of the New Testament Times.** The Time of Jesus. Trans. by the Revs. C. T. Poynting and P. Quenzer. 2 vols. 8vo, cloth. 12s. See Theological Translation Library, Old Series, p. 45.

HAWORTH (PAUL LELAND). Reconstruction and Union, 1865–1912. F'cap. 8vo, cloth. 2s. 6d. net.

HEATH (FRANCIS GEORGE). Nervation of Plants. By the well-known Author of "Our Woodland Trees," "The Fern World," etc. Well Illustrated. Crown 8vo. 3s. 6d. net.

—— **All About Leaves.** Well Illustrated, some in colours. 4s. 6d. net.

HEBREW TEXTS, in large type for Classes: Genesis. 2nd Edition. 16mo, cloth. 1s. 6d. Psalms. 16mo, cloth. 1s. Isaiah. 16mo, cloth. 1s. Job. 16mo, cloth. 1s.

HEESS (J. K., Ph.C.). Practical Methods of the Iron and Steel Works Chemist. Pp. 60. Cloth. 4s. 6d. net.

HENSLOW (Rev. G.). The Vulgate; The Source of False Doctrine. Crown 8vo, cloth. 2s. 6d. net.

HERDMAN (W. A.). Ascidia. With 5 Plates. 2s. net. See Liverpool Marine Biology Committee Memoirs, p. 42.

HERFORD (Rev. R. TRAVERS). Christianity in Talmud and Midrash. Demy 8vo, cloth. 18s. net.

—— **Pharisaism: Its Aims and its Methods.** Crown 8vo, cloth. 5s. net. Forming Vol. 35 in the Crown Theological Library, p. 36.

HERRMANN (Prof. WILHELM). The Communion of the Christian with God. Trans. from the new German Ed. by Rev. J. S. Stanyon, M.A., and Rev. R. W. Stewart, B.D., B.Sc. Cr. 8vo, cloth. 4s. 6d. net. Forming Vol. 15 in Crown Theological Library, p. 36.

HERRMANN (Prof. WILHELM). Faith and Morals.
New Edition. Crown 8vo, cloth. 4s. 6d. net. Forming Vol. 6 in
the Crown Theological Library, p. 36.

HEWITT (C. GORDON, B.Sc.). **Ligia.** With 4 Plates. 2s. net.
See Liverpool Marine Biology Memoirs, p. 43.

HIBBERT JOURNAL: A Quarterly Review of Religion
Theology, and Philosophy. Edited by L. P. Jacks and G. Dawes
Hicks. In quarterly issues, 2s. 6d. net; or yearly volumes bound
in cloth, 12s. 6d. net. Annual Subscription, 10s. post free.

**HIBBERT JOURNAL SUPPLEMENT, 1909, entitled
JESUS OR CHRIST?** Containing 18 Essays by leading
Theologians and Thinkers. Super royal 8vo, cloth. 5s. net.

HICKSON (SYDNEY J., D.Sc., F.R.S.). **Alcyonium.** With
3 Plates. Price 1s. 6d. net. *See* Liverpool Marine Biology
Committee Memoirs, p. 42.

HILL (ARTHUR E., Ph.D.). **Qualitative Analysis.** 12mo,
cloth. 4s. 6d. net.

HINDS (J. I. D., Ph.D., LL.D.). **Qualitative Chemical**
Analysis. 8vo, cloth. Pages viii + 266. 8s. 6d. net.

HINKS (A. R., M.A.). **Astronomy.** F'cap. 8vo, cloth, 1s. net;
leather, 2s. 6d. net. Forming Vol. 31 in the Home University
Library; for list, *see* p. 40.

HIRST (F. W., M.A.). **The Stock Exchange.** F'cap. 8vo,
cloth, 1s. net; leather, 2s. 6d. net. Forming Vol. 5 in the Home
University Library; for list, *see* p. 39.

HOBHOUSE (Prof. L. T., M.A.). **Liberalism.** F'cap. 8vo,
cloth, 1s. net; leather, 2s. 6d. net. Forming Vol. 21 in the
Home University Library; for list, *see* p. 40.

HOBSON (J. A., M.A.). **The Science of Wealth.** F'cap. 8vo,
cloth, 1s. net; leather, 2s. 6d. net. Forming Vol. 16 in the Home
University Library; for list, *see* p. 40.

—— **Character and Life.** *See* p. 5.

HÖFER (E.). Erzählungen. 3s. *See* Army Series of French
and German Novels, p. 35.

HOFF (J. H. VAN'T). Studies in Chemical Dynamics. Re-
vised and enlarged by Dr Ernst Cohen, Assistant in the Chemical
Laboratory of the University of Amsterdam. Translated by
Thomas Ewan, M.Sc., Ph.D., Demonstrator of Chemistry in the
Yorkshire College, Leeds. Royal 8vo, cloth. 10s. 6d.

HOLDERNESS (Sir T. W., K.C.S.I.). **Peoples and Problems**
of India. The Author is Secretary of the Revenue, Statistics, and
Commerce Department of the India Office. F'cap. 8vo, cloth,
1s. net; leather, 2s. 6d. net. Forming Vol. 37 in the Home
University Library; *see* p. 39.

HOLLINS (DOROTHEA). The Quest. A Romance of Deliverance. Demy 8vo, cloth. 4s. 6d. net.

HOME UNIVERSITY LIBRARY OF MODERN KNOW-LEDGE. Every volume is specially written for this Library by a recognised authority of high standing. Each volume is complete and independent, but the series has been planned as a whole to form a comprehensive library of modern knowledge. The Library is published under the direction of Professor Gilbert Murray and Mr Herbert Fisher of Oxford, Professor J. Arthur Thomson of Aberdeen, and Professor William T. Brewster of New York. Each volume consists of 256 pages and is issued bound in cloth at 1s. net, or in leather, 2s. 6d. net. For list of volumes, see p. 39.

HORNELL (JAMES, F.L.S.). Report to the Government of Baroda on the Marine Zoology of Okhamandal in Kattiawar. With Supplementary Reports on Special Groups by other Zoologists. Demy 4to, cloth, with full-page Plates. Part I. 15s. net.

HOWE (J. L., Washington and Lee University). **Inorganic** Chemistry for Schools and Colleges. Being a Second Edition of "Inorganic Chemistry according to the Periodic Law." By F. P. Venable and J. L. Howe. Demy 8vo, cloth. 12s. 6d. net.

HUGO (VICTOR). Les Misérables: Les Principaux Episodes. Edited, with Life and Notes, by the late J. Boïelle. 2 vols. 6th Edition. Crown 8vo, cloth. Each 3s.

—— **Notre Dame de Paris.** Adapted for the use of Schools and Colleges. By the late J. Boïelle. 2 vols. 2nd Edition. Crown 8vo, cloth. Each 3s.

HUNTER (Rev. J., D.D.). **De Profundis Clamavi, and** Other Sermons. Large crown 8vo, cloth. 5s. net.

—— **God and Life.** A Series of Discourses. Uniform with "De Profundis Clamavi." Cloth. 5s. net.

—— **The Coming Church.** A Plea for a Church simply Christian. Cloth. 1s. 6d. net.

ILBERT (Sir C. P., K.C.B.). **Parliament: its History, Con-**stitution, and Practice. F'cap. 8vo, cloth, 1s. net; leather, 2s. 6d. net. Forming Vol. 1 in Home University Library; for list, see p. 39.

IMMS (A. D., B.Sc. Lond.). **Anurida.** With 7 Plates. 4s. net. See Liverpool Marine Biology Memoirs, p. 43.

ISGROVE (ANNIE, M.Sc.). **Eledone.** With 10 Plates. 4s. 6d. net. See Liverpool Marine Biology Memoirs, p. 42.

JACKS (L. P.), Editor of the Hibbert Journal. **Mad Shepherds** and Other Human Studies. With a frontispiece drawing by Leslie Brooke. Crown 8vo, cloth. 4s. 6d. net.

—— **All Men are Ghosts.** 5s. net.

—— **Among the Idolmakers.** Crown 8vo, cloth. 5s. net.

—— **The Alchemy of Thought, and Other Essays.** Demy 8vo, cloth. 10s. 6d. net.

JEREMIAS (Prof. ALFRED). The Old Testament in the Light of the Ancient East. The Translation is edited by Professor C. H. W. Johns of Cambridge. With a large number of Illustrations. In two volumes, demy 8vo, at 25s. net. See Theological Translation Library, New Series, p. 45.

JOHNSTON (Sir H. H., K.C.B., D.Sc.). The Opening-up of Africa. (With Maps.) F'cap. 8vo, cloth, 1s. net; leather 2s. 6d. net. Forming Vol. 12 in the Home University Library; for list, *see* p. 39.

—— **Views and Reviews.** Essays on Racial, Political, and Colonial Questions. Crown 8vo, cloth. 3s. 6d. net.

JOHNSTONE (J.). British Fisheries: Their Administration and their Problems. A short account of the Origin and Growth of British Sea Fishery Authorities and Regulations. 10s. 6d. net.

—— **Cardium.** With 7 Plates. Price 2s. 6d. net. *See* Liverpool Marine Biology Memoirs, p. 42.

JONES. The Freezing Point, Boiling Point, and Conductivity Methods. 12mo. Pages vii + 64. 14 Illustrations. 3s. net.

JONES (Rev. R. CROMPTON). Hymns of Duty and Faith. Selected and Arranged. 247 pp. F'cap. 8vo, cloth. 2nd Edition. 3s. 6d.

—— **Chants, Psalms, and Canticles.** Selected and Pointed for Chanting. 18mo, cloth. 1s. 6d.

—— **Anthems.** With Indexes and References to the Music. 18mo, cloth. 1s. 3d.

—— **The Chants and Anthems.** Together in 1 vol. Cloth. 2s.

—— **A Book of Prayer.** In Thirty Orders of Worship, with Additional Prayers and Thanksgivings. 18mo, cloth. 2s. 6d. With Chants, in 1 vol. 18mo, cloth. 3s.

JONES (Rev. W. TUDOR, Ph.D.). An Interpretation of Rudolf Eucken's Philosophy. Crown 8vo. 5s. net.

JORDAN (DAVID STARR). The Stability of Truth. A Discussion of Reality as Related to Thought and Action. Crown 8vo, cloth. 3s. 6d. net.

JORDAN (HUMFREY R., B.A.). Blaise Pascal. A Study in Religious Psychology. Crown 8vo, cloth. 4s. 6d. net.

JOURNAL OF THE LINNEAN SOCIETY. Botany. At various prices. Index to Journal (Botany), 20s. **Zoology.** At various prices. General Index to the first 20 vols. of the Journal (Zoology) and the Zoological portion of the Proceedings, 20s.

JOURNAL OF THE QUEKETT MICROSCOPICAL CLUB. Nos. 1–26, 1s. net; Nos. 27–31, 2s. 6d. net. 1893, No. 32, and following Nos., half-yearly 3s. 6d. net.

JOURNAL OF THE ROYAL MICROSCOPICAL SOCIETY, containing its Transactions and Proceedings, with other Microscopical information. Bi-monthly. Previous to 1893 at various prices; after that date bi-monthly, each 6s. net.

KAPP (GISBERT, D.Eng., M.I.E.E., M.I.C.E.). Electricity. The Author is Professor of Electrical Engineering in the University of Birmingham. (Illustrated.) F'cap. 8vo, cloth, 1s. net; leather, 2s. 6d. net. Forming Vol. 58 in the Home University Library; *see* p. 41.

KAUFFMAN (RUTH and R. W.). The Latter Day Saints: A Study of the Mormons in the Light of Economic Conditions. Medium 8vo, cloth. 10s. 6d. net.

KAUTZSCH (E., Professor). **An Outline of the History of the** Literature of the Old Testament. With Chronological Tables for the History of the Israelites. Translated by John Taylor, D.Litt., M.A., etc. Demy 8vo, cloth. 6s. 6d.

KEIM'S History of Jesus of Nazara : Considered in its connection with the National Life of Israel, and related in detail. Translated from the German by Arthur Ransom and the Rev. E. M. Geldart. In 6 vols. Demy 8vo, cloth. 6s. each. *See* Theological Translation Fund Library, p. 46.

KEITH (A., M.D., LL.D.). **The Human Body.** The Author is Conservator of Museum and Hunterian Professor, Royal College of Surgeons. (Illustrated.) F'cap. 8vo, cloth, 1s. net ; leather, 2s. 6d. net. Forming Vol. 57, Home University Library ; for list, *see* p. 39.

—— **The Antiquity of Man.** With many Illustrations. 7s. 6d. net.

KENNEDY (Rev. JAS.). Introduction to Biblical Hebrew, presenting Graduated Instruction in the Language of the Old Testament. 8vo, cloth. 12s.

—— **Studies in Hebrew Synonyms.** Demy 8vo, cloth. 5s.

KER (Prof. W. P., M.A.). **English Literature : Mediæval.** F'cap. 8vo, cloth, 1s. net; leather, 2s. 6d. net. Forming Vol. 43 in the Home University Library ; for list, *see* p. 39.

KIEPERT'S Wall-Maps of the Ancient World— Wall-Map of Ancient Italy. Italia antiqua. For the study of Livy, Sallust, Cicero, Dionysius, etc. Scale 1 : 800,000. Mounted on rollers, varnished. 20s.

General Wall-Map of the Old World. Tabula orbis terrarum antiqui ad illustrandum potissimum antiquissimi ævi usque ad Alexandrum M. historiam. For the study of ancient history, especially the history of the Oriental peoples : the Indians, Medes, Persians, Babylonians, Assyrians, Egyptians, Phœnicians, etc. Scale 1 : 5,400,000. Mounted on rollers, varnished. 20s.

General Wall-Map of the Roman Empire. Imperii Romani tabula geographica. For the study of the development of the Roman Empire. Scale 1 : 300,000. Mounted on rollers, 24s.

Wall-Map of Ancient Latium. Latii Veteris et finitimarum regionum tabula. For the study of Livy, Dionysius, etc. Scale 1 : 125,000. With supplement : Environs of Rome. Scale 1 : 25,000. Mounted on rollers, varnished. 18s.

Wall-Map of Ancient Greece. Græciæ Antiquæ tabula. For the study of Herodotus, Thucydides, Xenophon, Strabo, Cornelius Nepos, etc. Scale 1 : 500,000. Mounted on rollers, varnished. 24s.

Wall-Map of the Empires of the Persians and of Alexander the Great. Imperia Persarum et Macedonum. For the study of Herodotus, Xenophon, Justinian, Arian, Curtius. Scale 1 : 300,000. Mounted on rollers and varnished. 20s.

KIEPERT'S Wall-Maps of the Ancient World—*continued.*

Wall-Map of Gaul, with Portions of Ancient Britain and Ancient Germany. Galliæ Cisalpinæ et Transalpinæ cum partibus Britanniæ et Germaniæ tabula. For the study of Cæsar, Justinian, Livy, Tacitus, etc. Scale 1 : 1,000,000. Mounted on rollers and varnished. 24s.

Wall-Map of Ancient Asia Minor. Asiæ Minoris Antiquæ tabula. For the study of Herodotus, Xenophon, Justinian, Arian, Curtius, etc. Scale 1 : 800,000. Mounted on rollers and varnished. 20s.

—— **New Atlas Antiquus.** Twelve Maps of the Ancient World, for Schools and Colleges. Third hundred thousand. 12th Edition, with a complete Geographical Index. Folio, boards. 6s. Strongly bound in cloth. 7s. 6d.

KING, THE, TO HIS PEOPLE. Being the Speeches and Messages of His Majesty George V. as Prince and Sovereign. Published by permission. Square 8vo, art canvas. 5s. net.

KITTEL (Dr RUDOLF, of Breslau**). A History of the Hebrews.** In 2 vols. 8vo, cloth. Each vol., 10s. 6d. Forming Vols. 3 and 6 of the Theological Translation Library, New Series; for list, *see* p. 44.

—— **The Scientific Study of the Old Testament:** Its Principal Results, and their Bearing upon Religious Instruction. Illus. 5s. net. Forming Vol. 32 in Crown Theological Library; for list, *see* p. 37.

KRAUSE (G.). Edited by. **Birds' Eggs.** Oologia universalis Palæarctica. Containing about 250 coloured plates with letterpress. English translation by O. G. Pike. To be completed in 150 parts, 4to, at 2s. net each part. Parts are not sold separately.

KRAYER (PETER J.). **The Use and Care of a Balance.** Small mo. Pages iv + 42. 3s. 6d. net.

KUENEN (Dr A., of Leiden**).** **The Religion of Israel to the** Fall of the Jewish State. Translated from the Dutch by A. H. May. 3 vols. 8vo, cloth. 18s. *See* Theological Translation Fund Library, p. 46.

—— **Lectures on National Religions and Universal Religion.** 8vo, cloth. 10s. 6d. Cheap Edition. 3s. 6d. *See* Hibbert Lectures, p. 38.

KYRIAKIDES (A.). **Modern Greek-English Dictionary.** With a Cypriote Vocabulary. 2nd Edition, revised throughout. Medium 8vo. 920 pages. Cloth. 15s. net.

—— **A Modern Greek-English and English-Modern Greek** Pocket Dictionary. In 2 vols., about 650 pp. each. 7s. net each vol.

—— **New Greek-English Dialogues.** 3s. 6d. net.

LAKE (KIRSOPP). **The Historical Evidence for the Resur-** rection of Jesus Christ. The Author is Professor of New Testament Exegesis in the University of Leiden, Holland. Crown 8vo, cloth. 4s. 6d. net. Forming Vol. 21 in the Crown Theological Library; *see* p. 36.

LAMMASCH (HEINRICH). Die Rechtskraft Internationaler Schiedsspruche. Vol. 4 of Publications de l'Institut Nobel Norvégien. 4to, sewed. 7s. 6d. net.

LANDOLT (Dr HANS). The Optical Rotating Power of Organic Substances and its Practical Applications. 8vo. Pages xxi + 751. 83 Illustrations. 31s. 6d. net.

LAURIE (Prof. SIMON). Ethica: or, The Ethics of Reason. By Scotus Novanticus. 2nd Edition. 8vo, cloth. 6s.

—— Metaphysica Nova et Vetusta: A Return to Dualism. 2nd Edition. Crown 8vo, cloth. 6s.

LEA (HENRY CHARLES, LL.D.). History of Sacerdotal Celibacy in the Christian Church. 3rd Edition. Thoroughly Revised and Reset. 2 vols. Medium 8vo, cloth. 21s. net.

LEAVENWORTH (Prof. W. S., M.Sc.). Inorganic Qualitative Chemical Analysis for Advanced Schools and Colleges. 8vo. Pages vi + 154. 6s. 6d. net.

LEBLANC (Dr MAX). The Production of Chromium and its Compounds by the Aid of the Electric Current. Demy 8vo, cloth. 5s. net.

LEIPOLDT (C. LOUIS, F.R.C.S. Eng.). Common - sense Dietetics. Strongly bound in Cloth. Crown 8vo. 2s. 6d. net.

LE ROY (EDOUARD). A New Philosophy: Henri Bergson. Translated by Vincent Benson, M.A. Crown 8vo, cloth. 5s. net.

LETHABY (Prof. W. R.). Architecture. Over 40 Illustrations. F'cap. 8vo, cloth, 1s. net; leather, 2s. 6d. net. Forming Vol. 39 in the Home University Library; for list, see page 40.

LEWIS (AGNES SMITH), Edited by. Old Syriac Gospels, or Evangelion Da-Mepharreshe. This is the Text of the Sinai Palimpsest, including the latest additions and emendations, with the variants of the Curetonian Text, corroborations from many other MSS., and a list of quotations from ancient authors. With 4 facsimiles. Quarto, bound half-leather. 25s. net.

—— Light on the Four Gospels from the Sinai Palimpsest. Cloth. 3s. 6d. net.

LLURIA (Dr ENRIQUE). Super-Organic Evolution. Nature and the Social Problem. With a Preface by Dr D. Santiago Ramon y Cajal. Large Crown 8vo. Illustrated. 7s. 6d. net.

LOBSTEIN (PAUL). The Virgin Birth of Christ: An Historical and Critical Essay. The Author is Professor of Dogmatics in the University of Strassburg. Edited, with an Introduction, by Rev. W. D. Morrison, LL.D. Crown 8vo. 2s. 6d. net. Forming Vol. 2 in the Crown Theological Library; for list, see p. 36.

LODGE (Sir O.). Life and Matter: An Exposition of Part of the Philosophy of Science, with Special References to the Influence of Professor Haeckel. Second Edition, with an Appendix of Definitions and Explanations. Crown 8vo, cloth. 2s. 6d. net. Popular Edition. Paper Cover. 6d. net.

—— School Teaching and School Reform. Four Lectures on School Curricula and Methods. 3s.

LONDON LIBRARY (St James's Square), **Catalogue of.** xiv + 1626 pages. 4to, bound in buckram. 42s. net. Supplements I.–VIII., bound in buckram, 5s. each.
—— **Subject Index.** 4to, bound in buckram. xxxviii + 1256 pages. 31s. 6d. net.

LONG (J. H.). A Text-book of Urine Analysis. Small 8vo. Pages v + 249. 31 Illustrations. 6s. 6d. net.

LORIA (ACHILLE). Les Bases Economiques de la Justice Internationale. 4to. 3s. 6d. net. Forming Vol. 2 of Publications de l'Institut Nobel Norvégien.

LYALL (Sir C. J., M.A., K.C.I.E.). Ancient Arabian Poetry, chiefly Præ-Islamic. Translations, with an Introduction and Notes. F'cap. 4to, cloth. 10s. 6d.

MACAN (R. W.). The Resurrection of Jesus Christ. An Essay in Three Chapters. 8vo, cloth. 5s.

MACAULAY (THOMAS BABINGTON). The Lays of Ancient Rome. With 8 Illustrations faithfully reproduced in colours, and a number in black-and-white, from original drawings by Norman Ault. Small 4to, cloth. 6s. net. Cheap Edition. 3s. 6d. net.

MACCOLL (HUGH). Man's Origin, Destiny, and Duty. Crown 8vo, cloth. 4s. 6d. net.

MACDONALD (J. RAMSAY, M.P.). The Socialist Move-ment. F'cap. 8vo, cloth, 1s. net; leather, 2s. 6d. net. Vol. 10 in the Home University Library; for list, see p. 37.

MACDONALD (WILLIAM). From Jefferson to Lincoln. F'cap. 8vo, cloth. 256 pp. 2s. 6d. net.

McDOUGALL (Prof. W., F.R.S., M.B.). Psychology: the Study of Behaviour. F'cap. 8vo, cloth, 1s. net; leather, 2s. 6d. net. Vol. 49 in the Home University Library; for list, see p. 41.

MACFIE (RONALD C., M.A., M.B.). Science, Matter, and Immortality. Crown 8vo, cloth. 5s. net.

MACGREGOR (Prof. D. H., M.A.). The Evolution of Industry. F'cap. 8vo, cloth, 1s. net; leather, 2s. 6d. net. Vol. 24 in the Home University Library; for list, see p. 40.

McKENDRICK (Prof. J. G., M.D.). The Principles of Physiology. F'cap. 8vo, cloth, 1s. net; leather, 2s. 6d. net. Vol. 44 in the Home University Library; for list, see p. 40.

MACKENZIE (W. LESLIE, M.D.). Health and Disease. F'cap. 8vo, cloth, 1s. net; leather, 2s. 6d. net. Forming Vol. 17 in the Home University Library; for list, see p. 40.

MAIR (G. H., M.A.). English Literature: Modern. F'cap. 8vo, cloth, 1s. net; leather, 2s. 6d. net. Forming Vol. 27 in the Home University Library; for list, see p. 40.
—— **English Literature.** A Survey from Chaucer to the Present Day. Illustrated. 6s. net.

MARETT (R. R., M.A., of Oxford). Anthropology. F'cap. 8vo, cloth, 1s. net; leather, 2s. 6d. net. Forming Vol. 41 in the Home University Library; for list, see p. 40.

MARGOLIOUTH (Prof. D. S., M.A., D.Litt.). **Mohamme-**danism. F'cap. 8vo, cloth, 1s. net; leather, 2s. 6d. net. Forming Vol. 15 in the Home University Library ; for list, see p. 40.
—— **Early Development of Mohammedanism.** *Vide* Hibbert Lectures, Second Series, p. 39.

MARKHAM (Sir CLEMENTS, K.C.B.). **Vocabularies of the** General Language of the Incas of Peru. Crown 8vo, cloth. 7s. 6d. net.

MARRINER (GEORGE R., F.R.M.S.). **The Kea: A New** Zealand Problem. With Illustrations. Demy 8vo, cloth. 7s. 6d. net.

MARTI (KARL, Professor of Old Testament Exegesis, Bern). **The** Religion of the Old Testament : Its Place among the Religions of the Nearer East. Crown 8vo, cloth, 4s. net. Forming Vol. 19 in the Crown Theological Library ; for list, see p. 36.

MARTINEAU (Mrs PHILIP). The Herbaceous Garden. Gives full particulars how to make and arrange hardy borders, and containing an alphabetical index of the most suitable plants. With a large number of illustrations and 2 plates in colour. Second Impression. Demy 8vo, cloth. 7s. 6d. net.

MARTINEAU (Rev. Dr JAMES). The Relation between Ethics and Religion. An Address. 8vo, sewed. 1s.
—— **Modern Materialism: Its Attitude towards Theology.** A Critique and Defence. 8vo, sewed. 2s. 6d.

MASEFIELD (JOHN). Shakespeare. F'cap. 8vo, cloth, 1s. net; leather, 2s. 6d. net. Forming Vol. 2 in the Home University Library ; for list, see p. 39.

MASON (W. P.). Notes on Qualitative Analysis. Sm. 12mo. 56 pp. 3s. 6d. net.

MATHIEU (C.). Para Rubber Cultivation. Manual of the Planter in Malasia. 4to, sewed. With Illustrations and Diagrams.

MEADE (RICHARD K., B.Sc.). **Chemist's Pocket Manual.** 16mo. Leather. Pocket Edition. Second Edition. 12s. 6d. net.
—— **Portland Cement: Its Composition, Raw Materials,** Manufacture, Testing, and Analysis. Second Edition. With 170 Illustrations. 20s. net.

MELDOLA (Prof. RAPHAEL, D.Sc., LL.D.). **Chemistry.** F'cap. 8vo, cloth, 1s. net ; leather, 2s. 6d. Forming Vol. 67 in Home University Library ; for list, see p. 41.

MELVILLE (HELEN and LEWIS). The Seasons. An Anthology in Prose and Verse. Forming an attractive volume, bound in art linen. 3s. 6d. net.

MERCER (Rt. Rev. J. EDWARD, D.D.). **The Soul of Pro-**gress. Being the Moorhouse Lectures for 1907. Cr. 8vo, cloth. 6s.

MERCIER (Dr C. A., F.R.C.P.). **Crime and Insanity.** F'cap. 8vo, cloth, 1s. net; leather, 2s. 6d. net. Forming Vol. 22 in the Home University Library ; for list, see p. 40.

MEREDITH (LEWIS B.). Rock Gardens. How to Make and Maintain them. With an Introduction by F. W. Moore, A.L.S., and an Alphabetical List of Plants suitable for the Rock Garden, with Notes on the aspect and soil they require. Second Edition. Demy 8vo, with Plates. 7s. 6d. net.

MERIMÉE (PROSPER). Le Coup de Pistolet, etc. 2s. 6d. *See* Army Series of French and German Novels, p. 35.

MIKAMI (YOSHIO). The Development of Mathematics in China and Japan. With 67 Figures in the Text. Royal 8vo, cloth. 19s. net.

MILINDAPAÑHO, THE. Being Dialogues between King Milinda and the Buddhist Sage Nāgasena. The Pali Text, edited by V. Trenckner. Crown 8vo, sewed. 21s.

MITCHELL(Rev. A. F.). How to Teach the Bible. 2nd Edition, thoroughly revised and reset. Cr. 8vo, cloth. 2s. 6d. net.

MITCHELL (Rev. C. W.). The Refutation of Mani, Marcion, and Bardaisan of St Ephraim. 21s. net. *See* Text and Translation Society, p. 43.

MOISSON (HENRI). The Electric Furnace. 8vo. Pages x + 305. 41 Illustrations. 10s. 6d. net.

MONTEFIORE (C. G.). Origin and Growth of Religion as Illustrated by the Religion of the Ancient Hebrews. The Hibbert Lectures, 1892. 2nd Edition. 8vo, cloth. 10s. 6d. Cheap Edition, 3s. 6d.

MOORE (Prof. BENJAMIN). The Origin and Nature of Life. F'cap. 8vo, cloth, 1s. net ; leather, 2s. 6d. net. Forming Vol. 62 in Home University Library ; for list, *see* p. 41.

MOORE (G. E., M.A.). Ethics. The Author is Lecturer in Moral Science in Cambridge University. F'cap. 8vo, cloth, 1s. net ; leather, 2s. 6d. net. Forming Vol. 54 in the Home University Library ; for list, *see* p. 41.

MOORE (Prof. George F.). The Literature of the Old Testa- ment. F'cap. 8vo, cloth, 1s. net ; leather, 2s. 6d. net. Forming Vol. 84 in the Home University Library ; for list, *see* p. 42.

MOULTON (Prof. J. H.). Early Zoroastrianism. Hibbert Lectures 1912. Cloth, 10s. 6d. net. *See* p. 39.

MUNRO (ROBERT, M.A., M.D., LL.D., F.R.S.E.). Prehistoric Britain. F'cap. 8vo, cloth, 1s. net ; leather, 2s. 6d. net. Forming Vol. 82 of the Home University Library ; for list, *see* p. 42.

MÜNSTERBERG (Prof. HUGO, of Harvard). The Ameri- cans. Translated by Edwin B. Holt, Ph.D., Instructor at Harvard University. Royal 8vo, cloth. 12s. 6d. net.

MURRAY (Prof. GILBERT, D.Litt., LL.D., F.B.A.), Editor of the Home University Library. For list, *see* p. 39.

—— **Euripides and his Age.** F'cap. 8vo, cloth, 1s. net ; leather, 2s. 6d. net. Forming Vol. 76 of the Home University Library ; for list, *see* p. 37.

MURRAY (Sir JOHN). The Ocean. A General Account of the Science of the Sea. F'cap. 8vo, cloth, 1s. net; leather, 2s. 6d. net. Forming Vol. 78 in the Home University Library; for list, *see* p. 42.

MYRES (J. L., M.A., F.S.A.). The Dawn of History. The Author is Wykeham Professor of Ancient History, Oxford. F'cap. 8vo, cloth, 1s. net; leather, 2s. 6d. net. Forming Vol. 29 in the Home University Library; for list, *see* p. 40.

NAVILLE (EDOUARD, Ph.D., Litt.D.). The Old Egyptian Faith. Translated by Colin Campbell, M.A., D.D. Illustrated. 4s. 6d. net. Vol. 30 in Crown Theological Lib.; for list, *see* p. 37.

NESTLE (Prof. EBERHARD, of Maulbronn). An Introduction to the Textual Criticism of the Greek New Testament. Translated from the Second Edition, with Corrections and Additions by the Author, by William Edie, B.D., and edited, with a Preface, by Allan Menzies, D.D., Professor of Divinity and Biblical Criticism in the University of St Andrews. With eleven reproductions of Texts. Demy 8vo, 10s. 6d.; half-leather, 12s. 6d. Forming Vol. 13 in the Theological Translation Library, New Series, p. 41.

NEWBIGIN (Dr MARION). Modern Geography. Illustrated. F'cap. 8vo, cloth, 1s. net; leather, 2s. 6d. net. Forming Vol. 7 in the Home University Library; for list, *see* p. 39.

NEW HEBREW SCHOOL OF POETS OF THE SPANISH-ARABIAN EPOCH. Selected Texts with Introduction, Notes, and Dictionary. Edited by H. Brodey, Ph.D., Rabbi in Lachod (Bohemia), and K. Albrecht, Ph.D., Professor in Oldenburg (Grand Duchy). English Translation of the Introduction, etc., by Mrs Karl Albrecht. Cloth. 7s. 6d. net.

NIBELUNGENLIED. "The Fall of the Nibelungens," otherwise "The Book of Kriemhild." An English Translation by W. N. Lettsom. 5th Edition. 8vo, cloth. 5s.

NIKAIDO (Y., B.Sc., M.A.). Beet-Sugar Making and its Chemical Control. With a number of valuable Tables and Illustrations. Demy 8vo, cloth. 12s. 6d. net.

NISSENSON. The Arrangements of Electrolytic Labora-tories. Demy 8vo. 52 Illustrations. 5s. net.

NOLDEKE (Prof. THEODOR). Compendious Syriac Gram-mar. With a Table of Characters by Julius Euting. Translated (with the sanction of the Author) from the Second and Improved German Edition by Rev. James A. Crichton, D.D. Royal 8vo. 18s. net.

—— **Delectus Veterum Carminum Arabicorum Glossarium** Confecit A. Muller. Crown 8vo, cloth. 7s. 6d.

NOYES (ARTHUR A., Ph.D.). Organic Chemistry for the Laboratory. Small 12mo. Pp. xii + 257. 22 Illus. 6s. 6d. net.

—— **and SAMUEL P. MULLIKEN, Ph.D. Laboratory** Experiments on Class Reactions and Identification of Organic Substances. 8vo. 81 pp. 2s. net.

O'GRADY (STANDISH H.). Silva Gadelica (I.–XXXI.). A Collection of Tales in Irish, with Extracts illustrating Persons and Places. Edited from MSS. and translated. 2 vols. royal 8vo, cloth. 42s. Or separately, Vol. 1, Irish Text; and Vol. 2, Translation and Notes. Each Vol. 21s.

OORDT (J. F. VAN, B.A.). Cape Dutch. Phrases and Dialogues, with Translations, preceded by short Grammatical Notes. Crown 8vo, cloth. 2s. 6d. net.

ORTH (SAMUEL P., Ph.D.). Socialism and Democracy in Europe. Demy 8vo. 360 pages. Cloth. 6s. net.

OSTWALD (WILHELM). Natural Philosophy. Translated by Thomas Seltzer. Crown 8vo, cloth. 4s. net.

OTTO (Prof. RUDOLF). Naturalism and Religion. Translated by J. Arthur Thomson, Professor of Natural History in the University of Aberdeen, and Margaret R. Thomson. Edited with an Introduction by Rev. W. D. Morrison, LL.D. Crown 8vo. 5s. net. Forming Vol. 17 in the Crown Theological Library; see p. 36.

PARKER (PERCY L.), Editor of "Public Opinion." **Character and Life.** A Symposium. Containing contributions by Dr Alfred Russel Wallace, John A. Hobson, Walter Crane, Harold Begbie, and the late Dr Emil Reich. Crown 8vo, cloth. 3s. 6d. net.

PAXSON (Prof. F. L.). The American Civil War. With Maps. F'cap. 8vo, cloth, 1s. net; leather, 2s. 6d. net. Forming Vol. 48 in the Home University Library; for list, see p. 39.

PEARSON (JOSEPH, M.Sc.). Cancer. With 13 Plates. 6s. 6d. net. See Liverpool Marine Biology Memoirs, p. 43.

PEDDIE (R. A.). Printing at Brescia in the Fifteenth Cen- tury. A List of the Issues. 5s. net.

PERCIVAL (G. H.). The Incarnate Purpose. Essays on the Spiritual Unity of Life. Crown 8vo, cloth. 2s. 6d. net.

PEROWNE (J. T. W., M.A.), Editor of the Army Series of French and German Novels. For list, see p. 35.

PERRIS (G. H.). A Short History of War and Peace. F'cap. 8vo, cloth, 1s. net; leather, 2s. 6d. net. Forming Vol. 4 in the Home University Library; for list, see p. 39.

PETERS (JOHN P., D.D.). Early Hebrew Story. Crown 8vo, cloth. 4s. 6d. net. Forming Vol. 7 in the Crown Theological Library; for list, see p. 36.

PETIT (ROBERT). How to Build an Aeroplane. Trans. from the French, with some additional matter, by Messrs T. O'B. Hubbard and J. H. Ledeboer. With nearly 100 Illustrations. Demy 8vo, cloth. 2s. 6d. net.

PFANHAUSER (Dr W.). Production of Metallic Objects Electrolytically. 5s. net.

PFLEIDERER (Dr O.). Lectures on the Influence of the Apostle Paul on the Development of Christianity. Translated by Rev. J. Frederick Smith. Being the Hibbert Lectures for 1885. Library Edition. Demy 8vo, cloth. 10s. 6d. Cheap Edition, cloth. 3s. 6d. See The Hibbert Lectures, p. 36.

PFLEIDERER (Dr O.). Paulinism : A Contribution to the History of Primitive Christianity. 2 vols. Demy 8vo, cloth. 12s. *See* Theological Translation Library, Old Series, p. 46.

—— **Philosophy of Religion on the Basis of its History.** In 4 vols. Demy 8vo, cloth. 24s. *See* Theological Translation Library, Old Series, p. 46. [Vol. 2 quite out of print.]

—— **Primitive Christianity : Its Writings and Teachings in** their Historical Connections. 4 vols. 10s. 6d. net each. *See* Theological Translation Library, New Series, p. 45.

—— **The Early Christian Conception of Christ : Its Signifi-** cance and Value in the History of Religion. 3s. net. *See* Crown Theological Library, p. 36.

PHILLIPPS (V., B.A.). A Short Sketch of German Litera- ture for Schools. 2nd Edition, revised. Pott 8vo, cloth. 1s.

PHILLIPS (FRANCIS C.). Methods for the Analysis of Ores, Pig Iron, and Steel. 2nd Edition. 8vo. Pages viii + 170. 3 Illustrations. 4s. 6d. net.

—— **Chemical German : An Introduction to the Study of** German Chemical Literature. Cloth. 8s. 6d. net.

PICTON (J. ALLANSON, M.A. Lond.). Man and the Bible. A Review of the Place of the Bible in Human History. Demy 8vo, cloth. 6s. net.

PIDDINGTON (HENRY). The Sailors' Horn-Book for the Law of Storms. Being a Practical Exposition of the Theory of the Law of Storms, and its uses to Mariners of all Classes in all Parts of the World. Shown by transparent Storm Cards and useful Lessons. 7th Edition. Demy 8vo, cloth. 10s. 6d.

PIGOU (Prof. A. C.). Unemployment. F'cap. 8vo, cloth, 1s. net; leather, 2s. 6d. net. Forming Vol. 85 in the Home University Library ; for list, *see* p. 39.

PLATTS (J. T., Hon. M.A. (Oxon.)). A Grammar of the Persian Language. Part I. Accidence. Broad crown 8vo. 10s. 6d.

POLLARD (Prof. A. F., M.A.). The History of England : A Study in Political Evolution. With a Chronological Table. F'cap. 8vo, cloth, 1s. net; leather, 2s. 6d. net. Forming Vol. 33 in the Home University Library ; for list, *see* p. 39.

PRANKE (EDWARD J.). Cyanamid (Manufacture, Chem- istry, and Uses). 8vo. Pages vi + 112. 8 Figures. 5s. net.

PRAY (Dr). Astigmatic Letters. Printed on Millboard, size 22 by 14 inches. 1s.

PROCEEDINGS OF INTERNATIONAL CONFER- ENCE under the Auspices of the American Society for Judicial Settlement of International Disputes, held at Washington, Dec. 1910. In 1 vol., sewed. 4s. net.

PROCEEDINGS OF THE ARISTOTELIAN SOCIETY FOR THE SYSTEMATIC STUDY OF PHILO-SOPHY. Old Series—Odd Numbers at various prices. New Series (yearly volumes bound in buckram)—Vols. I.-XI. ready, 10s. 6d. each net.

PROCEEDINGS OF THE OPTICAL CONVENTION,
No. 1, 1905. Crown 4to, cloth. 10s. net.

PROCEEDINGS AND PAPERS OF THE FIFTH INTERNATIONAL CONGRESS OF FREE CHRISTIANITY.
Held at Berlin, 1910. Edited by C. W. Wendte, D.D., and V. D. Davis, B.A. Medium 8vo, cloth. 9s. 6d. net. Sewed, 8s. 6d. net.

PUNNETT (R. C., B.A.). Lineus. With 4 Plates. 2s. net. *See* Liverpool Marine Biology Memoirs, p. 42.

RÆDER (A.). L'Arbitrage International chez les Hellènes. 4to, sewed. 10s. net. Being Vol. I. of Publications de l'Institut Nobel Norvégien.

REICH (Dr EMIL), Contributor to " Character and Life." *See* p. 5.

RENAN (E.). On the Influence of the Institutions, Thought, and Culture of Rome on Christianity and the Development of the Catholic Church. Translated by the Rev. Charles Beard. Being the Hibbert Lectures, 1880. 8vo, cloth. 10s. 6d. Cheap Edition (3rd Edition), 3s. 6d.

RENOUF (P. LE PAGE). On the Religion of Ancient Egypt. Hibbert Lectures, 1879. 3rd Edition. 8vo, cloth. 10s. 6d. Cheap Edition, 3s. 6d.

RÉVILLE (Dr A.). On the Native Religions of Mexico and Peru. Translated by the Rev. P. H. Wicksteed. Hibbert Lectures, 1884. 8vo, cloth. 10s. 6d. Cheap Edition, 3s. 6d.

—— **Prolegomena of the History of Religions.** With an Introduction by Prof. F. Max Müller. 8vo, cloth. 6s. *See* Theological Translation Library, Old Series, p. 45.

RÉVILLE (Prof. JEAN). Liberal Christianity : Its Origin, Nature, and Mission. Translated and Edited by Victor Leuliette, A.K.C., B.-ès-L. Crown 8vo, cloth. 3s. 6d. net. Forming Vol. 4 in the Crown Theological Library; for list, *see* p. 36.

RHYS (Prof. J.). On the Origin and Growth of Religion as Illustrated by Celtic Heathendom. Hibbert Lectures, 1886. 8vo, cloth. 10s. 6d. Cheap Edition, 3s. 6d.

RIEDEL (Prof. W.) and W. E. CRUM. The Canons of Athanasius of Alexandria, in Arabic, Ethiopic, and Coptic. 21s. net. *See* Text and Translation Society, p. 43.

ROBERTSON (Prof. J. G., M.A.). The Literature of Ger- many. F'cap. 8vo, cloth, 1s. net.; leather, 2s. 6d. net. Forming Vol. 65 in Home University Library; for list, *see* p. 39.

ROGET (F. F.). An Introduction to Old French. History, Grammar, Chrestomathy, and Glossary. 2nd Edition. Crown 8vo, cloth. 6s.

—— **First Steps in French History, Literature, and Philology.** For Candidates for the Scotch Leaving Certificate Examinations, the various Universities Local Examinations, and the Army Examinations. 4th Edition. Crown 8vo, cloth. 5s.

RUBINOW (I. M.). Social Insurance. The author is Chief Statistician Ocean Accident Guarantee Corporation. Demy 8vo, cloth. 12s. 6d. net.

RUFFINI (FRANCESCO). Religious Liberty. The Author is Ordinary Professor at the Royal University of Turin. With an Introduction by Prof. J. B. Bury of Cambridge. Demy 8vo. 12s. 6d. net. Forming Vol. 32 in the Theological Translation Library; see p. 44.

RUSSELL (Hon. BERTRAND, F.R.S.). The Problems of Philosophy. F'cap. 8vo, cloth, 1s. net; leather, 2s. 6d. net. Forming Vol. 40 in Home University Library; for list, see p. 39.

SABATIER (Late AUGUSTE). The Doctrine of the Atonement and its Historical Evolution; and Religion and Modern Culture. Translated by Victor Leuliette, A.K.C., B.-ès-L. Cr. 8vo. 4s. net. Forming Vol. 9 in the Crown Theological Library; see p. 36.

—— The Religions of Authority and the Religion of the Spirit. New impression. Demy 8vo, cloth. 10s. 6d. See Theological Translation Library, New Series, p. 44.

SADLER (Rev. Dr). Prayers for Christian Worship. Crown 8vo, cloth. 3s. 6d.

—— Closet Prayers, Original and Compiled. 18mo, cloth. 1s. 6d.

SADLER (GILBERT, M.A., LL.B.). A Short Introduction to the Bible. Crown 8vo, cloth. 2s. 6d. net.

SAGAS OF OLAF TRYGGVASON AND OF HAROLD THE TYRANT. A new translation, well illustrated with drawings by Erik Werenskiold, Christian Krogh, and others of the best Norwegian artists. In small 4to, comprising above 200 pages, bound with linen back and paper sides, in box. 12s. 6d. net.

SALEEBY (C. W., M.D., F.R.S.). Individualism and Collectivism. Crown 8vo, cloth. 2s.

SAUNDERS (T. BAILEY). Professor Harnack and his Oxford Critics. Crown 8vo, cloth. 1s. 6d. net.

SAYCE (Prof. A. H.). On the Origin and Growth of Religion as illustrated by the Religion of the Ancient Babylonians. 5th Edition. Hibbert Lectures, 1887. 8vo, cloth. 10s. 6d. Cheap Edition, 3s. 6d.

SCHLOSS (DAVID F.). Methods of Industrial Remuneration. 3rd Edition, revised and enlarged. Crown 8vo, cloth. 7s. 6d. Popular Edition. 3s. 6d.

SCHRADER (Prof. E.). The Cuneiform Inscriptions and the Old Testament. Translated from the Second Enlarged Edition, with Additions by the Author, and an Introduction by the Rev. Owen C. Whitehouse, M.A. 2 vols. With a Map. 8vo, cloth. 12s. See Theological Translation Library, Old Series, p. 46.

SCHREBER (D. G. M.). Medical Indoor Gymnastics, or a System of Hygienic Exercises for Home Use, to be practised anywhere, without apparatus or assistance, by young and old of either sex, for the preservation of health and general activity. Revised and Supplemented by Rudolf Graefe, M.D. With a large plate and 45 illustrations in the text. Royal 8vo, cloth. 2s. 6d. net.

SCHROEN (L.). Seven-Figure Logarithms of Numbers from 1 to 108,000, and of Sines, Cosines, Tangents, Cotangents to every 10 Seconds of the Quadrant. With a Table of Proportional Parts. By Dr Ludwig Schroen, Director of the Observatory of Jena, etc., etc. 5th Edition, corrected and stereotyped. With a description of the Tables by A. De Morgan, Professor of Mathematics in University College, London. Imp. 8vo, cloth, printed on light green paper. 9s.

SCHUBERT (HANS VON). History of the Church. Translated from the Second German Edition. By arrangement with the Author, an Additional Chapter has been added on "Religious Movements in England in the Nineteenth Century," by Miss Alice Gardner, Lecturer and Associate of Newnham College Cambridge. Demy 8vo, cloth. 10s. 6d. *See* Theological Translation Library, New Series, p. 41.

SCHURMAN (J. GOULD). Kantian Ethics and the Ethics of Evolution. 8vo, cloth. 5s.

—— The Ethical Import of Darwinism. Crown 8vo, cloth. 5s.

SCOTT (ANDREW). Lepeophtheirus and Lernea. With 5 Plates. 2s. net. *See* Liverpool Marine Biology Committee Memoirs on Typical British Marine Plants and Animals, p. 39.

SCOTT (Dr D. H., M.A., F.R.S.). The Evolution of Plants. Fully illustrated. F'cap. 8vo, cloth, 1s. net; leather, 2s. 6d. net. Forming Vol. 9 in the Home University Library; for list, *see* p. 39.

SCOTT (E. F., M.A.). The Apologetic of the New Testament. Crown 8vo, cloth. 4s. 6d. net. *See* Crown Theological Library, p. 36.

SEEBERG (Prof. R., of Berlin). The Fundamental Truths of the Christian Religion. Sixteen Lectures delivered before the Students of all Faculties in the University of Berlin. Crown 8vo. 350 pp. 4s. 6d. net. *See* Crown Theological Library, p. 37.

SEGER (HERMAN AUGUST), Collected Writings of. Papers on Manufacture of Pottery. 2 vols. Large 8vo. £3, 3s. net per set.

SEITZ (Dr ADALBERT). Edited by, with the assistance ot
Dr Jordan (Tring), W. F. Kirby (London), Warren (London), Hon.
W. Rothschild (London), and others. **Butterflies and Moths.**
The Macrolepidoptera of the World. A work of reference and identification, with 1000 coloured plates, depicting nearly 40,000 specimens,
with letterpress. To be completed in about 465 parts. 4to. The
work is divided into two Divisions. Division I., Fauna Palæarctica,
published in 4 vols., or 115 parts at 1s. net each. Orders are booked
for the whole division only. Division II., Fauna Exotica, published
in 12 vols., or 350 parts at 1s. 6d. net each. This division is divided
into Fauna Americana, Fauna Indo Australica, and Fauna Africana.
Each Fauna may be subscribed for separately, and subscriptions
will also be received for any of the classified groups, viz., Rhopalo-
cera, Bombyces and Sphinges, Noctuæ and Geometræ. Binding
covers for the work can be obtained after completion of each
volume. The latest prospectus should be applied for.

SELBIE (Principal W. B., M.A.). Nonconformity: Its Origin
and Progress. F'cap. 8vo, cloth, 1s. net; leather, 2s. 6d. net.
Forming Vol. 50 in the Home University Library; for list, *see* p. 41.

SHARPE (HENRY). Britain B.C.: As Described in Classical
Writings. With an Inquiry into the positions of the Cassiterides
and Thule, and an attempt to ascertain the ancient coast-line of
Kent and East Sussex. With Maps. Crown 8vo, cloth. 5s. net.

SHEARMAN (A. T., M.A.). The Development of Symbolic
Logic. A Critical Historical Study of the Logical Calculus.
Crown 8vo, cloth. 5s. net.

SIMKHOVITCH (Prof. V. J., Ph.D.). Marxism and Social-
ism. Demy 8vo, cloth. 6s. net.

SMITH (The Rt. Hon. F. E., K.C., M.P.). Unionist Policy
and Other Essays. Large 8vo, cloth. 5s. net.

SMITH (L. PEARSALL, M.A.). The English Language.
F'cap. 8vo, cloth, 1s. net; leather, 2s. 6d. net. Forming Vol. 45
in the Home University Library; for list, *see* p. 40.

SNELLEN'S OPHTHALMIC TEST TYPES. Best Types
for the Determination of the Acuteness of Vision. 14th Edition,
considerably augmented and improved. 8vo, sewed. 4s. Single
Sheets: E T B, M O V, B D E, ШШШ, and Large Clock Sheet.
8d. each. Small Clock Sheet and R T V Z. 4d. each.

SNYDER (HARRY, B.Sc.). Soils and Fertilisers. 2nd Edition.
8vo. Pages x + 294. 1 Plate, 40 Illustrations. 6s. 6d. net.

SODDY (F., M.A., F.R.S.). Matter and Energy. F'cap. 8vo,
cloth, 1s. net; leather, 2s. 6d. net. Forming Vol. 46 in the
Home University Library; for list, *see* p. 41.

SODEN (Prof. H. VON, D.D.). The Books of the New
Testament. Translated by the Rev. J. R. Wilkinson, and edited
by Rev. W. D. Morrison, LL.D. Crown 8vo, cloth. 4s. 6d.
net. *See* Crown Theological Library, p. 36.

SOLILOQUIES OF ST AUGUSTINE, THE. Translated into English by Rose Elizabeth Cleveland. With Notes and Introduction by the Translator. Small demy 8vo, cloth. 6s. net.

SOMERVILLE (Prof. W., D.Sc.). Agriculture. F'cap. 8vo, cloth, 1s. net; leather, 2s. 6d. net. Forming Vol. 26 in the Home University Library; for list, see p. 39.

SONNTAG (C. O.). A Pocket Flora of Edinburgh and the Surrounding District. A Collection and full Description of all Phanerogamic and the principal Cryptogamic Plants, classified after the Natural System, with an artificial Key and a Glossary of Botanical Terms. By the late C. O. Sonntag. F'cap. 8vo, limp cloth. 3s. 6d. net.

SORENSEN (S., Ph.D.), Compiled by. An Index to the Names in the Mahabharata. With short explanations. Royal 4to, in twelve parts, which are not sold separately, at 7s. 6d. per part net. Parts I. to VIII. now ready.

SOUTHWARK (Lady). Social and Political Reminiscences. Illustrated. 12s. 6d. net.

SPEARS (J. R.). Master Mariners. F'cap. 8vo, cloth, 1s. net; leather, 2s. 6d. net. Forming Vol. 55 in the Home University Library; for list, see p. 41.

SPENCER (HERBERT). A System of Synthetic Philosophy— Vol. I. **First Principles.** With an Appendix and a Portrait. Finally revised. New Edition, large crown 8vo, cloth. 7s. 6d. Specially printed cheap edition, bound in cloth. 2 vols. of 240 pages each. 1s. net per volume. Complete in one volume. 2s. net.

Vols. II. and III. **The Principles of Biology.** 6th Thousand. 8vo, cloth. Revised and greatly enlarged. 2 vols. 18s. each.

Vols. IV. and V. **The Principles of Psychology.** 5th Thousand. 2 vols. 8vo, cloth. 36s.

Vol. VI. **The Principles of Sociology.** Vol. I. Part 1, The Data of Sociology; Part 2, The Inductions of Sociology; Part 3, Domestic Institutions. 4th Thousand, revised and enlarged. 8vo, cloth. 21s.

Vol. VII. **The Principles of Sociology.** Vol. II. Part 4, Ceremonial Institutions; Part 5, Political Institutions. 3rd Thousand. 8vo, cloth. 18s.

Vol. VIII. **The Principles of Sociology.** Vol. III. Part 6, Ecclesiastical Institutions; Part 7, Professional Institutions; Part 8, Industrial Institutions. 2nd Thousand. 8vo, cloth. 16s.

Vol. IX. **The Principles of Ethics.** Vol. I. Part 1, The Data of Ethics; Part 2, The Inductions of Ethics; Part 3, The Ethics of Individual Life. 8vo, cloth. 15s.

Vol. X. **The Principles of Ethics.** Vol. II. Part 4, Justice; Part 5, Negative Beneficence; Part 6, Positive Beneficence; Appendices. Demy 8vo, cloth. 12s. 6d.

—— **A Rejoinder to Professor Weismann.** Sewed. 6d.

—— **Data of Ethics.** Reset uniform with popular edition of "First Principles." Sewed, 2s. 6d. net; cloth, 3s. net.

SPENCER (HERBERT). Descriptive Sociology; or, Groups of Sociological Facts. Compiled and abstracted by Professor D. Duncan of Madras, Dr Richard Scheppig, and James Collier. Folio, boards.

No. 1. **English.** 18s.

No. 2. **Ancient American Races.** 16s.

No. 3. **Lowest Races, Negritto Races, Polynesians.** 18s.

No. 4. **African Races.** 16s.

No. 5. **Asiatic Races.** 18s.

No. 6. **American Races.** 18s.

No. 7. **Hebrews and Phœnicians.** 21s.

No. 8. **The French Civilisation.** 30s.

No. 9. **Chinese.** Compiled and abstracted by E. T. C. Werner, H.M.'s Consular Service, China. 63s.

No. 10. **Greeks: Hellenic Era.** By Rev. Dr J. P. Mahaffy, and Professor W. A. Goligher, Trinity College, Dublin. 21s.

—— **Education: Intellectual, Moral, and Physical.** Popular Edition. Entirely reset. Crown 8vo, cloth. 2s. 6d. Cheap Edition, cloth, 1s. net.

—— **Essays: Scientific, Political, and Speculative.** A new Edition, rearranged, with additional Essays. 3 vols. 8vo, cloth. (Each 10s.) 30s.

—— **Facts and Comments.** Demy 8vo, cloth. 6s.

—— **Justice.** Being Part 4 of the Principles of Ethics. 2nd Thousand. 8vo, cloth. 6s.

—— **Reasons for Dissenting from the Philosophy of M. Comte.** Sewed. 6d.

—— **Social Statics.** Abridged and revised, together with " The Man v. The State." 8vo, cloth. 10s.

—— **The Man versus The State.** 14th Thousand. Sewed. 1s.

—— **The Study of Sociology.** Library Edition (21st Thousand), with a Postscript. 8vo, cloth. 10s. 6d.

—— **Various Fragments.** Uniform in Library binding. Demy 8vo, cloth. Enlarged Edition. 6s.

STATUTES, THE, OF THE APOSTLES. The hitherto unedited Ethiopic and Arabic Texts, with Translations of Ethiopic, Arabic, and Coptic Texts, by G. Horner, M.A.

STEPHEN (Rev. Canon REGINALD, M.A.). Democracy and Character. Being the Moorhouse Lectures for 1908. Crown 8vo, cloth. 5s.

STERNE (LAURENCE). A Sentimental Journey through France and Italy. With 12 Illustrations faithfully reproduced from water-colour drawings by Everard Hopkins. Cheap Edition in crown 4to, 6s. net.

STILLMAN (THOS. B., M.Sc., Ph.D.). **Engineering Chem-**
istry. 4th Edition. The 4th edition has been mostly rewritten
and altered to incorporate the latest approved methods of chemical
testing. Medium 8vo. With 147 Figures in the text. 21s. net.

STOCKER (R. DIMSDALE). Social Idealism. Crown 8vo,
cloth. 3s. net.

STRACHEY (G. L.). Landmarks in French Literature.
F'cap. 8vo, cloth, 1s. net; leather, 2s. 6d. net. Forming Vol. 35
in the Home University Library; for list, see p. 39.

TAYLOR (A. CAMERON). General Sir Alexander Taylor.
A Memoir by his Daughter. 2 vols. Demy 8vo, cloth. 25s. net.

TAYLOR (Rev. Dr J.). The Massoretic Text and the
Ancient Versions of the Book of Micah. Crown 8vo, cloth. 5s.

TEN SERVICES OF PUBLIC PRAYER, with Special
Collects. 8vo, cloth, 3s.; or 32mo, cloth, 1s. 6d.

—— **PSALMS AND CANTICLES.** 8vo, cloth. 1s. 6d. [cloth. 2s.

—— **PSALMS AND CANTICLES, with Anthems.** 8vo,

—— **SERVICES OF PUBLIC PRAYER, taken in Sub-**
stance from the Common Prayer for Christian Worship, with a few
additional Prayers for particular Days. 8vo, cloth, 2s. 6d.; or
32mo, cloth, 1s.

TENNYSON (ALFRED, LORD). The Princess: A
Medley. With Six Illustrations beautifully reproduced in colours,
and a number in black-and-white, from Original Drawings by
Everard Hopkins. Small 4to. 7s. 6d. net.

THOMSON (J. ARTHUR, M.A., LL.D.). **Introduction to**
Science. F'cap. 8vo, cloth, 1s. net; leather, 2s. 6d. net. Forming Vol. 32 in the Home University Library; for list, see p. 40.

—— **and Prof. PATRICK GEDDES. Evolution.** F'cap. 8vo,
cloth, 1s. net; leather, 2s. 6d. net. Forming Vol. 20 in the Home
University Library; for list, see p. 40.

—— Editor of the Home University Library; for list, see p. 39.

THURSTON (E. TEMPLE). The "Flower of Gloster."
By the well-known Author of "City of Beautiful Nonsense," "Sally
Bishop," etc. With six Illustrations faithfully reproduced in colours,
and other Illustrations in black-and-white, from drawings by W. R.
Dakin. Small 4to, cloth. 7s. 6d. net. Cheap Edition. 3s. 6d. net.

TISCHENDORF (C.). The New Testament. Novum Testa-
mentum Græce. 3 vols. 8vo. 70s. net.

TOLLINTON (Rev. R. B., M.A., B.D.). **Clement of**
Alexandria. A Study in Christian Liberalism. In two volumes.
Medium 8vo, cloth. 21s. net.

TOWER (CHARLES). Germany of To-day. F'cap. 8vo,
cloth, 1s. net; leather, 2s. 6d. net. Forming Vol. 71 in Home
University Library; for list, see p. 39.

TOWER (O. F., Ph.D.). The Conductivity of Liquids. 8vo. Pages iv + 190. 20 Illustrations. 6s. 6d. net.

TRANSACTIONS OF THE ROYAL DUBLIN SOCIETY. Issued in parts at various prices.

TRANSACTIONS OF THE ROYAL IRISH ACADEMY, DUBLIN. Vols. I.–XX. 4to. £22, 5s. 6d. Vols. XXI.– XXXI. Various prices.

TRANSACTIONS OF THE ROYAL SOCIETY OF EDIN-BURGH. Issued in parts at various prices. General Index to First Thirty-four Volumes (1783–1888), with History of the Institution. 4to, cloth. 21s.

TRENCKNER (V.). Pali Miscellany. Part I. The Introductory Part of the Milanda Panho, with an English Translation and Notes. 8vo, sewed. 4s.

TRENT (Prof. W. P.) and ERSKINE (Prof. J.). Great Writers of America. F'cap. 8vo, cloth, 1s. net; leather, 2s. 6d. net. Forming Vol. 52, Home University Library; for list, see p. 39.

TROELTSCH (Prof. ERNEST, of Jena). Protestantism and Progress : The Significance of Protestantism in the Rise of the Modern World. Translated into English by Rev. W. Montgomery, B.D. Crown 8vo, cloth. 3s. 6d. net. See Crown Theological Library, p. 36.

UPTON (Rev. C. B.). On the Basis of Religious Belief. Hibbert Lectures, 1893. Demy 8vo, cloth. 10s. 6d. Cheap Edition, 3s. 6d.

VEGA. Logarithmic Tables of Numbers and Trigonometrical Functions. Translated from the 40th, or Dr Bremiker's Edition, thoroughly revised and enlarged, by W. L. Fischer, M.A., F.R.S., Fellow of Clare College, Cambridge; Professor of Natural Philo sophy in the University of St Andrews. 75th Stereotyped Edition. Royal 8vo, cloth. 7s.

VEILED FIGURE, THE, and other Poems. Large post 8vo, buckram, gilt, cover designed by Mr T. Blake Wirgman. 2s. 6d.

VENABLE (T. C., Ph.D.). The Development of the Periodic Law. Small 12mo. Pages viii + 321. Illustrated. 10s. 6d. net.

—— **The Study of the Atom.** 12mo. Pages vi + 290. 8s. 6d. net.

VINCENT (JACQUES). Vaillante. 2s. 6d. See Army Series of French and German Novels, p, 35.

VINOGRADOFF (Prof. P., D.C.L.). Common-Sense in Law. F'cap 8vo, cloth, 1s. net; leather, 2s. 6d. net. Forming Vol. 83 in the Home University Library; for list, see p. 39.

WALFORD (Mrs L. B.). Recollections of a Scottish Novelist. With Portraits and other Illustrations. Demy 8vo, cloth. 10s. 6d. net.

WALLACE (Dr ALFRED RUSSEL). See Character and Life, p. 5.

WEBSTER (A. G.) The Dynamics of Particles and of Rigid, Elastic, and Fluid Bodies. Second Edition. Medium 8vo, cloth. 14s. net.

WEDMORE (Sir FREDERICK). Painters and Painting. (Illustrated.) F'cap. 8vo, cloth, 1s. net; leather, 2s. 6d. net. Forming Vol. 63 in Home University Library; for list, *see* p. 41.

WEINEL (Prof. H., of the University of Jena). **St Paul: The** Man and his Work. Translated by Rev. G. A. Bienemann, M.A. Edited by Rev. W. D. Morrison, M.A., LL.D. Demy 8vo, cloth. 10s. 6d. *See* Theological Translation Library, New Series, p. 44.

WEIR (T. H., B.D.). **A Short History of the Hebrew Text** of the Old Testament. By Thomas H. Weir, Assistant to the Professor of Oriental Languages in the University of Glasgow. 2nd Edition, with Additions. Crown 8vo, cloth. 6s.

WEISSE (T. H.). A Short Guide to German Idioms: being a Collection of the Idioms most in use. With Examination Papers. 3rd Edition. Cloth. 2s.

—— **Elements of German.** With a Course of Exercises instructing in Simpler Composition. Crown 8vo, cloth. 3s.

WEIZSÄCKER (Prof. CARL VON). The Apostolic Age. Translated by James Millar, B.D. Demy 8vo, 2 vols., cloth. Each 10s. 6d. *See* Theological Translation Library, New Series, p. 44.

WELD (A. G.). Glimpses of Tennyson and of Some of his Friends. With an Appendix by the late Bertram Tennyson. Illustrated with Portraits in photogravure and colour, and with a facsimile of a MS. poem. F'cap. 8vo, art linen. 4s. 6d. net.

WERNER (A.) and G. HUNT. Elementary Lessons in Cape Dutch (Afrikander Taal). 16mo, cloth. 1s. 6d.

WERNLE (PAUL). The Beginnings of Christianity. The Author is Professor Extraordinary of Modern Church History at the University of Basel. Revised by the Author, and translated by the Rev. G. A. Bienemann, M.A., and edited, with an Introduction, by the Rev. W. D. Morrison, LL.D. Demy 8vo. 10s. 6d. per volume. *See* Theological Translation Library, New Series, p. 44.

WHITEHEAD (A. N., Sc.D., F.R.S.). **Introduction to Mathe-** matics. With Diagrams. F'cap. 8vo, cloth, 1s.net; leather, 2s.6d.net. Forming Vol. 18 in the Home University Library; for list, *see* p. 40.

WILEY (HARVEY W., A.M., Ph.D.). **Principles and Prac-** tice of Agricultural Chemical Analysis. 3 Vols. 8vo. New Edition in preparation. Vol. I. Soils. Ready. 18s. net. Vol. II. Fertilisers. 20s. net. Vol. III. Agricultural Products. 26s. net.

WILLIAMS (ANEURIN, M.P.) **Co-Partnership and Profit-** Sharing. F'cap. 8vo, cloth, 1s. net; leather, 2s. 6d. net. Forming Vol. 80 in the Home University Library; for list, *see* p. 39.

WILLIAMS (The Right Rev. W. L., D.C.L.). **A Dictionary** of the New Zealand Language. 4th Edition. Edited by the Right Rev. Bishop W. L. Williams, with numerous additions and corrections. Demy 8vo, cloth. 12s. 6d.

—— **Lessons in Maori.** 3rd Edition. F'cap. 8vo, cloth. 3s.

WIMMER (R., Pastor of Weisweil-am-Rhein in Baden). **My** Struggle for Light : Confessions of a Preacher. Crown 8vo, cloth. 3s. net. *See* Crown Theological Library, p. 36.

WINSTEDT (E. O.), Edited by. **Coptic Texts on St Theodore** the General, St Theodore the Eastern, Chamoul and Justus. 21s. net. *See* Text and Translation Society, p. 43.

WOODS (C. E.). The Gospel of Rightness. A Study in Pauline Philosophy. 300 pages, cloth. 5s. net.

WRIGHT (Rev. C. H. H.). Light from Egyptian Papyri on Jewish History before Christ. Crown 8vo, cloth. 3s. net.

WRIGHT (G. H. BATESON, D.D.). **The Book of Job.** A new critically revised Translation, with Essays on Scansion, Date, etc. 8vo, cloth. 6s.

—— **Was Israel ever in Egypt?** or, **A Lost Tradition.** 8vo, art linen. 7s. 6d.

WRIGHT (W. ALDIS, LL.D.), Edited by. **A Rabbinic Com**mentary on the Book of Job, contained in a unique MS. at Cambridge. With Translation and Commentary. 21s. net. *See* Text and Translation Society, p. 43.

WUNDT (WILHELM). Outlines of Psychology. Translated, with the co-operation of the Author, by Charles Hubbard Judd, Ph.D., Instructor in the Wesleyan University. 3rd Enlarged Edition. Demy 8vo, cloth. 8s. net.

WYSOR (HENRY, B.S., Assistant Professor of Analytical Chemistry, Lafayette College). Metallurgy. A Condensed Treatise. Demy 8vo, cloth. 12s. 6d. net.

YOUNGHUSBAND (Col. Sir FRANCIS E., K.C.I.E.). Within : Thoughts during Convalescence. 3s. 6d. net.

COMPLETE LIST OF LIBRARIES AND SERIES ARRANGED IN ALPHABETICAL ORDER.

ARMY SERIES OF FRENCH AND GERMAN NOVELS.
Edited, with short Notes, by J. T. W. Perowne, M.A.

This series is equally well adapted for general reading, and for those preparing for the Army, Oxford and Cambridge Certificates, and other Examinations—in fact, for all who wish to keep up or improve their French and German. The notes are as concise as possible, with an occasional etymology or illustration to assist the memory. The books selected being by recent or living authors, are adapted for the study of most modern French and German.

Le Coup de Pistolet, etc. Prosper Merimée. 2s. 6d.

Vaillante. Jacques Vincent. 2s. 6d.

Auf Verlornem Posten and Nazzarena Danti. Johannes v. Dewall. 3s.

Contes Militaires. A. Daudet. 2s. 6d.

Erzählungen. E. Höfer. 3s.

CROWN THEOLOGICAL LIBRARY.

The only undertaking of its kind in the English language; each writer is at liberty to express his deepest convictions with absolute freedom—a freedom which is the only ultimate security of truth.

Vol. I.—**Babel and Bible.** By Dr Friedrich Delitzsch. 4s. 6d. net.

Vol. II.—**The Virgin Birth of Christ.** An Historical and Critical Essay. By Paul Lobstein. 2s. 6d. net.

Vol. III.—**My Struggle for Light.** Confessions of a Preacher. By R. Wimmer. 3s. net.

Vol. IV.—**Liberal Christianity.** Its Origin, Nature, and Mission. By Jean Réville. 3s. 6d. net.

Vol. V.—**What is Christianity?** By Adolf Harnack. 4s. 6d. net.

Vol. VI.—**Faith and Morals.** By W. Herrmann. 4s. 6d. net.

Vol. VII.—**Early Hebrew Story.** A Study of the Origin, the Value, and the Historical Background of the Legends of Israel. By John P. Peters, D.D. 4s. 6d. net.

Vol. VIII.—**Bible Problems and the New Material for their Solution.** By Prof. T. K. Cheyne, D.Litt., D.D. 4s. 6d. net.

Vol. IX.—**The Doctrine of the Atonement and its Historical Evolution,** and **Religion and Modern Culture.** By the late Auguste Sabatier. 4s. net.

Vol. X.—**The Early Christian Conception of Christ.** Its Significance and Value in the History of Religion. By Otto Pfleiderer. 3s. net.

Vol. XI.—**The Child and Religion.** Eleven Essays by Various Writers. 5s. net.

Vol. XII.—**The Evolution of Religion.** An Anthropological Study. By L. R. Farnell, M.A., D.Litt. 4s. 6d. net.

Vol. XIII.—**The Books of the New Testament.** By Baron Hermann von Soden, D.D. 4s. 6d. net.

Vol. XIV.—**Jesus.** By W. Bousset. 3s. 6d. net.

Vol. XV.—**The Communion of the Christian with God.** By W. Herrmann. Revised and much enlarged edition. 4s. 6d. net.

Vol. XVI.—**Hebrew Religion.** To the Establishment of Judaism under Ezra. By W. E. Addis, M.A. 4s. 6d. net.

Vol. XVII.—**Naturalism and Religion.** By Rudolf Otto. 5s. net.

Vol. XVIII.—**Essays on the Social Gospel.** By Dr Adolf Harnack and Dr Herrmann. 4s. net.

Vol. XIX.—**The Religion of the Old Testament.** By Karl Marti. 4s. net.

Crown Theological Library—*continued*.

Vol. XX.—**Luke the Physician.** Being Volume One of Dr Adolf Harnack's New Testament Studies. 5s. net.

Vol. XXI.—**The Historical Evidence for the Resurrection of Jesus Christ.** By Prof. Kirsopp Lake. 4s. 6d. net.

Vol. XXII.—**The Apologetic of the New Testament.** By E. F. Scott. 4s. 6d. net.

Vol. XXIII.—**The Sayings of Jesus.** Being Volume Two of Dr Adolf Harnack's New Testament Studies. 5s. net.

Vol. XXIV.—**Anglican Liberalism.** By Twelve Churchmen. 4s. 6d. net.

Vol. XXV.—**The Fundamental Truths of the Christian Religion.** By Dr R. Seeberg. 4s. 6d. net.

Vol. XXVI.—**The Life of the Spirit.** An Introduction to Philosophy. By Dr Rudolf Eucken. 4s. 6d. net.

Vol. XXVII.—**The Acts of the Apostles.** Being Volume Three of Dr Adolf Harnack's New Testament Studies. 5s. net.

Vol. XXVIII.—**Monasticism and the Confessions of St Augustine.** By Dr Adolf Harnack. 3s. 6d. net.

Vol. XXIX.—**Modernity and the Churches.** By Prof. Percy Gardner. 4s. 6d. net.

Vol. XXX.—**The Old Egyptian Faith.** By Prof. Edouard Naville. Illustrated. 4s. 6d. net.

Vol. XXXI.—**The Constitution and Law of the Church in the First Two Centuries.** By Dr Adolf Harnack. 5s. net.

Vol. XXXII.—**The Scientific Study of the Old Testament.** Illustrated. By Dr Rudolf Kittel. 5s. net.

Vol. XXXIII.—**The Date of the Acts and of the Synoptic Gospels.** Being Volume Four of Dr Adolf Harnack's New Testament Studies. Cloth. 5s. net.

Vol. XXXIV.—**The Religious Experience of St Paul.** By Prof. Percy Gardner. 5s. net.

Vol. XXXV.—**Pharisaism : Its Aims and its Methods.** By R. Travers Herford, B.A. Cloth. 5s. net.

Vol. XXXVI.—**Bible Reading in the Early Church.** Being Volume Five of Dr Adolf Harnack's New Testament Studies. Cloth. 5s. net.

Vol. XXXVII.—**Protestantism and Progress.** By Prof. Ernest Troeltsch of Jena. Cloth. 3s. 6d. net.

Vol. XXXVIII.—**Present Day Ethics.** By Prof. Rudolf Eucken. 3s. net.

Vol. XXXIX.—**Knowledge and Life.** By Prof. Rudolf Eucken. 5s. net.

Descriptive Prospectus on Application.

14 Henrietta Street, Covent Garden, London, W.C.

THE HIBBERT LECTURES.

Library Edition, demy 8vo.   10s. 6d. per volume.
Cheap Popular Edition, 3s. 6d. per volume.

Alviella (Count Goblet D').   Lectures on the Origin and the Growth of the Conception of God, as illustrated by Anthropology and History.   Translated by the Rev. P. H. Wicksteed.   (Hibbert Lectures, 1891.)   Cloth.   10s. 6d.   Cheap Edition, 3s. 6d.

Beard (Rev. Dr C.).   Lectures on the Reformation of the Sixteenth Century in its Relation to Modern Thought and Knowledge. (Hibbert Lectures, 1883.)   8vo, cloth.   10s. 6d.   Cheap Edition, 3s. 6d.

Davids (T. W. Rhys).   Lectures on Some Points in the History of Indian Buddhism.   (Hibbert Lectures, 1881.)   2nd Edition.   8vo, cloth.   10s. 6d.   Cheap Edition, 3s. 6d.

Drummond (Dr).   Via, Veritas, Vita. Lectures on Christianity in its most Simple and Intelligible Form.   (The Hibbert Lectures, 1894.)   10s. 6d.   Cheap Edition, 3s. 6d.

Hatch (Rev. Dr).   Lectures on the Influence of Greek Ideas and Usages upon the Christian Church.   Edited by Dr Fairbairn.   (Hibbert Lectures, 1888.)   3rd Edition.   8vo, cloth. 10s. 6d.   Cheap Edition, 3s. 6d.

Kuenen (Dr A.).   Lectures on National Religions and Universal Religion.   (The Hibbert Lectures, 1882.)   8vo, cloth. 10s. 6d.   Cheap Edition, 3s. 6d.

Montefiore (C. G.).   Origin and Growth of Religion as Illustrated by the Religion of the Ancient Hebrews.   (The Hibbert Lectures, 1892.)   2nd Edition.   8vo, cloth.   10s. 6d. Cheap Edition, 3s. 6d.

Pfleiderer (Dr O.).   Lectures on the Influence of the Apostle Paul on the Development of Christianity.   Translated by the Rev. J. Frederick Smith.   (Hibbert Lectures, 1885.)   2nd Edition.   8vo, cloth.   10s. 6d.   Cheap Edition, 3s. 6d.

Renan (E.).   On the Influence of the Institutions, Thoughts and Culture of Rome on Christianity, and the Development of the Catholic Church.   Trans. by the Rev. Charles Beard.   (Hibbert Lectures, 1880.)   8vo, cloth.   10s. 6d.   Cheap Ed., 3rd Ed., 3s. 6d.

Renouf (P. Le Page).   On the Religion of Ancient Egypt.   (Hibbert Lectures, 1879.)   3rd Edition.   8vo, cloth. 10s. 6d.   Cheap Edition, 3s. 6d.

Rhys (Prof. J.).   On the Origin and Growth of Religion as Illustrated by Celtic Heathendom.   (Hibbert Lectures, 1886.) 8vo, cloth.   10s. 6d.   Cheap Edition, 3s. 6d.

The Hibbert Lectures—*continued.*

Réville (Dr A.). On the Native Religions of Mexico and Peru. Translated by the Rev. P. H. Wicksteed. (Hibbert Lectures, 1884.) 8vo, cloth. 10s. 6d. Cheap Edition, 3s. 6d.

Sayce (Prof. A. H.). On the Religion of Ancient Assyria and Babylonia. 4th Edition. (Hibbert Lectures, 1887.) 8vo, cloth. 10s. 6d. Cheap Edition, 3s. 6d.

Upton (Rev. C. B.). On the Bases of Religious Belief. (Hibbert Lectures, 1893.) Demy 8vo, cloth. 10s. 6d. Cheap Edition, 3s. 6d.

Second Series.

Farnell (L. R., D.Litt., Wilde Lecturer in the University of Oxford). The Higher Aspects of Greek Religion. Lectures delivered in Oxford and London in 1911. Demy 8vo, cloth. 6s. net.

Moulton (Prof. J. H.). Early Zoroastrianism. Cloth. 10s. 6d. net.

Margoliouth (Prof. D. S.). Early Development of Mohammedanism. Cloth. 6s. net.

HOME UNIVERSITY LIBRARY OF MODERN KNOWLEDGE.

Editors: Prof. Gilbert Murray, D.Litt., LL.D., F.B.A., Herbert Fisher, M.A., F.B.A., LL.D., Professor J. Arthur Thomson, LL.D., and Professor Wm. T. Brewster. Each volume is written by an expert of the very first rank, and consists of 256 pages. Issued bound in cloth at 1s. net, or beautifully bound in leather, levant morocco grain, 2s. 6d. net.

Eighty-five Volumes Now Ready.

1. **Parliament.** Sir C. P. Ilbert, K.C.B.
2. **Shakespeare.** John Masefield.
3. **French Revolution.** (With Maps.) Hilaire Belloc, M.A.
4. **History of War and Peace.** G. H. Perris.
5. **Stock Exchange.** F. W. Hirst, M.A.
6. **Irish Nationality.** Mrs J. R. Green.
7. **Modern Geography.** (Illustrated.) Dr M. Newbigin.
8. **Polar Exploration.** (With Maps.) Dr W. S. Bruce.
9. **Evolution of Plants.** (Fully Illustrated.) Dr D. H. Scott, F.R.S.
10. **Socialist Movement.** J. Ramsay MacDonald, M.P.
11. **Conservatism.** Lord Hugh Cecil, M.A., M.P.
12. **Opening Up of Africa.** (With Maps.) Sir H. H. Johnston, G.C.M.G.

Home University Library of Modern Knowledge—*continued*.

13. **Mediæval Europe.** (With Maps.) H. W. C. Davis, M.A.

14. **The Papacy and Modern Times.** Rev. Dr W. Barry.

15. **Mohammedanism.** Prof. D. S. Margoliouth.

16. **The Science of Wealth.** J. A. Hobson, M.A.

17. **Health and Disease.** Dr W. L. Mackenzie.

18. **Introduction to Mathematics.** (With Diagrams.) A. N. Whitehead, Sc.D., F.R.S.

19. **The Animal World.** (With many Illustrations.) Prof. F. W. Gamble.

20. **Evolution.** Prof. J. A. Thomson and Prof. P. Geddes.

21. **Liberalism.** Prof. L. T. Hobhouse.

22. **Crime and Insanity.** Dr C. A. Mercier.

23. **History of our Time, 1885-1913.** G. P. Gooch, M.A.

24. **The Evolution of Industry.** Prof. D. H. MacGregor.

25. **The Civilisation of China.** Prof. H. A. Giles, LL.D.

26. **Agriculture.** Prof. W. Somerville, D.Sc.

27. **English Literature : Modern.** George Mair, M.A.

28. **Psychical Research.** Sir W. F. Barrett, F.R.S.

29. **The Dawn of History.** Prof. J. L. Myers.

30. **Elements of English Law.** Prof. W. M. Geldart, B.C.L.

31. **Astronomy.** A. R. Hinks, M.A.

32. **The Introduction to Science.** Prof. J. Arthur Thomson, M.A.

33. **The History of England :** A Study in Political Evolution. Prof. A. F. Pollard.

34. **Canada.** A. G. Bradley.

35. **Landmarks in French Literature.** G. L. Strachey.

36. **Climate and Weather.** (With Diagrams.) Prof. H. N. Dickson, D.Sc.

37. **Peoples and Problems of India.** Sir T. W. Holderness, K.C.S.I.

38. **The School.** An Introduction to the Study of Education. Prof. J. J. Findlay.

39. **Architecture.** (Over 40 Illustrations.) Prof. W. R. Lethaby.

40. **Problems of Philosophy.** The Hon. Bertrand Russell, F.R.S.

41. **Anthropology.** R. R. Marett, M.A.

42. **Rome.** W. Warde-Fowler, M.A.

43. **English Literature : Mediæval.** Prof. W. P. Ker.

44. **Principles of Physiology.** Prof. J. G. M'Kendrick.

45. **The English Language.** J. Pearsall Smith, M.A.

Home University Library of Modern Knowledge—*continued.*

46. **Matter and Energy.** F. Soddy, F.R.S.

47. **Buddhism.** Mrs Rhys Davids.

48. **The American Civil War.** (Maps.) Prof. F. L. Paxson.

49. **Psychology.** The Study of Behaviour. Prof. W. McDougall.

50. **Nonconformity,** Its Origin and Progress. Principal W. B. Selbie.

51. **Warfare in England.** (With Maps.) Hilaire Belloc, M.A.

52. **Great Writers of America.** Profs. W. P. Trent and J. Erskine.

53. **The Making of the Earth.** (With 38 Maps and Figures.) Prof. J. W. Gregory, F.R.S.

54. **Ethics.** G. E. Moore, M.A.

55. **Master Mariners.** J. R. Spears.

56. **Making of the New Testament.** Prof. B. W. Bacon, LL.D., D.D.

57. **The Human Body.** (Illustrated.) Prof. Arthur Keith, M.D., F.R.C.S.

58. **Electricity.** (Illustrated.) Dr Gisbert Kapp, D.Eng., M.I.E.E.

59. **Political Economy.** Prof. S. J. Chapman, M.A.

60. **Missions:** Their Rise and Development. Mrs Creighton.

61. **Napoleon.** (Maps.) Herbert Fisher, M.A., F.B.A.

62. **The Origin and Nature of Life.** Prof. Benjamin Moore.

63. **Painters and Painting.** (Illus.) Sir Frederick Wedmore.

64. **Dr Johnson and his Circle.** John Bailey, M.A.

65. **The Literature of Germany.** Prof. J. G. Robertson, M.A., Ph.D.

66. **The Navy and Sea Power.** David Hannay.

67. **Chemistry.** Prof. Raphael Meldola, D.Sc., LL.D.

68. **Comparative Religion.** Prof. J. Estlin Carpenter, LL.D.

69. **The Newspaper.** (Illus.) G. Binney Dibblee.

70. **The Victorian Age in Literature.** G. K. Chesterton.

71. **Germany of To-day.** By Charles Tower.

72. **Plant Life.** (Illustrated.) By Prof. J. B. Farmer, F.R.S.

73. **The Writing of English.** By Prof. W. T. Brewster.

74. **A History of Freedom of Thought.** By Prof. J. B. Bury, Litt.D.

75. **Ancient Art and Ritual.** By Miss Jane Harrison, LL.D., D.Litt.

76. **Euripides and his Age.** By Gilbert Murray, LL.D., D.Litt.

Home University Library of Modern Knowledge—*continued.*

77. **Shelley, Godwin, and their Circle.** H. N. Brailsford.

78. **The Ocean.** Sir John Murray.

79. **Nerves.** Prof. D. Fraser Harris.

80. **Co - Partnership and Profit - Sharing.** Aneurin Williams, M.P.

81. **Problems of Village Life.** E. N. Bennett, M.A.

82. **Prehistoric Britain.** Robert Munro, M.A., M.D., LL.D., F.R.S.E.

83. **Common-Sense in Law.** Prof. P. Vinogradoff, D.C.L., LL.D.

84. **Literature of the Old Testament.** Prof. George F. Moore, D.D., LL.D.

85. **Unemployment.** Prof. A. C. Pigou.

A Detailed List, containing Particulars of more than One Hundred Volumes, eighty-five of which are already issued, to be had upon application.

LIVERPOOL MARINE BIOLOGY COMMITTEE. MEMOIRS ON TYPICAL BRITISH MARINE PLANTS AND ANIMALS. Edited by W. A. Herdman, D.Sc., F.R.S. All demy 8vo, stiff boards.

1. **Ascidia.** By Prof. W. A. Herdman. With 5 Plates. 2s. net.

2. **Cardium.** By J. Johnstone. 7 Plates. 2s. 6d. net.

3. **Echinus.** By Herbert Clifton Chadwick, Curator of the Port Erin Biological Station. With 5 Plates. 2s. net.

4. **Codium.** By R. J. Harvey Gibson, M.A., F.L.S., and Helen P. Auld, B.Sc. With 3 Plates. 1s. 6d. net.

5. **Alcyonium.** By Sydney J. Hickson, D.Sc., F.R.S. With 3 Plates. 1s. 6d. net.

6. **Lepeophtheirus and Lernea.** By Andrew Scott, Resident Fisheries Assistant at the Peel Hatchery. With 5 Plates. 2s. net.

7. **Lineus.** By R. C. Punnett, B.A. With 4 Plates. 2s. net.

8. **Pleuronectes.** By Frank J. Cole, and James Johnstone, B.Sc. Lond. With 11 Plates. 7s. net.

9. **Chondrus.** By Otto V. Darbishire. With 7 Plates. 2s. 6d. net.

10. **Patella (the Common Limpet).** By J. R. Ainsworth Davis, M.A., and H. J. Fleure, B.Sc. With 4 Plates. 2s. 6d. net.

11. **Arenicola (the Lug-Worm).** By J. H. Ashworth, D.Sc. 8 Plates. 4s. 6d. net.

Liverpool Marine Biology Committee—*continued*.

12. **Gammarus.** By Margaret Cussans, B.Sc. 4 Plates. 2s. net.

13. **Anurida.** By A. D. Imms, B.Sc. (Lond.). 7 Plates. 4s. net.

14. **Ligia.** By C. Gordon Hewitt, B.Sc. 4 Plates. 2s. net.

15. **Antedon.** By Herbert Clifton Chadwick. 7 Plates. 2s. 6d. net.

16. **Cancer.** By Joseph Pearson, M.Sc. 13 Plates. 6s. 6d. net.

17. **Pecton.** By W. J. Dakin, M.Sc. 9 Plates. 4s. 6d. net.

18. **Eledone.** By Annie Isgrove, M.Sc. 10 Plates. 4s. 6d. net.

19. **Polychaet Larvae.** By F. H. Gravely, M.Sc. 4 Plates. 2s. 6d. net.

TEXT AND TRANSLATION SOCIETY. Established for the purpose of editing and translating Oriental Texts chiefly preserved in the British Museum.

The Sixth Book of the Select Letters of Severus, Patriarch of Antioch, in the Syriac Version of Athanasius of Nisibis. Edited and translated by E. W. Brooks, M.A. Vol. I. Text, Parts I. and II. Vol. II. Translation, Parts I. and II. 84s. net.

The Canons of Athanasius of Alexandria, in Arabic, Ethiopic, and Coptic. Edited and translated by Prof. W. Riedel (Griefswald) and W. E. Crum. 21s. net.

A Rabbinic Commentary on the Book of Job, contained in a unique MS. at Cambridge. Edited, with Translation and Commentary, by W. Aldis Wright, LL.D. 21s. net.

An Ancient Armenian Version of the Apocalypse of St John; also The Armenian Texts of Cyril of Alexandria, Scholia de Incarnatione and Epistle to Theodosius upon Easter, the former incompletely preserved in Greek, the latter unknown in Greek or Latin. All edited, with English versions, etc., by F. C. Conybeare, formerly Fellow of University College, Oxford.

Remnants of the Later Syriac Versions of the Bible. Part I. (Sixth Century). The Four Minor Catholic Epistles. Reconstructed Text, with Apparatus Criticus. Part II. (Seventh Century). Extracts, hitherto unedited, from the Syro-Hexaplar Text of Chronicles, Nehemiah, etc. All edited, with Greek versions, etc., by John Gwynn, D.D., Regius Professor of Divinity, Dublin. 21s. net.

Coptic Texts on St Theodore the General, St Theodore the Eastern, Chamoul and Justus. Edited and Translated by E. O. Winstedt, late Senior Demy of Magdalen College, Oxford. 21s. net.

The Refutation of Mani, Marcion, and Bardaisan of St Ephraim. Edited by the Rev. C. W. Mitchell. 21s. net.

Text and Translation Society—*continued.*

Euphemia and the Goth. With the Acts of Martyrdom of the Confessors of Edessa. Edited and Examined by Prof. F. C. Burkitt. 21s. net.

Two Commentaries on the Jacobite Liturgy. By George, Bishop of the Arab Tribes, and Moses Bār Kēphā. Together with the Syriac anaphora of St James and a document entitled the Book of Life. Texts and English translation by Dom. R. H. Connolly, M.A., and H. W. Codrington, M.A. 21s. net.

THEOLOGICAL TRANSLATION LIBRARY.

New Series. A Series of Translations by which the best results of recent Theological Investigations on the Continent, conducted without reference to doctrinal considerations, and with the sole purpose of arriving at the truth, are placed within reach of English readers.

Vols. I. and V.—**The Apostolic Age.** By Prof. Carl von Weizsäcker. Translated by James Millar, B.D. 2 vols. 10s. 6d. each.

Vols. II., VII., VIII., IX., X., XI., XII.—**A History of Dogma.** By Adolf Harnack, Berlin. Translated from the Third German Edition. Edited by the late Rev. Prof. A. B. Bruce, D.D. 7 vols. 10s. 6d. each.

Vols. III. and VI.—**A History of the Hebrews.**—By R. Kittel, Ordinary Professor of Theology in the University of Breslau. 10s. 6d. per volume.

Vol. IV.—**The Communion of the Christian with God :** A Discussion in Agreement with the View of Luther. By W. Herrmann, Dr Theol., Professor of Dogmatic Theology in the University of Marburg. 10s. 6d. net.

Vol. XIII.—**An Introduction to the Textual Criticism of the Greek New Testament.** By Prof. Eberhard Nestle, of Maulbronn. Cloth, 10s. 6d. ; half leather, 12s. 6d.

Vols. XV. and XVII.—**The Beginnings of Christianity.** By Paul Wernle, Professor Extraordinary of Modern Church History at the University of Basel. Vol. I. The Rise of the Religion. Vol. II. The Development of the Church. 10s. 6d. per volume.

Vol. XVI.—**The Religions of Authority and the Religion of the Spirit.** By the late Auguste Sabatier. 10s. 6d.

Vol. XVIII.—**Christian Life in the Primitive Church.** By Ernst von Dobschütz, D.D., Professor of New Testament Theology in the University of Strassburg. 10s. 6d.

Vols. XIX. and XX.—**The Mission and Expansion of Christianity in the First Three Centuries.** By Adolf Harnack, Berlin. Second, revised and much enlarged edition, 25s. net. Vols. not sold separately.

Vol. XXI.—**St Paul :** The Man and his Work. By Prof. H. Weinel, of the University of Jena. 10s. 6d.

Theological Translation Library—*continued*.

Vols. XXII., XXVI., XXVII., and XXXI.—**Primitive Christianity**: Its Writings and Teachings in their Historical Connections. By Otto Pfleiderer, Professor of Practical Theology in the University of Berlin. 4 vols. 10s. 6d. each net.

Vol. XXIII.—**The Introduction to the Canonical Books of the Old Testament.** By Carl Cornill, Professor of Old Testament Theology at the University of Breslau. 10s. 6d. net.

Vol. XXIV.—**History of the Church.** By Hans von Schubert, Professor of Church History at Kiel. 10s. 6d. net.

Vol. XXV.—**Ethics of the Christian Life.** By Theodor von Haering, Professor of New Testament Dogmatics and Ethics at Tübingen. 10s. 6d. net.

Vols. XXVIII. and XXIX.—**The Old Testament in the Light of the Ancient East.** By Alfred Jeremias, Pastor of the Lutherkirche, and Lecturer at the University of Leipzig. With numerous illustrations and maps, 25s. net. Vols. not sold separately.

Vol. XXX.—**The Truth of Religion.** By Dr Rudolf Eucken, Senior Professor of Philosophy in the University of Jena. 12s. 6d. net.

Vol. XXXII.—**Religious Liberty.** By Prof. Francesco Ruffini. With a Preface to the English Edition by Prof. J. B. Bury of Cambridge. Demy 8vo, cloth. 12s. 6d. net.

THEOLOGICAL TRANSLATION FUND LIBRARY.

Old Series. Uniform Price per Volume, 6s.

Baur (F. C.). **Church History of the First Three** Centuries. Translated from the Third German Edition. Edited by Rev. Allan Menzies. 2 vols. 8vo, cloth. 12s.

—— **Paul, the Apostle of Jesus Christ, His Life and** Work, His Epistles and Doctrine. A Contribution to a Critical History of Primitive Christianity. Edited by Rev. Allan Menzies. 2nd Edition. 2 vols. 8vo, cloth. 12s.

Ewald's (Dr H.). **Commentary on the Prophets of the Old** Testament. Trans. by the Rev. J. F. Smith. 5 vols. 8vo, cloth. 30s.

—— **Commentary on the Psalms.** Translated by the Rev. E. Johnson, M.A. 2 vols. 8vo, cloth. 12s.

—— **Commentary on the Book of Job,** with Translation. Translated from the German by the Rev. J. Frederick Smith. 8vo, cloth. 6s.

Hausrath (Prof. A.). **History of the New Testament** Times. The Time of Jesus. Translated by the Revs. C. T. Poynting and P. Quenzer. 2 vols. 8vo, cloth. 12s.

Theological Translation Fund Library—*continued*.

Keim's History of Jesus of Nazara : Considered in its connection with the National Life of Israel, and related in detail. Translated from the German by Arthur Ransom and the Rev. E. M. Geldart. Complete in 6 vols. 8vo. 36s. (Vol. I. only to be had when a complete set of the work is ordered.)

Kuenen (Dr A.). The Religion of Israel to the Fall of the Jewish State. Trans. from the Dutch by A. H. May. 3 vols. 8vo, cloth. 18s.

Pfleiderer (O.). Paulinism : A Contribution to the History of Primitive Christian Theology. Translated by E. Peters. 2nd Edition. 2 vols. 8vo, cloth. 12s.

——— Philosophy of Religion on the Basis of its History. Translated by Prof. Allan Menzies and the Rev. Alex. Stewart. 4 vols. 8vo, cloth. 24s. (Vol. I. out of print.)

Réville(DrA.). Prolegomena of the History of Religions. With an Introduction by Prof. F. Max Müller. 8vo, cloth. 6s.

Schrader (Prof. E.). The Cuneiform Inscriptions and the Old Testament. Translated from the Second Enlarged Edition, with Additions by the Author, and an Introduction by the Rev. Owen C. Whitehouse, M.A. 2 vols. With a Map. 8vo, cloth. 12s.

LIST OF PERIODICALS, REVIEWS, AND TRANSACTIONS AND PROCEEDINGS OF LEARNED SOCIETIES published by Williams & Norgate.

The British Review. With which is incorporated the Oxford and Cambridge Review. Monthly. 1s. net. Postage Inland 3d. ; Subscription covering 12 numbers post free, 15s. net.

The Hibbert Journal : A Quarterly Review of Religion, Theology, and Philosophy. Single numbers, 2s. 6d. net. Subscription, 10s. per annum, post free.

Journal of the Federated Malay States Museums. Issued quarterly. Single numbers, 1s. 6d. net. Subscription, 5s. per annum.

Journal of the Royal Microscopical Society, containing its Transactions and Proceedings, with other Microscopical Information. Bi-monthly. 6s. net. Yearly subscriptions, 37s. 6d., post free.

Journal of the Quekett Microscopical Club. Issued half-yearly, April and November. Price 3s. 6d. net. 7s. 6d. per annum, post free.

Linnean Society of London. Journal of Botany and Journal of Zoology. Published irregularly at various prices. Also Transactions, published irregularly.

List of Periodicals, etc.—*continued.*

Royal Society of Edinburgh. Transactions. Issued irregularly at various prices.

Liverpool Marine Biology Committee. Memoirs. I.–XIX. already published at various prices. Fauna of Liverpool Bay. Fifth Report, written by Members of the Commitee and other Naturalists. Cloth. 8s. 6d. net. *See* p. 39.

Publications de l'Institut Nobel Norvégien. Vol. I. L'Arbitrage International chez les Hellènes. Par A. Raedar. 4to. 10s. net. Vol. II. Les Bases Economiques de la Justice Internationale. By Achille Loria. 3s. 6d. net. Vol. III., Catalogue de la Bibliothèque de l'Institut Nobel Norvégien. 250 pages. 10s. net. Vol. IV. Die Rechtskraft Internationaler Schiedsspruche. Heinrich Lammasch. 4to, sewed, 7s. 6d. net.

Royal Irish Academy. Transactions and Proceedings issued irregularly ; prices vary. Cunningham Memoirs. Vols. I.–XI. already issued at various prices. *See* p. 31.

Royal Dublin Society. Transactions and Proceedings. Issued irregularly at various prices.

INDEX OF TITLES.

---

14 Henrietta Street, Covent Garden, London, W.C.

Christian Religion, Fundamental Truths of the. R. Seeberg, 28.

Christianity, Beginnings of. Paul Wernle, 34.

Christianity in Talmud and Midrash. R. Travers Herford, 12.

Christianity? What is. Adolf Harnack, 11.

Chromium, Production of. Max Leblanc, 19.

Church History. Baur, 2; Schubert, 28.

Civilisation of China. H. A. Giles, 9.

Climate and Weather. H. N. Dickson, 6.

Closet Prayers. Dr. Sadler, 27.

Codium. *Vide* L.M.B.C. Memoirs, 42.

Collected Writings of Seger, 15.

Colonial Period, The. C. M. Andrews, 1.

Coming Church. Dr. John Hunter, 15.

Commentaries on Jacobite Liturgy. Connolly and Codrington, 40.

Commentary on the Book of Job. Ewald, 8; Wright and Hirsch, 30; Commentary on the Old Testament. Ewald, 8; Commentary on the Psalms. Ewald, 8.

Common Prayer for Christian Worship, 5.

Common-Sense Dietetics. C. Louis Leipoldt, 19.

Common-Sense in Law. Prof. P. Vinogradoff, 33.

Communion with God. Wilhelm Herrmann, 13.

Comparative Religion. Princ. J. E. Carpenter, 4.

Conception of God. Alviella, 1.

Concrete, Reinforced. Colby, 5.

Conductivity of Liquids. Tower, 33.

Confessions of St. Augustine. Adolf Harnack, 12.

Conservatism. Lord Hugh Cecil, 4.

Constitution and Law of the Church. Adolf Harnack, 12.

Contes Militaires. A. Daudet, 35.

Co-Partnership and Profit-Sharing. A. Williams, 34.

Copenhagen and Norway, Guide to, 11.

Coptic Texts on St. Theodore. E. O. Winstedt, 35.

Crime and Insanity. Dr. C. A. Mercier, 21.

Crown Theological Library, 36.

Cuneiform Inscriptions, The. Prof. E. Schrader, 27.

Cyanamid, Manufacture, Chemistry, and Uses. Pranke, 25.

Cyperaceæ, Illustrations of. Clarke, 5.

Dante, Spiritual Message of. Bishop Boyd Carpenter, 4.

Date, The, of the Acts and of the Synoptic Gospels. Harnack, 12.

Dawn of History, The. Prof. J. L. Myres, 23.

Delectus Veterum. Theodor Nöldeke, 23.

Democracy and Character. Canon Stephen, 31,

Democracy, Socialism and, in Europe. Samuel P. Orth, 24.

De Profundis Clamavi. Dr. John Hunter, 15.

Descriptive Sociology. Herbert Spencer, 31.

Development of the Periodic Law. Venable, 33.

Differential and Integral Calculus, The. Axel Harnack, 12.

Dipavamsa, The. Edited by Oldenberg, 7.

Doctrine of the Atonement. A. Sabatier, 27.

Dogma, History of. Adolf Harnack, 12.

Dolomites, The, Practical Guide to, 11.

Dresden and Environs, Guide to, 11.

Dynamics of Particles. Webster, 33.

Early Hebrew Story. John P. Peters, 24.

Early Christian Conception. Otto Pfleiderer, 25.

Early Development of Mohammedanism. Margoliouth, 21.

Early Zoroastrianism. Moulton, 22.

Echinus. *Vide* L.M.B.C. Memoirs, 42.

Education. Herbert Spencer, 31.

Education and Ethics. Emile Boutroux, 3.

Egyptian Faith, The Old. Edouard Naville, 23.

Eighth Year, The. Philip Gibbs, 10.

Electric Furnace. H. Moisson, 22.

Electricity. Prof. Gisbert Kapp, 16.

Electrolysis of Water. V. Engelhardt, 8.

Electrolytic Laboratories. Nissenson, 23.

Eledone. *Vide* L.M.B.C. Memoirs, 43.

Elementary Chemistry. Emery, 7.

Elementary Organic Analysis. F. E. Benedict, 2.

Elements of English Law. W. M. Geldart, 10.

Engineering Chemistry. T. B. Stillman, 32.

England and Germany, 8.

English Language. L. P. Smith, 29.

English Literature, Mediæval. W. P. Ker, 17.

English Literature, Modern. G. H. Mair, 20.

English, The Writing of. W. T. Brewster, 3.

Enoch, Book of. C. Gill, 10.

Ephesian Canonical Writings. Rt. Rev. A. V. Green, 10.

Epitome of Synthetic Philosophy. F. H. Collins, 6.

Erzählungen. Höfer, 35.

Essays on the Social Gospel. Harnack and Herrmann, 12.

Essays. Herbert Spencer, 31.

Ethica. Prof. Simon Laurie, 19.

Ethics, Data of. Herbert Spencer, 30.

Ethics, Education and. Emile Boutroux, 3.

Ethics. G. E. Moore, 22.

Ethics, Principles of. Herbert Spencer, 30.

Ethics of the Christian Life. Prof. T. Haering, 11.

Ethics of Progress, The. Chas. F. Dole, 7.

Ethiopic Grammar. A. Dillmann, 7.

Eucken's Philosophy, An Interpretation of. W. Tudor Jones, 16.

Euphemia and the Goth. Prof. F. C. Burkitt, 4, 44.

Euripides and His Age. Prof. Gilbert Murray, 41.

Europe, Mediæval. H. W. C. Davis, 6.

Evolution. Thomson and Geddes, 32.

Evolution of Industry. Prof. D. H. Macgregor, 20.

Evolution of Plants. Dr. D. H. Scott, 28.

Evolution of Religion, The. L. R. Farnell, 9.

Exploration, Polar. Dr. W. S. Bruce, 4.

Facts and Comments. Herbert Spencer, 31.

Faith and Morals. W. Herrmann, 14.

Fertility and Fertilisers. Halligan, 11.

Fertilisers, Soil Fertility and. Halligan, 11.

First Principles. Herbert Spencer, 30.

First Three Gospels in Greek. Rev. Canon Colin Campbell, 4.
Flower of Gloster, The. E. Temple Thurston, 32.
Foundations of Duty, The. Bishop J. W. Diggle, 7.
Four Gospels as Historical Records, 9.
Four Gospels, Light on the. A. Smith Lewis, 19.
Free Catholic Church. Rev. J. M. Thomas, 32.
Freedom of Thought. Bury, 4.
Freezing Point, The. Jones, 16.
French Composition. Jas. Boïelle, 3.
French History, First Steps in. F. F. Roget, 26.
French Language, Grammar of. Eugène, 8.
French Literature, Landmarks in. G. L. Strachey, 32.
French Reader. Leon Delbos, 7.
French Revolution, The. Hilaire Belloc, 2.
Fundamental Truths of the Christian Religion. R. Seeberg, 28.

Gammarus. *Vide* L.M.B.C. Memoirs, 43.
Gaul, Wall Map of, 18.
General Language of the Incas of Peru. Sir Clements Markham, 21.
Genesis and Evolution of the Soul. J. O. Bevan, 2.
Genesis, Hebrew Text, 13.
Geography, Modern. Dr. M. Newbigin, 23.
Geometry, Analytical, Elements of. Hardy, 12.
German History, Noble Pages from. F. J. Gould, 10.
German Idioms, Short Guide to. T. H. Weisse, 34.
German Literature, A Short Sketch of. V. Phillipps, B.A., 25.
Germany, England and, 8.
Germany of To-day. Tower, 32.
Germany, The Literature of. Prof. J. G. Robertson, 26.
Glimpses of Tennyson. A. G. Weld, 34.
God and Life. Dr. John Hunter, 15.
Gospel of Rightness. E. C. Woods, 35.
Gospels in Greek, First Three. Rev. Colin Campbell, 4.
Grammar, Ethiopic. A. Dillman, 7.
Greek-English Dictionary, Modern, 18.
Greek Ideas, Lectures on. Rev. Dr. Hatch, 13.
Greek, New Testament. Prof. Edouard Nestle, 23.
Greek Religion, Higher Aspects of. L. R. Farnell, 9.
Greeks : Hellenic Era, 31.
Grieben's English Guides, 11.
Gymnastics, Medical Indoor. Dr. Schreber, 28.

Harnack and his Oxford Critics. T. B. Saunders, 26.
Health and Disease. Dr. W. L. Mackenzie, 20.
Hebrew, New School of Poets, 23.
Hebrew Religion. W. E. Addis, 1.
Hebrew Story. John P. Peters, 24.
Hebrew Synonyms, Studies in. Rev. J. Kennedy, 17.
Hebrew Texts, 13.
Hellenistic Greeks. Mahaffy and Goligher, 31.

Herbaceous Garden, The. Mrs. P. Martineau, 21.
Heredity in Relation to Eugenics. C. B. Davenport, 6.
Hibbert Journal Supplement for 1909, entitled : Jesus or Christ? 14.
Hibbert Journal, The, 14.
Hibbert Lectures, 38.
Highways and Byways in Literature. H. Farrie, 9.
Historical Evidence for the Resurrection. Kirsopp Lake, 18.
History of Dogma. Adolf Harnack, 12.
History of England. A. F. Pollard, 25.
History of Jesus of Nazara. Keim, 17.
History of Our Time. G. P. Gooch, 10.
History of Sacerdotal Celibacy. H. C. Lea, 19.
History of War and Peace. Perris, 24.
History of the Church. Hans von Schubert, 28.
History of the Hebrews. R. Kittel, 18.
History of the Literature of the O.T. E. Kautzsch, 17.
History of the New Test. Times. A. Hausrath, 13.
Holland, Practical Guide to, 11.
Home University Library of Modern Knowledge, 39.
House of Commons, The, from Within. Rt. Hon. R. Farquharson, 9.
How to Teach the Bible. Rev. A. F. Mitchell, 22.
Human Body, The. Prof. Arthur Keith, 17.
Hygiene, Handbook of. D. G. Bergey, 2.
Hymns of Duty and Faith. R. Crompton Jones, 16.

Idolmakers, Among the. Prof. L. P. Jacks, 15.
Immortality, Some Intimations of. Rt. Hon. Sir E. Fry, 9.
Incarnate Purpose, The. G. H. Percival, 24.
India, Peoples and Problems of. Sir T. W. Holderness, 14.
Indian Buddhism. Rhys Davids, 6.
Individual Soul, Genesis and Evolution of. J. O. Bevan, 2.
Individualism and Collectivism. Dr. C. W. Saleeby, 27.
Indoor Gymnastics, Medical. Dr. Schreber, 28.
Industrial Remuneration, Methods of. David F. Schloss, 27.
Infinitesimals and Limits. Hardy, 12.
Influence of Greek Ideas upon the Christian Church. Rev. Dr. Hatch, 13.
Influence of Rome on Christianity. E. Renan, 26.
Initiation into Philosophy. Emile Faguet, 9.
Initiation into Literature. Faguet, 9.
Inorganic Chemistry. J. L. Howe, 15.
Inorganic Qualitative Chemical Analysis. Leavenworth, 19.
Interpretation of Rudolf Eucken's Philosophy. W. Tudor Jones, 17.
Introduction to Biblical Hebrew. Rev. J. Kennedy, 17.
Introduction to the Greek New Testament. Prof. E. Nestle, 23.
Introduction to the Old Testament. Prof. Carl Cornill, 5, 45.

Introduction to the Preparation of Organic Compounds. Emil Fischer, 9.
Introduction to Science. Prof. J. A. Thomson, 32.
Irish Nationality. Mrs. J. R. Green, 10.
Isaiah, Hebrew Text, 13.

Jacobite Liturgy, Connolly and Codrington, 44.
Jesus. Wilhelm Bousset, 3.
Jesus of Nazara. Keim, 17.
Jesus or Christ? The Hibbert Journal Supplement for 1909, 14.
Jesus, Sayings of. Adolf Harnack, 12.
Job. Hebrew Text, 13.
Job, Book of. G. H. Bateson Wright, 35.
Job, Book of. Rabbinic Commentary on, 43.
Johnson, Dr., and His Circle. John Bailey, 2.
Journal of the Federated Malay States, 46.
Journal of the Linnean Society. Botany and Zoology, 16.
Journal of the Quekett Microscopical Club, 16.
Journal of the Royal Microscopical Society, 16.
Justice. Herbert Spencer, 31.

Kantian Ethics. J. G. Schurman, 28.
Kea, The. George R. Marriner, 21.
Kiepert's New Atlas Antiquus, 18.
Kiepert's Wall-Maps of the Ancient World, 17.
King, The, to His People, 18.
Kingdom, The Mineral. Dr. Reinhard Brauns, 3.
Knowledge and Life. Eucken, 8.

Laboratory Experiments. Noyes and Mulliken, 23.
Lakes of Northern Italy, Guide to, 11.
Landmarks in French Literature. G. L. Strachey, 32.
Latter Day Saints, The. Ruth and R. W. Kauffman, 16.
Law, English, Elements of. W. M. Geldart, 10.
Lays of Ancient Rome. Macaulay, 20.
Leaves, All about. F. G. Heath, 13.
Le Coup de Pistolet. Merimée, 22.
Lepeophtheirus and Lernea. Vide L.M.B.C. Memoirs, 42.
Letter to the "Preussische Jahrbücher." Adolf Harnack, 12.
Les Misérables. Victor Hugo, 15.
Liberal Christianity. Jean Réville, 26.
Liberalism. Prof. L. T. Hobhouse, 14.
Life and Matter. Sir O. Lodge, 19.
Life of the Spirit, The. Rudolf Eucken, 8.
Ligia. Vide L.M.B.C. Memoirs, 43.
Lineus. Vide L.M.B.C. Memoirs, 42.
Linnean Society of London, Journal of, 16.
Literature, English Mediæval. Prof. W. P. Ker, 17.
Literature, Highways and Byways in. Hugh Farrie, 9.
Literature, Initiation into. Faguet, 9.
Literature of Germany. Prof. J. G. Robertson, 26.
Literature of the Old Testament. Kautzsch, 15 ; Prof. G. F. Moore, 42.
Literature, The Victorian Age in. G. K. Chesterton, 5.

Liverpool Marine Biology Committee Memoirs, 42.
Liverpool Marine Biology Committee Memoirs, I.—XVII., 47.
Logarithmic Tables. Schroen, 28.
London. Sir. L. Gomme, 10.
London Library, Catalogue of, 20.
London Library Subject Index, 20.
Luke the Physician. Adolf Harnack, 12.

Mad Shepherds, and other Studies. Prof. L. P. Jacks, 15.
Mahabharata, Index to. S. Sorensen, 30.
Making a Newspaper. John L. Given, 10.
Making of the Earth. Prof. J. W. Gregory, 10.
Making of the New Testament. Prof. B.W. Bacon, 1.
Man and the Bible. J. A. Picton, 25.
Man versus the State. Herbert Spencer, 31.
Man's Origin, Destiny, and Duty. Hugh M'Coll, 20.
Maori, Lessons in. Right Rev. W. L. Williams, 34.
Maori, New and Complete Manual of. Williams, 34.
Marine Zoology of Okhamandal. Hornell, 15.
Marxism versus Socialism. Simkhovitch, 29.
Massoretic Text. Rev. Dr. J. Taylor, 32.
Master Mariners. J. R. Spears, 30.
Mathematics, Introduction to. A. N. Whitehead, 34.
Mathematics in China and Japan. Mikami, 22.
Matter and Energy. F. Soddy, 29.
Mediæval Europe. H. W. C. Davis, 6.
Metallic Objects, Production of. Dr. W. Pfanhauser, 24.
Metallurgy. Wysor, 35.
Metaphysica Nova et Vetusta. Prof. Simon Laurie, 19.
Midrash, Christianity in. Travers Herford, 13.
Milandapañho, The. Edited by V. Trenckner, 22.
Mineral Kingdom, The. Dr. R. Brauns, 3.
Mineralogy of Arizona. Guild, 11.
Mission and Expansion of Christianity. Adolf Harnack, 12.
Missions. Mrs. Creighton, 6.
Modern Greek-English Dictionary. A. Kyriakides, 18.
Modern Materialism. Rev. Dr. James Martineau, 21.
Modernity and the Churches. Percy Gardner, 10.
Mohammedanism. Prof. D. S. Margoliouth, 21.
Molecular Weights, Methods of Determining. Henry Biltz, 3.
Monasticism. Adolf Harnack, 12.
Moorhouse Lectures. Vide Mercer's Soul of Progress, 21 ; Stephen, Democracy and Character, 31.
Mormons, The. R. W. and Ruth Kauffman, 16.
Motor and the Dynamo. J. L. Arnold, 1.
Munich and Environs, Guide to, 11.
My Life, Some Pages of. Bishop Boyd Carpenter, 4.
My Struggle for Light. R. Wimmer, 35.
Mystery of Newman. Henri Bremond, 3.

Naples and Capri, Guide to, 11.
Napoleon. H. A. L. Fisher, 9.
National Idealism and State Church, 5; and the Book of Common Prayer, 5. Dr. Stanton Coit.
National Religions and Universal Religion. Dr. A. Kuenen, 38.
Native Religions of Mexico and Peru. Dr. A. Réville, 26.
Naturalism and Religion. Dr. Rudolf Otto, 24.
Nautical Terms. L. Delbos, 7.
Navy, The, and Sea Power. David Hannay, 11.
Nervation of Plants. Francis Heath, 13.
Nerves. Prof. D. F. Harris, 42.
New Hebrew School of Poets. Edited by H. Brody and K. Albrecht, 23.
New Testament, Making of. Prof. B. W. Bacon, 1.
New Zealand Language, Dictionary of. Rt. Rev. W. L. Williams, 34.
Newman, Mystery of. Henri Bremond, 3.
Newspaper, Making a. John L. Given, 10.
Newspaper, The. G. Binney Dibblee, 7.
Nibelungenlied. Trans. W. L. Lettsom, 23.
Noble Pages from German History. F. J. Gould, 10.
Nonconformity. Its Origin, etc. Principal W. B. Selbie, 29.
North Sea Watering-Places, Guide to, 11.
Norway and Copenhagen, Practical Guide to, 11.
Norwegian Sagas translated into English, 27.
Notre Dame de Paris. Victor Hugo, 15.
Nuremberg and Rothenburg, Guide to, 11.

Ocean, The. Sir John Murray, 42.
Old French, Introduction to. F. F. Roget, 26.
Ostend, Guide to, 11.
Old Syriac Gospels. Mrs. A. Smith Lewis, 19.
Old Testament in the Light of the East. Jeremias, 15.
Old Testament, Canonical Books of. Cornill, 6.
Old Testament, Prophets of. Ewald, 8.
Old World, The, Wall Map of, 17.
Ophthalmic Test Types. Snellen's, 29.
Optical Rotating Power. Hans Landolt, 19.
"Opus Majus" of Roger Bacon, 2.
Organic Analysis. Benedict, 2.
Organic Chemistry. A. A. Noyes, 23.
Organic Compounds. Emil Fischer, 9.
Origin and Growth of Religion. C. G. Montefiore, 22.
Origin and Nature of Life. Prof. Benjamin Moore, 22.
Outlines of Church History. Von Schubert, 28.
Outlines of Psychology. Wilhelm Wundt, 35.

Pages of my Life, Some. Bishop Boyd Carpenter, 4.
Pacific, The, Problems of. Frank Fox, 9.
Painters and Painting. Sir Fredk. Wedmore, 34.
Pali Miscellany. V. Trenckner, 33.
Papacy and Modern Times. Rev. Dr. Wm. Barry, 2.
Para Rubber Cultivation. Mathieu, 21.
Parliament, Its History, Constitution, and Practice. Ilbert, 15.
Pascal, Blaise. H. R. Jordan, 16.
Patella, 1. Vide L.M.B.C. Memoirs, 42.

Paul. Baur, 2; Weinel, 34.
Paulinism. Otto Pfleiderer, 25.
Pecton. Vide L.M.B.C. Memoirs, 43.
Persian Empire, Wall Map of, 17.
Persian Language, A Grammar of. J. T. Platts, 25.
Pharisaism. R. Travers Herford, 13.
Philo Judæus. Dr. Drummond, 7.
Philosophy, a New. Edouard Le Roy, 19.
Philosophy, Initiation into. Emile Faguet, 9.
Philosophy of Religion. Otto Pfleiderer, 25.
Plant Life. Farmer, 9.
Plants, Nervation of. Francis Heath, 13.
Pleuronectes. Vide L.M.B.C. Memoirs, 42.
Pocket Flora of Edinburgh. C. O. Sonntag, 30.
Polar Exploration. Dr. W. S. Bruce, 4.
Political Economy, Elements of. Prof. S. J. Chapman, 4.
Polychaet Larvae. Vide L.M.B.C. Memoirs, 43.
Portland Cement. Richard K. Meade, 21.
Prayers for Christian Worship. Sadler, 27.
Prehistoric Britain. R. Munro, 42.
Prehistoric Times. Lord Avebury, 1.
Present Day Ethics. Eucken, 8.
Primitive Christianity. Otto Pfleiderer, 25.
Princess, The. Alfred, Lord Tennyson, 32.
Principles of Physiology. Prof. J. G. MacKendrick, 20.
Printing at Brescia. R. A. Peddie, 24.
Prison, The. H. B. Brewster, 3.
Problems of Philosophy. Hon. Bertrand Russell, 27.
Problems of the Pacific. Frank Fox, 9.
Problems of Village Life. E. N. Bennett, 42.
Proceedings of the Aristotelian Society, 25.
Proceedings of the Optical Convention, 26.
Prolegomena. Dr. A. Réville, 26.
Protestantism and Progress. Ernst Troeltsch, 33.
Psalms, Commentary on. Ewald, 8.
Psalms, Hebrew Text, 13.
Psychical Research. Sir W. F. Barrett, 2.
Psychology. Prof. W. M'Dougall, 20.
Psychology, Principles of, Spencer, 30; Outlines of, Wundt, 35.
Public Schools and the Empire. Rev. Dr. H. B. Gray, 10.

Qualitative Analysis, Notes on. Prof. W. P. Mason, 21.
Quantitative Chemical Analysis. Gilman, 10.
Quest, The. Dorothea Hollins, 14.

Reasons for Dissenting from the Philosophy of M. Comte. Herbert Spencer, 31.
Recollections of a Scottish Novelist. Mrs. L. B. Walford, 33.
Reconstruction and Union. Paul Leland Haworth, 13.
Reformation of the Sixteenth Century. Rev. Dr. C. Beard, 2.
Refutation of Mani, Marcion, and Bardaisan. Rev. C. W. Mitchell, 20, 43.
Reinforced Concrete in Europe. Colby, 5.

Tourist Guides. Grieben's, 11.
Transactions of the Royal Dublin Society, 33.
Transactions of the Royal Irish Academy, 33.
Transactions of the Royal Society of Edinburgh, 33.
Truth, The, of Religion. Eucken, 8.

Unemployment. Prof. A. C. Pigou, 25.
Unionist Policy. Rt. Hon. F. E. Smith, 29.
Universal Christ. Rev. Dr. C. Beard, 2.
Universalism Asserted. Rev. Thos. Allin, 1.
Urine Analysis, A Text-Book of. Long, 20.

Vaillante, Vincent, 35.
Various Fragments. Herbert Spencer, 31.
Veiled Figure, The, 33.
Via, Veritas, Vita. Dr. Drummond, 7.
Victorian Age in Literature. G. K. Chesterton, 5.
Virgin Birth of Christ. Paul Lobstein, 19.

Vocabularies of the General Language of the Incas of Peru. Sir Clements Markham, 21.
Vulgate, The. Rev. G. Henslow, 13.

Wall Maps of the Ancient World. Kiepert, 17.
Warfare in England. Hilaire Belloc, 2.
Was Israel ever in Egypt? G. H. B. Wright, 35.
Water, Electrolysis of. Engelhardt, 8.
Weather, Climate and. Prof. H. N. Dickson, 7.
What is Christianity? Adolf Harnack, 12.
Winter Sports in Switzerland, Guide to, 11.
Within, Thoughts during Convalescence. Sir Francis Younghusband, 35.
Women's Suffrage. Helen Blackburn, 3.
World, The Old, Wall Map of, 17.
Writers, Great, of America. Profs. Trent and Erskine, 8, 33.
Writing of English. Brewster, 3.

Zoroastrianism. Moulton, 22.